Goals and Means

Anarchism, Syndicalism, and
Internationalism in the Origins of the
Federación Anarquista Ibérica

Goals and Means

Anarchism, Syndicalism, and
Internationalism in the Origins of the
Federación Anarquista Ibérica

Jason Garner

Goals and Means: Anarchism, Syndicalism, and Internationalism in the Origins of the Federación Anarquista Ibérica

© 2016 Jason Garner
This edition © 2016 AK Press (Chico, Oakland, Edinburgh, Baltimore).

ISBN: 978-1-84935-225-3
E-ISBN: 978-1-84935-226-0
Library of Congress Control Number: 2015942529

AK Press	AK Press
370 Ryan Avenue #100	PO Box 12766
Chico, CA 95973	Edinburgh EH8 9YE
USA	Scotland
WWW.AKPRESS.ORG	WWW.AKUK.COM
AKPRESS@AKPRESS.ORG	AK@AKEDIN.DEMON.CO.UK

The above addresses would be delighted to provide you with the latest AK Press distribution catalog, which features books, pamphlets, zines, and stylish apparel published and/or distributed by AK Press. Alternatively, visit our websites for the complete catalog, latest news, and secure ordering.

Cover and interior design by Margaret Killjoy: BIRDSBEFORETHESTORM.NET.

Printed in the USA.

CONTENTS

1870 and was evident from the beginning in the CNT, in which the majority of leading militants described themselves as anarchists. However, the CNT was not an exclusively anarchist organisation, nor could the Spanish anarchist movement be reduced to the CNT. It is the area in which working-class resistance was organised and united within the CNT, and intersected with the labour policy of the anarchist movement, that forms the heart of this study.

Both anarchism and syndicalism are ideologies with an internationalist outlook, and the Spanish movement was heavily influenced by ideas and events from outside its borders, albeit these were adapted to Spanish reality. There was dynamic interrelationship between the different national movements as well as between these and the international libertarian movement as a whole. The importance of events elsewhere can be gauged by the space given to them in the Spanish libertarian press, articles on them by leading anarchist and syndicalist militants, and the importance given to international meetings.[2] The almost constant repression faced by Spanish militants during the period under study, which sent hundreds into exile, meant that the flow of ideas back and forth across the Pyrenees was constant during this period. So any attempt to understand the relationship between anarchism and syndicalism in Spain cannot simply be based on national factors but must also take into account developments in the global libertarian movement. Moreover, it was the repercussions of international events, in particular the First World War and the Russian Revolution especially the latter's subsequent development and internationalization, and the wave of repression that spread across much of Europe that would cause such confusion and division within both syndicalism and the anarchist movement and would have a decisive impact on relations between the two.

Anarchism developed as an ideology in Europe in the second half of the nineteenth century due to the socio-economic changes brought about by the industrial revolution and the triumph of liberal political economy. It emerged as part of the universal socialist movement, which aimed at the overthrow of capitalism, concurrent with – and as a reaction to – the development of Marxism. Although sharing many Marxist criticisms of the capitalist system as well as the final goal of the Marxists – the creation of a classless society without the exploitation of one by another and where the state had withered away – anarchists differed from them in various aspects. They saw the poorer workers and agrarian workers as the most revolutionary sectors of the working class (although not simply lumpenproletariat as often claimed), believed in the possibility of achieving revolution immediately through insurrection instead of waiting for capitalism to mature and fulfill the supposed historic role assigned it in the preparation of the road towards socialism and, finally, rejected any role for the state in the transformation of society to socialism.

Anarchists opposed the state as they considered it an instrument of the dominant (capitalist) class to control society.[3] The state was not a natural phenomenon. It was human-made to achieve domination. Only with its complete destruction could society develop freely and naturally. The basic goal of anarchism is to achieve the maximum freedom for the individual so that all can develop to their maximum potential. However, anarchists do not conceive of humans living outside society. Human beings are social animals – society is their natural home – therefore, to be free they must live in a free society. The principal objective of the anarchist movement was to create such a society, organised from the bottom up. Organisations formed freely by individuals would be responsible for production and distribution, be organised horizontally (locally, regionally, and nationally according to the will of the people), and evolve, adapt, or disappear according to the needs of society. Of course, there was continuous debate as to exactly how this society should be (or should not be) organised, about the limits of individual and collective responsibility, et cetera, but fundamental to anarchists was their view of the state. A struggle against repression limited to an attempt to take control of the state was bound to be truncated. There was no guarantee that those victorious in a revolution would not simply become a new ruling class. Control of the state was neither a means nor an end to emancipation: the state had to be destroyed.

Anarchism as an ideology was born during the internal debates of the first-ever international labour organisation, the IWMA, and it was through this that its ideas first penetrated the Iberian peninsula. Anarchist philosophy developed in relation to the advance of capitalist society and human experience and knowledge, evolving into different tendencies, each with its own nuances, at times coalescing, at times dividing.

The reasons for the strength and persistence of anarchism in the Spanish working class have long been debated among historians.[4] Initial serious attempts to explain this phenomenon fell victim to Marxist sophistry or the patronising interpretations of liberal historians, which were often more anthropological than historical.[5] Blinded by their own ideology, Marxist historians, with Eric Hobsbawm at the fore, clung to simplistic, reductionist interpretations in which anarchism was presented as a utopian, primitive ideology, the reflection of a pre-industrial, backward labour movement which in the course of capitalist development would logically evolve towards Marxism.[6] The unsatisfactory conclusion was that the success of anarchism was either the result of a fanatical quasi-religious faith among the Andalusian peasantry, which slowly infiltrated industrialised areas through emigration in the early twentieth century, or of a specific 'Spanish temperament' which was somehow uniquely suited to an ideology whose origins lay in the French mutualism of Proudhon and the writings of the Russian aristocrat Mikhail Bakunin.[7] These deliberately simplistic interpretations have been superseded by more rigorous historical studies which, rather than basing their research on the peculiarity of the strength of anarchism in Spain, placed the appeal of anarchism among the working class within the economic and sociopolitical reality of a centralised yet culturally divided, economically backward yet modernising, military-dominated state.[8] As Josep Termes, one of the foremost historians of the Catalan and Spanish labour movement, clarifies, in Spain anarchism was "a response by the industrial workers to social inequality, [perhaps] utopian or idealistic, but no less rational and logical than that given to Europe by Marxist socialism."[9]

Spanish anarchism from its inception was organised within the labour movement, predominantly working-class (both in terms of number and culture) and internationalist in outlook. Anarchism in Spain began with the arrival there of Italian IWMA delegate Giuseppe Fanelli, amid the social and political confusion that followed Spain's September Revolution of 1868, which overthrew the Bourbon monarchy of Queen Isabella II. The revolutionary government persuaded Amadeo of Savoy to accept the throne in a constitutional monarchy.

However, the new king quickly became frustrated with the constant internal bickering of the government, and he abdicated in early 1873. After the collapse of the short-lived and inherently unstable First Republic (February 1873–December 1874), the Bourbon monarchy was restored, and Spain was then ruled by a government of oligarchs appointed by the king but responsible to parliament. This political arrangement, known as the Restoration, survived until September 1923, when General Primo de Rivera's pronunciamento, with the full approval of King Alfonso XIII, overthrew the parliamentary system.

The Restoration system functioned as a means of maintaining social peace between the different factions of the upper and middle classes. Under the so-called 'turno pacífico', power was interchanged between the two main parties, Liberals and Conservatives, which were merely groups of political bosses linked more by support for a particular leader than by any specific ideology.[10] The one definite aim of both parties was the maintenance of the existing social structures, with power remaining in the hands of a privileged oligarchy. Even though a number of advances were made in labour legislation from 1900 onwards, these were rarely enforced, and in general the conditions of the Spanish workforce were "degenerate in the extreme."[11] The workers were provided with no channel through which to articulate their needs, and any attempt by the workforce to organise in protest against their living and working conditions was met with repression. Labour protest was viewed simply as a question of law and order and dealt with accordingly, with the military often joining in the suppression of disputes in which it was not uncommon for workers to be injured or killed.[12]

The Restoration system managed somehow to survive the crisis of 1898, when Spain lost the last of its overseas colonies, and the social unrest of 1909, provoked by the decision to draft workers to fight in a colonial war in Morocco, but it proved totally incapable of dealing with the problems that resulted from the massive growth in industrial output during the First World War. Although Spain was neutral in the global conflict, the social and economic structure of the country was drastically affected by the huge demands on its industries from both belligerent countries and countries that Spain had previously supplied.[13] This reached a breaking point in 1917 when social, political, and military forces momentarily threatened to unite in a revolutionary movement against the state. The immediate danger was passed when the government gave in to the demands of the rebellious soldiers, and the army then joined in the suppression of labour protest. Nonetheless, from this moment on, the Restoration was in constant crisis until it was finally overthrown by a military coup in September 1923. Between 1917 and 1923, thirteen different governments held office, with an average life span of five months.

The rapid rise in industrial output brought with it a concomitant rise in union strength. Membership of the CNT, the Confederación Nacional del Trabajo, mushroomed from 15,000 in 1916 to 845,000 in 1919. However, the postwar period brought crisis to Spain as orders dried up. Falling prices and unemployment provided the backdrop for increasing social tension and a steep rise in labour unrest. From 1920 onwards, government repression and economic decline combined to decimate CNT numbers, especially in Catalonia.

Although Spain was theoretically a centralised state, the national government often had little control over law and order in the regions, particularly Catalonia, and was forced to follow the line adopted by civil governors, the Employers' Federation, or the military.[14] The Catalan Confederación Regional del Trabajo (CRT) was the CNT's main power base, and many of the CNT's leading figures either came from the region or gravitated toward it due to its employment opportunities and the relative strength of the unions there. Frequently during the period, Barcelona (or one of the surrounding towns) was the seat of the CNT's national committee and regional committee, the influential local federation of unions, and the CNT newspaper, *Solidaridad Obrera*. Outside Catalonia the CNT was also strong in Andalusia (although organisation proved a constant problem), the Levante, and Aragon. It also had influence in parts of Galicia (La Coruña and El Ferrol), and Asturias (Gijón and La Felguera).

National labour movements throughout Europe followed unique paths as a result of cultural, socioeconomic, and political differences and idiosyncrasies. However, there were also evident similarities. During the late nineteenth century, the labour movement in Spain had been heavily influenced by the same primary ideological currents as the rest of Europe: anarchism and orthodox Marxism. These two branches of socialism would eventually be represented by two national labour organisations, the revolutionary syndicalist CNT and the Unión General de Trabajadores (UGT). The UGT was dominant in the areas where the CNT was weakest, particularly in the mining region of the Basque country and in Madrid. Ideological divisions in the Spanish working-class movement were exacerbated by regional divisions.

The ideological origins of revolutionary syndicalism are to be found in the theories of Mikhail Bakunin and his supporters as elaborated in the original IWMA (1864–77) and subsequently developed by national trade union movements in the later years of the nineteenth century, especially in France. In essence revolutionary syndicalism was a fusion of Marxist economics and Pierre-Joseph Proudhon's rejection of politics, and it contained a number of concepts in common with Marxist theory: the acceptance of class struggle and the need to instil unity and consciousness among the working class. The ultimate goal was the libertarian communism – that is, anarchism – although for the revolutionary syndicalists the envisioned future society would be based around and organised by unions rather than simply communes, as proposed by leading anarchist thinkers of the late nineteenth century.[15] Tactics were defined within the concept of direct action, which essentially meant that the unions sought to solve their immediate demands directly with their employers, without involving the state.[16] This rejection of any form of negotiation or collaboration with the state included, most specifically, rejection of parliamentary politics.

Revolutionary syndicalism was born out of a rejection of the parliamentary collaboration of European social democratic parties in the decades before the First World War. The concentration on politics, the revolutionary syndicalists held, had led to the domination of the socialist movement by an elite made up of elements foreign to the working class: journalists, lawyers, intellectuals, and professional politicians. Likewise the socialist unions were governed by professional trade unionists bent on class collaboration for the sake of personal enhancement within the existing system, rather than acting in the best interests of the working class as a whole. In order to maintain their predominance over the working-class movement, this elite, revolutionary syndicalists argued, had imposed a centralised and bureaucratic mentality on the socialist movement which had "crushed individual initiative by lifeless discipline and bureaucratic ossification" which permitted no independent action.[17] To counter the formation of such an elite, revolutionary syndicalism was "based on the principles of federalism, on free combination from below upward, [which] put the right of self-determination of every member above everything else."[18] Therefore revolutionary syndicalism had a horizontal organisational structure, as opposed to the traditional vertical structure in which individual unions maintained independence of action and decision-making on issues that directly affected them. The decision-making process moved upwards through the organisation and was not dictated from above. Tactically (direct action), organizationally (bottom-up, decentralized structure) and politically (antipolitical, antistate), the areas of agreement between syndicalism and anarchism are obvious.

The basic unit of the CNT was the local union branch, which was divided into sections in accordance with trade (from 1918 onwards known as the *sindicato único*). These were then linked together within a local or provincial federation. The CNT divided Spain into seven regions (Andalusia, Catalonia, the North, Galicia, Castile, the Levante, and Aragón, La Rioja, and Navarra – the last three constituting one region) each of which, by 1923, had a regional confederation (CRT). The local and provincial federations of each region were linked through their respective CRTs.[19]

The sindicato único elected a section or administrative committee which was responsible for issues specific to the union. At the levels above the sindicato único, congresses were regularly held at which delegates of all member organisations would be present. National congresses were to be held every year, although due to repression only one congress, in 1919, was held between the national congress of 1911 and the advent of the Second Republic in 1931. The national congress had authority to make decisions of national interest on such issues as overall organisational structure, international relations, and confederation ideology. A decision by a national congress, where voting power depended on the number of members of each union, could only be overturned by a subsequent national congress. Due to the difficulties associated with organising congresses on regional and national levels, plenums were often held. At regional plenums, only delegates from the different local or provincial federations attended, whilst at national plenums delegates from the regional committees attended.

The regional and national congresses (or plenums) would decide the location of their relevant committees but not the committee members. These would be elected by the members of the area or town chosen. Typically the national committee resided in Barcelona, and its members would be selected from the unions of the local federation of the city and the regional committee of Catalonia. The performance of the national and regional committees would be assessed at both congresses and plenums, where they could be replaced. The national and regional committees were essentially administrative bodies, and their functions were limited to collecting statistics on the labour movement, organising propaganda trips, national congresses, or plenums, acting as liaisons between the different regional organisations, and maintaining contacts with the international movement. To avoid the creation of elites, committees were staffed by ordinary workers who did not receive a wage, with the exception of the national and regional secretaries.

Despite the CNT's emphasis on the individual and the equality of all members, it is noticeable that the same names appear again and again as members of the regional and national committees. Anna Monjo Omedes has divided CNT members into 'affiliates' and 'militants'. The former joined to "defend the workers' living conditions" whilst the latter hoped "for the revolutionary transformation of society."[20] The affiliates did not play a major role in the decision-making process of the unions and frequently declined to attend the assemblies or plenums at which the major decisions were made. However, the wide readership of the confederal press, the attendance of open-air conferences, and the support for strike movements shows that a large percentage did take an interest in the outcomes of debates. Although the militants could be seen as an ideological elite, they could not, even if they so wished, control the CNT. The committees were solely administrative, and even when they presented reports or motions at regional or national congresses these could be rejected – and often were. Nonetheless, although potentially all members had an equal say in union matters, the reality, in common with most political or labour organisations, was that some militants were more active than others.

These militants formed the ideological core of the CNT, and the vast majority were syndicalists sympathetic to anarchism.[21]

The CNT represented a specific branch of revolutionary syndicalism: anarcho-syndicalism. Anarcho-syndicalism was a hybrid of revolutionary syndicalism in which syndicalism provided the tactical means for achieving an anarchist goal, the triumph of the social revolution and the implantation of libertarian socialism – that is, anarchism. The difference between the two interpretations essentially relates to the role of politics within the unions.

Revolutionary syndicalism claimed that it was sufficient in itself to bring about and maintain the social revolution with no outside help from political parties.[22] Some revolutionary syndicalists went as far as interpreting this rejection of cooperation with political organisations to include anarchist groups. In theory, the anarcho-syndicalists agreed on the need to differentiate between anarchism and syndicalism, but what they rejected was that anarchism should be treated in the same way as the political parties of the left, whether socialist, republican, or communist. Most anarcho-syndicalists argued that anarchism and revolutionary syndicalism should cooperate as much as possible and that, as the two ideologies shared a common goal, anarchists should be allowed to propagate their ideas within the unions to prepare the workers for the future society. This did not mean that the unions should be open only to anarchists or even that ideological issues should take precedence over class issues in the day-to-day running of unions.

For anarcho-syndicalists, the workers' struggle was a result not of historical determinism but simply of an evil and corrupt system, capitalism. Industrialisation and economic centralisation had caused the workers to organise themselves so as to have the necessary strength to stand up to the capitalist overlords. Revolutionary syndicalism was thus simply a logical proletarian defence mechanism against repression. Confined to the sphere of economic relations, revolutionary syndicalism could not bring about the emancipation of humankind without having a clear political strategy. It was seen that this strategy should be influenced by anarchism.[23]

The tension within the syndicalist movement over the relationship between anarchism and revolutionary syndicalism was reflected within the anarchist movement as a whole. Overall there were three specific tendencies within the Spanish anarchist movement, with the lines between them often blurred: anarcho-syndicalism, anarcho-communism, and anarcho-individualism. In essence, the difference between the anarcho-communists and anarcho-syndicalists involved their ideas on the future society after the revolution. Whereas the anarcho-syndicalists saw the need for continuation of the unions, which would work hand-in-hand with communes in the tasks of production and distribution, the communists felt that the unions, as products of capitalism, had no role in any future society and would actually endanger the long-term survival of the revolution. In the pre-revolutionary period, many were suspicious of the reformist tendency they felt was inherent within the unions, which having been created to fight for or negotiate with the capitalist forces, would tend to look for accommodation with the capitalist system rather than its destruction. Nonetheless, anarcho-communists accepted the positive role that the unions could play in bringing about the revolution and educating workers and came to see that the active participation of anarchists would help defeat any reformist tendencies.

Therefore, although differences existed, there was some harmony between the communist and syndicalist tendencies. This was not the case with the individualists. As their name suggests, individualists vaunted the idea of individual freedom to such an extent that they denied that any benefits could be accrued through any form of organisation. By their very nature, anarcho-syndicalists believed in the strength of organisation and thus had little time for the egocentric interpretations of the individualists. In general the communists were also vehement in their condemnation of anarcho-individualism.[24] Although in areas relevant to personal experience, such as anarcho-naturism or free love, individualist writers did enjoy a certain influence within anarchist circles, their impact in other areas was negligible. Individualism had limited impact on the Spanish anarchist movement, especially in relation to the labour struggle, and was viewed as bourgeois by the predominantly working-class movement.[25]

The anarchist movement was organised on a much looser basis than the CNT. Prior to the formation of the Federación Anarquista Ibérica (FAI) there had been two other organizations or groupings that had aimed to link the anarchists of Spain: the Spanish section of Bakunin's Alliance of Socialist Democracy and the Organización Anarquista de la Región Española (OARE). Although relatively little is known about these organisations, both had close connections with the labour movement and saw it as the vital factor in any future revolution. Neither achieved the vitality, longevity, and influence of the FAI. With the exception of the few years these two organizations existed, in the period prior to the FAI's creation in 1927 there was no national organization to unite anarchists – contacts were maintained mainly via the libertarian press. Regional committees or organisations did exist, but these disappeared and reappeared with monotonous regularity due to government repression or, on occasion, the apathy of member groups.[26] However, the most important unit of the Spanish anarchist movement was the affinity group. An affinity group was made up of five to ten militants who joined together due to shared interest. There were groups dedicated to naturism (the appreciation of the relationship between humans and their environment including a mixture of nudism, ecology, healthy living and often vegetarianism), Esperanto, and violent revolution. Some came together in order to put on plays as a means of anarchist propaganda, others to produce a newspaper or journal.[27] The diverse nature of the affinity groups reflects the global reach of the Spanish anarchist movement, which was not confined to simply union or economic issues, hence the general feeling among many anarchists that the focus of syndicalism was too limited to constitute a fully fledged ideology and that there was a need for political guidance.

To present a complex array of information as clearly and understandably as possible, I focus in this book primarily on the decisions of Spanish national and regional congresses, manifestos of national and regional committees, and the opinions of leading militants of the different tendencies. The subject matter of the research centres around the general development of ideology in relation to CNT politics. Although it may seem that this represents a politically top-down approach, this is not the case. The internal dynamics of the CNT must be kept in mind. The very fact that the confederation was decentralised means that discussion in areas of global interest, such as ideology or international relations, which took place at a local level, was reflected in debates at a national level. Outside the congress decisions and committee manifestos, the evolution of the debates within the CNT can be traced through the articles of leading militants in the libertarian press. One further aspect to bear in mind is the scarcity of material available for any alternative approach to this area of research. For the pre-Republican era, information on individuals involved in Spanish unions is at a premium whilst, due to the passage of time, there are no longer living witnesses. A semi-chronological structure permits both analysis of the evolution of the relations between anarchism and syndicalism in Spain and comparison between the Spanish experience and that of the libertarian movements of Italy, Portugal, France, and Argentina, as well as the international movement represented by the new IWMA and the several international anarchist congresses that took place in the 1920s.

The first chapter of this book traces the birth of the anarchist movement and the arrival of anarchist ideas in Spain. It then charts the evolution of the movement internationally and in Spain before the creation of the CNT, covering the division between anarcho-collectivists and anarcho-communists as well as the dark years when the movement became submerged in the violence associated with the tactic of 'propaganda of the deed'. This chapter includes a general outline of the position of the different tendencies. For those who wish a deeper analysis of the positions of the prominent thinkers during this period, endnotes will act as a guide.

Chapter 2 focuses on the formation of the CNT and its formative years prior to the rapid growth in union membership brought about by economic growth during the First World War. Internationally it covers the first attempts to create a revolutionary syndicalist international, as well as the first steps towards the creation of an anarchist international prior to the October Revolution in Russia in 1917. During this period, some anarchists voiced concern about the reformist predilection they perceived within revolutionary syndicalism, but their warnings were ignored as others enthusiastically welcomed the opportunity to reconnect with the working classes after decades of socialist dominance in the unions.

Chapter 3 centres on the CNT's reaction to the rise of Bolshevism and the attempts to create a revolutionary syndicalist international, the Red Trade Union International (RTUI), in Moscow. Fears that the RTUI would be subordinate to the Comintern (the Third International) and the different national communist parties led a number of revolutionary syndicalist organisations, including the CNT, to reject the RTUI and create a truly independent international instead, independent from the control of political parties. The formation of this international in 1922 – the International Working Men's Association (IWMA) – and the continued impact of Bolshevism on both the international and Spanish movements, is the subject of chapter 4.

Chapter 5 concentrates on the anarchist movements in Spain and internationally in the light of the rise of Bolshevism, tracing the origins to the formation of the Spanish Committee of Anarchist Relations in 1923 and the attempts to create an anarchist international. Following the creation of the Committee of Anarchist Relations, there was a noticeable increase in tension between different sections within the CNT over the extent of anarchist influence in the confederation. After the seizure of power by General Primo de Rivera in September 1923 and the subsequent banning of the CNT in May 1924, the confederation was forced to operate underground. In this environment, ideological divisions widened as moderates looked for means of regaining the confederation's legal status whilst their opponents planned the revolutionary overthrow of the military dictatorship. These tactical divisions became identified with ideological differences, once again relating to the influence of anarchism in the unions.

Chapter 6 looks at the increasingly vitriolic conflict between anarchism and syndicalism during the two years following the ban on the CNT, including the intervention of militants from Argentina and Italy in ideological debates. A further result of the ban was the exodus of a large number of confederal militants to France. There Spanish exiles created both an anarchist and a syndicalist organisation and made contact not only with the French libertarian movement but with numerous exiles from other countries who were also based in France at the time. The experience of the exiled community in France provides the focus of chapter 7.

The book's chapter deals with the formation of an anarchist organisation independent of the CNT in Spain, the FAI, from its origins as part of a plan to create an Iberian Syndicalist Federation to the relationship between the anarchist federation and the CNT and attempts to reorganise the CNT in 1928, 1929 and again in 1930, following the collapse of the Primo de Rivera dictatorship. After six years of enforced absence, the CNT was finally able to reorganise legally, and the debates over the different approaches to the relationship between anarchism and syndicalism moved from the pages of the libertarian press, to the workshops, cafes, and *ateneos* of the working class.

nineteenth century. During the years of the First International and immediately after, anarchist thought was still in a period of initial evolution, and once the split with the Marxists in the International had been taken place, different ideological approaches began to emerge – although these would not become clearly apparent until the International had effectively collapsed. The importance of the International for the ideological advance of the Spanish labour movement cannot be overestimated for it was via the International, and the international contacts that it inspired, that anarchist ideas penetrated the Iberian peninsula.

An understanding of the ideological disputes that bedeviled the CNT throughout its existence requires an appreciation of the pre-history of the organisation and in particular the impact of the First International in Spain. A direct consequence of the International was the creation of the first national labour organisation in Spain, the Federación Regional Española (FRE). This initiated the close bond between anarchism and the Spanish trade union movement from this point until the end of the Civil War. Significantly, however, although anarchists represented the largest faction of the FRE, the federation was not a purely anarchist organisation and was open to workers of all political tendencies provided they accepted the basic principles of the IWMA. Both the FRE and its successor labour organisations, the Federación Regional de Trabajadores de la Región Española (FRTE) and the Federación de Resistencia al Capital – Pacto de Union y Solidaridad (known simply as the Pacto), adopted a policy of moderation, aiming to organise unions and unite all the working class under their wings, legally if possible. However, this policy of moderation was not reciprocated by the Spanish state or employers, who, whenever they felt it necessary, adopted a policy of repression, which included mass arrests of leading figures on trumped-up charges, forced confessions of guilt (induced by torture), and occasionally execution. This led to a further radicalisation of many anarchists, who, unable to act legally, engaged in violent retribution and individual acts of terrorism.

The collapse of the International in the 1870s and the failure of labour movements across the continent to advance in the face of violent repression in the wake of the Paris Commune provided the backdrop for the growing division in the anarchist movement in Spain and internationally. The division led to specific tendencies: anarcho-collectivism and communism.[1] Both rejected the state and parliamentary methods of liberation and advocated the social ownership of productive property and distribution, but they differed on one fundamental point – the way in which the products of labour should be shared. The collectivists argued for remuneration according to hours of labour, whilst the communists proclaimed the slogan "from each according to his means, to each according to his needs," thus abolishing wage differences, seeing that this would lead to the return of the divisions caused by capitalism. Moreover, communists saw that the complex nature of modern production made it next to impossible to determine a just remuneration system. This may seem an inconsequential difference but it had important tactical implications. Whereas the collectivists focused more on labour organizations as the means of bringing about the revolution, the communists, whilst not rejecting an important role for these organizations, generally preferred to limit organization to affinity groups. Some even showed a tendency towards, or support for, individualism, believing that revolution would result from a spontaneous revolt of the people and fearing that labour organisations could derail the revolution and help maintain or lead to the restoration of capitalist exploitation. After all, these organisations were a part of the capitalist system.[2] The stance taken towards organization had implications on the position adopted towards the use of violence. For collectivists seeking to unite the working class, being able to act openly and legally had evident benefits, although this does not mean they opposed illegal actions when the context demanded them. For communists, however, this was not such an important concern. Sectors of the communists became associated with or supported the tactic known as propaganda of the deed, which despite its initial ideological justification soon deteriorated into individual acts of violence. This provoked even greater state repression of both collectivists and communists irrespective of their support or involvement in the acts. This question of violence lay at the heart of the conflicts within the anarchist movement during this period in Spain and elsewhere. It was the all-absorbing factor that engulfed the movement in the final decade of the nineteenth century, weakening, dividing, and discrediting it in the eyes of the working class, which resulted in it becoming distanced, if not altogether estranged, from trade unions.

The First International and the Birth of the Anarchist Movement

Anarchism as a distinct ideology emerged during the debates between the supporters of Karl Marx and those of Mikhail Bakunin in the First International. Prior to these debates the First International had witnessed the birth of an embryonic form of syndicalism, the view that the emancipation of the working class would be achieved by their economic organizations, the unions, which would subsequently have a guiding role in the new society. The debate between these two grandees of nineteenth-century socialism would turn into vitriolic conflict. This clarified ideological positions distancing Marxists from anarchists, but it also initiated distrust, disrespect, and mutual recrimination that set the trend for future relations between the two socialist camps.

The main forces behind the creation of the International were English and French trade unionists, the latter heavily influenced by Proudhon. Other groups involved included Italian Republicans (followers of Giuseppe Mazzini), Owenites, Polish patriots, and even individual anarchists as well as German socialists. Marx was not involved in the preparations for organization of the International's first meeting at St Martin's Hall, London, in September 1864 Congress, but he was invited as a guest. At the congress he was elected to the General Council and was quickly able to dominate due to his undoubted intellectual and organizational ability. The council was seen, initially at least, as an "international agency between the different cooperating agencies" – but increasingly sought to centralise and increase its, and hence Marx's, influence. However, it needs to be clarified that despite his position on the General Council, the IWMA was not Marxist. Marx's skills were acknowledged, but this did not mean full support for his ideas, which, in any case initially were not well known.

At the Lausanne Congress of the International in 1867, Proudhonists appeared to have the upper hand. Proudhon, whose theories influenced both anarchists and Marxists, is best remembered for the condemnation of private ownership of production (he coined the phrase "property is theft"). Proudhon also analysed the exploitation that occurred in production, rejected wage labour, and developing a form of 'market socialism' known as mutualism, based on mutual banks and credit associations.[3] Proudhon and his followers stressed the need to build alternative economic relationships within existing capitalist society, such as cooperatives. Mutualism was anticapitalist but more reformist than strictly revolutionary, working towards building a new socialist society within the old capitalist one, a new society that would gradually replace the old rather than violently overthrow it.

At Lausanne, however, as well as recommending the creation of mutual aid societies, the congress also supported the creation of resistance societies (unions). This was a small step perhaps, but as Henryk Katz writes, "The discussions and the resolutions marked a departure from classical Proudhonism towards a semi-revolutionary syndicalism, a tendency that was to crystallize fully at a later time."[4] This departure would become more evident at the next congress, held in Basel in September 1869, with the adoption of a resolution that advised workers to form unions and urged those of the same trade to form national alliances. Furthermore, these alliances should advise "about measures to be executed in common, and [see] that they carried out, to the end, that the present wage system may be replaced by the federation of free producers." The resolution was presented by the Belgian delegate Eugen Hins, who in his speech argued that "the councils of the trade and industrial organizations will take the place of the present government, and this representation of labour will do away, once and forever, with the governments of the past." The seeds for the development of revolutionary syndicalism were not simply sown but sprouting shoots in the First International. What was required was a stronger and more unified labour movement to put the ideas into practice, and an economic and political situation conducive to its expansion. Hins's position was supported by the Spanish delegates, those from the Swiss Jura, and a considerable number of French sections.[5]

At Basel "collectivism and syndicalism were the victorious principles." The congress accepted that unions had a role in forging a future society. Unions and their federations would replace capitalist society with a federation of free producers.[6] Also supporting the resolution was Bakunin, attending his first and only IWMA congress. Inspired by the growth of the International and the direction it appeared to be taking, and reflecting on the evolution of his thought towards the revolutionary potential of the labour movement, Bakunin, along with eighty or so colleagues, formed the Alliance of Socialist Democracy, a secret organization to help ensure the revolutionary nature of the International. The Alliance aimed at "above all political, economic, and social equalization of classes and individuals of both sexes ... so that in future enjoyment be equal to each person's production, and so that ... the land [and] instruments of labour, like all other capital, on becoming collective property of the entire society, shall be used only by the workers, that is, by agricultural and industrial associations." Therefore, Bakunin and his supporters in the International were called, and called themselves, collectivists. Subsequently they would be called anarchists, but the idea of organizing society collectively remained central to Bakunin' creed. Indeed he "specifically rejected individualism of any kind and maintained that anarchism was a social doctrine and must be based on the acceptance of collective responsibilities."[7] The Alliance further accepted that only "international or universal solidarity of the workers of all countries" could provide a "final and real solution" to the social question.[8] The Alliance was collectivist and internationalist, and – as will be seen later – the influence of its Spanish section on the Spanish anarchist and the labour movement would be immense and enduring.

For Bakunin the Alliance would be "a necessary complement to the International," although he accepted that "the International and the Alliance, while pursuing the same ultimate goal, simultaneously pursue different aims. One has as its mission the gathering of the labouring masses ... transcending differences of nation and country, into one immense, compact body: the other one, the Alliance, has its mission as the endowment of those masses with a genuinely revolutionary direction." Their programmes too were different: "That of the International ... enshrines in germ, but only in germ, the entire programme of the Alliance. The Alliance's programme is a further expounding of the International's."[9] In summary, it was seen that the International should unite the workers in one movement, creating the force necessary to defeat global capitalism, with the Alliance providing ideological guidance.

The Alliance of Social Democracy then applied to be a member of the IWMA. Understandably, this request was turned down. The International was to group workers together, and lending institutional support to ideological organizations within its ranks, or even the appearance of such support, would cause internal conflict.[10] The Alliance soon disbanded, although many of the initial members in exile in Switzerland created the Geneva Section and applied as such to join the International, being accepted in by the General Council in July 1869. Meanwhile Marx tried to turn the International into a political faction.

Marx saw the Alliance and the alternative views that Bakunin and his supporters put forward as a threat to his and his supporters' control of the International. "I could not let this first attempt at disorganizing our society ... succeed," he wrote.[11] His use of the word 'our' is telling. These ideas, combined with Bakunin's successful performance at Basel, where his intervention helped defeat the Marxist position on inheritance, was perhaps too much for Marx, and he set about regaining the initiative. In reality Marx's objection to the Alliance entailed "not whether the International would have the dual purpose of bringing workers together and educating them, but who would do the educating," as Mark Leier writes in his book about Bakunin.[12]

At the International's London Conference of 1871, which had been called to discuss issues of organization and not ideology, Marx and his supporters had taken advantage of their temporary numerical domination (many of his followers were based in London whereas most of his opponents came mainly from southern Europe and found it difficult if not impossible to attend) to pass the Resolution on Working Class Political Action, which stated that against the "collective power of the propertied classes the working class cannot act, as a class, except by constituting itself into a political party, distinct from, and opposed to, all old parties formed by the propertied classes; (and) that this constitution of the working class into a political party is indispensable in order to ensure the triumph of the social revolution and its ultimate end – the abolition of classes."[13] Workers' actions in the economic sphere were vital, but it was the political party that would lead the way.

Marx's success in London provoked an immediate reaction from many sections, especially from southern Europe – the Spanish section severely reduced communication with the General Council whilst the Italians refused to even send a delegation to the next congress, and moves were made to organise an alternative congress of those opposing Marx. Confident after their success in London, Marx and his supporters organised the next congress, held in September 1872 in the Hague, a location that again made it difficult for many of the southern European sections to send delegates. At the congress, a commission was set up to examine the role of Alliance. The commission, dominated by Marx's allies, claimed that the Alliance of Social Democracy was a "secret agency aiming to seize supreme power in the International" (despite the fact that the commission's report accepted that it was not even sure the Alliance still existed) and proposed that Bakunin and other members of the Alliance be expelled from the International. Among the accused were three of the four Spanish delegates. The delegates that remained at the congress voted to expel Bakunin.

The decision of the Hague Congress caused an open breach between the supporters of Marx's politically orientated and centralised view of socialism and the supporters of the anti-authoritarian decentralisation of Bakuninism. From 1872 there existed two Internationals: one Marxist and the other anti-authoritarian. The Marxist International moved its headquarters to New York where it soon collapsed. According to Katz, the aim of moving the General Council to the United States was that Marx and Engels thought that it would leave important decisions in the "hands of their European plenipotentiaries, that is, themselves, helped by a small team of their most trusted partisans."[14] Actions speak louder than words. It was not simply the ideas that Marx and his followers put forward that raised objections, it was the calculated and scheming way they acted to ensure that their ideas dominated which helped to strengthen the belief that they represented a centralized, authoritarian approach intolerant of any opposition.

Following the Hague Congress, the anti-authoritarian wing of the International, including the Spanish FRE, quickly organised a congress at Saint-Imier (Switzerland), which began its deliberations only eight days after the Hague congress had ended. The delegates at the congress sought to distance themselves from the political predilection of their opponents at the Hague Congress, declaring, "All political organisations can be no more than the organisation of domination in favour of one class to the detriment of the masses and ... if the proletariat were to want to seize power, it would automatically become a dominating class and therefore exploiters. ... The hopes of the proletariat can have no other objective than the establishment of absolutely free economic organisations and federations, based on the labour and equality of all and absolutely independent of all government policy. ... The organisation of labour is the indispensable condition of the true and complete emancipation of the worker."[15]

Emancipation through the state was a delusion. The state was oppression, no matter who was at the helm. Emancipation could only be achieved by the destruction of the state, and this could only be achieved by the working class acting through its economic organisations. Furthermore, the structural base of these organisations needed to reflect their goal: it had to be decentralised, egalitarian, and independent from political organisations that favoured the parliamentary path to emancipation.

The anti-authoritarian International held further congresses until 1877.[16] In the future when the anarchists referred back to the IWMA, they had in mind the collectivism of the anti-authoritarian wing and its policies regarding the labour movement. Both Marxist and collectivist Internationals then collapsed in the face of increasing repression, directed against the International itself and against the working class across Europe. The divisions created in the First International would continue to grow, however, and the two factions would become violent enemies. This was a disaster for the labour movement, although it is hard to see how it could have been avoided given the extent of the differences between their two positions.

Both Marx and Bakunin looked to influence the direction and politics of the International. Bakunin looked to increase the influence of his ideas, whereas Marx was intent on ensuring his control and ill prepared to allow alternatives to challenge his position. That Marx was happy to split the International instead of allowing alternative views to emerge is consistent with his intolerant nature. After all, he and not the others "held the patent on the scientific truth of the future of society," as Alexandre Skirda puts it.[17] Nonetheless, as much as Marx's behaviour in the International created divisions, it was the deliberate misinterpretations and falsifications of his followers in their analysis of the reasons for the split that helped maintain and deepen these splits. As Leier writes, "The interpretation of the history of the International was disingenuous and distorted. Political action had not been the creed of the International; it had been the subject of intense debate and dispute from the very beginning."[18]

This is not to claim that Bakunin was a totally innocent bystander, but the starting point to too many studies is that the First International was Marxist, which it was not. Nor was it Bakuninist, of course, but Bakunin and his supporters had every right to put forward their ideas, as did Marx and his followers. Before analyzing the differences, it is important to point out a fact often forgotten or overlooked: that on many points there was clear agreement between the two socialist thinkers. They agreed on the critique of capitalist exploitation and on the type of society that should eventually replace it. In fact Bakunin acknowledged "the great service he (Marx) has rendered to the socialist cause," accepting or agreeing with much of his analysis of the nature of capitalism.[19]

Marx, Bakunin accepted, "was on the right path. He established the principle that religious, political and juridical evolutions in history were not the cause, but the effect, of economic evolution. This is a great and fruitful concept … and he is to be credited for solidly establishing it and having made it the base for his economic system."[20] Nonetheless, a theory may help explain a phenomena but that does not mean that it is the only truth, and Bakunin, whilst accepting the basic premise of historical materialism, rejected it as a closed dogma: "The political state in every country, [Marx] says, is always the product and faithful reflection of its economic structure; to change the former, one has to change the latter. This is the whole secret of political evolutions according to Herr Marx. He pays no heed to the elements in history, such as the effect – obvious though it is – of political, juridical and religious institutions on the economic situation."[21]

So Bakunin accepted the importance of economic relations but did not see this as the be-all and end-all or even the decisive factor in each and every case.[22] As Bakunin wrote, Marx "says that 'hardship produced political slavery – the State', but does not allow for the converse: 'Political slavery – the State – reproduces and maintains hardship as a condition of its existence, so that in order to destroy hardship the State must be destroyed."[23] The destruction of oppression cannot be achieved by using the tools of oppression. On paper, perhaps, the argument for the need for a dictatorship of the proletariat to help defeat capitalism and organize the transition to communism may appear to have a certain rationale, although the nature of this was ill defined by Marx himself and in reality it is impossible. The seizure of the state by the working class by through a dictatorship of the proletariat could not achieve freedom, "no dictatorship ... can have any other objective than to perpetuate itself," Bakunin asserted.[24] Such a dictatorship would be elitist, lacking faith in the capacity of the workers for self-management of the workers, showing a desire to govern, control, and guide that would never disappear. A dictatorship that frees the people is a deception. As Bakunin wrote, "We are convinced that freedom without Socialism is privilege and injustice, and that Socialism without Freedom is slavery and brutality."[25] For Bakunin and his followers, the destruction of all state power needed to be the first aim of any revolution, and as the evolution of collectivist ideology during the years of First International suggested, the new society should be based on the economic organizations of the working class.

Marx's 'scientific socialism' was too rigid, too doctrinaire for the Russian, who had far greater physical contact with the realities of class conflict than Marx, whose main source of knowledge was the library of the British Museum. Of course neither one was working class, but whereas Bakunin was a man of action, after 1848 Marx was happier with his books than with active revolutionaries.[26] Marx's system was more clearly set out, offered a more profound analysis of the causes of capitalism, and claimed 'scientific' truth for his belief that emancipation would come via the political path. It worked perfectly on paper but hasn't in real life. Bakunin's ideas were less systematic and not so clearly laid out, though it would be incorrect to see Marx as the intellect and Bakunin simply as a revolutionary with a few scarcely thought out ideas. Bakunin was far more than this.

Central to Bakunin's position was the rejection of the parliamentary path towards emancipation in favour of spontaneous revolutionary action by the workers themselves in the economic field, which would destroy the state, making political action irrelevant.[27] This rejection of the political road to emancipation (the struggle to take power through the state, rather than simply destroying it) was the main difference between the two factions. However, other aspects should be taken into account, especially as the conflict developed over time. Bakunin shares Marx's belief in class conflict but differs from Marx in that he does not assign the revolution to the proletariat alone, seeing 'revolutionary potential' in other classes as well, most specifically the peasantry and the lumpenproletariat. But the anarchist rejection of Marxism is not simply based on a political disagreement over tactics, it embraces a specific ethical and metaphysical approach that finds the tactics of scientific socialism objectionable.

Marx aimed to uncover the contradictions of capitalism that, he argued, must lead to conflict and the dialectic advance to another stage of societal development, whereas Bakunin, also an avid reader of Hegel in his youth, condemned capitalism on moral grounds, saying simply that it ought to be overcome. The two had different conceptions of human nature and the natural world. For Bakunin human nature was fixed, whereas for Marx it was controlled by social relationships and evidently the mode of production predominant at the time. Hence Bakunin saw human beings as a "constituent part of the natural world and in no way distinct from it."[28] The 'scientific socialism' of the anarchists is therefore that of the natural sciences, articulated principally during this period by Peter Kropotkin and Élisée Reclus, who, as well as being anarchists, were both widely respected scientists in their own fields.[29] Kropotkin wrote that "anarchism represents more than a mere mode of action and a mere conception of a free society ... it is part of a philosophy, natural and social" and embraces "the whole of nature ... including ... the life of human societies and their economic, political and moral problems." In short, "the theory of anarchy rests on science, in particular the science of evolutionary biology."[30]

The aim of anarchism is to achieve the greatest freedom possible for the individual. However, the individual does not and cannot live outside society. "Man does not voluntarily create society; he is involuntarily born into it," Bakunin wrote. Indeed, "man" is "a social animal. ... Only in society can he become a human being," as such "freedom ... is the product of the collectivity."[31] The task of the anarchist is therefore to create a society that permits the individual the freedom to develop to her or his maximum potential, without restricting the freedom of anyone else.

Kropotkin rejected the common idea of the period, integral to the capitalist creed, that interpreted Darwin's theory of evolution to show that human progress depended on competition, the survival of the fittest. He argued that natural selection favoured societies in which mutual aid (cooperation) thrived and that "individuals in these societies had an innate predisposition to mutual aid." In short, cooperation was a natural action and helped create a cooperative culture, and it was this and not competition which was necessary for the evolution of mankind and society (you can't have one without the other): "Competition is always injurious to the species, and you have plenty of resources to avoid it! That is the tendency of nature, not always realized in full, but always present. ... Therefore combine – practice mutual aid! That is the surest means for giving to each and to all the greatest safety, the best guarantee of existence and progress, bodily, intellectual, and moral."[32]

Kropotkin did not claim that competition did not exist in nature but simply that it was not beneficial to progress. In fact, it was the very opposite, as his anarchist colleague Errico Malatesta argued: "If the history of mankind had been limited to struggle and competition, humanity would have remained in its barbarous state."[33] Both cooperation and competition could be found in nature, but in human societies social factors determined which dominated. Contemporary capitalist society stressed the latter.

But while society is a natural phenomenon, the state and its coercive institutions are not. These are the creations of ruling elites to ensure their domination of others. They are artificial, unnatural, and pervert human evolution. Kropotkin further argued that humans are moral by nature and by living in society they develop a natural collective sense of justice and morality. Capitalism repressed this, he believed, creating its own self-interested morality that represented and reinforced the values of the ruling class.

In short, the progress of the human race depends on the cooperative nature of society as opposed to the competitive. Since contemporary society stressed the reverse and the state and other institutions enforced this position, these institutions had to be destroyed. The anarchist rejection of capitalism and the nation-state system that maintained it was therefore scientific (its logic coming from nature) and moral. As Malatesta wrote, "Anarchism was born of a moral revolt against social injustice."[34]

In anarchism there is no grudging respect for capitalism. There is no belief that capitalism must fulfill any specific mission or that there is one unique, unalterable road to emancipation. Capitalism is immoral. It perverts the development of the individual and humankind. It must be overthrown to allow the full development of society and therefore the individual, and this can only occur in a free society. The sooner this is created the better, and anarchists should work to make it sooner rather than later. They must do so in line with their own moral values, for unjust means will create unjust societies. For many anarchists, the Marxist 'scientific' approach, involving entering in the capitalist political game, trying to take over its tools of oppression, sitting at the negotiating table with the those who repressed the workers, et cetera, was not simply unlikely to work, it was morally incorrect. "For Bakunin ... social revolution requires a total transformation of [the] world condition – not, for example, a 'mere' change of governing or administering class, as with Marx."[35] This moralistic view of Marxism as a cold, emotionless ideology, obsessed with internal scientific logic that often justified collaboration with capitalism or immoral acts committed against the working class, however exaggerated it may be, had an immense impact on anarchists' relations with Marxists. And the behaviour of the political organizations inspired by Marx, reformist, orthodox, or revolutionary, only served to entrench these feelings in the years to come.

The First International in Spain

Prior to the creation of the Spanish section of the International, the Federación Regional Española (FRE), embryonic labour organizations had existed in the country since the 1830s, mainly in Catalonia. They limited their activities to issues such as wages (preventing cuts as well as requesting raises) and the collection of funds for members for times of hardship, such as illness or unemployment, with their main demand being for the simple right to exist legally – that is, the right of association. In general these organisations were 'friendly societies' or cooperative organizations influenced by the ideas of the French utopian socialists Fourier, Cabet, and Saint-Simon.[36] The appeal of the utopians was undoubtedly enhanced by the almost nonexistent prospects for advancement presented to the labour movement by the political parties that dominated during the years prior to 1868 (the working class did not have the vote), misleadingly labelled moderates and progressives. These nascent labour organisations tended to favour democrats and republicans or to eschew involvement in politics altogether. They did not see their struggle in terms of class politics or propose the revolutionary overthrow of the state. Their action was confined to limited demands related to working conditions. It was the First International that would introduce socialism as a doctrine of class struggle to the Spanish labour movement and arm it with clear ideas and tactics aimed to bring about its rapid emancipation.

The year 1868 was transcendental. The Glorious Revolution finally put an end to the ancien régime and opened the door for the first time to the organization of a national labour movement in Spain. As important as the ideas that came with the First International was its timing. The first representative of the International to visit Spain, Giuseppe Fanelli, would arrive almost two months after General Juan Prim's pronunciamento had put an end to the reign of Queen Isabella, installing a theoretically constitutional monarchy under Amadeo de Savoy and introducing a period of political and social unrest. The continuous quarrels between the political factions that had combined with Prim led the new king to abdicate in 1873, thus bringing about, by accident rather than design, the Federal Republic. A chaotic and weak regime survived less than a year, before a military coup led by General Manuel Pavía installed a more conservative regime. Spain continued without a monarch until, in accordance with common practice in nineteenth-century Spain, a further military rising, this time by General Martínez Campos, restored the Bourbons to the throne, and Alfonso XII, Isabella's son, became the new king in January 1875. The juxtaposition of the most advanced ideas of the international labour movement on an already revolutionary situation would leave a deep and lasting impression on the Spanish labour movement: "it transformed the perspectives of the labour struggle, and modified its ideological content."[37] The political and social turmoil provided the backdrop for the expansion of the First International to Spain, where if found fertile terrain.

In 1866, the International created a corresponding secretary for Spain within the General Council, with the position given to Paul Lafargue, Marx's future son-in-law, due to his linguistic skills. In 1868, Antonio y Anglosa attended the Brussels Congress as a delegate of Catalan workers' societies.[38] As mentioned, that same year a representative of the IWMA visited Spain for the first time. Crucially, that representative, the Italian Giuseppe Fanelli, was also a member of Bakunin's Alliance of Social Democracy. Within months of Fanelli's arrival in Spain, branches of the International were created in both Madrid and Barcelona. The Federación Regional Española (of the International) was created at the first-ever Spanish Labour Congress in Barcelona in June 1870. The federal council was based in Madrid, whilst the Catalan sections were responsible for the publication of its main organ, La Federación. The influence of collectivism was reflected in a speech made by Rafael Farga Pellicer, president of the FRE, about the aims of the new organisation: "We want the end of the capitalist empire, of the state and of the church, in order to build on its ruins anarchy, the free federation of free workers' associations."[39] The FRE accepted the authority of the General Council in London, whilst at the same time condemning political action. Membership was open to "all Spanish workers" who wanted to be emancipated by the means proposed by the IWMA. At this stage no one was claiming that this should not be the case. For Marxists and Bakuninists alike, class unity was the sine qua non, without which the revolutionary potential of the working-class movement would be fatally reduced.[40] It was the 1871 London Conference that forced the FRE to clarify its position. Marx and Engels tried to gain the support of the Spanish delegate, Anselmo Lorenzo, claiming, somewhat hypocritically, that Bakunin simply wanted to create an elite revolutionary organization to guide the passive working class. Lorenzo was not convinced and indeed felt that the International had already been taken over by "elements alien to the working-class" – most delegates in London, obviously including both Marx and Engels, were not working-class. Following Lorenzo's report on the conference, the FRE greatly reduced its contacts with the General Council.

Even before the final showdown between collectivists and Marxists in the IWMA, the victory of the former in Spain was assured. A small pro-Marxist section within the FRE evolved in Madrid following the arrival in Spain in December 1871 of Lafargue, one of many communards to flee across the Pyrenees. The New Madrid Federation had its own newspaper, *La Emancipacion*, in which readers were informed of Marx's ideas and the evolution of the Marx-Bakunin struggle in the IWMA. However, the group enjoyed little support, and their vitriolic attacks against the FRE leaders only succeeded in hastening their expulsion from the FRE in June 1872. The Marxists held a congress in 1873, but only five local federations attended. The New Madrid Federation soon broke up, and *La Emancipacion* also disappeared due to lack of funds. Nonetheless, Lafargue's work did bear fruit in the long run: the Spanish socialist movement evolved from the Madrid Marxists. At the Hague Congress, the FRE was represented by Morago, Marselen, Farga Pellicer, and Alerini, with Lafargue representing the pro-Marxist section from Madrid – the first three being charged alongside Bakunin of being members of the Alliance. All but Lafargue would then represent the FRE at the Saint-Imier Congress of the collectivist International.

Within the FRE the followers of Bakunin represented one of the stronger factions but did not enjoy an overall majority.[41] However, their influence became more noticeable as the years passed, and at the Valencia Conference of September 1871 the FRE declared that "the true federal democratic Republic is [represented by] collectivised property, anarchy and economic federalism, in other words the free universal federation of free industrial and agricultural workers' associations."[42] According to Josep Termes, the balance of power within the FRE was held by a conglomeration of Bakuninists (antipolitical collectivists) and apolitical unions or societies (Termes uses the term '(apolitical) syndicalist', but this is anachronistic – syndicalism as an ideology or movement did not exist until later), a position that, allowing for the evolution of both tendencies, would be repeated within the CNT. Alongside these tendencies there were other labour organizations that supported political action as well as supporters of cooperativism. The antipolitical-apolitical collaboration was reflected in the decision to adopt an apolitical rather than antipolitical stance, which in essence meant that, although the FRE would not intervene in politics, individual members did not have to abstain from joining political parties.[43]

Following the Paris Commune the FRE was the target of government repression, which caused the General Council to flee to Portugal in June 1871. The same year, the FRE's room for operation was strictly limited, as the combination of workers to demand better wages was declared a crime. Just when the repression seemed to be easing in July 1873, the Cantonist movement broke out, the failure of which precipitated the restoration of the Bourbon monarchy. The FRE had at best a minor role in the movement that was led mainly by Republicans, but despite this the FRE would be the main victim of the repression that followed, being declared illegal in 1874. The repression only served to strengthen the hand of those radicals who had argued all along that the working class could expect nothing from the Republicans, democrats, and radicals of the middle classes. Forced to operate clandestinely, the radicals proposed a straightforward insurrectionist policy and became increasingly doubtful and suspicious of the revolutionary nature of unionism, a belief strengthened by unsuccessful attempts of the syndicalists to act legally. Moreover, these differences in approach merged with the growing dispute between collectivists and communists, although in Spain the former represented the majority. Riven by internal divisions and paralysed by government repression, the FRE was voluntarily dissolved in 1881 after having been forced by government repression to act underground since 1874.

In reality the strength of the FRE was ethereal – it could not even meet its postal expenses. Rather than trade unions, it was made up predominantly of small-scale professional guilds. The basic unit of the FRE was the trade section, which grouped together workers of the same profession in the same town. Given its relatively short and turbulent life, the FRE was not able to fully implement the organizational guidelines it had set for itself, therefore the level of organization differed from region to region and from city to city. Significantly, Catalonia was by far the strongest region for the FRE, accounting for roughly two-thirds of its membership.[44] Other regions that had a relative strength within the movement were Andalusia, Valencia, and Aragon, which, along with Catalonia, would later provide the strongest support for the CNT. Organisationally, the aim was that all the sections of a specific trade would be grouped together, creating a national trade federation that would have responsibility for strikes. The different trade sections of a specific town would group together to form a local federation. The grouping together of all the local federations would create the regional federation (that is, the FRE). These regional federations would then unite to create a world federation. These different federations would form the embryo of the local and national administrations of the future society that would be based on their production.

The FRE was succeeded by the Federación de Trabajadores de la Región Española (FRTE) – a name that shows the continued affiliation to the International and its ideals even though it no longer existed. The FRTE survived from 1881 to 1888, like the FRE falling victim to repression despite its leaders favouring a moderate and legal approach. The constant repression combined with the failure of industrialisation in Spain, in comparison with most other European nations, was reflected in the failure of both collectivists and the Marxist labour organisation, the Unión General de Trabajadores (UGT) founded in 1888, to attract a large membership until the second decade of the next century.[45]

When the FRTE was dissolved in 1888 it was replaced by two organisations: the Federación de Resistencia al Capital – Pacto de Unión y Solidaridad (Pacto) and the Organización Anarquista de la Región Española (OARE). The Pacto was based around seven basic principles, which included the aim to unite the working class through a common action against capitalism, including, when necessary, strike action. Far less influential than its predecessors, the Pacto disappeared in 1896, crushed under the weight of government legislation and repression.[46]

According to Álvarez Junco, the OARE was the continuation of the Alliance and the precursor to the FAI, operating as a form of "party" alongside the Pacto as part of an "organizational revolutionary-syndicalist double project." However, the exact intricacies of the relationship between the two organisations are unclear.[47] Given the date and the reference to the Valencia Congress, it appears that the Cuban-born anarchist Fernando Tarrida del Mármol was writing about the OARE when he recommended to his French colleagues that they too should organize themselves, irrespective of their different approaches to anarchism, adopting a policy of "anarchy without adjectives."[48] The OARE was made up of affinity groups in which there was "no authority," with each member undertaking a certain role (treasurer, secretary, et cetera), meeting weekly or fortnightly or more frequently in urgent cases. These groups created a national "commission of relations" in order to save on work and expenses and as means of mutual assistance in case of persecution. Collectivists and communists coexisted in the OARE. Similar to the Alliance before it, the OARE's objective was to allow anarchists to exchange ideas and maintain contact, but the real "field of action" was "among the proletarian masses": "This is our place. By abandoning them … they will become the meeting places of charlatans who speak to the workers of 'scientific socialism' or practicism, possibilism, cooperation, accumulation of capital to maintain peaceful strikes, requests for aid and the support of the authorities etc., in such a way that will send the workers to sleep and restrain their revolutionary urges."[49] This was happening in other countries, and it was in danger of happening in Spain with the formation of the UGT and Partido Socialista Obrero Español (PSOE) as well as the creation of Alejandro Lerroux's Radical Republican Party. Tarrida's comments describe an attempt to maintain coexistence of tendencies, counter to those who portray the period as one of out-and-out conflict between communism and collectivism. The majority of Spanish anarchists desired a close, active relationship with unions, a reflection that Spanish anarchism had been born within the labour movement and was predominantly made up of workers. Conflict between tendencies did exist, but its immediate cause was fallout from the adoption of propaganda of the deed and the concurrent growth in repression. The OARE did not last long, whilst Tarrida himself would be forced into exile from Spain in 1897, having previously been imprisoned. Nonetheless the Spanish section of the Alliance appears to have only disbanded sometime during the 1880s. The importance given to relations with the unions and the fact that some militants were members of both the Pacto and the OARE suggests that the latter was in many ways a continuation of the Alliance but one which aimed to overcome the differences that had emerged in the 1880s between the different anarchist tendencies.

Division, Wilderness and Violence – Propaganda of the Deed

Conflict between collectivists and communists came into the open almost immediately after the death of Bakunin in 1876. At the Verviers Congress in 1877 (the last congress before the IWMA disappeared), delegates agreed that anarcho-communism should be the movement's goal. Significantly, the Spanish delegates defended the anarcho-collectivist position, a reflection of the dominance this had in the country's labour movement, as demonstrated by efforts to maintain the FRE, FRTE, and Pacto in the extremely unfavourable conditions created by the Spanish authorities.

Nonetheless, the collectivist position was seriously weakened by the wave of repression that spread across Europe following the Paris Commune. The hopes of the First International quickly disappeared: "In this climate in which the exaltation and impotence dragged them to long for a short cut, the most impatient sectors believed that in the violent action of a few people they had found the pickaxe that would start the demolition of the social order."[50] This shortcut was the adoption of a tactic of violence: propaganda of the deed.

Propaganda of the deed appears to have originated in Italy, where Carlo Pisacane, a revolutionary nationalist and socialist, declared that "ideas spring from deeds, not the other way round." This was taken by the Italian anarchist Carlo Cafiero to show that "just as the deed gave rise to the revolutionary idea, so it is the deed again which we must put into practice."[51] In 1877 Cafiero and Malatesta provoked a peasant uprising in southern Italy, in which Malatesta and thirty others, armed and following red flags, seized the village of Lentino, issued arms to the population, and put the public records to the torch. The army quickly retook the city from them. This insurrectionary tactic, whereby militants travelled through the countryside encouraging repressed groups to rise against their repressors and organize themselves in communes, was in essence a form of revolutionary training (similar to the tactic 'gimnasia revolucionaria' – revolutionary gymnastics – adopted by radical anarchists during the Second Republic).[52] Anarchists would not simply sit back and talk about revolution to overthrow oppressive regimes, they would actively provoke rebellion, showing the masses that they were on their side, inspiring them not to accept their fate, and showing them the path towards their own emancipation. Even though the episodes were brief, the precedent had been set: the peasants had seen an alternative, the seeds of revolution were sown, and there would be no return to quiet submission. This was the idea.

A further aspect of the tactic was the assassination of prominent figures directly associated with the repression of the working classes. Here the influence of the violent programme adopted by the Russian revolutionary movement Narodnaya Volya (People's Will) was evident.[53] Their campaign of assassinations of leading figures in the tsarist regime reached its height when Tsar Alexander II was killed by a bomb in 1881. The very same year the London International Congress of anarchists endorsed the tactic of propaganda of the deed, although the concept remained 'imprecise' – the use of violence was accepted but no limitations where specified.[54] The congress advised anarchists "to give weight to the study and application of ... the technical and chemical sciences ... as a means of attack and defense," in other words, the manufacture of explosives.[55] The belief in 1881 was that capitalist society was in crisis, the excessive repression was seen as proof, and it just needed a push to topple over. Propaganda of the deed was seen as a way of doing this. Despite the ideological justification, the tactic was based on an erroneous understanding of the revolutionary potential of unorganised, or scarcely organised, workers and peasants. The basic pretence, spurred by a "naïve revolutionary optimism," was that the acts would "awaken the masses, making the injustice of the society even more evident, attack the symbols of authority ... showing the bourgeois that they were also vulnerable," and thus somehow, it was never really clarified how, would bring about a revolution.[56] What alternative existed for those who sought the overthrow of capitalism? The creation of a revolutionary organization of the masses was next to impossible. Even communication between militants was complicated. The congress also proposed the creation of a central bureau of information, but this was not acted on. Such was the police infiltration of the international movement that Malatesta commented, "It is not by an International League, with endless letters read by the police, that the conspiracy will be mounted [but by] isolated groups."[57] The repression left militants isolated, and they felt forced to act alone or ideologically convinced themselves of the need for this. Basing their faith in a spontaneous insurrection of the impoverished and repressed masses that would lead to revolutionary change, but seeing that this had not occurred, the supporters of propaganda of the deed concluded that it was necessary to provide the spark for the fuse, rather than analyse more deeply the reason why the masses had failed to rise against the oppressors.

No clear definition of propaganda of the deed was ever made, and therefore there is a lack of clarity about what actually constitutes the tactic: insurrectionalism, assassinations of prominent political figures, or bomb attacks that target the bourgeois? This explains much of the confusion about who supported the tactic. For example, Kropotkin and Malatesta had no problem supporting peasant risings such as in Lentino and even justified the assassination of presidents or monarchs directly responsible for the repression of the working masses, but they do not ever appear to have supported apparently indiscriminate bomb attacks and assaults on the general public.[58] Nonetheless, the reference to "technical and chemical sciences" at the London Congress clearly relates to the use of explosives, and it is bombings that have become most associated with propaganda of the deed. It was this violence that would cause serious divisions within the anarchist movement. Some saw the perpetrators as martyrs and heroes helping to bring about the revolution. Others viewed the tactic as ridiculously optimistic and detrimental to anarchism, creating either association in the public's mind between anarchism and violence rather than its ideals. Still others simply felt that there could be no justification for the attacks – that violence of this nature and its exaltation were contrary to anarchist morality.

In Spain as early as 1876 the tactic had apparently been discussed at a meeting in Barcelona, although little information is available and no decision appears to have been made. Moreover it is difficult to distinguish between those acts of violence inherent in the labour struggle against a repressive government and those inspired by the very idea of propaganda of the deed. In any case, it was not until 1886 that the first attacks with explosive devices on buildings belonging to the Catalan employers' organization occurred. The strength of the collectivist position reflected in the policies adopted by the FRE and FRTE had advanced what seemed a more positive option. Nonetheless, by the time of this first attack the collectivist alternative had struck the wall of government repression.

In late 1882 agrarian workers in the province of Cadiz organised in the Unión de Trabajadores del Campo began to plan a strike as part of an attempt to improve the desperate conditions in which they worked. Early in 1883 the authorities in the area suddenly began rounding up anarchists, accusing them of membership of an illegal terrorist organization, la Mano Negra. The existence of la Mano Negra has never actually been proven (and indeed it seems likely that such an organisation did not exist – prominent anarchists in the area claimed that they had no knowledge of any such group). Nonetheless the 'discovery' of the secret organisation was used as a justification for mass repression. The denunciation by an employer or the police or even the mere suspicion of a neighbour were excuse enough to arrest workers.[59] Within a few weeks over three thousand militants were arrested. It is likely that the 'terrorist plot' was invented to justify the repression – to end the dangerous precedent of agrarian workers organizing themselves and preparing for a strike for better conditions and wages. Moreover, in the short term at least, the repression worked. In 1891 Andalusia suffered near famine conditions, and rations had to be distributed to the peasants. The economic crisis and vast inequality in living conditions in the area led to an uprising early the following year in Jerez. The revolt was quickly put down, but the subsequent reprisals by the authorities were extreme, even by the standards of the Spanish state. Hundreds were detained, and eventually four men were executed by garroting. It is worth describing this procedure, as it provides ample proof of the inhumane treatment the Spanish state meted out to those who dared challenge or even question the dominant classes control of society: "Strapped to seats, facing a crowd of soldiers and spectators, a rod was inserted into a cord looped around their neck and slowly rotated to strangulate them. Slower than hanging, far less clinical than the guillotine, it was a punishment that spoke of a governing elite who viewed anarchists as little better than vermin."[60]

It should not therefore be too much of a surprise that some anarchists began to support the idea of responding to violence in kind, "without a thought, starting from the premise that the fallen were 'martyrs' who demanded revenge."[61] Previously there had been bomb attacks against buildings of institutions associated with capitalism. But in the 1890s the targets changed. The period 1893–97 is said to be the 'classic period' for propaganda of the deed in Spain (and more specifically Catalonia), although attacks and assassinations of leading political figures occurred in subsequent years.[62] In September 1893 Paulino Pallás threw two bombs at the *capitan general* of Catalonia, Arsenio Martínez Campos. The bomb missed its target but killed two people. Pallás was executed but not before promising that "vengeance will be terrible." Within a month Santiago Salvador had thrown two bombs into the crowd at the Liceu (opera house) in Barcelona, killing some twenty people and leaving many more injured. Two years later twelve people were killed when a bomb was thrown at a religious parade on Calle de los Cambios Nuevos in the same city. The bombings sowed fear into the ruling classes, confirmed their belief that all anarchists were terrorists, but also horrified many of those the perpetrators aimed to attract, including workers and anarchists themselves, and showed no signs of precipitating a revolutionary insurrection.

On this latter point Nuñez Florencio points out that "the vast majority of the libertarian movement kept well away from the criminals … many others distanced themselves theoretically or ideologically and even within the movement itself there continued to exist a pacifist current as important, if not more so, than this bloody faction."[63] According to José Álvarez Junco the main position within the anarchist movement in Spain was opposition based on the impracticability of the attacks. Anselmo Lorenzo argued that the anarchists had to "convince people, not terrify," whilst Ricardo Mella argued that "an act of violence does not convince anyone, rather it supposes the loss of sympathetic elements who withdraw [from the movement]" and railed against the "blind and barbaric violence" of those "who think that the problem of emancipation can be simply resolved by pruning and cutting the rotten branches of the social tree" and who due to "error or short-sightedness attribute to violence the most lofty of revolutionary virtues ... forgetting that every power and tyranny had been constituted and affirmed by violence."[64] The most critical position was that taken by the anarchist newspaper *La Tramontana*: "The authors of such repugnant acts [who] try to cover their madness or vileness under the façade of ideas that they neither understand, practice, know, nor study should know and understand that the principled people who do share these ideas spit in their faces."[65] It appeared to their opponents within the movement that the supporters of violence had lost both their heads and their hearts.

But opposition from anarchists to the attacks did not save them from the repercussions. The reaction of the authorities was as to be expected, not simply an increase in repression but the effective banning of anarchism as a movement or even ideology. Of course, the repression was not limited simply to those who carried out or supported the actions. The weight of the law fell most specifically on prominent militants of the labour movement and the unions and those anarchists opposed to the violence. In 1894 a law against "attacks with explosives, the fabrication and sale of explosives, and against conspiracy, threat, apology for and any association with such crimes" was passed. A further law in 1896 increased even further the sentences for the authors, accomplices, and those who help cover up crimes. This law was used in 1896 against anarchists accused in relation with the attack on Campos Nuevos earlier that year – even though no one knew who had thrown the bomb and the fact that victims were at the end of the procession, and therefore from the working class, led many to doubt it was even an anarchist. Over four hundred militants were rounded up, imprisoned in Montjuïc Castle in Barcelona, and tortured. Eventually 305 people were charged and 8 sentenced to death, with others saddled with life sentences. Outside of Montjuïc, unions were closed and the libertarian press shut down. Banned, imprisoned, exiled, disillusioned by the lack of action of the masses, and distanced from the labour movements, many anarchists retreated to an intellectual purism detached from contemporary realities.

The tactic of the propaganda of the deed was an unmitigated disaster practically and morally and left the Spanish libertarian movement "without a strong organization … progressively distanced from the labour movement … the few mass actions that it produced; with an unrealistic revolutionary optimism and a great faith in the individual; … and provoking for itself an increasing repression as the attacks continued." Those anarchists "who favoured the tactic didn't want to see what had been obvious from the very start: that this tactic was above all a tragic demonstration of their impotence."[66]

Elsewhere propaganda of the deed brought similar misery to the movement. Anarchism was effectively made illegal by laws in France (les lois scélérates), Italy (Crispi Laws), Argentina (Ley de Residencia, Ley de Defensa Social), and other countries. In 1898 representatives from twenty-one nation-states attended an anti-anarchist conference in Rome to discuss how to end the anarchist threat. They agreed to sharing of information between national police forces and enacting new legislation to facilitate the suppression of anarchy. Subsequently, in 1904, ten countries signed a 'Secret Protocol for the International War on Anarchism' in Saint Petersburg, and Spain went along.[67] The US president, Theodore Roosevelt, declared anarchism "a crime against the whole human race."

Nuñez Florencio has noted that "justifications of the propaganda of the deed normally came from the anarcho-communist sector." Specifically it was the influence of individualism that penetrated the communists more than the collectivists and led many to think that an individual act could light the spark that would lead to revolution, whereas "the collectivists completely rejected the tactic."[68] This is not surprising, given that as a general rule the collectivist revolution was based on the organised forces of the labour movement, whilst the communists put their faith in spontaneous rebellion of the people aided by the independently organised affinity groups. But one should not oversimplify the case. Those individuals and groups more directly involved in the violence may have been closer to the communists but represented an individualist current on the extreme edges of the ideology. Prominent communists, such as Malatesta and Kropotkin, both highly regarded and widely read in Spain, never denied the importance of the labour organizations but did not see them as the only revolutionary path open to the masses. They were aware of the potential of unions to become bureaucratized or to accept their role as moderators between capitalist and working class, rather than trying to destroy the former. Furthermore, despite accepting the need for some measure of violence in the revolutionary struggle of the working class, they both condemned the individual acts of violence and bomb attacks that by the 1890s were the cornerstone of propaganda of the deed. For Malatesta the perpetrators of the attacks were not guided by "a love for the human race ... but the feeling of vendetta joined to a cult of an abstract idea, of a theoretical phantasm."[69] Kropotkin warned against the "illusion that one can defeat the coalition of exploiters with a few pounds of explosives," arguing that the anarchists should "be with the people, who no longer want isolated acts, but want men of action inside their ranks."[70]

The anarcho-communists needed to reestablish bonds with the collectivists, strengthening the relationship between anarchism and the labour movement. The calamitous results of propaganda of the deed only served to demonstrate the fallacy of the belief in the overthrow of capitalism by the spontaneous insurrection of the masses. Both internationally and nationally the capitalist states had increasingly well-structured defence mechanisms. Moreover, following the formation of the Second International in 1889 and the growth of universal male suffrage across most of the continent, social democratic parties based on the model provided by the orthodox Marxist Social Democratic Party of Germany (SPD) had seen their vote increase dramatically. The legal, peaceful, collaborationist path to emancipation appeared to be bearing fruit.[71] A revolutionary ideology needs a revolutionary force, and in the context of the growth of industrial capitalism that force had to be the unions. It was obvious to most anarchists that if they remained divided and isolated they would not be able to influence the advance of the working-class movement or even the direction it took. At the same time the increasing complexities of international capitalist production as well as the gradual deskilling in the workplace made the collectivist goal of a society in which wages were decided 'to each according to his labour' more problematic. The communist alternative, outlined with great clarity in the works of Kropotkin – *The Conquest of Bread* and *Fields, Factories and Workshops* – provided an ideological solution to these complexities. Although mutual suspicions continued, the following decades would see a form of collectivist-communist synthesis: anarcho-syndicalism. Collectivist tactics would be used to achieve the communist goal.[72]

2.

THE EARLY YEARS OF
THE CNT: GERMINATION

The birth of revolutionary syndicalism, with origins in the IWMA, reunited the anarchist movement with the labour movement. This was apparently a synthesis not simply of communists and collectivists but also of workers who distrusted the political machinations of the so-called workers' parties (or simply wanted to keep open their options) with the anarchist movement as a whole. Revolutionary syndicalism essentially bridged the anti-authoritarian wing of the IWMA – with its stress on the economic path to emancipation and in which the Spanish section played a leading role – with the economic and political realities of an industrialising society in which the political system did not help workers' standards of living or working conditions. But syndicalism did not bridge the division between those who felt that ideas should dominate in the unions and those who gave priority to strength, bringing all workers together in one organization. In the short term, however, the rapid surge of syndicalism in the years before the First World War patched some of the cracks in this relationship, creating a force that could demand reforms but was yet not prepared to directly challenge the continuation of the capitalist state.

The growth of syndicalism internationally was impressive. Whereas in 1906 the French CGT – Confédération Générale du Travail – had been the "only avowedly syndicalist labour organization in Europe," by 1912 there were syndicalist organizations throughout Europe as well as North and South America.[1] The French CGT led the way, claiming over six hundred thousand members by 1912, while Italy the same year saw the foundation of the Unione Sindacale Italiana, with eighty thousand members, a figure that would rise to one hundred thousand the next year, and syndicalist organizations in Scandinavia, Germany, the United Kingdom, the United States, and Latin America enjoyed similar fortunes. In Spain, Solidaridad Obrera had been formed in Catalonia in 1907, and by 1908 this regional syndicalist organization boasted almost forty thousand members before being devastated by government repression.[2]

Nonetheless, whilst accepting the revolutionary potential of syndicalism, many Spanish anarchists warned against the bureaucratic and reformist tendencies they believed endemic in trade unions, voicing their fears about the potential dangers of anarchists becoming consumed in the economic day-to-day struggles of the unions. But rather than sit on the sidelines, they actively joined in the labour struggle. The strength of the anarchist movement and its suspicions about revolutionary syndicalism were evident at the founding congress of the CNT in 1910, at which the newly created revolutionary syndicalist organisation was given a clearly anarchist outlook.

Although in Spain industrialisation developed at a painstakingly slow pace until the First World War, the growth of unionism elsewhere inevitably had an influence on Spanish in Spain. As it transpired, the greatest influence on the Spanish labour movement came from an organisation that itself had been inspired by the anti-authoritarian wing of the First International and whose organisational base owed much to the FRE and the First International.[3] The French CGT, founded in 1895, updated the collectivist ideas of the First International, developing a coherent body of policies relevant to an industrialising society, emphasising the independence of the trade unions from political parties, the necessity of class unity, and the use of direct action, with the general strike as the ultimate means of bringing about the social revolution.[4] To avoid individuals using the unions as steppingstones to further their political careers, or the unions becoming simply an appendage of a political party (the French Socialist Party), the unions were to be independent of all political institutions whilst, by adopting an organisational structure based on a bottom-up approach, giving each individual union autonomy, it was hoped to avoid the creation of a domineering elite with a vested interest in affairs other than the immediate good of those they represented.

Operating according to this new plan, the trade unions, Fernand Pelloutier (secretary responsible for the section of the Bourses, a pivotal section of the CGT) argued, could become "the practical school of anarchism." Georges Yvetot, another leading figure within the CGT, went as far as arguing that syndicalism was simply a branch of anarchism.[5] Speaking at the CGT's 1910 congress, Yvetot said, "I am reproached with confusing syndicalism and anarchism. It is not my fault if they have the same end in view. Anarchism pursues the integral emancipation of the individual; syndicalism the integral emancipation of the working man. I find the whole of syndicalism in anarchism."[6] Nonetheless, for the majority of anarchists who saw the potential of the revamped unionism, the reverse was not true.

However, as with the FRE, the CGT was not an anarchist organisation. It was a working-class organisation open to all workers with the goal of gathering together in one economic organisation all the working class, irrespective of their political persuasion. To maintain working-class cohesion among the different ideological groups within the unions and attract new members that were needed to make direct action a practical tactic, the CGT needed to appeal to all and upset none, a difficult feat that was achieved by the adoption of an apolitical position, rather than an openly anti-parliamentary one. So, although many anarchists entered the unions, this does not mean that the unions themselves became anarchist or that the activity of these militants was in favour of anarchism.

The compromise over political relations was implicit in the Charter of Amiens (1906), a statement of principles that gave each individual member complete liberty "to participate, outside his union, in whatsoever forms of struggle conform to his political or philosophical views" whilst in turn "requesting that he, in exchange, not introduce into his union the opinions he holds outside it." The charter also repeated the CGT's commitment to the double task, *double besogne*, by which it was responsible for the coordination of the workers to help achieve their day-to-day demands as well as preparing for "complete emancipation, which can be realised only by expropriating the capitalist class; it sanctions the general strike as its means of action and it maintains that the trade union, today an organisation of resistance, *will in the future be the organisation of production and distribution, the basis of social reorganisation.*"[7]

The *double besogne* was the basis for the CGT motto that syndicalism *'suffit à tout'* – was sufficient in itself – and required no outside assistance in the achievement of short-term and long-term aims. For the CGT, revolutionary syndicalism provided the perfect combination of ideology and action, a praxis that not only contained the means to bring about and defend the revolution, but also would create the base and driving force for the future society that this would inaugurate. The dependence on the spontaneous organisation of the masses to create the new society was thus replaced by the force of the independent and organised labour movement. The Charter of Amiens finally laid down on paper the ideological basis for a new movement that had been developing within the CGT since its formation: revolutionary syndicalism. The charter was the blueprint for the revolutionary syndicalist organisations that developed across the continent and beyond in the years before the outbreak of the First World War.[8]

However, the charter was flawed from birth. The compromise over political relations involved an evident contradiction between the interests of party and union. It was the union, in which political discourse was forbidden, that was to be the basis of the future society and which, apparently, *'suffit à tout'*. Thus, theoretically, CGT members who also had party political affiliations would be expected to concede automatically to the will of the union should there be conflict with the party. In the extreme case of revolution this would mean that they would have to acquiesce in the disappearance of their parties, as these were to have no role in a future syndicalist society. If the party involved did not share the same opinion, as could be expected, an inevitable struggle would arise between party and union loyalties. If the CGT was *suffit à tout*, then clearly its policies were at odds with the parties that attracted working-class support at the time, be they liberal, radical, or socialist. By avoiding divisive debate over political matters, political disputes could be avoided.

While the revolution remained a distant dream, blind faith in the revolutionary potential of the general strike concealed the contradictions at the heart of the Charter of Amiens. The organisation of the revolution and post-revolutionary society were political acts. Therefore, obviously, the unions needed to take an active interest in political issues and the question of political power, taking politics as not simply the battle between parties but the organization and administration of society. By not having a clearly defined political programme (which evidently included the rejection of party politics), the CGT created a void that could be, and indeed was, filled by the political parties and the state. Political neutrality left the unions at the mercy of political parties which did not hesitate to point the direction that the workers should follow. Once the socialists' predilection for parliamentary politics had led them to collaborate with the state, conflict between the different political factions in the CGT could no longer be avoided. This resulted in the CGT splitting in two in 1922, between moderate and revolutionary syndicalists. However, the close collaboration between the state and leading syndicalists of the CGT during the First World War suggested that neutrality was no longer a viable option, a fact that became obvious during the social unrest of the latter period of the war and in the period following the October Revolution in Russia. Revolutionary syndicalism, as defined in the Charter of Amiens, was only revolutionary in non-revolutionary situations.

But this was all for the future. In the years immediately preceding the war, the need for working-class unity overrode ideological considerations. Nonetheless, even during this period political neutrality soon became political vacuity. The reformism that would make collaboration possible during the war was evident on an international level with the CGT's refusal to become involved in the moves to form a

revolutionary syndicalist International, preferring instead to sit alongside the reformist organisations in the International Secretariat of
National Trade Union Centres (ISNTUC).[9]

The differences between the CGT's vision of politically neutral revolutionary syndicalism and the anarchist interpretation of syndicalism
were demonstrated in the 1907 International Anarchist Congress in
Amsterdam.[10] The CGT was represented at the congress by Pierre
Monatte. In the discussion about anarchism and syndicalism, Monatte
claimed that revolutionary syndicalism was the movement of the future, an essential weapon for the working class in its struggle against
the modern industrialised state.[11] According to Monatte, syndicalism,
"unlike socialism and anarchism which *preceded it*," was based "on
actions not theories." United together in a great federation, the workers could *faire parler les faits* – let the facts do the talking. Monatte
outlined CGT policy as stated in the Charter of Amiens and advocated this as the basis for other syndicalist organisations. Anarchists
should join the unions alongside other anti-authoritarian socialists,
as exploited workers and not due to ideological beliefs. Monatte also
stressed that "anarchy is our final aim" and said that he still considered
himself an anarchist.[12]

Errico Malatesta countered Monatte's thesis, holding to the established anarcho-communist criticism that trade unions in themselves
were actually conservative and bureaucratic institutions born from
the capitalist system. Malatesta questioned how syndicalism could be
expected to overthrow capitalism when it was itself a creation of capitalism. Although he accepted that syndicalism could emancipate the
workers, it could not liberate everyone, and, as such, the claim that
syndicalism was sufficient in itself was false. Malatesta warned against
the potential of syndicalism to engulf anarchism, resulting in those
anarchists who joined the unions being forced to place economic concerns above moral issues to such an extent that the latter would be
forgotten altogether.[13]

Malatesta was not arguing that anarchists should remain indiffer-
ent or opposed to the syndicalist movement. What he rejected was
the idea that syndicalism represented a specific ideology and was not
simply a means by which anarchy could be achieved: "We [anarchists]
are convinced supporters of the labour movement, or if you prefer, the

syndicalist movement … but we are not syndicalists, if by syndicalism one means that doctrine which gives syndicalism alone a special virtue that must automatically … lead us to emancipate ourselves from the yoke of capitalism and to build a new society." Anarchists should join the unions but not aim to control them or attempt to limit membership according to ideology. He argued that the unions should be neutral, open to all workers irrespective of ideological or party affiliation:

> With political and religious neutrality, the masses, or a large part of the masses, can join together for the purposes of propaganda and revolutionary action. If this were not the case, they would be controlled by the politicians and the priests; we want them [the unions] to be neutral because they cannot be anarchist. And they cannot be anarchist, because this would require the whole mass [of the working class] to be anarchist, and in this case the union could merge with the anarchist group and there would be no need to try and convince the stragglers and lead them in the battle.[14]

For Malatesta, rather than attempting to take over the unions, anarchists should work to ensure that no other political or religious group did so.[15] Furthermore, in order to prevent the formation of an elite of functionaries within the unions, anarchists should work to guarantee that all administrative tasks were carried out voluntarily by an alternating group of militants, who, where possible, would not be paid. However, in working to achieve this, the anarchists should not undertake any official position within the unions. Their task was to set an example for the workers and be the first to take risks and make sacrifices when necessary.

So, although Malatesta was critical of syndicalism, he also viewed active anarchist involvement in the labour movement as essential to reacquaint the working class with anarchist ideals and to ensure it was not won over again by the socialists: "According to our way of seeing things, the anarchists must take the side of those organisations that are closest to their methods and ideals, and in the periods of active struggle, be with those who are fighting. … [We must] fight the disease, in the labour organisations, of the politicians and social climbers who want to use the workers as a footstool to fashion themselves a position in the bourgeois world."[16]

The unions represented simply one sphere, a very important one in the contemporary conditions, in which the anarchists should operate. In the end, the Amsterdam congress supported Malatesta's position and passed a motion that supported the entrance of anarchists into the unions, whilst advising them that their action there be limited to ensuring that the principles of direct action were observed. The motion concluded by reminding anarchists that, although syndicalism was a powerful means for revolution, it was not a substitute for it.[17] Syndicalism may have provided the force to destroy the old capitalist society but it did not necessarily have the ideas to create a fairer new one.

Although the next years witnessed a rapid growth in the number and size of organised revolutionary syndicalist movements across Europe and the world, it would be erroneous to suggest that the decisions at Amsterdam played an important role in this – the international anarchist movement did not enjoy such influence.[18] The relevance of the debates lies more in the different positions of the two main protagonists than in the motion passed: Monatte represented what would become the classic revolutionary syndicalist position. Malatesta reflected the position of those anarchists who accepted the revolutionary potential of the labour movement but were also wary of the dangers it presented to their movement, a position that would have important ramifications in Spain more than in his homeland, Italy. The fact that both supported the entrance of anarchists into the unions and both defined themselves as anarchists, when they actually represented very different positions towards syndicalism, provides an early example of the problems involved in defining the different currents within the revolutionary syndicalist movement.

Tierra y Libertad, the main anarchist weekly newspaper in Spain at the time, supported the position defended by Malatesta at Amsterdam. Following the Amsterdam congress, articles by Malatesta on syndicalism appeared regularly in the Spanish libertarian press.[19] Wariness by certain sections of the Spanish anarchist movement towards syndicalism would increase as the strength of the syndicalist movement in

Spain grew. The limitations to Malatesta's position – what happened when internal debate was limited or banned by a dominant faction? – would only become clear after the Russian Revolution and the subsequent creation of communist parties throughout Europe and the world, and even the Italian would update his ideas in light of events.[20]

The need to clarify the relationship between anarchism and syndicalism was also one of main reasons that led Amédée Dunois, a French anarchist who was also a member of the CGT, to argue for the need to create an international anarchist organisation independent of the unions. He did this in his speech on 'anarchist organisation' at the congress. Dunois argued that since the turn of the century a "decisive evolution" had occurred in the "minds and practices" of the anarchists that had resulted in them joining the workers movement "actively" and participating "in peoples lives." Dunois continued, "We have overcome the gap between the pure idea, which can so easily turn to dogma, and real life [and] have become less and less interested in the sociological abstractions of yore and more and more interested in the practical movement, in action." Syndicalists argued that the anarchists needed to join the unions, as these were the "living bud[s] of the future society." This connection with the people, the workers, was vital, for, Dunois continued, "No matter how backward and limited the people may be, it is they, and not the ideologue, who are the indispensable force of every social revolution. … We willingly assign pride of place in the field of action to the workers' movement, convinced as we have been for so long that the emancipation of the workers will be at the hands of those concerned or it will not be."[21]

Again there is clear acceptance that the workers' movement was the most likely revolutionary force and as such must be as strong as possible, hence the need to try to unite all workers together in one union. Anarchists needed to "create a link" and "provide constant support" for the labour organization. There needed to be a symbiotic relationship. This would be mutually beneficial: the anarchists would become stronger due to daily contact with the realities of the working class organizations: "The stronger we are – and we will only become strong by organizing ourselves – the stronger will be the flow of ideas that we can send through the workers' movement, which will thus slowly become impregnated with the anarchist spirit."[22] Meanwhile anarchists would provide the intellectual and ideological accompaniment to the labour struggle.

Anarchists needed to leave their ivory towers and reconnect with the labour movement. They could not and should not dominate the movement, as this had its own internal logic – to unite as much of the working class together in one organization strong enough to challenge the rule of capitalism – but should work to see that their ideas eventually prevailed among the unions. The best way to do this was to organise outside the unions, thereby presenting a unified front strong enough to impress, through argument and organization, the workers to follow their lead.

Although most delegates were clearly in favour of closer organisation, the debate on the question demonstrated the confusion and potential for disunity that the question of individualism posed for the movement. In fact many individualist anarchists had refused to attend the congress, precisely because it was organised to discuss the need to establish an international anarchist organization. Their position was neatly summed up by Hynan Croiset, who did turn up and who argued, "My motto is: Me, me, me ... and then the others. ... Organisations ... have the inevitable result of limiting the freedom of the individual to a greater or lesser degree. Anarchy is therefore contrary to any permanent system of organisations. ... Anarchist ideas must preserve their ancient purity, instead of trying to become more practical. Let us return to the ancient purity of our ideas."[23]

Individualism is a concept shared by both anarchism and liberalism, but the difference is simple. Liberals believe that humans create society and that this is nothing more than a loose collection of individuals who come together when they need to achieve some specific function. For liberals, people are motivated by pure self-interest, hence the need for a state to regulate relations. As opposed to self-indulgent individualism, which can lead to extreme exploitation by one over another, anarchist individualism did not place the individual above or outside society. As described in chapter 1, in the view of anarchists, society creates the individual. No individual can and does live entirely alone and disconnected to society, nor can humans progress if society does not advance. All individuals are naturally part of society, and their freedom depends upon them working together to ensure that this society is as free as possible. This is the basis of the anarchist concept of individualism, often confused or not clarified by historians of anarchism in general.

Most general histories of anarchism mention the writings of the German philosopher Max Stirner (Johann Kaspar Schmidt), including *The Ego and Its Own*, in which he took individual self-interest to its extreme, advocating that individuals form 'unions of egotists' to achieve goals only when they deem it necessary. In Stirner's ideal world there are no moral restraints to egoism – there is no morality at all. Stirner was an extreme individualist and not an anarchist, although some aspects of his arguments influenced individuals on the periphery of the movement. Bohemian artistic circles of the turn of the century which showed an interest in anarchism were peopled by middle-class intellectuals who had little or no contact with the anarchist and labour movements. The influence of Stirner's thinking was highly limited, mainly the preserve of radical middle-class or artistic circles at the turn of the century who mixed Stirner's ideas with the nihilism of Nietzsche – an academic fringe largely irrelevant to the anarchist movement, especially that associated with the labour movement. This is not to say that no anarchists found his ideas of interest, but in general he was ignored, and his ideas are anathema to the main proponents of an organised anarchist movement. This was even more the case in Spain than elsewhere.

In the 1920s many Spanish anarchists had close contacts with prominent French and Belgian individualist anarchists due to being exiled in these countries, but there is little evidence that this represented acceptance of, or support for, their ideas in general (see note 69 to chapter 7). The main influences on Spanish anarchism came from Bakunin and Kropotkin. For Kropotkin, true individuality could only be realized "through practicing the highest communist sociability." The basis of anarchist morality was solidarity.[24] Bakunin similarly linked the rights of an individual to his or her duties to society. At the 1907 International Anarchist Congress, Malatesta, who would be the most widely published international anarchist in the pages of the Spanish libertarian press during the early years of the CNT, clarified the position: "All anarchists, whatever tendency they belong to, are individualists in some way or other. But the opposite is not true; not by any means. Man 'alone' cannot carry out even the smallest useful, productive task ... that which frees the individual, that which allows him to develop all his faculties, is not solitude, but association." Those who did not accept the principle role given to society were individualists but not anarchists. Malatesta concluded:

> It is time for all of us to work together in order to exert an effective influence on social events. It pains me to think that in order to free one of our own people from the clutches of a hangman it was necessary for us to turn to other parties instead of our own. Ferrer would not then owe his freedom to masons and bourgeois free thinkers, if the anarchists gathered together in a powerful and feared International had been able to run for themselves the worldwide protest against the criminal infamy of the Spanish government. ... Let us ensure that the Anarchist International finally becomes a reality. To enable us to appeal quickly to all our comrades, to struggle against the reaction and to act, when the time is right, with revolutionary initiative, there must be an International![25]

Tellingly, Pierre Ramus supported the formation of an international organization but warned, "As for the aim of the new International, it must not act as an auxiliary force of revolutionary syndicalism. It must occupy itself with the propaganda of anarchism in its entirety."[26]

In the end the congress voted in favour of an amended motion put forward by Dunois that advised "comrades from every country to proceed to form anarchist groups and federate the groups once they had formed." An addendum by Malatesta and the Czech anarchist Karel Vohryzek was also approved: "The Anarchist Federation is an association of groups and individuals in which no-one can impose his will nor belittle the initiative of others. Its goal with regard to the present society is to change all the moral and economic conditions and accordingly it supports the struggle with all appropriate means."[27] This represented an extremely general basis for a programme.

The next session of the congress discussed the creation of such a federation and founded the Anarchist International, which was to be made up of the anarchist organizations that already existed and groups and individuals (endorsed by organizations) that would be able to join subsequently. An International Bureau was set up, with five members to be based in London and with the aim of creating an international anarchist archive and establish relations with anarchists globally. In the end, only this bureau showed any sign of life after the congress.

In Spain, the real problem was not so much extreme individualism – though this did exist – but the fact that many anarchists saw the labour unions as the natural place for anarchist organisation and therefore did not feel the need to create a separate anarchist organisation. If anarchists could ensure that the labour movement was faithful to anarchist goals, there was no need to organise themselves at a national level beyond this.

The Formation of the CNT

Syndicalist ideas emanating from across the Pyrenees found immediate acceptance among a number of respected militants in the Spanish anarchist movement, most notably Francesc Ferrer, Ricardo Mella, Anselmo Lorenzo, and José Prat.[28] For Lorenzo, a veteran of the First International, "modern syndicalism" was simply "the International itself reappearing after a cease-fire in history."[29] The Catalan Prat, although enthusiastic about the potential of syndicalism, qualified his support, arguing that syndicalism "was not a theory, but a fact" and simply an immediate consequence of the capitalist system. As such, it was not inherently revolutionary, but, spurred on by anarchists, it could be so. He therefore urged anarchists to join the unions because union members were "in the end workers like us."[30] Moreover, the Radical Party, preaching a demagogic anti-clericalism, was increasingly popular among the Catalan working classes, whilst the socialists, despite a limited support base, were also looking to increase its influence in the region. If the anarchists continued to stay aloof from the workers' organisations, others were prepared to fill the void.[31]

Syndicalism received immediate approbation largely due to the fact that the rise of the CGT in France occurred at the same time as a noticeable upsurge in labour unrest in Spain. A short-lived economic boom at the turn of the century created the climate for rapid growth in union organisation although the unions remained predominantly small, craft-based, and localised organisations. In particular, the years 1900–1903 witnessed a sudden growth in labour unrest.[32] In 1900, at a regional congress of labour societies in Madrid, the FRE was reborn. Although a pale version of the original, it managed to celebrate annual congresses until 1906.[33] However, the fact that outside of Catalonia the FRE enjoyed meagre support suggested that it would be better to organise the workers initially on a regional basis.

In 1904 attempts were made at reorganising the labour unions in Barcelona and the surrounding area, but with little success. Finally, the failure in 1906 of an attempted general strike in favour of the eight-hour workday forced the realization that the labour movement needed to be better coordinated. A commission was created to draw up the statutes of the new union, and these were published in *Tierra y Libertad* in July 1907 and formed the basis of a new regional syndicalist federation, Solidaridad Obrera (SO).[34] SO was actually an amalgam of those with differing left-wing views, including anarchists, republicans, and socialists, and it was militants from the latter group who provided the initiative for its formation, in particular Antonio Fabra Ribas and Antonio Badía Matamala.[35] The socialist UGT had also benefitted from the growth in union activity, but regional politics, an aversion to the political influence of the socialist Partido Socialista Obrera Español (PSOE), and the reformist policies enforced by the Madrid-based union leadership meant that it was unable to attract much support in Catalonia.[36] Fabra and Badía were attempting to remedy the failure of the orthodox Marxist UGT to win support in the most industrialised region of Spain. The anarchists also wanted to ensure the support of the Catalan working class. Alongside SO an Ateneo Sindicalista (Syndicalist Athenaeum) was founded that "offered a tribune to colleagues who wished to propagate revolutionary syndicalism in order to facilitate the creation of syndicalist anarchists who could orient [SO] conscientiously and revolutionarily."[37]

In July 1909, a popular revolt broke out against the call-up of reservists (who came predominantly from the working class) for the colonial war in Morocco. Protests soon took the form of a general strike, with barricades put up in working-class neighbourhoods across the capital and throughout Catalonia and assemblies or councils set up to coordinate events. The revolt was not anarchist-led but popular, including republicans and socialists as well as those of no clear political orientation. This period of social unrest (July 26–31) and the resultant government repression against the general strike and those opposed to the call-up was dubbed the Tragic Week by the Catalan bourgeoisie but known as the July Revolution to many in the working class. During the disturbances a number of churches were burnt to the ground, due to the Catholic Church's association with the state and its support of the war. The government used the violence against the church during the Tragic Week as an excuse to launch a crackdown against anarchists in Barcelona. Francesc Ferrer, the pioneer of the rational schools, was accused of being the organiser of the violence and was executed. The charges were false. If anything, the violence was not organised (hence the need for a stronger working-class organisation). Ferrer was targeted by the Church, which feared that the influence of his schools endangered its monopoly on education.[38] Moreover, Ferrer had generously funded SO as well as the pro-syndicalist newspaper *Huelga General*.

There were lessons to be learnt. The July Revolution was said to be "the last romantic revolution" and "a glance back at the nineteenth century, to traditional popular protest."[39] The spontaneous insurrection, it had been hoped, would lead to full-blown revolution. But it had failed, and the vengeful repression was successful. New tactics were needed.

The Semana Tragica had also resulted in the weakening of the Radical Republican Party's influence among the workers, as many Republican workers rallied to the protests only to see the party hierarchy distance itself, with prominent members playing an important role in the justification for the repression that followed. "Lerroux's Party was given a death blow. It forever ceased to be a party of the masses, and was reduced … to being a conglomerate of political climbers which was no longer fed by the wisdom of the masses."[40] Indeed, during the Second Republic, the Radical Party would joined forces with the parties of reaction, with Lerroux still at the helm.

The revolt had caused the postponement of a congress called by SO which was due to be held in September 1909. SO initiated steps to link up with associations from across the country that shared the same ideas in order to create a new national organisation, but this was unacceptable to the socialists, who saw no reason for the creation of an alternative to the UGT. Pressure from Madrid resulted in the socialist presence noticeably weakening in SO, and so subsequently socialist involvement in the newly created national organisation was virtually negligible.[41]

When organisations gathered for the 'Foundation Congress' of the Confederación Nacional del Trabajo in Barcelona from October 30 to November 1, 1910, they represented different schools of syndicalism, but the influence of anarchists predominated. In the discussion over whether syndicalism was "the means of the ends of the workers' emancipation," the resolution approved by the congress made clear that syndicalism "must not be considered as a social goal, must not be interpreted as an ideal, but as a means of [class] struggle."[42] For the CNT, syndicalism was simply a means, not an end in itself. The end would be clarified at the Madrid congress in 1919.

The 1910 congress did not represent an organisation in action, as none existed, which explains the vague nature of many of the decisions adopted and makes it impossible to draw any precise conclusions about the overall ideological direction of the CNT.[43] The task of adding meat to the bones of the decisions made in 1910 began in earnest following an extraordinary meeting of 'juntas and delegates' on January 5, 1911.[44] Following the meeting, a manifesto was issued that called on the unions to organise on a geographical basis, as opposed to by profession, creating local and then regional federations, and finally a national federation. The manifesto also spoke of the need to base the social struggle in "the purest economic field" and of the role that would be played by a conscious proletarian minority to avoid the pitfalls inherent in stepping outside a purely economic sphere.[45]

At a conference held in Barcelona in August 1911, which was presided over by José Negre, delegates of the CNT, the UGT, and the French CGT discussed the relative differences in tactics of the different organisations. Negre drew on the similarities between the CGT and the CNT, focusing especially on the adoption of direct action.[46] The stress on the use of direct action is important as it drew a clear line between the tactics of the UGT and those of the CNT. The adoption of direct action as the exclusive tactical base of the CNT, as opposed to action built on what was termed a 'multiple base', was the most important decision of the CNT's first congress, held in Barcelona, September 8–10, 1911.[47] Syndicalism's '*a base multiple*' included corporatist as well as reformist tactics, such as the building of strike funds or pensions and other means which it was felt would stifle the potential for spontaneous action by the unions, softening the nature of the class struggle and leading the CNT towards an acceptance of capitalism.[48] Despite distancing itself tactically from the UGT, the CNT maintained the syndicalist (and, of course, Marxist) desire for class unity, and the congress agreed that once the CNT had reached numerical parity with the UGT, the two organisations should merge.

Even in this early period the CNT made a number of decisions that set it apart from the pure revolutionary syndicalism of the French CGT. The adoption of direct action and the rejection of political action in favour of economic action were consistent with the Charter of Amiens, but the rejection of syndicalism as an end in itself was not. For the revolutionary syndicalists, syndicalism was sufficient in itself, whilst the inaugural congress of the CNT had made clear that syndicalism was simply a means, a new tactic towards an old goal, a point emphasised by Negre: "The emancipation of the workers must be accomplished by the workers themselves. … The most convenient tactic is determined by the circumstances and the moment: the orientation and the final goal is always the same."[49]

The goal was the same as that outlined by Farga Pellicer at the first Spanish Labour Congress in 1870: anarchism. Although it could be argued that anarchism – libertarian communism – was also the ultimate goal of the CGT and would be that of Lenin and the Bolsheviks (once the state had withered away), Negre's use of the word 'orientation' is highly relevant. Anarchism was not simple the goal but the guiding force. So although it may be premature to talk of the CNT as an anarcho-syndicalist organisation in its early years, it was evident that it represented a very Spanish interpretation of revolutionary syndicalism, in which the influence of anarchism was strongly evident.[50]

The exact nature of the CNT's ideology at this early stage cannot be clearly defined, as revolutionary syndicalism in Spain was still in its infancy, and thus the differentiation between specific factions had not reached a level at which such clarification became necessary. Indeed, the term 'anarcho-syndicalism' does not appear in early articles in either *Solidaridad Obrera* or *Tierra y Libertad*. The one position that was clear was the difference in approach between the revolutionary syndicalism of the CNT and the evolutionist socialism of the UGT, although the CNT hoped to be able to bridge the tactical divide between the two in the future.

Nonetheless, what was important at this stage was not endless discussion about ideological nuances within the syndicalist school but action against the state and employers. In Spain prior to the First World War, the CNT did not have the time or the strength of numbers to experience the potential conflicts that existed between revolutionary syndicalism, anarcho-syndicalism, and anarchism. The Spanish working class was not as large or as politicised as it would be following the industrial growth and unrest generated by the war, which would be reflected in the sharp rise in CNT membership in the years following 1916. In the pre-war years the CNT enjoyed only a brief legal existence. Almost immediately following its first congress, the CNT called a general strike in support of strikers in Bilbao and in protest against the colonial war being fought in Morocco. As a result, in September 1911 the CNT was declared illegal, its leaders detained, *Solidaridad Obrera* suspended, and its unions closed.[51]

Elsewhere, the years immediately prior to the outbreak of the war represented the heyday of the syndicalist movement, as blind faith and enthusiasm covered the cracks in the ideological base of revolutionary syndicalism. The existence of rival social democratic unions provided syndicalists of all shades with a common enemy they could unite against. It was the desire to distance themselves from the reformist organisations whilst at the same time contacting like-minded organisations that gave rise to calls for an international alternative to the social democrat–controlled ISNTUC.

During the Amsterdam International Anarchist Congress in 1907, a number of delegates, including Fritz Kater from Germany, Christiaan Cornelissen from the Netherlands, the Italian anarchist Luigi Fabbri, and Pierre Monatte, had held two private meetings at which it was decided to establish an international press bureau headed by Cornelissen which would be responsible for publication of the

Bulletin international du mouvement syndicalist.[52] The *Bulletin* kept the syndicalist militants up to date with the progress of fellow organisations across the globe. Among its collaborators were José Negre and Anselmo Lorenzo, who kept militants in other countries informed about developments in Spain.[53] However, revolutionary syndicalism was very much in its infancy in 1907, and six more years were necessary before the national organisations felt sufficiently equipped to expand their interests into the international arena.

The London International Syndicalist Congress, September 1913

The first international syndicalist congress was organised by the Industrial Syndicalist Education League (ISEL) in England together with the Dutch National Arbeids Secretariaat (NAS), with the former winning the honour of being the host although depending on finances from the latter.[54] The ISEL invitation, addressed to "the members of labour unions and syndicalist propagandist bodies everywhere," severely criticised the existing international organisation (the ISNTUC), saying it was composed of "glib-tongued politicians" and run by "conservative" officials or "reactionaries" who did not represent the common worker. What was needed was "a congress of the rank and file, not of officials. We want to confer on means of action, not merely on pious resolutions. We want common action against war, not parliamentary palaver. We want international solidarity expressed in direct action."[55]

For the CNT, domestic considerations meant that the ISEL invitation could hardly have arrived at a more fortuitous moment. The CNT had remained disorganised since 1911, but moves to reorganise its scattered forces began in Catalonia in late 1912.[56] The attempted reorganisation initially provided the backdrop against which deliberations about the proposals and delegations to be sent to London took place. When, in August 1913, the reorganisation was cut short following a strike by manufacturing unions in Catalonia, it was the need for solidarity with their international comrades that became of paramount importance (although the decisions made at the London congress might have influenced a future attempt to rebuild the national movement in Spain).[57]

The London congress was thus a significant event for the CNT for both domestic and international considerations. The reaction of the anarchist and syndicalist press was unsurprisingly enthusiastic. An editorial in the first number of *Solidaridad Obrera* to appear following eighteen months of suspension spoke of the preparations being made for the congress that would see the rebirth of the "International Pact."[58] The hope was that a new IWMA would restore Spanish labour's international contacts.

Further editorials spoke of the "vivificante oxígeno" (life-giving oxygen) that the congress could give to the international proletariat and urged readers to take time off from their daily struggles to put forward initiatives for the Spanish delegates to take to London.[59] The paper also stressed the impact that the congress could have upon the CNT itself: "In no other country does the proletariat find itself more isolated than in ours. ... Isolated by our mental weakness from the world of the proletariat, we need to rub shoulders with them; it is of the utmost importance that we offer a hand of friendship in a formal act such as the congress of London of the proletariat of the New and Old Worlds."[60]

Referring to the congress, José Negre spoke of the need for revolutionary syndicalism to take "new directions," a feeling echoed by Antonio Babra, who argued that the CNT had to attend in order to mix with the more modern trends of syndicalism.[61] The importance of the congress was such that a proposed propaganda excursion organised by J. Suárez Duque, one of the eventual CNT delegates who attended the congress, was postponed until after the congress, in order to include what had been learnt in London.[62]

The reaction of the anarchist periodical *Tierra y Libertad* was even more welcoming than that of the syndicalist paper: "Spanish and American Workers! ... to the Syndicalist Congress of London! ... Trade unionists, trade union federations, diverse trades, old and new societies now held in bondage by political federations, exercise your primitive right of autonomy; obey that impulse towards freedom that has never been allowed to die — to the Syndicalist Congress of London!"[63]

The organisers requested that those who wished to attend the congress select their delegates and send in their resolutions. Unfortunately, due to the inefficiency of the ISEL, the provisional agenda was only dispatched to participating organisations shortly before the congress, giving no time for prior discussion of the contents at a domestic level, and many of the proposals do not appear to have been addressed at the congress itself. Among the differing groups whose proposals appeared on the agenda, three were from Spain.[64]

When the London congress began on September 27, 1913, representatives of twelve countries attended, including the Swedish Sveriges Arbetares Centralorganisation (SAC), the Dutch NAS, the Unione Sindicale Italiana (USI), the Federación Obrera Regional Argentina (FORA), and the German Freie Vereinigung Deutscher Gewerkschaften (FVDG) – the forerunner of the Freie Arbeiter-Union Deutschlands (FAUD) – who were all future members of the revolutionary syndicalist IWMA founded in 1922. The Norwegian syndicalists were represented by the SAC, and Russian anarcho-syndicalist Alexander Schapiro, along with Cornelissen a remnant from the 1907 Amsterdam congress and a pivotal player in the formation of the revolutionary syndicalist IWMA, was also present.[65] The French CGT did not attend, though a number of independent unions from France did.

The CNT was represented at the congress by J. Suárez Duque, representing thirteen associations from La Coruña (Galicia); José Rodríguez Romero, representing thirteen associations from the Balearics; and José Negre, representing the Catalan Regional Confederation of Labour (CRT).[66] Both Negre and Suárez Duque were living in exile in Paris.[67] Dr. Pedro Vallina, who was living in London, represented the Ateneo Sindicalista in Barcelona (possibly the same ateneo established at the time of SO), as a fraternal delegate. The congress organisers also invited the veteran Anselmo Lorenzo to preside over the inaugural session to demonstrate the continuity between the congress and the First International. However, ill health kept him in Spain, so he sent a greeting to the congress which was read out at the opening session.[68]

The congress took two important steps towards the formation of a revolutionary syndicalist International: the creation of an information bureau, which was to act as an information centre to foster international solidarity and organise future congresses, and the drawing up of a Declaration of Principles accepted by the different organisations.[69] The Declaration of Principles began by stressing the *double besogne* of the unions: "This congress ... declares that the class struggle is a necessary result of private property in the means of production and distribution, and therefore declares for the socialisation of such property by constructing and developing our Trade Unions in such a way as to fit them for the administration of these means in the interest of the entire community." But the most significant aspect of the declaration, when compared with the Charter of Amiens, was in relation to its attitude towards political organisations: "This congress ... recognises that, internationally, Trade Unions will only succeed when they cease to be divided by political and religious differences; declares that their fight is an economic fight, meaning thereby that they do not intend to reach their aim by trusting their cause to governing bodies or their members, but by using direct action, by workers themselves relying on the strength of their economic organisations. ... to obtain their emancipation from capitalism and the State.[70]

Emancipation could only be achieved through economic organisations. Yet all the delegates gathered, including the Spanish, agreed that these organisations should be open to workers of all political creeds.[71] What the declaration did not include, but which was made implicit during the congress, was that anyone holding a political office could not hold office in the unions. This point had been the focus of a major dispute when it was discovered that one of the joint presidents of the congress, Jack Wills, as well as being the delegate for the Bermondsey Trades Council was also a local councilor in London. The Spanish delegation was among those demanding that he step down. Revolutionary syndicalism was supposed to be independent of party politics and, as such, the majority of delegates voted for Wills to be replaced by another English delegate, Jack Tanner. But as this point was not included in the declaration, the latent contradiction remained of an apolitical organisation containing members with positions in, and therefore loyalty to, political parties which preferred the parliamentary path to emancipation.[72]

Overall, the congress was not a great success as much time was wasted on personal recrimination and factional infighting. However, it did form the basis for future agreements, whilst the bureau represented a commitment to the future establishment of a revolutionary syndicalist International.[73] In their reports on the congress, both Negre and Duque stressed that the most important aspect of the congress had been the decision to create a new International. Duque claimed that, taken together, the establishment of the bureau and the agreement on a declaration of principles was tantamount to the creation of a new International.[74] Negre was equally optimistic: "The bases for an international understanding between all the syndicalist forces are in place. From today forward, the scattered revolutionary elements of the different countries will no longer fight in vain."[75]

On returning to Barcelona, Negre gave a further report on the congress in an assembly held at the Workers' Centre there on November 16. Once more he was very positive about the future, looking forward to the next congress, which would create a new International, "the direct descendent of the great, of the disappeared, International." The new International, he added, could serve, as had the original, to gain international respect and influence for the Spanish labour movement.[76] However, following the publication of a circular by the information bureau in November, no further mention was made of either the congress or the bureau in the Spanish syndicalist or anarchist press. Plans to organise a further congress and to proceed towards the creation of the hoped-for International were ruined by the outbreak of the First World War.[77]

Anarchist Internationalism before the First World War

The war also ended the faltering moves towards the holding of a second international anarchist congress. The Amsterdam congress of 1907 had decided to establish an Anarchist International, and a bureau was set up to prepare the way for its creation.[78] However, enthusiasm for the International did not survive long.[79] The follow-up congress due for 1909 never occurred and, the same year, in response to the apathetic response to its work, the bureau gave up its activities.[80]

Three years later, moves to hold an international anarchist congress were relaunched by the Action Libre group of Bordeaux, which was made of Spanish exiles.[81] The initiative received responses from groups in Argentina, New York, Canada, Lisbon, Elche, and Madrid, among others, and the Action Libre group requested that *Tierra y Libertad* and *El Libertario* (Gijón) dedicate space in their papers to a plebiscite on the location and themes of the congress.[82] However, there were very few responses to the plebiscite in either of the papers as attention centred on the proposed international syndicalist congress.

Nonetheless, the approach of the new Liberal government of Count Romanones, less repressive than that of his predecessor, Jose Canalejas, permitted an environment in which the anarchist organisation could grow across Spain in 1913.[83] Anarchist federations were created in the Basque region, Valencia, and Catalonia, and steps were taken towards the formation of federations in Andalusia and Extremadura.[84] In September *Tierra y Libertad* proposed the creation of a national pact between the regional groups, although it admitted that it felt that such a move was still premature.[85] Nonetheless the creation of different regional organization clearly suggests that an important number of Spanish anarchists had accepted the need for closer organization.

The previous month the French anarchists had agreed to the formation of a national organisation, the Fédération Communiste Révolutionnaire Anarchiste (FCRA), at a congress in Paris.[86] The FCRA established an international anarchist bureau to enter into relations with anarchist organisations in other countries.[87] The FCRA then joined with the German anarchists and the Anarchist Federation of London to organise the long-awaited international anarchist congress, to be held in London from August 29 to September 6, 1914.[88] The congress was eventually postponed due to the war.[89]

The debates leading up to the congress illustrate a growing disquiet among certain anarchists about revolutionary syndicalism. An editorial in *Tierra y Libertad* argued that the relationship between anarchism and syndicalism should be one of the principal points discussed at the congress.[90] This was echoed by others in the following weeks.[91] An article by Gilimón (Eduardo Gilimón), a Catalan exile living in Buenos Aires whose political ideas had evolved from socialism to anarchism, expressed concern about the decline in the influence of anarchism over workers and their unions. The author argued, "It is a contradiction, an absurdity, to expect that the workers who are members of these unions whose practices are so authoritarian, in which discipline is everything, will become anarchist ... their methods of behaviour can in no way be anarchist."[92]

Gilimón had come to fear the way that the unions were absorbing anarchists who now simply limited their ideas to the economic field. His views provided a foretaste of what would later become the FORA V in Argentina, which advocated a purely anarchist labour movement, an idea which would have an important impact on debates within the CNT in the 1920s (see chapter 6). Commenting on the article, *Tierra y Libertad* added that the theme required serious study and emphasised that the subject had to be dealt with at the congress, which should serve as a forum to "study problems related to tactics, means of struggle and propaganda." *Tierra y Libertad* itself unwittingly had provided an example of the growing importance of syndicalism within the anarchist movement by its relatively low-key reaction to the anarchist congress, which was in stark contrast to the way it reacted to the London syndicalist congress.[93]

The El Ferrol International Congress of Peace, 1915

The outbreak of war in Europe in August 1914 not only put a halt to both the syndicalist and anarchist attempts to form their respective Internationals, but also demonstrated the abject failure of social democratic internationalism. The myth of working-class unity had collapsed in the face of basic national chauvinism. In the belligerent countries the unions lined up to support the war effort, throwing years of antiwar rhetoric to the wind. Even in anarchist circles a number of leading figures, including Kropotkin, supported the Allies, a position that was echoed by a small minority of anarchists in neutral Spain (most notably Ricardo Mella and Federico Urales), although the vast majority adopted the orthodox anarchist position of total rejection of the war.

Internationally, the opposition to Kropotkin's position was led by Malatesta and Sébastien Faure, the director of the French anarchist newspaper *Le Libertaire*. Faure's opposition to the war inspired members of the Syndicalist Ateneo in El Ferrol (Galicia) to organise an

International Congress of Peace.[94] The aims set out in the initial congress agenda focused on issues directly related to the war, although, as it transpired, the congress focused predominantly on labour organisation and the means for ending all wars, not simply the present one.[95] The agenda was included in a manifesto sent out by the Syndicalist Ateneo in which it was also suggested that "in neutral countries the workers might boycott all goods destined to help the belligerent countries to continue the butchery, and that later the general strike might be tried."[96]

Eusebio Carbó, at the time editor of the anarchist publication *Regeneración* in Sabadell, claimed that worker and anarchist organisations from across Europe were making preparations to send delegates to the congress.[97] However, passport problems meant that many of those invited were unable to attend.[98]

On April 29, 1915, the first session (of two) of the International Congress of Peace was opened despite the Spanish government having banned the meeting. Forty-seven delegates attended, the majority from Spain, although there were also representations from Portugal, Brazil, and France. Following the first session, the delegates with foreign passports were expelled by the police whilst, after the second session, Carbó and López Bouza (of the organising committee) were detained and were not released until the middle of May.[99]

The congress made a number of important decisions, some of which were intended for immediate effect, while others looked more towards the postwar world.[100] The former included a call for a series of general strikes and the formation of a permanent committee of the International Congress of Peace which would undertake to send revolutionary tracts to the fighting soldiers.[101] The latter category included a decision to create a labour International and, as a means of giving this new organisation strength, a decision to relaunch the CNT.

The labour International, to be composed of delegates from Portugal and Spain, undertook to link closer together "the proletariat of both countries, creating in this way the Iberian Federation, the initial cell of the International Federation of Workers' Unions, against the war, against all wars, against the tyranny of the State."[102]

Following a suggestion by Carbó, it was decided that there was no need to write new statutes for the International, as those of the

First International would be more than adequate, although with slight modifications. Perhaps the most notable modification to the old statutes was that "The economic emancipation of the workers is the great objective to which all political movement must be subordinate" became "The economic and social emancipation of the workers is the primary objective which every movement must aim for," obviously a statement against reformist socialism.[103] The International, which carried the title International Working Men's Association in homage to the full name of the First International, was to reside in El Ferrol, with López Bouza as secretary.[104] The first manifesto of the new IWMA was published in early July 1915 and included the organisation's statutes. The last sign of life of the short-lived IWMA was a call to the workers of Spain and Portugal to be on guard against forces within their countries that wanted to pressure the national governments to end their policy of neutrality in the war.[105]

Despite its fleeting existence, the new IWMA did have one important consequence. During the congress, Angel Pestaña, representing both *Solidaridad Obrera* and the Catalan CRT, suggested that the reorganisation of the CNT would give greater force to the International.[106] The congress agreed, and it was decided that the committee in charge of the reorganisation should be based in Barcelona.

Solidaridad Obrera published a manifesto announcing its intention to reorganise the CNT in early June 1916, followed by a series of articles explaining why it was essential that this should occur.[107] The process of reorganisation was relatively slow, especially in comparison to the CNT's growth. Membership had risen from roughly thirty thousand mid-1915 to fifty thousand in May 1916.[108] During the early period of the reorganisation, the close relationship between the CNT and the anarchists was immediately noticeable.[109] Putting aside earlier concerns, *Tierra y Libertad* came out strongly in favour of revolutionary syndicalism: "There is no incompatibility — as some believe — between anarchism and revolutionary syndicalism: in fact a complementary relationship exists. We understand that there can be no philosophical or political emancipation, if before or at the same time, the economic problem is not resolved. Therefore we are enthusiastic supporters of the organisations that, like the National Confederation, … recommend autonomy among their members, raise the spirit of and educate the multitudes, directing them toward ideological discovery, awaking in them the feeling of dignity, vital for the development of individual strength, the foundation and guarantor of a future based on equality."[110]

Such apparently unquestioning support for revolutionary syndicalism from the anarchist newspaper had been lacking before. This temporary change in view most probably resulted from the significant role played by anarchists in the reorganisation that followed El Ferrol. Manuel Buenacasa, who would become the CNT's general secretary for a short period in 1919 and was a leading proponent of anarchism in the CNT, later attested to this: "When the march of the Spanish labour federation was renewed, in the year 1916, my friends and I drove that organisation in a clearly anarchist sense."[111] Alongside Buenacasa, at the forefront of the reorganisation was a new generation of militants (Angel Pestaña, Eusebio Carbó, Joan Peiró, Salvador Seguí, Salvador Quemades, and others) who were all active in the unions and described themselves as anarchists.

Parallel to the reorganisation of the CNT, moves were also made towards the formation of a national anarchist organisation. Alongside the committee of the International Congress of Peace and the IWMA, a further organisation with international pretensions was established at El Ferrol. Benefiting from the fact that various representatives of anarchist groups and periodicals had gathered in El Ferrol, Constancio Romero from the Cantabrian Anarchist Federation organised a meeting at which he proposed the formation of a new anarchist International.[112] The meeting agreed to the establishment of the Spanish committee of the anarchist International, which was to be based in Barcelona and administered by the editorial group of *Tierra y Libertad*.[113] A committee of five members was eventually established following an agreement between *Tierra y Libertad* and the Catalan Federation of Anarchist Groups that clarified their immediate aim as the creation of "a confederation of Spanish-speaking federations, groups and individuals."[114] The committee was soon complaining of the poor reaction to their first circulars, although subsequently the response rate was more positive. By November three individuals, eleven groups, and the anarchist federations of Cantabria and Castile had joined the Catalans in the committee.[115] Reports in *Tierra y Libertad* of increased anarchist activity came to an abrupt end in November as the periodical's pages were increasingly occupied by news of a crackdown on libertarian groups which was linked with a propaganda tour by leading confederal militants following the El Ferrol congress.[116]

Working-Class Unity: Revolutionary Syndicalism and Reformist Socialism

The reorganisation of the CNT nonetheless continued. It was the economic expansion associated with World War I that transformed the CNT into a mass movement. Although Spain remained neutral, it benefitted greatly from the increase in demand from the belligerent countries and from their former markets. However, the benefits were not evenly spread and, especially in Catalonia, the increased profits did not filter down to the working class. Parallel to the growth in demand from abroad came a sharp rise in the cost of living in Spain, as wages failed to keep pace with the rise in prices, in particular of essential goods.[117] The logical corollary of this was a rapid rise in labour unrest and an interrelated growth in labour organisation.[118] In response to this, a cost-of-living committee was established in 1915, composed of representatives of the CNT, the UGT, and other labour organisations. The committee organised a conference in Valencia on May 13, 1916, to discuss tactics for dealing with the rising cost of living, and a direct consequence was the Zaragoza Pact between the UGT and the CNT of July 17, by which the two organisations agreed to organise a twenty-four-hour strike on December 18 to protest against the government's inability to control the rise in prices.[119] In terms of numbers and solidarity, the strike was said to be "the most successful national protest action yet undertaken by the labour movement" and provided a foretaste of what was to come, but it did not lead to a change in government policy.[120] The strike had demonstrated the potential of labour unity, but subsequent attempts at joint action between the CNT and UGT in the future would fall victim to ideological differences and mistrust.

The year 1917 was one of crisis for the Restoration system by which Spain had been governed since 1875, with revolutionary change appearing a real possibility as, against the backdrop of increasing labour unrest, other forces in Spain were stirring.[121] First, sections of the military and then factions of the Republican (bourgeois) political parties openly challenged the government. Realising which group presented the greatest threat, the government agreed to the demands of the protesting soldiers (who had organised themselves in *juntas de defensa*) for better wages, and it withdrew plans to change the military promotion system. With the army won over and the political opposition increasingly disunited, for all intents and purposes any threat of a revolution died. Nonetheless, although it did survive the immediate crises, the weakness of the Restoration system and its dependence on the military for its survival was evident, and the period of political disintegration that began in 1917 continued until general Primo de Rivera's pronunciamento in September 1923 (during which period thirteen different governments held office).

During the unrest of 1917 the socialists followed a dual strategy: on the one hand, the PSOE joined in alliance with the Republican parties in June with the aim of imposing a new government that would organise a Constituent Cortes (a constituent assembly of Spain's parliament) ; whilst, on the other, the UGT threatened a revolutionary strike, in tandem with the CNT, to achieve this end. However, what may have seemed a logical policy to the socialists was seen as proof of their duplicity by the CNT. The contact initiated between the CNT and UGT the previous year continued and, in March, representatives from the two unions again signed a joint manifesto critical of the government's inability to alleviate the labour crisis and threatening a general strike of an undefined duration across the entire country.[122] A national assembly of CNT and UGT delegates was held in Madrid on April 25 to discuss in more detail the proposed strike. In the months that followed, the CNT put increasing pressure on the UGT to call the general strike, but the UGT vacillated before making a decision, hoping that the Republican movement would triumph, thus making a strike unnecessary. The Republican opposition called an alternative parliamentary assembly which was quickly dispersed. The socialists could no longer prevaricate and, in effect, were forced by one of their own unions into supporting the call for a general strike on August 13, the railway workers' union in Valencia, which had gone on strike three days earlier and had demanded that a general strike be declared. The strike was a failure. The military, now firmly behind the new conservative government of Eduardo Dato, violently repressed the movement, which petered out within five days.[123] The failure of the strike spelt the end of the close contact between the CNT and the UGT. *Tierra y Libertad* blamed it on the fact that the leaders of the UGT were "essentially politicians." They were therefore not true syndicalists.[124]

The bitter recrimination following the failed general strike of 1917 did not end the attempts to unify the working-class movement but does demonstrate why subsequent attempts at unification all failed — the CNT was uneasy about the political relationship of the UGT with the PSOE.[125] Essentially the prospect of unification or united action with the UGT placed two key principles of revolutionary syndicalism in direct conflict: the desire for class unity and the rejection of parliamentary politics. Whilst the UGT refused to distance itself from the moderate socialist politics of the PSOE this conflict could not be solved. Revolutionary syndicalism had been born out of a rejection of the tactics of parliamentary socialism. For the CNT, unification with the UGT was possible only if it also rejected the political path to emancipation. The aim of uniting all the working class under one roof and thus creating a force strong enough to destroy capitalism was a logical one, except that now social democracy had evolved towards a position of accepting capitalism – indeed during the war it had fought for it in the form of the nation-states that helped maintain the system. Uniting workers opposed to capitalism with those that appeared happy to accommodate themselves with it in return for moderate improvements in the utopian hope that such collaboration weakened capitalism – this made no sense at all. Such an organization could not present a united force, and it was the creation of such a force that was the sine qua non of revolutionary syndicalism. The syndicalists would need to concentrate on uniting the revolutionary sectors of the working class and hoped the reformists would awaken from their delusions when the time came.

Nonetheless, both unions continued to call for the unification of the Spanish working class movement. The Sans Congress of the Catalan CRT, held at the end of June 1918, called for the celebration of an assembly "with the aim of achieving the unification of the Spanish proletariat."[126] In response, the thirteenth UGT congress, held in

Madrid in September 1918, agreed on the need to unite the Spanish proletariat. The UGT general secretary, Largo Caballero, therefore sent a letter to the secretary of the CNT, Manuel Buenacasa, stating that the UGT wished to start proceedings towards "the fusion of the Spanish labour force in one sole national organisation." Buenacasa replied, saying that the CNT agreed with the idea in principle but that the issue would have to be discussed at a national congress first as this alone had the authority to decide.[127] This relative lack of urgency on Buenacasa's part most probably resulted from the fact that, from 1916 onwards, the CNT had continued to grow in strength and now outnumbered the UGT by more than three to one. Inspired by the revolution in Russia, many in the CNT now began to think in terms of their own social revolution, and to be tied down by a pact with the reformist UGT was not an attractive option. What they wanted was not the UGT but its members, and this was reflected in the motion adopted at the CNT's Madrid congress in December 1919, which gave members of the UGT three weeks in which to join the CNT or face being declared "yellow" and not part of the labour movement.[128] Rather than fusion, the Congress agreed to absorb the UGT.

In 1919, the CNT was at the height of its pre–Second Republic strength. However, extreme repression enforced in Catalonia in the aftermath of the Canadiense strike (see chapter 3), which then spread throughout the country, would soon severely weaken the CNT and lead its national committee to approach the UGT one last time in September 1920.[129] The result was a circumstantial pact which would "stand up to the reactionary and repressive action being practised in Spain by political elements and the employers." The CNT hoped that the UGT would join them in a general strike, the aim of which was "to return [Spain] to constitutional legality." However, when the CNT called the strike, the UGT refused to second it and in some areas actively opposed it. This prompted the CNT to issue a manifesto accusing the UGT of betrayal and renouncing the pact.[130] The UGT and CNT would not act together again until forced to do so by the Civil War.

The UGT was at heart a reformist union, a fact amply demonstrated by its collaboration with the Primo de Rivera dictatorship in the 1920s. Its leaders were predominantly moderates and took their lead from the PSOE, in which many UGT members were also lead-ing figures.[131] Revolutionary syndicalism had been born as a reaction against the increasingly reformist tendency of orthodox Marxist par-ties of the Second International, and during the pre–First World War period it essentially defined itself in relation to the parliamentary pre-dilection of the socialist movement. However, the growth of revolu-tionary socialism during the war, and especially following the October Revolution in Russia, inaugurated a period of confusion within the revolutionary syndicalist movement, in which it was forced to reap-praise its ideological stance towards politics. Initially, however, the similarity of the revolutionary rhetoric used by both revolutionary syndicalists and socialists masked ideological differences.

Along with the growth in its membership dating from 1916 came a growth in the confidence of CNT militants. The congress at El Ferrol had decided that if the Spanish government should break with its policy of neutrality, then this should be opposed by use of the most extreme measures, including, if possible, a general strike. At the time the CNT was in no situation to enforce this threat, but, from August 1916 onwards, *Solidaridad Obrera* was warning that any move by the government to involve Spain in the war would not go unanswered by CNT: "If the government tries to get us 'involved' against other peoples who we will always consider as brothers, we will 'involve' our-selves against the government, as this [government] is the factor that has caused the slaughter that has led to such pain and shedding of tears. Workers! We are ready! Down with the possible order of mobi-lisation, the revolution! Down with the capitalist war, the social war, the class war!"[132]

The proposal to transform the European war into a social war was shared by others, most famously the Bolsheviks and revolution-ary Marxists of the Zimmerwald Left. The Zimmerwald conference, which gathered together the socialist minorities opposed to the war for the first time since the conflict began, had little impact in Spain, al-though it was welcomed by *Tierra y Libertad*.[133] No revolutionary syn-dicalist organisations were invited to Zimmerwald, with the exception of the French CGT, a decision that raised complaints from the Italian USI.[134] There were no Spanish representatives at either Zimmerwald or Kienthal (the second conference of the minority left organisations), the Spanish socialists being predominantly in favour of an Allied victory. The CNT's ignorance of Bolshevik ideology would become clear in the days immediately following the October Revolution. This, coupled with the fact that the discussions at El Ferrol showed that the confederation was already leaning towards a revolutionary position against the war, suggests that the impact of Zimmerwald was negligible.[135] The view that war was a result of the capitalist system had always been an integral part of anarchist and syndicalist ideology, and it had been generally accepted by most, if not all, schools of socialist thought since the First International.

Rather than the CNT's slogans mimicking those of Lenin and his followers, by 1917 many of the Bolshevik slogans seemed to echo those of the anarchists and syndicalists. Revolutionary syndicalism had evolved as a reaction against the increasingly reformist policies of the social democrats. The growth of a revolutionary wing within the social democratic parties sowed confusion in the ranks of the CNT, especially during the period between the Russian Revolution and the formation of the Spanish Communist Party, during which time many of Lenin's supporters in the country found themselves increasingly attracted to the revolutionary activism of the CNT.

Within the CNT, the divisive nature of the question of political relations on the revolutionary wing of the working class had not yet become apparent. In the years prior to the Russian Revolution, ideological arguments had centred on differences between the socialists and the syndicalists rather than the differences between factions within the revolutionary syndicalist movement itself. Fears had been voiced by some anarchists about the potential of anarchism to be engulfed by syndicalism, but their warnings had been drowned out by the enthusiasm of the majority who welcomed the possibilities syndicalism presented for reacquainting the labour movement with anarchist ideology. Change in the economic base of the country, increasing industrialization, was evident in the workshops and factories of Barcelona and Bilbao but also in cities with less heavy industry, such as Seville. A stronger, more industrialized working class meant stronger unions and potentially, finally, a force strong enough to overthrow the Restoration system. It is not surprising that new generations of anarchists should see in the labour movement the means to their goal.

This enthusiasm had led many anarchists not only to join the CNT but to take an active role in union matters. The result was a particularly Spanish version of revolutionary syndicalism that was strongly influenced by anarchism from the beginning, and even more so during the early months of the reorganisation that began in 1915. The reorganisation coincided with a sharp growth in union numbers and social unrest, which in turn resulted in a dramatic increase in CNT membership. From a small and relatively inexperienced association of craft-based localised unions, the CNT was suddenly transformed into a mass organisation at the forefront of a revolutionary movement. The experience of the years of revolutionary turmoil would bring to the fore the ideological conflicts within the unions and the contradictions inherent in the political neutrality of revolutionary syndicalism and its revolutionary aims.

3.

REVOLUTIONARY POLITICS AND REVOLUTIONARY SYNDICALISM

In May 1917 a manifesto signed by the secretary of the CNT, the Catalan CRT, and the CNT members of the joint UGT/CNT committee created in 1916 echoed the decisions of the El Ferrol congress, calling for the formation of an International once the war was over that would be "the spur to the Social Revolution."[1] Support, but not action, for the creation of an International gathered pace following the October Revolution in Russia, most particularly from the pen of the leading CNT militant and sometime national secretary, Manuel Buenacasa. The honour of organising the revolutionary International was eventually conceded to the Bolsheviks due to the success of the revolution, though it was not until 1919 that the Third International (Communist International, or Comintern) finally held its first congress. The CNT was represented at the second congress, in 1920, and again at the inaugural congress of the Red Trade Union International (RTUI, sometimes referred to as Profintern) in 1921. Yet by the end of 1922 the confederation had cut all ties with Moscow. Early praise for the Bolshevik role in the revolution had been replaced with abject condemnation of what was seen as the political deviation enforced on a social revolution by Lenin and his followers, most specifically in the adoption of the 'dictatorship of the proletariat'. The CNT vowed to resist political interference from all parties, including communists, in their struggles in Spain and rejected any revolution that had the strengthening of the state as a by-product.

Initial Reaction to the Bolshevik Revolution

The vehement nature of the CNT's rejection of Moscow was in sharp contrast with the initial warm welcome it gave the Bolshevik seizure of power in November 1917, news of which arrived in Spain at a time of growing social conflict. Reaction to the Russian Revolution passed through three phases, although the difficulties in receiving reliable information on the events in Russia, combined with the effects of the repression unleashed on the CNT by the authorities, make it hard to pinpoint the specific time that a shift in opinion took place.[2] Initially militants of all persuasions within the CNT welcomed the Bolshevik seizure of power enthusiastically, but this support became increasingly qualified from late 1918 onwards as more information became available about the exact nature of Bolshevism.[3] The revolution was still championed, but its defenders in the CNT no longer proclaimed that Bolshevism was analogous to revolutionary syndicalism or shared the same goals as the confederation. The final phase began in late 1920, with the formation of the Partido Comunista Español (PCE), which happened just as the CNT received the invitation to attend the inaugural congress of the Profintern and the anarchist and syndicalist press was becoming more noticeably critical of Bolshevism. Just as syndicalists of all shades within the confederation had welcomed the revolution in 1917, by 1922 all but a small pro-communist section unequivocally rejected Bolshevism.

News of the October Revolution arrived in Spain at a time of growing social tension, largely caused by rapid industrialisation which occurred during the First World War. A taste of what was to follow had been provided by the unsuccessful general strike of August 1917. For the next three years Spain was gripped by a spectacular upsurge in social unrest and agitation in both industrialising and rural areas, which resulted in a rapid expansion in confederation membership. The CNT's reaction to the events in Russia must therefore be seen in relation to the political and economic crises in Spain and the resultant increase in social unrest.

The initial reaction of both the confederation's daily newspaper, *Solidaridad Obrera*, and the anarchist *Tierra y Libertad* to the October Revolution was, not surprisingly, favourable.[4] For the workers in Spain involved in their own struggle against the state, the exact nature of Bolshevism was of secondary importance. What mattered was that a revolutionary movement of workers had overthrown a tyrannical regime and that the workers were now in control of their own destiny. Anarchist support for the revolution was more vociferous than that of the CNT, as reflected in *Solidaridad Obrera*.[5] The recently formed Catalan Federation of Anarchist Groups met on December 9, 1917, and decided to organise acts in sympathy with the Russian revolutionaries and immediately identified with the events in Russia, going as far as to accept the Bolshevik tactic of the dictatorship of the proletariat, although they did not state clearly what they felt the term meant.[6] The federation's position was confused, referring to the Bolsheviks as if they shared anarchist goals and not mentioning specifically the Communist Party or assigning a role within the revolution to any political organisation. An editorial in *Tierra y Libertad* in December echoed the Federation's approach, demonstrating that confusion about Bolshevism was widespread.[7]

Buenacasa, the confederation's most prolific writer on international affairs and a member of the national committee, was initially one of the strongest supporters of the Bolsheviks. In late 1918, he wrote favourable articles on Lenin and Trotsky and gave a brief background to their involvement at Zimmerwald and Kienthal in which he stressed how the Russian revolutionaries had shared the CNT's policy of transforming the imperialist war into a social revolution. However, although giving full support to the Bolshevik Revolution, Buenacasa did differentiate clearly between Bolshevism and syndicalism. 'Bolshevism', he stated, was 'state socialism', which represented a lesser ideology than syndicalism, as the latter gave the "workers control of administrative functions" and was, in comparison with syndicalism, "even further removed from anarchism."[8]

Nonetheless, there was no question of withdrawing support for the Russian Revolution. It reflected support for a workers' revolutionary struggle against bourgeois capitalism. Furthermore, the success of the Bolsheviks had a part to play in the eventual victory of the Spanish workers. As revolution spread westward across central Europe in 1918, both Buenacasa and *Solidaridad Obrera* spoke of the 'revolución universal' that would bring about the triumph of revolution in Spain.[9] The Russian Revolution was the first phase of a revolutionary process that would have a domino effect on other countries. This was certainly the opinion of the national committee of the CNT, whose members welcomed the end of the First World War with calls for the creation of a Labour International that would "continue the social war against capitalism, already triumphant in Russia and spreading across the empires of Central Europe on all fronts" so that soon "Spain's turn will come."[10]

Belief in the victory of the Russian Revolution meant belief in the victory of a Spanish revolution. However, from late 1918 onwards the supporters of the October Revolution began to differentiate between support for the social revolution in Russia and support for Bolshevism as a political ideology. This was most evident in the pages of *Solidaridad Obrera* where, as Antonio Bar has pointed out, a series of editorials had been equally qualified in their treatment of the revolution, praising its achievements whilst using language that made the 'statist' orientation of the Bolsheviks clear by constant reference to the 'dictatorship of the proletariat', seizure of power, 'government of the people,' et cetera.[11]

This change in attitude was also evident in anarchist circles. In November 1919, the Catalan Anarchist Federation reappraised its previous ideological stance vis-à-vis Bolshevism in a manifesto which differentiated between economic and political organisations: "Syndicalism – a means of struggle based on direct action – ends in the implantation of libertarian communism … whilst State socialism – a means of labour struggle based on multiple action – ends in the implantation of authoritarian communism."[12] The essential point in all the ideological debates was the growing realisation that Bolshevism did not encompass the libertarian principles of Spanish revolutionary syndicalism. However, this did not lessen support for a revolutionary overthrow of an imperialist state. Whatever the arguments surrounding the merits of the Bolsheviks, the CNT's connections with Russia remained at the level of press commentary and factory debate. Beyond the solidarity of one revolutionary workers' force with another there was no contact. This changed as news of the decision to establish a new International in Russia arrived in Spain.

The CNT's membership of the new International was discussed at its national congress held in Madrid in December 1919, the first since 1911. The dramatic rise in social agitation had led to a sharp increase in membership of the CNT. The congress provided a necessary forum for taking stock of the changes that had occurred both in Spain and within the CNT's own ranks since 1911. As if to emphasise the confederation's priorities, the main debate of the congress revolved not around Bolshevism but the proposed unification of the CNT and the socialist Unión General de Trabajadores (UGT). After the debates over the situation in Spain and internal CNT matters, the congress turned its attention to the Russian Revolution.

A resolution on Russia was split into two parts. The first referred to the means of combating the blockade of Russia by international capitalism whilst the second dealt with international relations, specifically whether or not the CNT should join the Third International. Buenacasa opened the debates with a strong defence of the revolution as a fact in itself but did not broach the question of the International, which was surprising, given the attention he had given to the issue in the pages of *Solidaridad Obrera* since 1917. The debates also demonstrated that information about the exact nature of Bolshevism was still scarce. Hilario Arlandis from the Levante urged that the CNT unconditionally join the Comintern. Basing his arguments almost entirely on a report on the first Comintern congress (held in March 1919), he accepted that differences existed between the Bolsheviks and the CNT but felt that this was because it was "very difficult to find a concrete formula to unite all the proletariat of the world and satisfy all the tendencies." However, he concluded, the Third International "exemplifies all our aspirations,"[13] Significantly, Andreu Nin, at this point a member of both the Socialist Party and the CNT, concurred: "I am a supporter of the Third International because it is a reality, because above the ideologies it represents a principle of action, a principle of coexistence between all the clearly revolutionary forces who aspire to implant communism immediately."[14] Both Arlandis and Nin would soon become staunch supporters of Moscow.

Doubts about the dictatorial tendency inherent in Bolshevism were raised by the Asturian Eleuterio Quintanilla. Quintanilla agreed that the CNT should welcome the Russian Revolution but also argued that the revolution did not "embody, in principle, the ideals of revolutionary syndicalism." The CNT needed to be wary of the Bolshevik Party's principles because "the way in which the Russian dictatorship has acted represents a serious danger to us." His main point was the evident conflict between the tactics and aims of revolutionary syndicalism and Bolshevism. The followers of the latter believed that the unions should be "subject to the demands of the state and offered themselves to it unconditionally," he said. The Comintern, Quintanilla continued, was simply Bolshevism on an international level, and, as such, was a "specifically political organisation ... where we have no reason to be represented." Instead the CNT should help to build a "pure" International that was "specifically syndicalist [and] would conserve CNT principals and follow the tradition of the First International."[15]

Salvador Seguí, the most respected and influential militant of the Catalan section of the CNT, accepted Quintanilla's criticism, but argued that the CNT must be represented in the Third International. "Not due to its theories which we oppose, but for the need to be realistic, we support entering the Third International because this is going to endorse ... the call that the CNT is going to make to the syndicalist organisations of the world to form the true, the unique, the genuine workers' International."[16] Furthermore, he argued, as the CNT was the largest labour movement in Spain, its position needed to be recognised internationally, and being associated with the International in Moscow would reinforce its revolutionary credentials. In the end, the congress compromised, *provisionally* adhering to the Comintern whilst at the same time stressing that support for the Comintern was due to its revolutionary and not ideological character and stressing that the CNT's ideological base rested on the anti-authoritarian wing of the First International:

> The National Committee ... with reference to the theme of the Russian revolution, proposes the following:
>
> First. That the Confederación Nacional del Trabajo declares itself a firm defender of the principles that guided the First International, as conceived by Bakunin.
>
> Second. Declares that it affiliates, provisionally, with the Third International, due to its revolutionary character, whilst the International Congress is organised and held in Spain, to define the basic principles that will govern the true International of workers.[17]

The affiliation of the CNT with the new International did not represent an acceptance of the principles of Bolshevism as was clear from the adoption of a motion put forward by various delegates (and supported by the national committee) which was attached to the resolution on the Comintern:

> Bearing in mind that the tendency that has the greatest force at the heart of the workers' organisations of all countries is that which leads to the complete, total, and absolute liberation of humanity morally, economically and politically, and considering that this objective cannot be achieved until the land and the instruments of production and exchange are socialised, and the tyrannical power of the state disappears, propose to the congress, that in agreement with the essence of the

proposals of the workers' International, [it] declares
that the ultimate goal of the Confederación Nacional
del Trabajo in Spain is libertarian communism.[18]

So at the very moment that the confederation agreed to join the
Comintern, it made a clear commitment to an ideology that was fundamentally at odds with the centralised and politicised doctrine of
the Third International's founders. This contradiction can only be explained by the continuing confusion over Bolshevism, the belief that
revolution in Spain was imminent, and more specifically the belief that
the Comintern would be an autonomous revolutionary International
and not be dominated by the Bolsheviks. Having decided to join
the International, the CNT then had to select delegates to go to
Moscow to present its membership as well as to find out more about
the Bolshevik regime. At first, Quintanilla and Pedro Vallina (who
had attended the International Revolutionary Syndicalist Congress in
London in 1913) were chosen but both declined, so instead the committee chose Eusebio Carbó (a prominent member of the Valencian
region of the CNT who spoke both French and Italian) and Salvador
Quemades (a member of the committee of the Catalan CRT).

Parallel to the proposed trip of these two delegates, the CNT national committee decided to appeal to the workers in neighbouring
countries to boycott Spanish goods as a protest against the increasingly repressive nature of the Spanish authorities and employers. Shocked
by the success of the CNT in Catalonia, whose growing strength had
been amply demonstrated during the strike at the Ebro Irrigation and
Power Company (known as the Canadiense as it was part-owned by
Canadians), the Employers' Federation decided that the relentless rise
in confederal numbers in the region would have to be stopped.[19] The
strike, which had lasted for forty-four days between February and
March of 1919, and had left large parts of Catalonia, including the
capital Barcelona, without power, was the greatest victory in Spanish
labour history, and the employers had been forced to give in to all the
CNT's demands. The victory at La Canadiense marked the pinnacle
of CNT strength prior to the Spanish Civil War. However, the captain general of Catalonia, Lorenzo Milans del Bosch, reneged on the
agreement to release a number of the strikers who had been detained

during the strike, and the confederation again called a general strike. This time the employers were prepared, and, in collaboration with the military in the region, forced the Madrid-appointed civil governor, who was attempting to negotiate a settlement to the dispute, and the police governor out of office in April. Attempts by the central government to reach a negotiated agreement between employers and the CNT by means of the creation of a mixed commission of workers and employers who would discuss the dispute also failed in the face of the employers' refusal to participate in it. Instead, in October 1919 the second congress of the Employers' Federation decided to "destroy the workers organisation ... liquidating it by use of a lockout" which closed down factories and shops from November 3, 1919, to January 26, 1920. The result of the lockout was severe privation of the workforce and weakening of the unions.[20]

Parallel to the lockout, in December 1919 a new civil governor, Francisco Maestre Laborde (Count Salvatierra) who had been responsible for a similar repression against the unions in Seville, enforced a further crackdown on confederal militants. In January 1920, Count Salvatierra ordered the closure of confederation unions and the dissolution of the Catalan CRT, proclaimed a state of war, and suspended constitutional guarantees – on January 18 – that would not be reestablished until March 31, 1922. As if this were not enough, the Employers' Federation had also begun to employ armed militia to deal with confederal militants who operated alongside the paid gunmen of the Sindicatos Libres (Free Unions), an extreme right-wing Catholic union which had been created in 1919 in opposition to the CNT.

As a result of the increasingly oppressive climate, the CNT had to act clandestinely whilst the continued detention of leading militants led to constant changes within the national and regional committees. The authorities took advantage of events in Barcelona and a general strike in Seville to justify closing down CNT unions and press across the country.[21] Communication between regions became impossible due to the repression. In regional plenums not all regions were always represented, whilst the constant change in personnel meant that the different delegates often did not even know each other. However, the most visible reaction was the rise in violence in the Catalan capital, where the CNT became involved in Chicago-style gang warfare with armed gunmen in the pay of the Employers' Federation in which many of its leading figures would lose their lives. Although intermittent until late 1920, this repression formed the background to the CNT's involvement in the Bolshevik International. In such a desperate situation, confederal militants looked abroad for hope, to Russia and to the solidarity of their fellow syndicalists in Europe. Therefore, beyond a simple appeal for a boycott, the delegates who were to go to Russia were also given instructions to make contact and strengthen relations with the revolutionary syndicalist organisations in neighbouring countries. To this end prior to going to Russia, Carbó was sent to Italy, Salvador Quemades to Portugal, and Angel Pestaña, another leading figure of the Catalan CRT, to France.

The Delegation to the Second Comintern Congress

In France, Pestaña met with the anarchist Sébastien Faure and Pierre Monatte who represented the revolutionary wing of the French CGT. Monatte helped organise a meeting for the CNT delegate with the leadership of the CGT to discuss the boycott and the proposals for the creation of a congress of Latin unions.[22] Pestaña's presence in Paris soon attracted the attention of the authorities, and, thanks to the assistance of Monatte, an unnamed Russian he met in Paris, and friends from the anarchist paper *Le Libertaire*, he managed to secure passage to Berlin en route for Russia. Given the difficulties that militants faced in simply crossing the Spanish border, it was decided that, having made it as far as Paris, Pestaña should join up with Carbó and Quemades and go to Moscow.[23] Pestaña kept in contact with Carbó in Italy via letter but relied on the national committee to keep him in touch with Quemades. Carbó was himself in Paris in March 1920, arriving in Italy some time during April.[24] In Italy, Carbó met with delegates from the USI as well as the editorial board of the anarchist publication *Umanita Nova*.[25] His interview with Errico Malatesta provided one of the first direct ideological criticisms of Bolshevism published in the Spanish press by a prominent international anarchist.[26] Carbó never arrived in Moscow. In an article written in mid-June, he told of how the Italian authorities were searching for him.

By mid-August, Carbó was writing articles from jail in Valencia.[27] Little is known of the adventures of Quemades, but he likewise failed to reach Moscow.

Pestaña was the only official delegate of the CNT to reach Russia, arriving on June 26, 1920, and eventually leaving on September 6.[28] The day after he arrived in Petrograd he travelled to Moscow. By chance Zinoviev (the president of the Comintern) was travelling on the same train and, informed of Pestaña's presence, he asked to see him. On arriving in Moscow they went directly to a meeting of the executive committee of the International. Zinoviev proposed that the CNT should be admitted to the Third International. The proposal was accepted, and on June 27, 1920, the CNT finally joined the Third International.[29]

In the same meeting Solomon Lozovsky, the Bolshevik spokesman on international trade union policy, proposed that an international conference of revolutionary syndicalist organisations be held in order to constitute the 'Revolutionary Syndicalist International'. The proposal was accompanied by a draft of the Statutes of the Provision Council of the Red Trade Union International (Profintern). Pestaña's criticism of the document was threefold: its criticism of 'apoliticism' (unions with no party or political affiliation); the acceptance of political interference in union matters; and the defence of the dictatorship of the proletariat. This criticism was consistent with the basic principles of revolutionary syndicalism which rejected political interference in the unions and denied any constructive role for the state during the revolution, worker's dictatorship included. The preamble to the statutes claimed that the apoliticism or neutrality of the unions in the majority of the belligerent countries had resulted in these unions becoming the "slaves of capitalist imperialism" during the Great War and had thus delayed the emancipation of the workers. As Pestaña pointed out, such a claim was erroneous, as only in France was the union apolitical, whilst many 'political' unions in the neutral countries also took sides. The logical corollary of the rejection of apoliticism was the need for political influence in the unions. According to the statutes, the unions were to work "in close relation" with the "political organisation of the international communist proletariat" and were to "create within the unions a nucleus of communists whose unrelenting effort would lead to the imposition of our point of view." This assumed that the union's point of view would be the same as that of the political organisations and, given how the relationship between union and party had developed in Russia, essentially meant party domination of union matters.[30]

The statutes further proclaimed that the dictatorship of the proletariat was both a "decisive and transitory" requirement. Pestaña pointed out that this would prove unacceptable to the CNT, but Lozovsky informed him that no changes to the paragraphs relating to the conquest of political power or the dictatorship of the proletariat would be accepted.[31] Clearly seeing the direction in which the Profintern was going, Pestaña urged that, for the sake of its autonomy, the first congress of the Profintern be held outside Russia in Italy or Sweden, but to no avail. Despite his objections, Pestaña signed the document which had the support of the majority of those present, leaving it to the CNT to decide on his return to Spain whether it could accept the terms. As Lozovsky claimed that the document was only provisional and would be open to discussion at the inaugural congress of the Profintern to be held on January 1, 1921 (later changed to July 1), the document was not final, at least in theory. However, his later experience at the congress, and some heavy prompting from Armando Borghi, the delegate of the USI, eventually led Pestaña to withdraw his signature from the document.[32]

Despite his disagreements with the Bolsheviks, Pestaña continued to attend the meetings of the Third International. He became increasingly disillusioned with the evident gap, both tactical and ideological, between syndicalism and Bolshevism, and what he perceived as the manipulation of the debates by the communists only helped to reinforce his misgivings about Bolshevik intentions for the Profintern.[33] His experience on the Commission of Union Issues presided over by the "rabid anti-syndicalist" Karel Radek was typical. Radek's position, Pestaña argued, was that "if the unions do not serve the Communist Party, they have no reason for existing." Pestaña's complaints were ignored to such an extent that he eventually stopped attending the commission's meetings. When the commission's paper was finally discussed by the Comintern, Pestaña, fed up with whole process, did not even vote. The coup de grace was delivered in the last session of the International, in which it was decided that henceforward the unions would be represented in the Comintern by the delegates of the Communist Party of their country. Once more Pestaña protested, along with delegates from other revolutionary syndicalist organisations, but again to no avail. The CNT was effectively relegated to the second division of the International.

In August, Pestaña, Borghi, Augustin Souchy (delegate of the German revolutionary syndicalists), and the American syndicalist delegates were presented with a convention drawn up by Alfred Rosmer, a former French syndicalist and now a Bolshevik stalwart, which was to be adopted by the member organisations of the Profintern. The convention contained eight articles which would have committed the signatories to "close cooperation" with the Communist Party. A bureau was to be established by the syndicalist organisations in each country in cooperation with the relevant communist party, with members being elected by the unions but with the approval of the party and its executive committee. The bureau would also effectively control international relations. Not surprisingly, Pestaña and his fellow revolutionary syndicalists refused to sign the document.[34] All in all, Pestaña's experience in Russia simply served to demonstrate the ideological gulf between Bolshevism and the revolutionary syndicalism of the CNT.

Having achieved his principal goal, the affiliation of the CNT to the International, Pestaña left Russia on September 6 with the promise of an invitation to the CNT to attend the inaugural congress of the Profintern. Whilst passing through Italy in October en route to Spain he was detained by the police and relieved of all the documents he was carrying.[35] In December he was deported to Spain amid extreme security and placed in the Modelo prison in Barcelona. Here he would take a year to finish his report, which would only be made public the following year in the Madrid-based anarchist paper *Nueva Senda*, although a rough copy was somehow smuggled to the CNT national secretary Evelio Boal.

Meanwhile, in Spain the anarchist and syndicalist press was slowly turning against Bolshevism. Early in 1920, following Quintanilla's intervention at the Madrid congress, articles appeared in both *Fructidor* (Tarragona) and *Rebelión* (Cadiz) criticising the state-centric and dictatorial policy of the Bolsheviks.[36] Carbó's interview with Malatesta, possibly the most popular foreign anarchist in Spain and certainly the most widely published in the anarchist press, published in *España Nueva*, provided a more complete critique to a potentially larger readership.[37]

However, the real turning point came with the formation of the Partido Comunista Español (PCE) by radical members of the PSOE in April 1920 and the introduction of Bolshevism directly into Spanish political life.[38] The newly formed PCE published a manifesto in *España Nueva* in July alongside the publication of the famous nineteen points (later twenty-one) laying out the rules governing the Comintern. Article 5 stated that the proletariat could not achieve the revolution if it did not first form a Communist Party. However, it was article 6 which referred to the role of the communists in the unions, which proved most problematic for the militants of the CNT: "To avoid these organisations [the unions] falling into the hands of the enemies of the revolutionary proletariat, the best communist elements should direct the ... organisation and education of these organisations."[39]

The PCE was now the official Spanish representation in the Comintern and so, in accordance with the proposed statutes of the Profintern, if the confederation was to belong to the International it would have to accept direct communist intervention in union matters. Many of the new communists were simply old socialists, with a predetermined ideological animosity to revolutionary syndicalism, and this augured ill. In fact one of the party's first acts was to issue a manifesto in which they claimed that the inability of the confederation to overcome the repression of the Spanish authorities was a result of its flawed ideology (revolutionary syndicalism). A policy of direct confrontation with the leaders of the CNT with the aim of winning over the confederation's members was doomed to failure from the beginning and brought only contempt from confederation militants.[40]

Although the PCE as a party could not hope to overturn the CNT's position, individual members of the CNT sympathetic to the communists could. The struggle between those who favoured the CNT's membership in the Communist International and subsequent close collaboration with the communists was an internal one. The sympathisers, labelled 'communist-syndicalists' by historians (due to their position with in the CNT and their support of the communists), were able to reach a level of importance within the CNT out of all relation to their actual support base within the CNT due to the undoubted talent of two of its leading representatives, Joaquín Maurín and Andreu Nin, although it was mainly as a consequence of the repression of prominent CNT militants at the time.

Pestaña's detention had been part of the ongoing repression. At the beginning of November 1920 General Severiano Martínez Anido was appointed civil governor and was given full power to deal with the unions as he pleased. With his chief of police, Colonel Miguel Arlegui, who took pleasure in personally torturing his CNT prisoners, Martínez Anido introduced an unprecedented era of violent repression that was to last until early 1922. On November 30, 1920, there began a new wave of detentions, and thirty-six CNT leaders were transferred to a prison in Mahon (Menorca). At the beginning of 1921, the CNT was practically leaderless, which resulted in a constant change in membership of the national and regional committees in Catalonia.[41] Once again this repression would all but force the CNT underground, loosening the links between regions and strengthening the independence of the national committee based in Catalonia.[42] The repression in Barcelona resulted in much of the confederal activity being transferred to Lleida (Lérida) in the west of Catalonia, where in early 1920 Maurín had been elected secretary of the provincial federation of the CNT and director of its newspaper, *Lucha Social*.[43] Such was Maurín's influence in a region which historically had favoured socialism over anarchism that anarchists baptised the town 'Mauringrado'.[44] At the same time the constant arrests of leading militants made previous anonymity in the movement a positive attribute for anyone wishing to become a member of the regional and national committees. In early 1921, Maurín formed part of the restructured Catalan regional committee. On March 2, 1921, the CNT secretary, Boal, was arrested. His replacement was Andreu Nin.[45]

The Delegation to the Inaugural Profintern Congress

The invitation to attend the inaugural congress of the Profintern arrived in Spain against the backdrop of repression and an increased criticism of Moscow in the anarchist and syndicalist press.[46] The plenum organised to discuss the invitation, held in Barcelona on April 19, 1921, was attended by Nin for the national committee; Jesus Ibáñez representing Asturias; Maurín representing Catalonia; Arlandis representing Valencia; Arturo Parera, editor of the anarcho-syndicalist newspaper *El Comunista*, for Aragón; Atenas for Galicia; as well as delegates from the north, Castile and León, and Palencia (the Andalusian delegate arrived after the plenum had finished).[47] The plenum decided to send a delegation of five to Russia, choosing four of those in attendance – Maurín, Arlandis, Ibánez, and Nin – as well as Quintanilla, who was later replaced by the French-born but Barcelona-based anarchist Gaston Leval (real name Pierre R. Piller) who was chosen by the Libertarian Communist Federation in Barcelona.[48]

According to Jaime Salan (who used the pseudonym Wilkens), a member of the Intersyndicale Ouvrière de Langue Espagnole en France (an organisation of confederation militants exiled in France), the CNT had originally decided not to send a delegation to Moscow due to the imprisonment of its leading militants. Wilkens, who had been in Russia during the second congress of the Comintern, claims that he had written to the national committee proposing that they send a delegation of five members to the inaugural congress. Having met Pestaña and the delegates of the other revolutionary syndicalist organisations in Russia and again in Berlin, Wilkens could not have known that the communist-syndicalists now ran the national committee and most probably suggested such a large delegation in the hope that they would be better able to defend the revolutionary syndicalist position in Moscow.[49] Whether, the committee was responding to Wilkens's suggestion or not, it is still surprising that such a relatively large delegation, including the national secretary, should leave for Russia at a time when the confederation needed all the help it could muster at home. It is also not clear whether Wilkens made his criticisms of the Comintern clear in his invitation, but in any case Nin had already seen Pestaña's draft report, which had been passed to Boal on his return to Spain, and was thus aware of his negative opinion of the Profintern. He made no mention of this to those present.

The plenum mandated the delegation to support the principle of the dictatorship of the proletariat to be exercised by the unions and not a party, to defend the autonomy of the CNT, and to accept an exchange of delegates between the Comintern and the Red Trade Union International. The delegation claimed that it would be loyal to the Berlin declaration which had been signed by representatives of various revolutionary syndicalist organisations following a congress in Berlin in December 1920, vowing to defend the autonomy of the revolutionary syndicalist movement at the Profintern congress.[50] Following their arrival in Russia, the delegation participated in the third congress of the International which began on June 22, 1921, but their action was of secondary importance as, in line with the decisions of the previous congress, Spain was represented by the PCE.[51]

The inaugural congress of the Profintern opened on July 3, 1921, continuing its deliberations for the following fifteen days.[52] The delegation (except Leval, who distanced himself from his colleagues and soon became embroiled in the debates over the treatment of anarchists in Russia) was noticeable for its strong support of the Profintern and Bolshevism.[53] For the Russians, their pliability made a welcome change to the criticisms of Pestaña. In Spain, as occurred in revolutionary syndicalist organisations elsewhere, there was an outcry over the statutes of the Profintern that were finally agreed on at the congress. The principal objection related to the motion on relations between the Comintern and the Profintern signed for Spain by Nin and Maurín, which stated that "the closest ties possible should be established with the Third Communist International [Comintern], vanguard of the revolutionary workers' movement throughout the world, based on a reciprocal representation in the executives of the two organisations. … This link must be organic and technical in character, [and it] should be shown in the joint preparation and realisation of revolutionary acts on a national and international level."[54] This meant that the links between the Comintern and the Profintern would be reflected on a national basis by the "establishment of a close and genuine link" between the unions and the Communist Party – a position that Pestaña had rejected in 1920.[55]

In Spain, the northern region of the CNT (the Basque Country and Santander) responded immediately to the publication of the resolutions agreed to in Moscow, demanding that the national committee "disqualify its delegates."[56] A campaign against the Profintern delegation was immediately launched in the pages of the anarchist newspapers *Nueva Senda* (Madrid) and *Redención* (Alcoy). *Nueva Senda* spelt out the fundamental contradiction involved if the CNT joined the Profintern: "If the objective of the CNT is the destruction of the State, it cannot collaborate with the State. It cannot work with the State even under the pretext of reforming it or … defending the workers. … [F]rom the moment that the CNT joined the Profintern of Moscow, which is under the hegemony of a socialist party, and therefore, in favour of the State, it renounced its ideology and as a consequence its tactics."[57]

Being a member of the Profintern, its opponents argued, meant that the unions would be subordinate to the political machinations of the Comintern in the international arena and to its representatives, the PCE, at home. The CNT had previously dismissed proposals to unite its forces with the socialist-dominated UGT due to the latter's political connections with the PSOE, and it was therefore highly unlikely to accept that a party, the PCE, formed by erstwhile socialists, should interfere in its affairs. A plenum was held in Madrid on August 14 to discuss the resolutions of the Moscow congress and the activity of the CNT delegation. Unlike at the April plenum, all the regions of Spain were represented, with a total of twenty-seven delegates present. The plenum agreed to postpone any final decision until the delegation had returned but disqualified them "in principle," pending the holding of a further plenum at which they could defend themselves.[58] The meeting reaffirmed the "autonomous and independent character" of the CNT in relation to all political parties, including "the so-called communists," rejected any pacts or alliances with political parties, and once more stressed that the goal of the CNT was libertarian communism.[59]

The opposition to the communist-syndicalists' position within the CNT was not limited to militants in Spain. There were also other CNT militants in Moscow who kept their colleagues in Spain informed of the delegation's progress. Their reports were not favourable. In early 1921, exiled CNT militants in Paris who had fled the repression in Spain had formed the Intersyndicale Ouvrière de Langue Espagnole en France (IOE) in order to publish a version of *Solidaridad Obrera* in the French capital. The IOE also published CNT national committee manifestos in the foreign libertarian press to inform them about what was happening in Spain.[60] Articles and manifestos from the IOE appeared in the anarchist press in France, Italy, Argentina, Portugal, Uruguay, and Spain. One of the members of the organisation was Wilkens, who had represented the IOE at the international syndicalist congress in Berlin in 1920, which discussed the position that the revolutionary syndicalists should take towards the Profintern. From Berlin he travelled to Russia, where he met Pestaña, among others. Wilkens, a member of the construction workers' union of Chauny (Aisne, France), had been mandated by the Trade Union Committee for the Defence of Spanish Workers of the Nord region of France to travel to Russia and report back his impressions. Wilkens stayed in Russia for several months on an educational tour and had a number of articles on different aspects of Soviet Russia published in *Le Libertaire.* He was, he claimed, in close contact with the national committee of the CNT. Due to the imprisonment of Pestaña, he was the first representative of the CNT to publish an eyewitness account of Bolshevism in action.[61]

Whilst in Russia, Wilkens interviewed Lenin, who told him, "We created the syndicalist International out of opportunism; because we know that there are many convinced revolutionary workers in the unions, ready for action, but who, due to a remnant of anarchist mentality, do not accept that they should enter the Communist Party. Once they are in the Communist International, through the intermediary of the syndicalist International, it will be much easier for us to direct them to follow our tactics and methods."[62]

Whether Lenin had been this honest or not – Wilkens arrived in Russia a fervent supporter of the Russian revolution – this simply reinforced what many in Spain were beginning to believe.[63] Alongside Wilkens, at least three other exiled CNT militants also visited Russia and sent back critical reports of the Profintern delegation: José Pedro Carlos Foix (using the pseudonym Leon Xifort), who also had close contacts with the IOE; Bruno Lladó (secretary of the IOE); and Francisco Durán, an anarchist from Barcelona, who met the delegation whilst they were in Russia.[64] Jemmy Troitzsch, a Polish anarchist who had spent many years in Spain and was now living in Lithuania, also sent articles critical of the delegation's position to the anarchist press. Their reports brought the activities of the Profintern delegation and the opinion of the other revolutionary syndicalist organisations to the attention of CNT militants in Spain through the pages of *Nueva Senda*. In August, the IOE launched a manifesto claiming that the four delegates had betrayed the principles of the CNT by accepting the statutes of the Profintern and added its voice to those calling for the disqualification of the delegation, declaring "null and void all the agreements that have been signed in the name of the CNT."[65]

The only support for the position adopted by the delegation in Russia came in the pages of the periodical *Lucha Social* of Lérida, which remained loyal to its director, Maurín. An editorial rejected claims that the Profintern would be subservient to the directives of the Comintern.[66] However, the article continued, it was ridiculous to rule out dealings or pacts with the communists as, although it was "obvious that the space between the ideologies of communism and revolutionary syndicalism is great, they coincide on one point that is of real importance: the preparation and execution of the revolution as soon as possible."[67] The influence of the newspaper was limited, however. The lack of references to *Lucha Social* in other syndicalist newspapers suggests strongly that it was not widely read outside of Lérida.[68] The task of defending their actions therefore fell predominantly on the delegates themselves.

Whilst returning from Moscow, Leval, Arlandis, and Nin were arrested in Berlin. On his release, Nin immediately returned to Moscow. Only Ibáñez and Maurín were able to return directly to Spain, where the former was immediately arrested, leaving only Maurín to argue in favour of the positions adopted in Moscow.[69] This was not necessarily a disadvantage, as Maurín was easily the most pro-syndicalist of the delegates. Maurín took over Nin's position as secretary to the national committee on his return.[70]

Of the four delegates, Maurín's position is perhaps the most interesting as it demonstrates not only the lack of homogeneity among the communist-syndicalists but also an alternative, political form of revolutionary syndicalism, which was in essence a mixture of revolutionary syndicalism and revolutionary politics. Maurín developed his 'political revolutionary syndicalism' from reading the works of the 'textbook' theoretician Georges Sorel and the Italian socialist syndicalists Arturo

Labriola and Errico Leone.[71] Maurín did see the potential dangers inherent in the dictatorial tendencies within Bolshevism but was won over by the mere fact of the triumph of the revolution in Russia. He had been the only one of the four communist-syndicalists to present any consistent opposition in Moscow, joining with others to create an Association of Revolutionary Syndicalist Workers of the World within the Profintern as a liaison centre for militants who opposed political influence within the Profintern. [72] The association had an office in Paris, but it proved to be a short-lived phenomenon, and, significantly, Maurín did not even mention his role in this group on his return.[73]

The plenum to discuss the "disqualification in principle" of the Profintern delegation was eventually held in Barcelona on October 15–16, 1921, but, thanks to the intervention of Maurín, this again vacillated and delayed taking any final decision on both the delegation and relations with the Profintern until a future national congress.[74] The failure to take a decisive stand at the October plenum brought the threat of a split within the CNT from the local committee of Guipúzcoa (Basque Country, part of the northern CRT), enraged by the decisions taken (or not taken) at the October plenum. The Basques were the first of a number of organisations that threatened to split from the confederation, joined later by Pamplona, La Coruña, and the Levante CRT.[75] The response from the national committee (probably written by Maurín) accused the Basques of wanting to make the confederation a "sectarian grouping" open only to anarchists, arguing that the Comité Syndicaliste Révolutionnaire (CSR) – the revolutionary syndicalist wing of the CGT in France – and the USI in Italy had demonstrated that anarchists, revolutionary syndicalists, and communists could coexist in the same organisation.[76] Maurín continued his defence of the Profintern in a series of articles published towards the end of 1921.[77] The link between the Comintern and the Profintern, he claimed, was necessary to maintain class unity and did not represent the subordination of the latter to the former, or, on a national basis, of the unions to the parties. For the CNT, the only alternatives were Amsterdam, the home of the reformist socialist International, or Moscow. The CNT belonged in the latter, he argued, as the Profintern was a truly revolutionary International based on action and not ideology. Action in the form of organised revolutionary violence by a united working class was the sine qua non of the triumph of the revolution. The CNT, he argued, should gather together all the forces of the working class under its banner, including communists. In doing so, it would not weaken its autonomy, it would strengthen its ranks.

What mattered more was what he did not say. Characteristically, Maurín avoided mentioning that the Comintern had set the PCE the task of conquering the unions. In his attacks on his opponents in the confederation, Maurín simplified the ideological debate to one between two tendencies. The first felt that the unions should be class-focused, involved in a class struggle of the masses joined with other such bodies internationally. The second saw the CNT as a sectarian organisation, whose tactics were based on individual action which was bound to fail and whose ideological base was inevitably leading the confederation towards doctrinaire reformism. The first represented those who favoured Moscow and the second those who opposed it.[78]

This argument was based on an evident misrepresentation of the opponents of Moscow. The need to resort to such oversimplification may have resulted not simply from Maurín's dislike of anarchism but also from his desire to avoid focusing on the central issue, Bolshevik anti-syndicalism.[79] José Alberola, a leading anarchist militant in the CNT, dissected Maurín's ideological position, attacking first his sub-ordination of ideology to action: "The desire for triumph at all costs without worrying about means is a dangerous tactic which gives false results. … [T]he principle that the end justifies the means disgusts all rational and reasonable minds. … We anarchists don't want to fragment the organisations. What we desire is that they do not serve as a footstool for certain nascent dictators and future despots."[80]

For Alberola, it was the communist designs on the revolutionary syndicalist organisation that were the root causes of Maurín's and his associates' attempts to portray the dispute as one between the differing revolutionary and anarcho-syndicalist ideologies. Referring to the political past of Maurín, Nin, and Arlandis, Alberola railed against the "neophytes who have adopted syndicalism at the eleventh hour … [who] are looking to find arguments for justifying the metamorphosis of revolutionary syndicalism … so that it can serve state communism. … The Communist Party will be nothing without managing to take hold of the organisation, and it is clear that it is remorselessly trying to do this to achieve its goals."[81]

As the communist-syndicalists' attempts to gain support for their position by means of ideological argument had failed, they increasingly resorted to a policy of slandering their opponents. Pestaña, Leval, Wilkens, Xifort, and José Duran were all the subject of slander campaigns by the pro-Bolsheviks on their return from Moscow. Typically the accusations were that individuals had been influenced by anarchists in Russia or had requested money to visit Russia and, this being refused, had turned against the Bolsheviks.[82] This brought a highly critical response from the Levantine CRT in a manifesto published in December: "The National Committee with singular inhibition and as its unique argument slanders all those who raise any criticisms, no matter how reasoned or calm these are of its woeful performance. ... We assert that the performance of the Committee is frankly disturbing, contradicts the Confederation's history, distorts its spirit, and twists the trajectory that it had always followed." The Levantine CRT also questioned how the national committee could justify its decision to be represented (by Arlandis) on the Profintern executive committee when the revolutionary syndicalist organisations from France, Italy, and Portugal had all refused to do so. Repeating the position adopted by Pamplona, they argued that, until another national congress met and decided to change the decisions of 1919, the CNT's ideology was libertarian communism, and the national committee should act accordingly. The manifesto concluded that "the only positive service that the Confederal Committee can do for the organisation is to resign."[83]

The national committee responded to Levante's criticism in a private letter dated January 5, 1922. The secretive manner of the reply was viewed with such suspicion by Eusebio Carbó, who had spoken in favour of Bolshevism at the national congress in 1919, that he published the letter in *Redención* under the title "Against Secret Diplomacy" and complained of the committee's mania to keep private to a small number of people information that should be open to all.[84] Carbó added his voice to those who complained about the national committee's attempts to silence debate within the CNT and reminded them that the national committee was not an executive but more a liaison committee and responded to the wishes of local and regional organisations and not vice versa. In its letter, the national committee once more claimed that its opinion was the same as that of the revolutionary syndicalists in France, Portugal, and Italy, especially after the last plenum when they had agreed to withdraw Arlandis from the executive of the Profintern. However, the committee made no mention of the fact that Nin had taken up a leading position in the Profintern. Unconvinced, the unions of the Levantine CRT threatened en masse to withdraw from the CNT if the confederation did not withdraw from the Profintern.[85]

This did not happen. The communist-syndicalists' control of the national and Catalan Committees had been dependent on the detention of leading militants and the repression in Catalonia. Carbó was one of the many leading CNT militants released in early 1922, while Maurín finally fell victim to the government repression, being detained in February 1922.

The new national committee (elected after the detention of Maurín) quickly defined itself as "essentially anarchist" in a manifesto in *Acción Social Obrera* on March 1, 1922, and went on to declare: "We reject all means of struggle that are not direct action and that do not pursue as their goal the establishment of libertarian communism. ... We are and will always be irreconcilable enemies of all dictatorships whatever label they carry. ... We believe in federalism. We recognise that freedom goes from the individual to the community. ... We are and always will be enemies of the state and its institutions. And our principles are those of the CNT."[86] The CNT's brief membership of the Profintern was now drawing to an end, and in late March, the new secretary of the national committee, Joan Peiró, announced that a national congress was being prepared to discuss the issue.

The Zaragoza National Conference, the largest CNT gathering between 1919 and 1931, began on June 11, 1922.[87] Thanks to the lull in the government repression of the organisation, most of the leading CNT militants had been released from prison and were thus able to attend (although the majority of delegates came from northern Spain: Catalonia, Aragón, Basque country, Galicia, Asturias, and Valencia). The deliberations of the conference were started by Pestaña, who read out his official report on his experiences in Russia, telling how he had gradually become so disillusioned with the International that he had withdrawn his signature from the document on the formation of the Profintern when he realised that this was contrary to the libertarian principles of the confederation. Pestaña argued that the CNT should break from the Third International. Pestaña's speech was welcomed with great enthusiasm by the vast majority of the delegates. Arlandis, who followed Pestaña, was not given so warm a reception. Arlandis read out his report on the Profintern congress which stressed the need for the CNT to have close relations with the world's proletariat and said that, as the Profintern was not subordinate to the Comintern, the CNT should remain in the Profintern. However, Arlandis began by attempting to justify the performance of the delegation to the Profintern. This he did with reference to the decisions made at the April plenum of the previous year at which he claimed it was agreed that the delegation should defend the dictatorship of the proletariat. This decision was based on the approval given by the Madrid congress of 1919 when it gave an "enthusiastic welcome" to the revolutionaries in Russia. Such a tenuous and twisted interpretation brought uproar from the conference.[88] The legality of the April plenum was once again questioned. Parera, the representative for Aragón at the April plenum, claimed that the plenum did not accept the dictatorship of the proletariat but a syndicalist dictatorship, a position supported by the contemporary evidence, and questioned the whole procedure by which the delegates at the plenum appointed themselves as delegates for the Profintern congress. Parera added that Arlandis had kept secret the fact that he had become a member of the PCE before being appointed a delegate and had known that he was going to Russia even before the April plenum. The national committee of the CNT concluded that the delegation had been "irregular."

However, there was some doubt as to whether the conference had the right to overturn the CNT's affiliation with Moscow, as this had been decided by a national congress, and, in accordance with confederation rules, such a decision could only be overturned by a future national congress. This problem was overcome by the decision to hold a referendum among the unions. The final proposal, approved by the conference and drawn up by Pestaña and Seguí, stated that the decision to adhere to the Third International owed more to "the sympathy between the proletariat of Spain and the world" than a "sharing of principles." The later confusion over the Madrid motion resulted, it argued, from the abnormal situation in Spain, which also played an important part in the decision to send the second delegation. The CNT "could not subscribe to or accept the decisions taken by that delegation." Having tackled these two issues, the proposal then moved on to the question of the Third International, which it described as "clearly political," "party-oriented," and "fundamentally at odds with the principles sustained by the CNT." Taking all this into account, the conference accepted in principle the separation of the confederation from the Profintern and submitted for the consideration of all its members "the definitive separation of the CNT from the Profintern and the Third International and the affiliation of the CNT with all attempts that are made for the organisation of a revolutionary syndicalist International, independent of all political parties, irrespective of their nature." The CNT withdrew from the Comintern due to its political content, the rationale given in the proposal being clearly in line with revolutionary syndicalist doctrine (although clearly acceptable to the anarchists as well). The proposal was accepted by the vast majority of delegates at the conference, and the subsequent referendum gave resounding support for separation from Moscow.[89]

Separated by an Ideological and Tactical Chasm

The period covering the CNT's membership of the Comintern and then the Profintern is one of confusion, not least due to the repression throughout the country and especially in Catalonia. The forced demise of the majority of newspapers and periodicals, as well as the scarcity of surviving editions of those that did manage to be published, have made it difficult to present a clear picture of the evolution of the confederation's reaction to Bolshevism. Those historians who have covered the period in depth have often done so without consulting all the available material, such as the acts of the Zaragoza conference, copies of *Acción Social Obrera* and *Redención* (which are available only at municipal archives), and foreign anarchist and syndicalist papers which published copies of articles from the Spanish press.[90] The result has been that the activities of the delegation and their followers have been given a more favourable treatment than is perhaps deserved, and the debates over the delegation to the Profintern have been presented as a conflict between anarchism and Bolshevism rather than as a logical corollary of the traditional revolutionary syndicalist rejection of political interference in union matters.

It has been claimed that the communist-syndicalists represented a planned Bolshevik infiltration of the CNT from the beginning.[91] The contemporary evidence is not conclusive, although there is room for suspicion. Clearly the communists were interested bringing the unions within their sphere of influence – this would seem both a logical and justifiable position. The problem was not of ends – every party has the right to try to attract unions to its position – but of means. As they proved unable to win over the majority of militants through argument, they adopted tactics that would lead some to conclude that a policy of secret infiltration was being followed. Bruno Lladó obtained a copy of an agreement reached between the delegates of the PCE and the CNT in Moscow (the existence of this agreement was subsequently confirmed by the general secretary of the RTUI, Lozovsky, in a speech to the Confédération Générale du Travail Unitaire (CGTU) Congress in Saint-Étienne in June 1922). The agreement stipulated that the communists in the socialist UGT were to continue working to win support for Moscow within the reformist organisation but would also "coordinate their activity with the Confederation." If the communists were expelled from the UGT, they would automatically be incorporated into the CNT.[92] The Levantine CRT published extracts of the decisions taken at the congress which supported Lladó's assertions.[93] This suggests that the PCE and CNT would work closely together but also could be read to imply that the direction of the CNT was clearly pro-communist. Nin's position is difficult to justify given that he appears to have seen Pestaña's critical report prior to going to Moscow and kept its findings a secret. He did not return to Spain, for fear of arrest, and became a key figure in the Profintern leadership and Trotsky's secretary.[94] Arlandis and Ibáñez's credibility throughout the events must be questioned as it appears that both had become members of the PCE in 1920 – a fact they consistently neglected to mention.[95] There were simply too many misrepresentations and too much secrecy.

It is possible that the communist-syndicalists were also simply driven by their own ideological persuasions, albeit they must have known that these were not those held by the majority of confederal militants and that the ideological positions put forward at the Profintern congress were contrary to those adopted at the Madrid congress of 1919. Nonetheless they did not let this inhibit their actions in Russia. Despite Bar's claim to the contrary, the activities of the delegation in Russia were not consistent with the decisions of the Madrid congress and in fact showed a flagrant disregard for the ideological independence of revolutionary syndicalism.[96] The actions of the delegation in Moscow could not conceivably be justified with reference to those taken in Madrid in 1919 which formed the basis upon which the delegation should have been acting. The delegation acted disregarding their position as representatives of a national organisation, preferring to follow their own agenda. Clearly they had a right to defend their ideas within the CNT but not to represent its membership in disregard for its principles. They acted according to their own agenda and not that of the organisation they were supposed to be representing.

The delegation to the Profintern had left Spain promising to protect syndicalist autonomy yet seemed to have forgotten this almost as soon as they arrived in Russia.[97] Why did the delegation act this way? Perhaps the clearest explanation was given by Bruno Lladó, the secretary of the IOE, who was in Russia at the time of the congress: "Perhaps the only reason for such an attitude … is that none of them are revolutionary syndicalists: that they are not anarchists or libertarians; that, on the contrary, they are social democrats, who have become Bolsheviks or authoritarian communists."[98]

Maurín was a Marxist in syndicalist clothing – "Doctrinally I found myself close to the Socialists … [but] in practical terms the syndicalists seemed to me more realistic, more daring, younger."[99] He looked for a middle way between the two positions. He advocated a close relationship between communist party and unions while maintaining autonomy and claimed this was the Profintern position. He was not believed.[100] Despite his doubts about Bolshevism, he had been won over by its revolutionary success. Nin had been a former member of both Republican and Socialist parties and had an evident predilection towards party, rather than union, politics. Ibáñez had been a member of the UGT and along with Arlandis had joined the PCE in 1920, whilst Arlandis's ideology could at best be described as confused (passing from individualist anarchism to Stalinism in the course of his adult life).[101]

On returning to Spain, Maurín and Arlandis had been economical with the truth and later (along with Nin writing from Moscow) had resorted to simplistic interpretations and slander and at all times kept quiet about any contacts with the communists. All this was to cover up one simple fact: Bolshevism and revolutionary syndicalism were incompatible doctrines. One required the complete centralisation of all authority within a political elite that would seize the state for the purposes of defending the revolution. The other believed that it was the state itself which was the enemy that must be defeated if the revolution was to succeed. The unions contained not only the means to bring about the revolution, but also the means to protect it, and they needed to be independent from the influence of all political parties which would seek to divert the revolution for their own purposes. The CNT withdrew from the Profintern because, in line with revolutionary syndicalist doctrine, the vast majority of its members opposed party political influence in the unions. The weakness of the communist-syndicalist position was amply demonstrated when a lull in the repression against the CNT in early 1922 led to the release of the detained militants and as a result they were abruptly removed from their positions and their policy towards Moscow overturned. To stress the syndicalist rationale behind this decision, it should be noted that many of the leading figures who spoke out against the CNT's membership of the Comintern, Pestaña, Quintanilla, Seguí, and the national secretary at the time of the Zaragoza conference, Joan Peiró, would soon become the target of anarchist attacks for their defence of a pure syndicalist doctrine and the independence of the CNT from the anarchist groups.[102] As Seguí proclaimed at Zaragoza, the CNT's split from the Profintern resulted from the fact that "a chasm separates us from Russia, both in ideology and in tactics."[103]

4.

AN INDEPENDENT REVOLUTIONARY SYNDICALIST INTERNATIONAL

THE CNT WAS NOT THE ONLY ORGANISATION THAT TURNED ITS BACK on Moscow. Significantly the majority of the organisations that attended the London congress of 1913 (or their successor organisations) could be found among those that would eventually form a new International Working Men's Association (IWMA) at the Berlin congress of December 1922 to January 1923. Even before the Comintern had held its inaugural congress in March 1919, moves had begun to renew the prewar efforts to establish a truly independent revolutionary syndicalist International that would be based on the principles of union independence, federalism, and anti-statism. The invitation to the second congress of the Comintern and the subsequent formation of the RTUI that followed effectively sidetracked the plans of the revolutionary syndicalist organisations. Just as had occurred with the majority of CNT militants, members of the other organisations underwent a gradual evolution from outright support for both the Russian Revolution and Bolshevism to a position whereby they differentiated between the aims of the former and the politics of the latter. Disenchantment with Moscow led to the conclusion that the revolutionary syndicalist International could not be formed in Moscow and would actually have to be formed *against* Moscow. The new IWMA was the revolutionary syndicalist alternative to the discredited RTUI, although its origins predated the formation of the RTUI. The result of the conflict with Moscow was that postwar revolutionary syndicalism was markedly more antipolitical than it had been prior to the First World War.[1]

Ironically, at the very moment that moves towards the creation of an independent revolutionary syndicalist International were reaching a successful conclusion, the CNT, which had for so long called for such an organisation, hesitated before giving its allegiance and even contemplated returning to the RTUI. The reasons for this were twofold. First was the fear that as the other leading union organisations headed for the reformist International in Amsterdam or the Communist version in Moscow the CNT would become isolated on the international stage, confined to a second-rate International. Second and more important, the vacillation was symptomatic of the ideological confusion in which the moderate elements of the confederation, in both the national and the Catalan regional committee, found themselves as they attempted to defend the old-style apolitical syndicalism. The moderates hoped in this way to maintain the unity of the confederation in the face of an increasingly bitter ideological struggle within the ranks over the influence of anarchism in the movement. For the moderates, the new International's rejection of prewar political neutrality was unwelcome.

The historiography of the IWMA is extremely limited, apart from in contemporary articles. Only one book covers the birth of the organisation, and there is an almost complete dearth of in-depth research on the latter trajectory of the International.[2] Generally in Spanish texts the IWMA is ignored except when referring to the Zaragoza conference's decision to withdraw from the Comintern and send a delegation to Berlin in June 1922. Virtually no reference is made to the CNT's role in the formation of the IWMA from the congress in London in 1913 to the founding congress that opened in Berlin on Christmas Day, 1922. This creates the impression that the IWMA was simply a short-term reaction to the formation of the Comintern instead of the conclusion of a drawn-out process interrupted by the war and the Russian Revolution. The CNT's affiliation with the IWMA is thus seen simply as a negative, the rejection of Moscow, rather than indicating a positive relationship with its fellow revolutionary syndicalist organisations. To show how the confederation's position towards the creation of a revolutionary syndicalist International independent of Moscow developed, it is necessary to chart the CNT's involvement in, and reaction to, the moves that culminated in the formation of the IWMA. This, taken in tandem with the CNT's proclaimed position in London in 1913, demonstrates that the IWMA was more than a knee-jerk reaction to the RTUI but instead the culmination of a long-term desire to be united with kindred organisations. The RTUI divided and confused but ultimately could not prevent the IWMA's creation.

However, for much of the period immediately prior to the formation of the IWMA, the CNT was forced to play a secondary role due to the continued repression it faced in Spain. During most of the period from 1920 to mid 1922, apart from the ill-fated delegation to the RTUI, the national committee was limited to sending increasingly desperate manifestos to its international comrades, informing them of the relentless repression at home and requesting a full boycott of Spanish goods.[3] Nonetheless the rationale of the organisations that played a principle role in the International's creation closely mirrored the ideas of the CNT.

Revolutionary Syndicalist Internationalism following the London Congress, 1913

Although the war had cut the links between the revolutionary syndicalist organisations of the peninsula and the rest of Europe, the call

made by the delegates from Spain and Portugal at El Ferrol in favour
of an international congress once the carnage had ended was echoed
by other organisations. In May 1915, although unable to attend the
invitation to El Ferrol, the USI sent its support by post.[4] In a meeting
of the general council the same month, Armando Borghi reported on
the developments of the USI's international relations, most specifically with the German syndicalist minority, the CNT, the labour organisations in Portugal, and the revolutionary syndicalist minority in
France. The extract of Borghi's report that appeared in the press sheds
little light on the exact nature of these contacts, but the council did
agree that the general executive should make sure that the USI would
be present at any future "international labour congress."[5]

At the end of 1916 the Dutch National Arbeids Secretariaat (NAS)
sent a circular to all the revolutionary syndicalist organisations, proposing the celebration of a new congress as soon as the war ended.
In February 1919 syndicalists from Norway, Denmark, and Sweden,
meeting in Copenhagen, agreed on the need to convoke a new international congress and approached the NAS to ask if they could organise it. Following this, a second revolutionary syndicalist International
congress was scheduled to be held in Amsterdam in August that year.[6]
However, whereas a congress of the reformist unions of the old Second
International took place in the Dutch capital in September, the revolutionary syndicalist congress had to be cancelled, as foreign delegates,
including a delegation from the CNT, were unable to gain access to
the country.[7] Nonetheless, the differing syndicalist organisations were
once again increasing their international contacts, including with the
CNT. Speaking at a conference in Madrid in early October 1919,
Salvador Seguí claimed that the CNT had relations with colleagues in
France, Portugal, Holland, Belgium, and just about "everywhere" and
was working to deepen these connections.[8]

In the first half of 1920 the Catalan CRT appointed delegates
to visit a number of European countries. According to a report by
the Naval attaché in Madrid, Vich Ramasoff was to visit Greece,
Romania, and Bulgaria; Eusebio Carbó was to travel to Italy,
Austria, and Germany; Salvador Quemades was to go to Switzerland,
Germany, Bulgaria, Poland, and Finland; Vicente Gil was to visit Portugal; and Angel Pestaña was to go to France, Switzerland,

Belgium, Holland, and Denmark.[9] Nothing is known of Ramasoff's and Quemades's journeys, and nothing is known about Ramasoff at all. Carbó did reach Italy but got no farther. Gil met representatives of the Portuguese Confederaçào Geral do Trabalho, and Pestaña attended a meeting of the administrative commission of the French CGT. It appears that relations with the French CGT were strongest although ultimately of little significance due to the reformist nature of the French organisation (see chapter 2).[10] However, given the international climate and the corresponding difficulty of travel, the CNT was unable to play a leading role in attempts to create a revolutionary syndicalist International.

Due to the impossibility of holding a revolutionary syndicalist congress in Amsterdam, the NAS limited its actions to an interchange of ideas with German syndicalists. At a national congress in December 1919, the disparate forces of the revolutionary syndicalists in Germany formed the Freie Arbeiter-Union Deutschlands (FAUD) – the Free Labour Union of Germany. The congress mirrored that held by the CNT in the same month by declaring its solidarity with the Russian Soviet Republic and calling for the establishment of a syndicalist International.[11] In response to the NAS move, the FAUD decided that it should contact the NAS to convoke an international congress in 1920.[12] In the summer of 1920, whilst passing through Berlin on his way to Moscow, Armando Borghi, the delegate of the USI to the Comintern congress, met up with the leading figures of the FAUD in Berlin and was given the task of consulting the syndicalist organisations in Moscow about the congress proposed by the NAS.[13]

The revolutionary syndicalist movement finally gathered in Moscow at the second congress of the Comintern from July 19 to August 7, 1920. The agreement to form a syndicalist International, made at the second Comintern congress, led to confusion in the syndicalist camp. As has been seen, the CNT delegate Pestaña at first signed the document relating to the formation of the RTUI, before withdrawing his signature after consulting with Borghi.[14] According to Borghi, Pestaña's room in the congressional delegates' hotel was the meeting place for the various "companions of the libertarian tendency" who were unhappy about the Bolshevik proposals for the RTUI.[15] At a meeting held in Moscow in September, Pestaña and

Borghi, with Jules Lepetit and Marcel Vergeat – the delegates of the French Comité Syndicaliste Révolutionnaire (CSR) – the revolutionary wing of the CGT, Souchy, and a delegate of the International Workers of the World agreed that the inaugural meeting of the RTUI should take place outside Russia, as in Moscow it would not be possible to constitute the true syndicalist International independent of all political parties.[16] Lepetit and Vergeat were both anarcho-syndicalists and critical of what they found in Russia. However, both died whilst returning to France by boat via Murmansk and the Baltic. Why they should have been forced to take this route has never been discovered – other delegates returned via more straightforward routes – and led to claims that the boat had been deliberately sunk to avoid their critical reports reaching the French workers, although suspicion was not backed by evidence.[17]

Following this, the FAUD organised a conference of the revolutionary syndicalist organisations.[18] The conference took place December 16–21, 1920, with representatives from the United States (IWW), Argentina (FORA), France (CSR), England (shop stewards' movement), Sweden (SAC), and Holland (NAS), as well as delegates of the Russian communist party and the provisional council of the RTUI in attendance.[19] The USI and the Portuguese CGT were unable to send members due to their respective domestic situations but declared themselves in agreement with the holding of the conference. The domestic situation in Spain forced the CNT to do likewise, although Wilkens claims to have represented the confederation at the congress.[20] Messages of sympathy were also sent by syndicalists from Norway and Denmark.

The principal aim of the congress was for the different organisations to agree to a joint policy that they would follow at the inaugural congress of the RTUI to be held in May 1921. This objective was eventually achieved but not until it became clear that there were differences of opinion over two key issues: the acceptance and exact meaning of the term 'dictatorship of the proletariat' and what relations, if any, the RTUI should have with the Comintern. On the first issue, the American and English delegates felt that the conference should endorse dictatorship of the proletariat as the Russian Revolution had shown that it was necessary to ensure the defeat of the forces of reaction following the revolution.[21] They faced strong disagreement from the German and Swedish delegates until it was eventually established that the proponents of dictatorship of the proletariat did not intend to establish a new state but only shared land and means of production by the revolutionary workers' economic organisations (trade unions, in essence a dictatorship of the soviets). Finally the disagreement was resolved, with the delegates supporting the principle of 'the domination of the working class' and rejecting the dictatorship of the proletariat due to its political implications. On the issue of Comintern-RTUI relations, Belinsky, the delegate of the RTUI, proposed that the new International should "do their practical work in contact with the Third International." Only the English delegate supported him, and the proposal was rejected.[22]

Nonetheless, it was obvious that for many of the representatives of the different organisations the revolutionary attraction of Moscow persisted. No breach with Moscow was suggested. The final outcome of the meeting was the Berlin Declaration, which called on the revolutionary syndicalist organisations to attend the inaugural conference of the RTUI, where they were to defend the principles of revolutionary syndicalism outlined in the declaration itself.[23]

The Berlin Declaration contained no direct criticism of Moscow, and although emphasising that it was unions, acting as autonomous organisations in accordance with the tactics of direct action, that were to play the pivotal role in the emancipation of the working class, the door was left open for joint action with communists. The final objective of the syndicalists remained the installation of a free communist society (libertarian communism). The limited and general scope of the six points of the Berlin Declaration reflected the confusion created among revolutionary syndicalists by the success of the Russian Revolution, its perceived political nature, and its implications for any future syndicalist International.

The revolutionary syndicalist organisations had hoped to organise an additional meeting before the inaugural congress of the RTUI, at which the USI and the CNT could be fully represented. Apparently CNT leaders were consulted and agreed. The bases of this meeting were to be the six points agreed to in December.[24] However, it proved impossible to organise a second meeting.

By the time the RTUI finally held its constituent congress in June 1921, the situation was far less favourable for Moscow's supporters. More was now known about Bolshevik union policy, and as a result many revolutionary syndicalist organisations were able to see clearly the differences in their positions and those of Moscow. Moreover, the true nature of the Bolshevik regime and its intolerance to opposition from peasants and workers alike was becoming abundantly clear following the crushing of the Kronstadt rising in March of the same year, which added to the growing knowledge of communist repression directed against anarchists and alternative workers' organizations from mid-1918 onwards and especially after the victory in the Civil War.[25] The Comintern policy of communist party infiltration of the unions and the pretence that the 'organic link' between the two Internationals would not restrict the autonomous nature of the RTUI convinced only those who accepted party infiltration in the first place. The RTUI congress clearly had not satisfied the requirements drawn up at Berlin, and once the results of the congress were known at home they were quickly rejected by the more independently minded organisations. The French CSR rejected the statutes of the RTUI at its congress in Lyon in November 1921. The Spanish and Italian delegations were disowned by their respective organisations on their return home.[26] The Portuguese CGT withdrew its membership at a national congress in October 1922, whilst the German FAUD had refused to even attend the RTUI inaugural congress.[27]

The Formation of the New IWMA

At the FAUD's thirteenth congress, held in Dusseldorf in October 1921, an extraordinary meeting was held with a number of representatives from the Netherlands, Germany, Sweden, Czechoslovakia, and the United States in attendance (the USI and various minority organisations also sent in their written support).[28] The meeting agreed that as the RTUI congress had not resulted in the formation of an "effective revolutionary syndicalist international," the syndicalists should move ahead to organise a further international syndicalist conference, the bases for which were to be the first five points approved at the 1920 December congress.[29]

The conference was eventually organised by the USI with the help of the FAUD and held in Berlin June 16–19, 1922.[30] Delegations came from the French CSR, the FAUD, the USI, the CNT, the SAC, the Marine Union from the Netherlands, the deported remnants of the Russian syndicalist minority, and a representative of the All-Russian Trade Unions.[31] The Portuguese CGT, the FORA, the NAS, and the IWW sent communiqués but, along with the revolutionary syndicalists from Denmark, were unable to attend. The Dutch were unwilling to attend as they were in the middle of a referendum on membership of the RTUI. The Spanish delegation, Florentino Galo Díez and Avelino González Mallada, chosen at the Zaragoza Conference, arrived on the final day, were quickly brought up to date with the proceedings, and approved the resolutions made.[32] These included the adoption of ten principles and tactics of revolutionary syndicalism, which represented an updated version of the Charter of Amiens, modified in the light of the First World War and the Russian Revolution. Whereas prewar syndicalism was apolitical, its postwar descendant was more clearly antipolitical. The role of the state and political parties in the emancipation of the workers was rejected:

> Revolutionary syndicalism is the unqualified opponent of all economic and social monopolies ... [and] is subordinate to no political power or party. Against the politics of states and parties it sets the economic organisation of labour; against the government of men, the administration of things. For this reason it does not aspire to the conquest of political power but the elimination of every state function from the life of society. It is of the opinion that together with the monopoly of property, the monopoly of power must also vanish, and that the state in every form, even in the form of the so-called 'Dictatorship of the Proletariat', can never be an instrument for the liberation of labour but always only the creator of new monopolies and new privileges.[33]

In line with the prewar revolutionary syndicalism, the statutes accepted that revolutionary syndicalism was based on class struggle (principle 1), and adopted the *double besogne* of the Charter of Amiens (principle 3) as well as the tactics of direct action (principle 8). The International was to have a federal structure (principles 4 and 6), based on the "voluntary federation of all forces on the foundation of mutual interests and common convictions."

The conference did not establish a new International, as had been hoped by the Spanish delegates, deferring such a move until after the newly formed CGTU (CGT Unitaire, representing the French syndicalists that had split from the reformist CGT) had held its inaugural congress at Saint-Étienne, and until after the second congress of the RTUI.[34] However, a Provisional International Bureau was created that included Pestaña (who was unable to carry out much work after he was the victim of an assassination attempt on August 25, 1922).[35] The bureau was made responsible for the organisation of a world congress of revolutionary syndicalist organisations (originally scheduled for November but postponed until December to await the results of the second RTUI conference) and for communicating to the RTUI the decisions made in Berlin.

Following the Berlin conference, both Borghi and Galo Díez attended the Saint-Étienne congress and spoke in support of the decisions made at Berlin, calling for the establishment of an independent International.[36] Neither were given much of a hearing in comparison to the RTUI representative, Lozovsky, who had been a member of the French CGT before the war and was a close colleague of leading CGTU militants.

It is worth focusing a little on Lozovsky's speech in which the general secretary traced the formation of the RTUI as well as the origins and reasons for, in his opinion, the anarchist objection to this. He also sought to justify the dictatorship of the proletariat and argue for the need for a clear relationship between revolutionary parties and revolutionary unions. The arguments were not new but no weaker for that. In Russia the anarchists had been unrealistic. Their devolved power system based on factory committees would not and could not have supplied the necessary unity of purpose to defend the revolution against the bourgeois forces of reaction. But not to fear, once the class war had been won, the state would wither away and society would apparently be organised along syndicalist lines – the productive forces organizing the economy. Some anarchists in Russia, Lozovsky claimed, had been more realistic in supporting the revolution, because they felt: "Certainly, our position is more just and the society that we want to build more equal: But, for the moment, the best elements of the working class are struggling and sacrificing themselves in fighting against our class enemies. Our place is there where the struggle leads due to our communist ideals." Why, he asked, don't the European anarchists follow their lead? The reason was jealousy. The Russians had succeeded where syndicalists and anarchists had failed. Lozovsky claimed that criticism of Moscow had only really started after the collapse of revolutionary movements in Spain, Italy, and France in 1919–20. He further claimed that at the second congress of the Comintern, at which the creation of the RTUI was agreed, Pestaña and Borghi had raised no objection to the dictatorship of the Proletariat. As has been seen, this last point is somewhat disingenuous. There had been criticism, and Lozovsky knew it and ignored it (see chapter 2 and note). But the key point was that the RTUI was a force that could scare the bourgeois with 2.5 million members worldwide, whilst any anarcho-syndicalist international would be perhaps free and independent but with "autonomy of inaction and the independence of weakness." The argument had much merit but only if there would be tolerance, debate, and freedom of movement for the unions of the RTUI. The point is that its opponents didn't think this would exist, saw the link with the Comintern as a means of ensuring that it did not, and had more than enough evidence of what happened to dissenting voices in the workers' struggles in Russia.[37]

The CGTU, now heavily under the influence of the communists who were supported by the communist-syndicalists associated with the paper *La Vie Ouvriere*, had previously asked the RTUI to change its statutes over relations between the RTUI and the Comintern.[38] In expectation of the changes, the Saint-Étienne congress voted overwhelmingly in favour of Moscow. There were two reasons for this vote. The first was that the syndicalist wing represented by Besnard was at the time in favour of joining the RTUI as long as there was no 'organic link' between the party (Comintern) and the union internationals. Perhaps more important, as the historian David Perry points out, was "the continuing prestige of the Russian Revolution and of its leaders and the refusal of many sympathizers with Moscow to face facts when it came to hard evidence of the realities of political repression." People did not yet understand why the anarchists were so opposed to Moscow. Were they simply jealous that the Bolsheviks had succeeded where they hadn't?[39]

At the second congress of the RTUI, held in November, the reference to an organic link between the Comintern and the RTUI was changed to "an agreement between the different groups of the labour movement and, above all, between the Comintern and the RTUI." The changes to the statutes of the RTUI not only won over the French syndicalists but also had the desired effect on the Dutch NAS, forcing the revolutionary syndicalists who favoured adhesion to Berlin to split away and form the NSF (Norsk Syndikalisk Federation). Apart from the French and Dutch, most of the organisations that had attended or supported the Berlin conference, seeing the changes as simply another Bolshevik ploy to divide them, now saw no reason to procrastinate further.[40]

After almost three years of waiting, an independent revolutionary syndicalist International was finally founded at the Berlin congress of December 25, 1922, to January 2, 1923.[41] Delegates from the FAUD, FORA, SAC, Norway, the NSF, the USI, and the French Comité de Défense Syndicaliste (CDS) – which had been set up by those members of the CGTU opposed to adhesion to the RTUI – attended.[42] The CNT delegates were arrested in Paris whilst on their way to Berlin.[43] The delegation had been given three directives by the national committee:

1. To work for the creation of the revolutionary syndicalist International based on the principles that governed the First International.
2. To adhere, in principle, to the revolutionary syndicalist International created in Berlin.
3. And in the case that this international assembly decides to adhere to the RTUI ... in view of the absolute disagreement of our organisation with this decision, [to] refuse to continue collaborating in the rest of the sessions of the congress.

Quite clearly the CNT saw the new International as a continuation of the old, non-authoritarian First International, supported its creation, and were not prepared to countenance a return to Moscow.

A new Berlin Declaration, approved at the end of the congress, combined with the adoption of the ten principles agreed upon in July and re-adopted in December, showed the progress made since 1913.[44] The new International stood "against the capitalist offensive and the politicians of all classes." It was to be "a true international association of workers in which each member knows that his ultimate emancipation will only be possible when the workers themselves, as workers, are prepared in their economic organisations not only in order to take possession of the land and the factories, but also to preside over them … in such as way as to be able to continue production."[45]

The rejection of Moscow appeared to be complete. However, a "Resolution on Revolutionary Unity" called for the secretariat of the new International to make one final effort to come to an understanding with Moscow for the benefit of unity.[46] The door was thus still theoretically left open to an amalgamation with Moscow. However, in reality, there could be no turning back since the principles of the new IWMA encapsulated a complete rejection of the political dictates of Bolshevism. Furthermore, the Berlin Declaration decried the Bolshevik seizure of power as the "deviation of a social revolution into a political revolution," saying that it had "resulted in a hypertrophy of state socialism whose outcome has been the development of a capitalist system just as exploitative and dominating as any other system of bourgeois origin."[47] The resolution on unity was simply a sop to the French CDS, which had put forward a resolution to the congress in favour of "the unity of the world's revolutionary forces." This gave the IWMA the mandate for an exchange of opinions with the RTUI in order to realise "international trade union unity." The congress accepted the resolution, hoping that such an approach might win support for the CDS within the CGTU.[48] However, communist domination in France was strengthened at the Bourges congress of November 1923 which rejected affiliating with the IWMA by 962 votes to 219. So the contradiction with the principles of the organisation was overturned at a plenum of the IWMA held in Innsbruck in December 1923, and contacts with the RTUI were finally broken.[49]

The federalist nature of the International evidently meant that its ideological base would reflect the nature of its adherents. Thus the principles of the International had to reflect the full range of the policies of member organisations, so long as they accepted the basic principles and tactics outlined in the adopted principles of revolutionary syndicalism. This left ample room for interpretation, with one area in particular remaining to be clarified – the relationship between revolutionary syndicalism and anarchism. The revolutionary syndicalism espoused by the IWMA aimed to reorganise "the whole of social life on the basis of free communism through the collective revolutionary action of the working class itself. ... strive[d] for their elimination by means of economic communes and administrative organs of industrial and field workers on the basis of a free council system [and argued that] ... only in the revolutionary economic organisations of the working class lies the means for its liberation, and the creative energy for the reconstruction of society in the direction of free communism."[50]

No direct mention was made of anarchism, although clearly the term "free communism" clarified that the final goal was that shared by anarchists and syndicalists alike. Many organisations and their members took it for granted that the new International would warmly welcome the influence of anarchists within its ranks as long as these anarchists were workers. Those organisations that had little contact with the anarchists in their country, the Dutch NAS being the clearest example, could rest assured that membership in the IWMA was confined to unions and that the International's decentralised structure left them in control of domestic relations with anarchists. They would not be forced into any relationship with 'political' elements as had occurred with Moscow.

Nonetheless, connection between the IWMA and anarchism was evident for all to see.[51] The principles of the organisation had been drafted by Rudolf Rocker of the FAUD, who was a well-known and respected anarchist.[52] The FAUD was instrumental in the creation of the IWMA being aided by deported Russian anarchists and anarcho-syndicalists. A number of prominent figures, such as Gregory Maximoff, Volin, Alexander Schapiro, Nestor Makhno, Peter Arshinov, Emma Goldman, and Alexander Berkman had fled Russia from 1919 onward, arriving in Berlin, which soon became the "nerve centre of the international Russian anarchist movement."[53] Maximoff and especially Schapiro played significant roles in the formation of the IWMA. Alongside the CNT, the French CSR, the USI, the FORA, and the Portuguese CGT all counted anarchists among their leading figures (although the extent of anarchist influence was different in each case).

Reaction to the IWMA within the CNT

In Spain the opponents of the IWMA within the CNT focused their attacks on anarchism. Nin chastised the CNT for adhering to the Berlin International. Writing from Russia, he laughed at the club of "vegetarians, neo-Malthusians, and supporters of universal peace." The former secretary general of the CNT claimed that anarcho-syndicalism was a "dead doctrine" that did not respond to the necessities of the postwar world. The IWMA's programme was based on "the prewar principles of anarcho-syndicalism, unshakable in spite of the butchery of 1914–18 and the Russian revolution," he wrote, and allowed "absolute freedom for the member organisations to do what they wanted." "This," he fumed, "is impotence. And this is what is called an International."[54] The power of the revolution was everything. Ethics and ideals were secondary. The Bolsheviks had taken power, no other revolutionary left group had done so, and that was enough. A lack of understanding of the Bakuninist theory of the state, and perhaps something of a schoolteacher mentality, blinded Maurín to the fact that the taking of power and centralizing it was not the aim but rather its redistribution and decentralization along democratic lines among the productive society.

Maurín was equally dismissive of the new International with its "minuscule organisations."[55] There were, he argued, only two real internationals, Amsterdam and Moscow, and "whoever is not with Moscow is against Moscow, and therefore is in favour of Amsterdam and capitalism."[56]

The RTUI did not accept the CNT decision, addressing a manifesto to confederal members "above the heads of our leaders" in which it criticised the CNT leaders for having "learnt nothing" from recent international events or from the recent experience in Spain and accusing them of leading the confederation down the path to reformism.[57]

Both Nin and Maurín lambasted the CNT for falling into the grips of "anarcho-reformists": "Contrast the decision made by the CNT at Zaragoza with that made by the French at their constitutive congress. Whilst the true syndicalists are going to Moscow, we have made the decision to oppose Moscow!"[58]

The reference to the CGTU's attitude towards Moscow was indicative of the policy that the communist-syndicalists in Spain would follow. Those militants within the French CGT who opposed the decision at the Lyon congress of September 1919 to join the Amsterdam International set up the Comité Syndicaliste Révolutionnaire (CSR). The CSR represented an uneasy mix of communists, anarcho-syndicalists, and revolutionary syndicalists. The first secretary general was the communist-syndicalist Pierre Monatte, although between May 1920 and July 1921 Monatte was replaced by the anarcho-syndicalist Pierre Besnard. The CSR was finally expelled from the CGT in February 1922, and at the Saint-Étienne congress a breakaway confederation, the CGT Unitaire (CGTU), was officially founded. The Saint-Étienne congress also represented a defeat for the anarcho-syndicalist wing, which lost control of the organisation to the communists.[59] This was reflected in the congress's decision in favour of joining the RTUI.

Maurín and his followers hoped that the success of the CSR in France would be repeated in Spain. The communist-syndicalists did not send a delegation to the second congress of the RTUI that began in Moscow on November 1922, concentrating instead on organising their supporters within the CNT in order to fight to change the decisions adopted at Zaragoza.[60] In November the first manifesto of the Spanish Comités Sindicalistas Revolucionarios (CSR) was published.[61] The manifesto contained all the usual criticism of the reformist leaders of the CNT as well as the typical Maurínesque vaunting of the central position of "collective violence" within the ideology of revolutionary syndicalism. The Zaragoza conference was denounced as a "meeting of pedagogues," unrepresentative of the workers, "pedagogues" who had decided to "renounce the class struggle" in favour of "an era of submission." By withdrawing from the RTUI, the CNT was opposing the Russian Revolution itself, and this was "the crowning moment of the march towards the Right." For Maurín, the RTUI "based in the country that made the social revolution, [was] a guarantee of the revolutionary resolve", whilst the IWMA was simply an attempt by anarchists to channel revolutionary syndicalism along sectarian lines.

The constituent assembly of the Spanish CSR was held in Bilbao in December 1922, and the representatives agreed on the five policies that the CNT should adopt. First:

1. The CNT must not be a sectarian organism ... but a strong revolutionary class organisation, without ideological distinctions.
2. [It] must escape from evolutionary verbalism and return to the class struggle, opposing all the recent formula[s] of intervention with the doctrine of collective violence.

In addition, to combat the growing centralisation of capitalist forces, the CNT should

3. support the formation of the United Front of the Proletariat[,]
4. move towards the fusion of all the working class in one class organisation[, and]
5. affiliate with the RTUI.[62]

The majority of the groups and organisations that sent delegates to the inaugural congress were controlled by the PCE, with most coming from Vizcaya (Basque country), where the CNT had little influence. The one main exception was Lleida (Lérida), Catalonia, Maurín's power base, where *Lucha Social* had been published.

In essence, the CSR programme was simply that of the RTUI, and indeed there is strong evidence to suggest that the impulse for the formation of the CSR in Spain came from Moscow.[63] Quite clearly the position adopted at Zaragoza and in the anarchist and syndicalist press before and after the conference demonstrated that it was generally agreed that the RTUI was itself a front organisation for a sectarian group (the communists) and that thus points 1 and 5 contradicted each other. Point 2 was an obvious attack on the moderate leadership of the CNT, whose views had triumphed at the Zaragoza conference. Meanwhile points 3 (the United Front) and 4 (syndicalist unity), however desirable they may have appeared – the CNT had twice voted in favour of creating a national labour organisation that would unite the forces of the CNT and the UGT, at its congresses in 1911 and 1919 – were wishful thinking given relations between the UGT and the CNT.

In December 1921 the executive of the Comintern had called for a united front against capitalism that, besides communists, would include social democrats and "workers supporting anarcho-syndicalist organisations." The call was a response to concerns that Moscow was losing its hold on the revolutionary organisations of western Europe. Coming as it did after the less-than-positive response to the inaugural congress of the RTUI, many saw the tactic as a further ploy to permit Bolshevik infiltration of the unions. This certainly was the opinion of the CNT expressed in early 1922: "The Confederación Nacional del Trabajo of Spain will not act as an extra in the machinations of those elements that might represent a nation but cannot claim for itself the representation of the proletariat."[64]

The assault on revolutionary syndicalism launched by the PCE on confederal leaders and revolutionary syndicalism from 1920 onwards, combined with the communist-syndicalists' subterfuge whilst in charge of the national committee, meant that every policy proposed by the communists was viewed with suspicion, something that would not change in the future. Beyond this, the call made little sense as the CNT and the UGT had twice before come to an agreement over joint action (in 1916 and 1920) and twice the CNT had felt betrayed by the UGT's political ties to the PSOE (see chapter 2). For the CNT, both the United Front and syndicalist unity were desirable goals, but experience had shown their impracticality, if not impossibility. Given that the two organisations differed on tactical and ideological questions, as had been amply demonstrated by the previous attempts at joint action, it was highly unlikely that the aim of all the revolutionary workers uniting in one union would be realised.[65] However, the programme of the CSR was not rejected due to its impracticability but because the committees were seen simply as an attempt by Moscow to infiltrate the confederation.

Even before the creation of the CSR, the connections between the communist-syndicalists and the PCE were becoming increasingly evident. Despite the CNT's clear rejection of the RTUI at Zaragoza, Maurín represented the Moscow International at the Portuguese CGT congress in October.[66] *Acción Sindicalista*, which replaced *Lucha Social* (which was forced to close down due to lack of funds) not only openly supported the RTUI but was actually financed by Moscow.[67] *La Batalla*, founded in December 1922 as a continuation to *Acción Sindicalista*, supported the line of the CSR for an independent CNT and affiliation with the RTUI. Among the CSR members were a number of leading militants of the PCE, and indeed the first article written on the CSR came from the pen of Luis Portela, a member of the central committee of the PCE.[68]

The communist-syndicalists had still not come to terms with the fact that they could not simply transpose an alien political system onto the Spanish working class. The importation of a state-centric ideology in which all power was wielded by a centralised political elite was foreign to the culture, tradition, and experience of certain sections of the Spanish workforce, particularly in Catalonia. Although politically Spain was a highly centralised state, it was also a culturally and socially divided nation, in which the working class neither respected nor trusted the state and the political structures that maintained it.

Whereas the historical weakness of unions in Russia, not to mention police infiltration and control, may have led the Bolsheviks to argue for the necessity of a political entity to represent the workers, in Spain the unions had always been the centre of working-class activity. Even socialist leaders such as Francisco Largo Caballero placed union interests ahead of party interests. Indeed the syndicalist movement in Russia, although retarded due to tsarist repression, had begun to grow and organised itself during the revolutionary year of 1917, only to be subsequently emasculated by the Bolshevik party. As was so clearly occurring in Russia, the introduction of political direction could only serve to divert the workers from the task of self-emancipation and lead to a centralised dictatorship, every bit as repressive as the system it had replaced. The economic reductionism of revolutionary Marxism, in which social and cultural issues were secondary to the all-powerful economic imperative, combined with immediate and direct political direction imposed by Leninism, was alien to a country as culturally diverse as Spain, which had a history of active labour organization dating back to the 1840s. The Bolshevik Russian model at first took little account of history, tradition, or culture but perhaps in the end depended a little too much on tsarist history, tradition, and culture – coming to emulate it. Furthermore, the revolutionary surge of the postwar period had passed. As opposed to Russia in 1917, in Spain the forces of reaction had not been decimated by three years of war. The military formed an integral part of the political system, as had been demonstrated by the plague of pronunciamentos in the nineteenth century. The middle and upper classes saw the army as a means of career enhancement, not simply a fighting force for the defense of the nation, a fact reflected in its top-heavy structure in which almost 20 percent of soldiers were officers.[69] It was neither a revolutionary force in the socialist sense, nor could it be easily won over to the cause of the working class.[70] The demands of the *juntas de defensas* during the revolutionary year of 1917 had referred to professional issues, and, once these had been granted, the army sided with the state in violently repressing the social unrest. The strength of the employers and state combined were amply demonstrated by their successful crushing of the strike movements of 1919. The decline into acts of individual violence that followed was in part a response to the impossibility of overthrowing the state by other means at that stage. It was time to take stock, consolidate the movement, and educate the workers in their revolutionary task.

The CSR in Spain did not have a realistic chance of emulating the success of their French colleagues. The logic of numbers was clearly against them. Although *La Batalla* claimed that the decision to break with the RTUI was unpopular with a large part of the CNT masses, the reality was somewhat different.[71] This large number was imaginary, a point that Maurín later admitted.[72]

The meagre support that the CSR enjoyed resulted in a number of inconsistencies between the words and actions of their principal figure, Maurín. He criticised openly the 'anarcho-reformists' who had taken control of the CNT and were leading the confederation away from the revolutionary path, whilst at the same time attempting to show the similarity of their position to his and chastising the overt sectarianism of the more radical anarcho-syndicalists.[73] But his greatest inconsistency was the claim that the RTUI and by inference the CSR were independent of communist control, when this was evidently not so.

Maurín was once more caught in the middle. His belief in a Marxist interpretation of revolutionary syndicalism and the potential of the Russian Revolution was limitless. Yet the ideological basis of the latter was in conflict with that of the former. Despite all his protests it had become abundantly clear that no communist party would allow the union movement independence of action. The very weakness of his support in Spain drew him inevitably towards the communists. He needed communist financial support to be able to defend his arguments yet continued to pretend that the platform he supported would maintain union autonomy. His position within the CNT was scarcely credible, and few believed him. The arguments surrounding the CSR simply reflected the conflict between pro-Bolsheviks and anti-Bolsheviks that had broken out in 1921. The real battle had already been won at Zaragoza. The CSR simply provided an epilogue.

At a regional plenum in Barcelona on February 17–19, 1923, the CSR was condemned as having been organised "under the aegis of, and funded by, Moscow." The plenum concluded that the confederation could not "recognise any group created in the heart of the organisation that does not accept implicitly the principles of the CNT ... and [recognises] that it is necessary to undertake an intense labour in ... economic, revolutionary, and ideological fields in order to counteract the work of proselytism undertaken by the communists."[74]

Despite this effective ban, the CSR continued its campaign in favour of the five points in its programme but was increasingly ineffectual. Although the CSR's main strength within the CNT was in the Basque country, they were easily defeated at the Extraordinary Congress of the Confederation of the North held in Bilbao in April 1923 that ratified the agreements reached at the Zaragoza conference and agreed that the CNT should make permanent its provisional membership in the IWMA.[75] In Catalonia they were roundly defeated at the regional congress in Granollers in December 1923, which also spelt the end for the newspaper *Lucha Obrera*, a collaboration between the communist-syndicalists and militants from the confederation, which it later transpired was funded by money expropriated from the Metal Workers' Union.[76] At a regional assembly in Catalonia in May 1924 Maurín was thrown out as the assembly agreed that the organisation he claimed to represent "did not exist."[77] By now the CSR was clearly little more than an appendage of the PCE, and Maurín had given up all pretence of autonomy by joining the communist party in 1923.[78]

The final admission of the failure of the CSR's plans to win over the CNT to their programme came at the third congress of the RTUI, which decided that anarcho-syndicalism was to be combated "without respite, rest or pity." Maurín, representing the CSR at the congress, declared that his experience in Spain had convinced him "that the struggle against anarcho-syndicalism is a necessary pre-condition of all other revolutionary action."[79] All pretence at unity between communists and syndicalists was finally ended. Joan Peiró concluded, "If the pro-Bolsheviks have accepted this Muscovite motto ... how can we accept a jot of sincerity in their campaign for a united front, and how can we believe that it is not this, but their hegemony ... which they are pursuing?"[80] Following the ban on the operation of the CSR within the CNT, and the rejection of the United Front, the later attempts by the PCE to seize control of the confederation would be by subterfuge rather than direct confrontation.[81] Suspicion and distrust simply furthered the ideological divide between communists and revolutionary (and anarcho-) syndicalists.

The CSR criticism of the increasingly reformist tendency among leading militants within the CNT touched a raw nerve. The failure of the revolutionary period in Spain to result in any long-term benefits for the working class had led many of the leading figures in the Catalan region (Seguí, Pestaña, Peiró, Adrián Arnó, Angel Abella, and others) to adopt more moderate positions. These moderates maintained close contact with liberal politicians whilst, paradoxically, at the same time shying away from ideological issues within the unions and emphasising the apolitical and class basis of revolutionary syndicalism. The syndicalism that the moderates espoused is often referred to as 'pure' syndicalism as opposed to anarcho- or communist-syndicalism. It was more evolutionary than revolutionary. The so-called pure syndicalists were not a homogenous group, as would become apparent in the late twenties, but on the central issue of ideological influence within the CNT they were all agreed. They supported the platonic ideal of class unity above all other issues. In the highly politicised atmosphere of the postwar years this often seemed equivalent to procrastination, especially given that by 1922 the CNT had distanced itself first from the UGT and then from the communists. The confusion between the ideal of unity and the reality of the ideological splits in the labour movement was evident in the decisions regarding the CNT's affiliation with the IWMA. Although the Zaragoza conference of June 1922 agreed to withdraw the CNT from the RTUI and sent delegates to support the creation of the new revolutionary syndicalist International, it was not until September 1923 that *Solidaridad Obrera* finally carried the words "Adherida à la Asociación Internacional de los Trabajadores" ("Affiliated with the International Working Men's Association").[82]

The resolution adopted at Zaragoza spoke of a referendum among the unions over the withdrawal of the CNT from the RTUI and the Comintern and "the adherence of the CNT to all the attempts made to organise an autonomous Red Syndicalist International, free from all political parties."[83] To this end, leading moderates argued fervently for the rejection of the political machinations of Moscow and in favour of Berlin.[84] In the referendum, almost all of the organisations consulted supported the confederation's provisional affiliation with the International that was to be created at the Berlin congress of December 1922 to January 1923.[85] Yet, days before the Berlin congress began, the national committee of the CNT sent a circular to its member organisations suggesting that if the Berlin congress did not result in the formation of a new International (or if the new International was composed solely of the FORA and the Portuguese CGT) it should re-affiliate with the RTUI, as long as it accepted certain propositions that would safeguard syndicalist independence and the RTUI's autonomy from the Comintern.[86] On January 9, just days after the Berlin congress had finished, the confederation's national committee released a manifesto which hardly resonated with support for the newly created IWMA: "Our credo and our ideology are not subject ... to international fluctuations; and they do not need to be strengthened by any International."[87]

The committee's position may have resulted from a fear that in rejecting the RTUI they might be isolated, especially following the CGTU's decision to join the RTUI and the crushing of the USI by the Fascists in Italy. Nonetheless, their action was a clear breach of the mandate given to the delegations to both the June and December congresses, which stated clearly that if no International was created, then the CNT would stand alone.

A proposed return to the RTUI was tantamount to total ideological surrender in the face of the Bolsheviks and contrary to the stated views of the member organisations, as the referendum made clear. Whatever the reasoning behind the committee's actions, it could only serve to raise fears that there was an ideological vacuum at the head of the confederation. These fears were heightened when Maurín claimed that before Salvador Seguí's death at the hands of gunmen of the Sindicatos Libres (Free Unions) in March 1923, Seguí had been preparing to travel to Moscow to negotiate the readmission of the CNT to the RTUI.[88] The CNT immediately refuted the allegations.[89]

Despite the national committee's temporary ideological paralysis, member organisations of the confederation showed no such uncertainty. At the regional plenum in February 1923 that effectively outlawed the CSR, the question of the International was again discussed. The plenum discussed the modifications made to the statutes of the RTUI at its second congress which, according to the Asturian delegate, was "a trap set to catch those organisations recalcitrant to the influence of Moscow."[90] The plenum agreed that the final decision on permanent membership in the IWMA should be the subject of a further referendum, the results of which would then be discussed at the next congress of the CNT, due to be held in Madrid in June 1923.

The results of the second referendum were once more overwhelmingly in favour of the CNT joining the IWMA.[91] However, the result was not ratified as it proved impossible to convene the national congress due largely to the transport strike in Barcelona that lasted for three months from May until July. Following Primo de Rivera's pronunciamento in September 1923, the CNT found it impossible to organise a national congress. The next one was not held until 1931.

The CNT remained provisionally rather than fully affiliated with the IWMA, and, although it was treated as a full member, permanent affiliation was still not resolved by the time of the 1931 national congress in Madrid, despite the fact that the IWMA's fourth congress was held in Spain a month later.[92] The permanent affiliation of the confederation, agreed upon at a regional level in 1923, was never debated at a national congress.

Despite the delayed and provisional nature of the confederation's membership in the IWMA, the International was to play an important role in the trajectory of the CNT in the years to come.[93] However, this was not so much due to the influence of the International itself as to its role as a link between the different national organisations. The IWMA acted as a liaison office, facilitating the development of relations between like-minded organisations. Limited contacts had existed previously through individuals or press coverage. However, the IWMA held biannual international conferences and provided a press service, which kept the differing organisations up to date with both events and ideological and tactical developments elsewhere. The International was influential in the creation of an action committee in Paris in 1926 which brought together exiles from Italy, Spain, Portugal, and Poland. It facilitated the entrance of exiled CNT militants into the French Confederation Generale de Travail Syndicaliste Revolutionnaire (CGTSR), which was itself created as a direct result of the action and emigration committees set up by exiles in France.

However, the creation of the second IWMA did not come at the most propitious moment. The revolutionary fervour of the postwar years had long since died and been replaced by widespread repression as governments and employers recovered confidence in their ability to control the workers. The loss of the CGTU to the RTUI and the dissolution of the USI following November 1922 further weakened the revolutionary syndicalist movement.[94] In Spain, the unremitting violence of both state and the Sindicatos Libres, sponsored by the employers and acting at the discretion of the authorities, had a noticeable effect on the CNT. A number of leading militants of both the national committee and the Catalan CRT (who had already shown an evident predisposition towards moderation), having all but defeated the challenge of the communist-syndicalists at Zaragoza, now sought to reduce ideological interference in union matters. Thus, despite the fact that the IWMA represented the very revolutionary syndicalist

International that the CNT had called for at its Madrid congress in 1919, there was an evident hesitation towards Berlin immediately prior to its creation, hesitation that was probably inspired by fears that the International would contain little more than the confederation itself. This subordination of qualitative or ideological considerations to quantitative ones provided a further example to those who feared that the apolitical stance of the moderate leadership was leading the CNT towards reformism or was opening it up to potential communist domination. This was a possibility that the moderates' opponents within the confederation were not prepared to accept.

5.
EARLY CONFLICTS BETWEEN ANARCHISM AND SYNDICALISM

Just as revolutionary syndicalism had been forced to reappraise its ideological position in the light of the Russian Revolution by adopting a more clearly antipolitical stance, the Bolshevik victory had also made apparent certain deficiencies in the anarchist revolutionary doctrine. The two vital lessons that the anarchists learnt from the Russian experience were the need to ensure that anarchists had direct contact with the forces that would bring about the revolution – the working classes – and the necessity of greater organisation among anarchists in order to propagate the anarchist idea among the workers more effectively. So, whilst the revolutionary syndicalists had adopted a position towards politics that coincided with that of the anarchists in general, the anarchists had in turn moved further towards syndicalism. The revolution might be spontaneous, but the masses needed to be organised and prepared to seize the moment when it arrived so as to avoid falling into the hands of those that wished to divert the revolutionary masses for their own political agendas.

Anarchism is not a dogma but an ideology that is open to a variety of interpretations, nowhere more so than in relation to syndicalism. This has led to much confusion about the nature of the internal conflicts within syndicalist organisations, especially in Spain. Initial historical interpretations of the different tendencies within the CNT employed the tactic of talking of 'anarchists' (representing the more radical wing of the CNT) and 'syndicalists' (the moderates). Although helpful in making a complex situation more understandable, this approach is open to misinterpretation.[1] More recently historians who have studied the CNT during the 1920s as a preliminary to more in-depth analysis of the internal divisions during the Second Republic have suggested that there were at least three tendencies, although disagreement remains over their exact definition.[2]

The communist-syndicalists were the smallest of the general tendencies within the CNT during this period. Eulàlia Vega suggests that there were three main tendencies: neutral syndicalists, who wanted the unions to be open to all workers and favoured the use of direct action; anarcho-syndicalists, who agreed with the above but felt that the confederation needed ideological *content* and that this should be anarchism; and anarchists who thought the unions should be openly anarchist.[3] This analysis is supported by Monjo Omedes, although she describes the third tendency as 'radical anarcho-syndicalists' (as they supported the need for organization and action through the unions), and it is this that seems the most appropriate in relation to the ideological divisions during the period under study. These positions evolved throughout the 1920s in reaction to events in Spain and abroad, especially the Russian Revolution and its aftermath. The three tendencies all agreed that the unions should remain independent of political groups (although the syndicalists viewed the anarchists as a political group and argued that the unions must be free from their direct influence as well).[4]

It would be premature to ascribe a specific identity to the moderates and the radicals before the ideological debates of the Primo de Rivera dictatorship. To provide a clear account of the early stages of the evolution of these positions, it is more helpful to simplify the situation as one between syndicalists (the moderate wing of the CNT) and anarchists (the radicals), with the anarcho-syndicalists caught in the middle. This is based on focusing on the role of anarchism within the unions and the position of the CNT towards the state. Many militants who supported the syndicalist position within the unions still regarded themselves as anarchists. On other issues, militants from both tendencies were agreed, or differences of opinion did not necessarily reflect the tendency to which they subscribed.

Within the confederation, syndicalists and anarchists did not represent two distinct ideologies but rather two distinct approaches. Members of both tendencies accepted that the ultimate goal of the confederation was anarchism (libertarian communism – it was the syndicalists who proposed the motion adopted at the 1919 congress), rejected party politics, and supported the principle of direct action. Most significantly, both groups referred to themselves as anarchists (although this position changed for some during the 1930s). At heart, the disagreements were similar to those within social democratic circles prior to the First World War over revolutionary and evolutionary Marxism. In the revolutionary environment of 1917–19, anarchists within the unions were increasingly drawn into more active roles within the confederation, more often than not simply as a result of the revolutionary situation itself. During this period many believed that the revolution was close at hand and that all that was required was to strengthen the unions, which, by force of numbers, would bring about the collapse of capitalism. The finer points of ideology were secondary. But the revolution never came. Instead many anarchists who had joined during this period had become 'syndicalised' by their experience in the unions (as had occurred in France during the CGT's prewar expansion).[5] Protection of the confederation now became more important than the pursuit of the revolution.

Although certain anarchist suspicions about syndicalism had existed since the birth of the CNT, friction between the syndicalists and anarchists did not come to the fore until late 1919 when the confederation's meteoric rise came to a sudden halt and the revolutionary élan was replaced by a defensive war against the state and employers.

The ensuing unrelenting persecution of confederal militants combined with economic decline during the years 1920–22 resulted in a discernible decline in membership. Traumatised by the violent reaction and the fall in membership, moderates within the confederation sought a period of social peace to reorganise and take stock of what had occurred. To secure this required a less overtly revolutionary programme, and moderates such as Seguí and Pestaña began to talk of the need to educate the workers, not simply in terms of their revolutionary task in overthrowing the capitalist system but also in the operation of the specific industries in which they were involved and their position within the overall economic system. This could be achieved by organising the unions to defend immediate material gains for the workers, rather than pursuing revolutionary tactics, whilst the work of education was taking place.[6]

As their position evolved, the moderates increasingly stressed the predominance of economic over ideological issues within the unions, reverting to a form of 'pure' syndicalism divested of all political interference (including from anarchists).[7] In this context, the terms 'moderate' and 'syndicalist' clearly overlap. But it is the lack of a specific ideology or rather the attempt to define syndicalism as such that was of crucial importance as this was the point that their opponents within the confederation focused on. Therefore the term 'syndicalist' refers to those 'syndicalised' anarchists who felt that, in the unions, the demands of the class struggle should take precedence over all other matters, that politics should be kept outside the unions, and that the specific task of the unions was to unite all workers in the struggle against capitalism and build, through this unity and the experience of struggle, a class-conscious movement that could finally bring about its own emancipation. The initial success of the 1919 strike action had showed the potential of syndicalism to force the employers back, and after a decade of struggle the eight-hour day had been achieved in many areas, but the radicals had then pushed too far and provoked the fierce reaction. Hence the stress on education, organisation, and the need for restraint in labour disputes. In the short term, this required the confederation to work together with other workers' organisations and even political parties, without compromising the basic principles of the unions, and not to give too dogmatic an interpretation to the principles of direct action where the situation demanded.[8]

Radical members of the CNT, the so-called anarchists, had drawn very different conclusions from the failure of the revolutionary period. The inability of the confederation to resist the repression resulted, they felt, from the lack of ideological commitment of confederal members. The concentration on creating class unity through the means of strikes based mainly on material demands had resulted in the formation of an ideological void in the unions, and this, the anarchists argued, could only be overcome by increasing the influence of anarchism within the unions. The reaction of the employers, supported by the state, was inevitable if they were given time to restock and reorganize. Therefore in situations such as the 1919 strikes it was necessary to ensure that this did not occur, by radicalising labour action in the hope that it would lead to revolution that would overthrow capitalist domination. Strikes for material gains were acceptable, as they showed workers the inequality inherent in capitalism and trained them in the art of resistance, but more important were strikes for solidarity and other rights that trained them to see each other as kin and prepared them mentally for a new, fairer, and more just society. Besides, any gains won in the short term would inevitably be taken away in the long term if the workers weren't constantly vigilant. Collaboration or negotiation with the state and the apparatus for labour control involved accepting the economic logic that these represented – in effect workers were negotiating their own subservience. Unions collaborated in maintaining capitalism when the aim was to crush it. Moreover, they feared that prominent syndicalist leaders had become too accustomed to positions of responsibility and had began to act in a way similar to union leaders of the UGT, seeing the unions as a springboard to political office. (Pestaña would eventually form a syndicalist political party in 1932.) The unions, and syndicalism in general, were a means of creating the revolution. The confederation should not forget that it was simply a revolutionary organisation whose primary goal was the overthrow of the existing society as soon as possible.

As the aim of the confederation was the victory of libertarian communism (anarchism), anarchism should be accepted as the guiding political principle of the confederation rather than simply treated on a par with other socialist political ideologies. Strikes should remain true to anarchist tactics, which meant that the confederation should maintain its refusal to work directly with political parties and remain unbending in its commitment to the principles of direct action – two points on which the syndicalists were prepared to compromise if they deemed it necessary to do so for the benefit of the confederation.

Following the reestablishment of constitutional guarantees by the Liberal-dominated Sánchez Guerra government, which came to power on March 1922, the syndicalists dominated both the national and the Catalan regional confederations. Not surprisingly, the radical anarchists became increasingly suspicious about the aims of the syndicalist leadership. Once the immediate danger of the communist-syndicalists had been expunged and there was a relative respite in repression, the anarchist movement was finally able to organise itself outside the unions regionally and then nationally. This process culminated in the formation of a national organisation in 1923 that coincided with a marked increase in anarchist activity within the CNT. As in parts of northern Europe, in particular in the east, there was a brief resurgence in revolutionary aspirations among the working class in 1923, which in Spain only served to increase the tension between the different factions in the CNT.

Much of this tension resulted from the introduction of an extremist faction within the anarchist tendency of the CNT, the so-called anarcho-Bolsheviks. The anarcho-Bolsheviks were a small group of militants dedicated to revenging fallen comrades as well as bringing the revolution about through violent means as quickly as possible. Their apparently contradictory name was given to them by their opponents and was derived from their ill-defined plans to create a revolutionary workers' army to overthrow the state and introduce a form of dictatorship of the proletariat.[9] However, beyond revolutionary activism combined with blind faith in anarchism, in practice their ideological position was at best simplistic. In many ways the terminology also reflects the ideological confusion created within the CNT in the period following the Russian Revolution. Such unqualified support for revolutionary activism could also be found in the writings of Maurín, as could the call for collective violence enforced by a militarised workforce. However, the anarcho-Bolsheviks were clearly anarchists, accepting no masters and equally refusing to lead the workers in anything but example.

This extremist faction, which was centred around the affinity group Los Solidarios, hoped to convince both the independent anarchist movement and the CNT to adopt a violent strategy that would bring about an immediate revolution.[10] Their position was initially rejected by both the national anarchist congress of March 1923 and the CNT. However, as social tension increased in Catalonia as a result of a wave of strikes throughout the summer of 1923 and with rumours of a potential military coup growing daily, the anarcho-Bolsheviks' position gained increasing support within the CNT until finally it prevailed, mainly as a result of the increasing violence and desperation of the situation. Almost immediately, however, Los Solidarios were weakened when leading figures were arrested, and by 1924 most were either in jail or had fled abroad and would not play a significant role in the CNT again until the Second Republic.

The initial period of anarchist organisation prior to 1923 has often been overlooked, as historians have naturally concentrated on the CNT. Even those who mention the national anarchist congress of 1923 do so only as part of the prehistory of the formation of the Federación Anarquista Ibérica (FAI) in 1927. Little attention is given to the surge in regional organisation that preceded it, with the exception of Andalusia.[11]

Anarchist Reaction to the Rise and Demise of the CNT, 1918–1922

Given the strength of the Spanish anarchist movement, it may seem strange that the 1923 national congress was only the second occasion since the formation of the CNT that anarchists had been able to meet together outside the confederation. The reason for this was the existence of the CNT itself. The previous national anarchist congress, held at the end of 1918, had been inspired by the rapid reorganisation of the confederation. It came following the Sans congress of late June and early July 1918 in Barcelona, which had relaunched the Catalan CRT and declared that the CRT viewed anarchism "with sympathy" but that anarchists were not to "directly intervene in the affairs of the unions" and should "work outside the unions in favour of the emancipation of the working class."[12] Despite the difficulties, organizing and acting in labour unions had certain advantages over doing so in regional or national anarchist groupings, which would be easier targets of repression and police infiltration. Meanwhile, to an extent, the anarchist press acted as a space for affinity groups and individuals to keep in touch and share their ideas with their colleagues. The Sans congress provided the basis for the rapid rise in confederal numbers throughout Spain, and, at the national CNT congress in Madrid in December 1919, the confederation ratified the decisions made at Sans in relation to organisation and tactics – the adoption of the Sindicato Único and a renewed emphasis on the use of direct action.

In response to the decisions made at Sans, and as a result of the revolutionary atmosphere prevalent in Spain at the time, many anarchists felt the need for a more active role within the unions to help bring about the revolution. This was reflected by the decision of a national congress of anarchists held in Barcelona in December 1918, which, according to Manuel Buenacasa, recommended that all libertarian workers in Spain should "enter and participate directly and immediately in the labour unions."[13] Buenacasa further claimed that until then many anarchists had remained on the sidelines of the labour movement, being simply members of the unions without assuming positions of responsibility, in line with the position proposed by Malatesta. As has been seen, this is not exactly true, as many anarchists had been active in the movement from the beginning.[14] What Buenacasa seems therefore to be suggesting is that the December 1918 anarchist congress encouraged even those who had remained suspicious of syndicalism to enter the unions because, in so doing, they could ensure the influence of anarchism with the CNT.

The 1918 national anarchist congress does not appear to have discussed the creation of a national anarchist organisation, preferring to concentrate on anarchist activity in the unions. Another reason could be that at this point it was simply impractical. In May 1918, the Catalan anarchists had resurrected the Spanish Committee of the Anarchist International (now called the International Committee of Relations) created following the El Ferrol congress, with the aim of organising an anarchist International as well as acting as a liaison point for Spanish anarchists.[15] The International Committee had been created following the dissolution of the Catalan Anarchist Federation, which had itself been reorganised in late 1917.[16] However, the attempts to create an international body prior to the existence of national or even regional bodies proved premature.[17] This point was accepted by the group Juventud Anarquista (Anarchist Youth), also known as Juventud Acrata, from Barcelona in October, which then took the initiative to propose the unification of "all Spanish anarchists" but stated that this should start at the bottom, with the creation of a regional federation in Catalonia.[18] The anarchist periodical *Acracia* supported the group's call for a national organisation in a letter to "all the anarchist groups of Spain," proposing the holding of a national congress that would exchange ideas about the policies to be adopted in the present revolutionary situation.[19] By mid-December 1918, the Regional Anarchist Federation of Catalonia had been reformed, and, in the same month, the national anarchist conference, referred to by Buenacasa, was held in Barcelona.[20]

The anarchist congress took place as the CNT was reaching the height of its pre–Civil War strength. The rapid rise in industrial output brought with it a concomitant rise in union strength. Membership of the CNT, till then relatively insignificant, mushroomed from 15,000 in 1916 to 714,028 (427,086 in Catalonia) in 1919.[21] A nationwide propaganda tour by leading CNT militants had been planned for early 1919. State authorities reacted by suspending constitutional guarantees throughout Spain, closing down *Solidaridad Obrera*, and arresting a number of leading CNT members.[22] Weeks later, the strike at the Canadiense led to a general strike in Barcelona that closed the city. As has been seen, the initial stage of the strike was successful, with the employers giving in to the CNT's demands (see chapter 2). However, backlash was not long in coming. The authorities reneged upon the agreement to release those imprisoned during the strike, and the CNT once more called the workers out on strike, despite the opposition of Seguí and other moderates who saw the employers' actions as a deliberate attempt to provoke the unions into overstretching their ability to sustain strikes economically. In this they were right, although history had showed that it was only a question of time before the employers, united in their own federation, sought to regain lost ground. This time the employers were prepared and, with the support of the authorities in the region, adopted a policy of repression and revenge. The reaction led the moderate sectors of the CNT to accept the creation in October of a mixed commission of union representatives and employers, to help in the resolution of labour conflicts.[23] This was a clear breach of the dictates of direct action but, given the conditions, was deemed necessary. However, the employers were unmoved and adopted a policy of lockouts aimed at starving the workers into submission. The lockouts lasted until January 1920 and were successful in forcing the Catalonia regional confederation to its knees. This put a sudden end to the rapid rise of the CNT, whose numbers diminished rapidly, especially in Catalonia, as the unions became involved in a virtual civil war fought on the streets of the Catalan capital against gunmen in the pay of the Employers' Federation, whilst leading militants feared for their lives or spent months in prison cells.[24] Between 1920 and 1923, 104 CNT militants in the region were murdered and 33 injured. Newspapers were forced to close down or operate clandestinely.

In October 1919, at the height of the lockout in Catalonia, Seguí and Pestaña travelled to Madrid where they gave a series of conferences defending the role of the Catalan CRT in the social unrest in the region as well as their acceptance of the mixed commission. Seguí, in particular, also argued in favour of the preponderance of syndicalism over anarchism in the class struggle and in the creation of a future society.[25] Seguí's increasing tendency to define syndicalism as an ideology in its own right brought criticism both from the Madrid-based anarchist periodical *Espartaco* and, more significantly, from the Catalan Federation of Anarchist Groups:

> Syndicalism – a means of struggle based on direct action – ends with the implantation of libertarian communism. ... Syndicalism as a goal in itself, is nothing. ... [If it were, still] the task would be only half-finished, and a new more or less despotic power ... would weigh down on mankind. This is the danger of guiding syndicalism according [to the principle of] *non plus ultra*. ... [T]he so-called pure syndicalists tend to be interested only in the economic struggle. And we

feel that if things continue like this, the abyss of corpo-
ratism or of reformism awaits the unions.[26]

The Catalan federation called upon anarchists to act within the
unions to ensure that syndicalism did not become reformist and reminded their opponents that not only were almost all Spanish anarchists members of the CNT, but that they made up the majority of
its leading figures.

Thus, the battle between moderates and the radical elements within the CNT was well under way even before the Madrid congress of
1919.[27] In fact, the resolution approved at Madrid, which adopted
'libertarian communism' as the ultimate goal of the confederation,
probably represented an attempt at reconciliation, since among the
names of those who drew it up were a number of leading moderates.
The reconciliation was the result of the success of the repressive measures adopted by the authorities in Catalonia and Andalusia but only
represented a lull in the evolving conflict between syndicalists and
radical anarchists within the CNT.

As has been seen, following the Madrid congress the CNT was
immersed in a battle for survival against the combined forces of the
state and the employers as well as an ideological struggle within the
unions, provoked by the communist-syndicalists. However, differences between the radicals and syndicalists were never far from the surface, especially as Seguí's reformist predilection became increasingly
apparent. In a conference held in prison in the Balearics in December
1920, Seguí appeared simply to be paraphrasing Monatte's speech at
the 1907 International Anarchist Congress: "The professional organisation of syndicalism, with a revolutionary and libertarian orientation, is close to anarchism. ... Syndicalism, let's be clear now, is the
advance of anarchism."[28] Also in late 1920, Seguí spoke of the need
for the confederation to contribute to an increase in national production and, in a letter published in the Madrid-based independent
newspaper *El Sol* under the title "Possibilist Syndicalism," appeared
to argue in favour of a Liberal government.[29] Possibilist syndicalism
was simply a moderation of the CNT's revolutionary activity in the
light of events. It did not represent a specific ideological position but
established the basis for the ideological evolution of the revolutionary

syndicalist position elaborated later by Joan Peiró and Angel Pestaña. Meanwhile, rumours and allegations abounded about Seguí and Pestaña's possible collaboration with the political forces of the Catalan Left.[30] The rumours, it appears, were unfounded. However, the close friendship of both men with prominent figures of the Catalan Left was enough to raise doubts among those already suspicious of the direction the leading figures in the Catalan CRT were proposing.

After the Liberal-led government came to power in March 1922, constitutional guarantees were restored and the persecution of the confederation eased but did not disappear. The first national meeting of leading CNT delegates since 1919 was held in Zaragoza in June 1922. As has been seen, the Zaragoza conference focused predominantly on the question of the Internationals. Besides the defeat of the communist-syndicalists, a further important decision made at Zaragoza was the adoption of the so-called 'Political Motion.' The motion argued that the CNT had to involve itself in the politics of the nation, not politics as defined by the other political parties but politics in general, all issues that affected the lives of the members of the confederation:

> We are obliged to bring forward solutions ... for all moral, cultural, economic, political and social problems ... being a thoroughly revolutionary organisation that rejects, absolutely ... parliamentary action and collaboration with political parties, which is at the same time wholly and absolutely political, since [our] mission is to conquer the rights of [intervention and surveillance] with respect to the evolving values of national life; and to such an end, [our] duty is to exercise positive action by means of coercion derived from the resources and manifestations of strength of the CNT.[31]

The motion, drawn up by Pestaña, Seguí, Josep Viadiu, and Peiró was passed unanimously, although it appears that little time was given to discussion about its meaning.[32] The exact remit of the motion was the subject of much confusion. The anarchist Max Stephen saw in the generalised nature of the language an attempt to hide the fact that the motion represented a clear move away from the "pure norms of revolutionary syndicalism."[33] Gaston Leval fumed over the adoption of the Political Motion. Politics, he argued, meant "the art of governing a State, a people or a nation," and the CNT would have nothing to do with this. Much of his anger was aimed directly at Seguí and Pestaña. Leval savagely criticised both, claiming their ultimate aim was to achieve political office on the back of the confederation.[34]

However, it is possible to give the motion a very different interpretation. An editorial in *Redención*, although lamenting the lack of clarity in the motion, argued that in approving it the confederation was accepting "sole responsibility for its action" and rejecting completely contact with any political party. According to the editorial, the CNT must have an opinion and a policy for all the problems that arise in national life, and this policy should be guided by the principles of libertarian communism. This was vital for the preparation of the working masses for the revolution.[35]

Valeriano Orobón Fernández, one of the most outstanding theorists of the Spanish and international anarcho-syndicalist movements, saw the motion as a reflection of the ideological advances the CNT had made in the light of lessons they had learnt since the end of World War I:

> The evolution of politics following the war has spelt the end of the syndical neutrality of the Amiens Charter. In the whole world there is not a syndicalist organisation existing today that does not practise politics, either directly or as an appendage of a political party. The CNT brought itself up to date with this international trend, adopting at the congress at La Comedia [Madrid 1919] an ideological platform, and, at the Zaragoza conference, a political platform. The CNT is therefore a complete organisation. Whereas pure syndicalism is not 'sufficient in itself', anarcho-syndicalism clearly is.[36]

This was not the same position as Seguí's, as Orobón Fernández is accepting the predominance of anarchism within the unions, in line with the stated final goal. Orobón Fernández had earlier been one of the first anarchist theorists to take on board the lessons of the Russian Revolution.[37] In an article published in *Solidaridad Obrera* (Bilbao) in late 1920, he argued that a Spanish revolution would need to be protected from the forces of reaction that made a transitory period of dictatorship a necessity. The dictatorship would be carried out by the unions – "the genuine representation of the proletariat ... if the motto of the Russian Revolution was 'All power to the Soviets!', ours must be 'All power to the unions!' – but these should always act in accordance with their final goal, anarchism.[38] By 1922 this position enjoyed wide support among anarchists. In January 1922, the Catalan Libertarian Communist Federation published a manifesto in *Acción Social Obrera* in which they announced: "We accept syndicalism as a means of struggle to achieve the implantation of libertarian communism *as quickly as possible*. We accept the principle of a transitory dictatorship to sustain the social revolution. ... Our strength is in the labour organisation; we must channel our efforts in this direction."[39]

Later that year the recently formed Levante Federation of Anarchist Groups also clarified their position toward syndicalism: "We do not consider syndicalism as a goal, but as a means. ... [and] so that it responds to these [our] ends, it is necessary to instil [the unions] with libertarian and revolutionary principles."[40]

The Levante federation also warned that anarchists working within the confederation should not forget that "above all, we are anarchists." This was undoubtedly a reference to those anarchists who had forgotten their principles on entering the unions – that is, the syndicalists.[41] The fear of the growing 'syndicalisation' of anarchist militants in the CNT prompted the Catalan Anarchist Federation to propose the holding of a national anarchist congress as early as 1920 to discuss the questions that had arisen in relation to syndicalism since the previous congress in 1918. The Catalan initiative was supported by a number of leading anarchist publications, but the moves came to nothing due to "government sanctions."[42] Further attempts to organise a national congress in 1920 and again in 1921 failed in the face of the repression.[43] A Spanish Committee of Anarchist Relations, based in Barcelona, sent a letter detailing the repression in Spain to the International Anti-Militarist Congress in March 1921. However, no further reference to this committee appears in the Spanish press.[44] Throughout the years 1920–22, regional anarchist bodies in Catalonia appeared and disappeared as a result of the unrelenting repression in the region.

The International Anarchist Congresses of 1921 and 1923

As conditions in Spain made it impossible to organise at a regional level, let alone the national level, the announcement of the forthcoming International Anarchist Congress to be held in Berlin in December 1921 provided a welcome distraction for the country's anarchists.[45] Not surprisingly, attempts to hold a national congress to discuss the mandate of any Spanish delegation again proved impossible.[46] In the end, the Spanish anarchists were represented in Berlin by Bruno Lladó, whilst the newly formed Local Federation of Anarchist Groups of Madrid sent a report to the congress.[47]

In general, the calibre of the delegates was not as high as had been hoped, due to the difficulty in acquiring passports and gaining entry to Germany, as well as the continent-wide repression that the anarchists faced.[48]

The congress, held in Berlin from December 25, 1921, to January 2, 1922, was the first international anarchist congress since the Amsterdam congress of 1907. It was organised following a request by the Unione Anarchica Italiana (UAI), which hoped it would help to create an anarchist International.[49] Similarities with the revolutionary syndicalist attempts to create a revolutionary syndicalist International were immediately apparent, and it was even suggested that the true revolutionary syndicalist conference might arise from this congress.[50] The congress was held at the home of the industrial unions of Berlin, with Rudolf Rocker of the FAUD (later to be the first secretary of the new IWMA) giving the opening speech.

As at the Amsterdam congress of 1907, one of the major topics of debate was the unresolved problem of the anarchist position toward syndicalism.[51] Although the Spanish anarchists had been unable to meet to discuss their opinions on the issues, articles by individuals and regional organisations in the press had made clear that their views had changed since the prewar period. Greater anarchist involvement in the syndicalist movement had also been accepted by other national organisations. At its national congress held in Lyon in November 1921, the Union Anarchiste Française (UAF) had advised anarchists to enter the unions in order to lead the struggle against the influence of reformists and political parties, even so-called proletarian ones (that is, communist parties).[52] The same month, the UAI had advised its members to take part in the labour movement, either in the USI or the reformist CGL, to avoid any party creating a dictatorship within the two unions.

These views were supported by the congress and the resolution adopted on 'Anarchism and Syndicalism', which accepted that syndicalism was not only a means to achieve the revolution, but was to be "the economic base of the new society." As such, anarchists must play a leading role in the unions:

> All economic organisations that are battling for the creation of a new social order … should have the anarchist influence brought to bear upon them. Anarchists, therefore, should penetrate such organisations, in order to propagate our ideals and make them conversant with it; but it should never be forgotten that such organisations are not specifically anarchist, and that libertarian communism is anarchism's sole economic aim. Comrades who enter these organisations ought to defend in them federalist and anti-bureaucratic ideas.[53]

In comparison with the position adopted in 1907, the resolution represented a far greater acknowledgment of the revolutionary potential of syndicalism. Anarchists were no longer simply to act within the unions to ensure that revolutionary syndicalism remained true to the principles of direct action. They were now to act to make the influence of anarchism directly felt within the unions. Anarchists should defend their positions and work to ensure that others did not take control or subserve the unions to the demands of a political party. They should not seek to control but guide. Of course, to opponents there was a thin line between these two points. But it was no longer feasible to stand aside whilst others sought to accommodate the unions with the state (socialists) or with state-centric ideologies (communism). To an extent, internal struggle was inherent, but if all sides abided the goals and played fair, this could work. However, suspicions remained. Syndicalism was still confined to the economic sphere. Only anarchism could bring full emancipation in economic, political, and social spheres, but to achieve this required better organisation: "Political parties are strongly organised, and exercise thereby a great influence on the working-class movement. It appears, therefore, to be all the more necessary for anarchists to organise."[54]

To this end, the various federations in each country were advised to move toward the formation of a national anarchist union. At the international level, the congress recommended that anarchists "assist every project that may have as its aim the formation of a truly revolutionary syndicalist International which will be independent of all external influences." An International Anarchist Bureau was created (based in Sweden) with the purpose of organising a specifically anarchist International. As with the bureau created following the 1907 congress, which had the same objective, it enjoyed a brief and unsuccessful existence.

The creation of an anarchist International would be discussed again, at the international anarchist congress held in Paris in October 1923.[55] This congress would be a disappointment, with few militants of any real standing attending.[56] Once again a correspondence bureau would be established, this time based in France, with the French anarchist Lucien Haussard acting as secretary. The congress would also found the Union Anarchiste Universelle, although, due to the sparse participation in Paris, it was agreed that a new congress be called as soon as possible to discuss the basis upon which the International was to function.[57] A further congress was planned for early 1925, but, in the end, the next international anarchist congress was not held until 1927.[58] According to Haussard, the reason for this was because after 1923, in international affairs, anarchists focused their attention on either the IWMA, Bolshevism, or an international platform (see chapter 7).[59]

The invitation to attend the 1923 international congress in Paris had arrived in Spain whilst the anarchists were still occupied with the formation of their own national organisation.[60] Following a suggestion by the Northern Federation of Anarchist Groups, anarchists sent their opinions as to whether or not Spain should send a delegation to Berlin (where such a congress was originally to be held in January 1923) to the anarchist papers *La Tierra* (La Coruña) and *Redención*.[61] The majority view was that it would be pointless to send a delegation whilst no national organisation existed. It made more sense to concentrate on creating a national federation of anarchists – as proposed by the previous international congress and increasingly necessary given the situation in Spain and with the internal conflicts developing in the CNT – before becoming involved in an international organisation.[62]

The Madrid National Anarchist Congress, 1923

At the beginning of March 1922, the Libertarian Group of La Felgura (Asturias) proposed that the anarchists of Madrid create a Preparatory Committee of the Spanish Anarchist Federation. The Local Federation of Anarchist Groups of Madrid responded by suggesting that it would be better if this task was assigned to the anarchists of Levante or Asturias where, they claimed, regional organisations already existed and where there were more militants.[63] The Asturian federation had been formed towards the end of 1921 whilst the Federation of Anarchist Groups of Levante would be founded at an assembly in either late June or early July 1922.[64] The assembly nominated a Council of Relations that was to be in regular contact with all the anarchists of the region, Spain and abroad. At roughly the same time, regional federations were created in Aragón, Rioja, and Navarra (one federation for the three regions), Andalusia, and the north, whilst the Catalan Anarchist Federation was reconstituted in late 1922.[65]

The increase in organisation at a regional level inevitably led to calls for the holding of a national congress.[66] Initially the Levante federation undertook to organise the congress, and a meeting was called to discuss the matter on October 21, 1922.[67] Meanwhile, a provisional committee of the 'Anarchist Union' had been established in Barcelona in September with the immediate aim of creating a Catalan Regional Federation, which would then help in the preparation for the holding of a national congress.[68] Abel Paz, who bases his information on the eyewitness accounts of Aurelio Fernández, claims that a Regional Commission of Anarchist Relations was created at a conference of Catalan and Balearic anarchists.[69] The meeting must have taken place toward the end of 1922, when there was a lull in the repression in the region following the dismissal of the civil governor Martínez Anido.[70] At the end of January 1923, the commission addressed a letter to the anarchists of the region, calling for the holding of a regional congress to be held before the national congress. The regional congress was held in March 1923.[71]

In the end, neither the Catalan nor the Levante anarchists organised the congress. At an assembly in January 1923, the anarchists from Zaragoza (Aragón) decided to take responsibility for the organisation of the national congress (with cooperation from the Madrid federation), and a proposed agenda for the congress was published the same month.[72] An organisational commission, comprising Nicasio Domingo, Francisco Soni, and the ubiquitous Manuel Buenacasa, was established, whilst correspondence was to be sent to the offices of *Tierra Libre* in Madrid.[73] The congress eventually took place in Madrid on March 18 and over the following days.

The congress agenda listed ten subjects for discussion, including organisation (local, regional, and national) and the anarchist position in relation to syndicalism.[74] The congress agreed to the creation of the National Committee of Anarchist Relations and to the publication of a national anarchist periodical *Crisol* (which began publication in August).[75] The committee was to be based in Barcelona, sharing the same address as the recently revived *Solidaridad Obrera*.[76] National organisation was limited to the Committee of Anarchist Relations rather than a national federation because, according to Mauro Bajatierra, it was judged more important that members should seek to influence actions in their specific regions by acting within their specific affinity groups, as this would help maintain their freedom of activity and would allow them to act voluntarily rather than through the direction of a national body.[77] The National Committee of Anarchist Relations (and the various regional committees) would coordinate but not direct anarchist activity across regional and local borders. In any case, the anarchists already had a national organisation: "The CNT constitutes and represents our revolutionary organisation. Here in Spain, it is the only organisation that, without euphemisms, without political intentions, without parliamentary aspirations, is carrying out a completely libertarian programme."[78]

If, as was constantly claimed, all the leading anarchists were also active within the CNT, there was no need for a further national libertarian organisation. At its inaugural congress, the CNT had declared that syndicalism was nothing more than a means of bringing about the revolution, and in Madrid in 1919 it had agreed that the aim of the revolution would be the implantation of libertarian communism throughout the country. As the anarchist revolution depended on the confederation, anarchists had an indisputable interest in ensuring that it did not deviate from the revolutionary line it had adopted in 1919.[79]

However, the 1923 national congress rejected the proposal made by a new radical sector, the anarcho-Bolsheviks, who proposed that all anarchists in the country unite in an armed struggle against the state. The anarcho-Bolsheviks, as described above, were a small number of militants centred around the affinity group Los Solidarios, which was made up of young militants who had begun their adult life in the postwar union struggles. Their revolutionary activism had evolved from the gang warfare between the CNT and the paid gunmen of the Employers' Federation, which had gone hand in hand with the labour struggle from 1919 onwards (although the first killings occurred before this date, the most intensive period of warfare started in late 1919 or early 1920).[80] The violent tactics of these anarchists had much in common with those adopted by the more violent proponents of the propaganda of the deed in the years before the turn of the century and were spurred on by the twin forces of desperation and vengeance. An added ingredient was that revolution had seemed possible both nationally and internationally, with 1923 marking the end of the period of revolutionary uprisings that followed the Bolshevik Revolution in central and eastern Europe. However, at heart the violence was part of the class war that was occurring in Spain, most specifically in Catalonia.[81] The resort to violence and assassination had been adopted by certain sectors of the CNT and had even, in certain cases, been funded and organised by the confederation, but these had been predominately defensive tactics or used as for vengeance following the violence of their opponents. It would be incorrect to describe this violence simply as a tactic of the radical anarchists, since militants of all persuasions were involved.[82] But whereas violence had been originally employed as a defensive, revenge-based policy, it was transformed by the members of Los Solidarios into a means of bringing about social revolution. Rather than ideologues, the anarcho-Bolsheviks were activists, a sort of revolutionary vanguard, albeit with a somewhat simplistic view of how the revolution could be achieved. Their proposal was rejected at the national anarchist congress. In the months that followed, when, after a two-year lull, the CNT once again returned to the offensive, it would become a significant force. However, this would only be a temporary phenomenon which resulted from the exceptional circumstances brought about by the rise in social conflict in Catalonia. This conflict was accompanied by almost daily acts of violence in the months preceding the military seizure of power in September 1923.

The Growth in Anarchist Activity in the Unions in 1923

In the months that followed the Madrid congress, there was a discernible increase in anarchist activity in the CNT, reflecting a more radical approach not only by the anarcho-Bolsheviks but also by the syndicalists' opponents in the confederation. Although the members of the initial National Committee of Anarchist Relations were quickly obliged by the situation in Barcelona to leave the city at the end of May, new members were appointed and the committee remained in Barcelona.[83] The first manifesto published by the National Committee of Anarchist Relations was couched in untypically vague terminology. The manifesto spoke of the "principle of the ultimate goal" and "the possession of an ideal," which led to the conclusion that the revolution was "the only way." The manifesto was tantamount to a call to revolution. "Society," it concluded, "must be ours, that is, it must belong to the workers."[84]

A general statement of intent might be expected in the first manifesto of an organisation, but the timing, the title ("The Anarchists and the Present Movement"), and the fact that the manifesto was cosigned by the Catalan committee suggest strongly that it was specifically a battle cry for anarchists involved in the ongoing transport strike in Barcelona.[85] According to Camil Piñón, the president of the transport union at the time, the strike was "after La Candiense, the most important [strike] of the period" and carried out at a time of resurgent gang warfare following the murder of Salvador Seguí in March.[86] It started in the port after a number of workers had been sacked for not turning up to work on May Day, which was not at the time an official holiday. On May 14 an assembly of the Transport Union decided to call a general strike, which continued until July 12, when the employers agreed to reinstate workers.[87] However, it was a pyrrhic victory for the CNT. The transport strike was one of a series of labour protests occurring during the summer of 1923 which left the workers exhausted, the unions penniless, and the CNT more divided than ever. As a result of the explosive social situation provoked by the labour unrest, relations between syndicalists and anarchists (of which the anarcho-Bolsheviks can be considered an extremist faction) in the CNT became so heated that both the national and regional committees were moved from the Catalan capital.[88]

The most significant factor of the renewed social unrest in Catalonia was the increasing role of the anarchists within the CNT. At the end of May, *Tierra y Libertad* published a manifesto (which had previously been read out at a meeting of anarchist groups in the regional capital) in which they complained, "The failures of the labour organisation are all too frequently blamed on extremist elements. … And this, as well as being unfair, is false. For a long time now, anarchists as a unit have had no influence and have not intervened in the labour movement."[89]

The manifesto admitted that individuals who called themselves anarchists had acted within the movement, but anarchists as a group had not. The intention of the paper, it claimed, was simply to "make note of the fact and nothing more." But simply by stating the fact, the manifesto was suggesting that an alternative policy needed to be adopted. This certainly seems to have been the interpretation of many anarchists in the city.[90] In early June, Jaime Rotger, a correspondent for *El Libertario* (the newspaper of the Alianza Libertaria Argentina) who was visiting Spain at the time, interviewed a 'Giménez', who, according to Rotger, was the general secretary of the CNT. Giménez told him that the national committee of the confederation had "close relations" with the Committee of Anarchist Relations.[91]

The extent of anarchist involvement in the affairs of the Catalan confederal organisation became clear at a regional plenum held in Barcelona on June 29.[92] At the plenum, the CRT secretary, Roigé, reported that the regional committee had been "mutilated" because the unions had withdrawn their respective delegations due to the animosity between differing unions in the capital.[93] The local federation of Barcelona severely criticised the performance of the committee of the Catalan CRT, whilst a representative of the anarchist groups added that the committee had "violated the basic principles" of the confederation, resulting in the failure of the syndicalist organisation. In particular, the delegate of the anarchist groups, whose criticism was supported by a number of others, condemned the visits of leading figures of the regional committee of the CRT to a minister and the civil governor.[94] The plenum agreed that the regional committee should be transferred from Barcelona to Manresa.

In the days leading up to the regional plenum, the anarcho-Bolsheviks, bolstered by the revolutionary tension in the city and rumours of a potential military coup that were now openly circulating throughout both the city and the country, called a meeting of leading CNT members at which they put forward their plan to launch an "assault on power."[95] At the meeting held sometime between June 18 and 28 in the woods near Las Planas (just outside Barcelona), Juan García Oliver told those gathered (who included Pestaña, Piñón, and Peiró) that the bourgeoisie was on the brink of collapse and that now was the time for revolution. If the CNT could provide the action groups (Los Solidarios and two or three others) with the means (that is, arms), they would bring it about. Again the meeting rejected the proposal, with Peiró declaring that García Oliver was proposing "an adventure whose results were less than certain and in which any error might have fatal consequences." A lack of faith in revolution, although perhaps realistic, only served to further the extreme elements in their belief that the moderates had lost their revolutionary zeal.

Despite this setback, the anarcho-Bolsheviks did not give in and attended the national plenum held in Valencia July 22–24 en masse, where their ideas finally enjoyed success. At the plenum, the anarcho-Bolsheviks proposed that the CNT support assaults on banks and other financial institutions in order to buy guns and be in a position to resist any potential military coup. There is only limited information available on the deliberations of the plenum, which was held in secret, but it appears that this proposal was accepted. Furthermore, the plenum agreed that the national committee should move to Seville, where initially it was comprised of activists who supported the anarcho-Bolshevik position.[96] However, this new committee, led by Manuel Adame, was detained on August 16 after a failed armed attack and was eventually replaced by a moderate and legally constituted committee in the Andalusian capital, with Paulino Díez as secretary.[97] At the beginning of September the leading figures of Los Solidarios were arrested or forced to flee the country after they attacked the Bank of Spain in Gijón.[98] The anarcho-Bolsheviks would not have such a direct influence on the CNT again until the Second Republic.

During the transport strike the action of the Catalan Employers' Federation had been notable for two reasons: their opposition to central government's attempts to mediate and, following the negotiated settlement, an increasingly harmonious relationship with military forces in Catalonia, in particular with Captain General Primo de Rivera. In fact, the strike had been prolonged deliberately by the Employers' Federation to create the right atmosphere for a military coup.[99] The social violence that accompanied the strike was one of the excuses used by Primo de Rivera to justify his pronunciamento of September 13, 1923, launched from the Catalan capital, which brought to an end the parliamentary system that had governed Spain since 1875, a system which had represented a small oligarchy of vested interests rather than the nation as a whole. King Alfonso XIII immediately gave his blessing to the general, as Primo De Rivera promised to conceal information on his involvement in a military fiasco at Annual, Morocco (Alfonso would lose his crown in 1931 due to his connection with the dictatorship), and two days later, the Military Directorate established by Primo de Rivera to govern the country suspended constitutional guarantees, dissolved the Cortes, and extended the state of war throughout Spain.[100]

The CNT's immediate reaction was to invite the UGT to join them in a united front against the pronunciamento. This was rejected by the UGT, who, alongside their political allies, the PSOE, would soon embark on a process of open collaboration with the dictatorship. The opposition of the socialists meant that the general strike called by the CNT for September 14 failed to materialise.[101]

The CNT was not immediately banned, maintaining a theoretically legal status until May 1924. However, for all intents and purposes, the functioning of the confederation was made impossible by government legislation and press censorship.[102] The position of the Primo de Rivera regime toward the confederation became clear on September 24 with the appointment of Martínez Anido as undersecretary of the interior. Three days later, Arlegui was made director general of public order. The two men who had presided over the brutal repression of the Catalan federation in 1919–12 were now civil governor and chief of police in Catalonia. Following their appointment, numerous militants were detained or forced into exile, whilst the pages of *Solidaridad Obrera* often contained articles that had been completely blanked out by the government censor.

On September 29 Martínez Anido sent a circular to the various civil governors, ordering them to give unions eight days to place themselves on a legal footing by presenting their books and accounts to the governors. This would require the unions to provide the authorities with a complete list of not only their activities but also their members, including the position they held in the unions and their home addresses.[103] On October 3, fearing, with some justification, that such information would be used by the authorities to persecute militants, the local federation of Barcelona decided that the unions in the capital should go underground.[104] The federation suspended publication of *Solidaridad Obrera* two days later.[105] However, the policy was not popular with all the unions in the capital or with leading syndicalists, although it would be too simplistic to suggest that all anarchists supported illegality and all syndicalists opposed it.[106] Nonetheless, it was a further cause of friction that the communists attempted to exploit, launching, as part of a joint project with moderates on the directorial board of *Solidaridad Obrera*, a daily newspaper, *Lucha Obrera*.[107] Fearful of yet another communist attempt to split the CNT, the local federation agreed to a change of policy. *Solidaridad Obrera* reappeared on November 24, whilst a regional plenum held in Mataró in early

December decided that the Catalan CRT should be reconstituted.[108] It was agreed that the internal conflict in Barcelona, over whether the unions should act legally or not, should not be discussed at the plenum and should instead be the subject of an assembly of unions from the Catalan capital. The CRT committee was meanwhile to be established in Mataró.[109] The new position of the Catalan CRT was that the unions should remain open and act legally for the present but should go underground if there was an increase in repression. Germinal Esgleas, an anarchist, became the new secretary of the CRT, whilst the new treasurer, Adrián Arnó, was in the syndicalist camp.[110] Once again, fear of communist infiltration of the CNT had served to soothe the discord between syndicalists and anarchists, albeit only for the time being.

Solidaridad Obrera initially appeared to be following a middle path between the proponents of legality and illegality in Barcelona and called for "tolerance among the workers."[111] But, by early December, the paper was evidently under the influence of radical anarchists:

> The CNT, an organisation that has a concrete goal … cannot continue to call itself a syndicalist organisation. Syndicalism, an ideal that is still not clearly defined, is the opposite of anarchy. And if the aim of the confederation is the organisation of society based on anarchist principles, the means employed to achieve this must be anarchism. … The union is a means, better than others, perhaps, where anarchism can be enacted, and if it is successful … the union becomes an element of libertarian action and emancipation. However, when the syndical environment, with all its vices, absorbs the anarchist personality, it becomes an obstacle … to the realisation of the ideal.[112]

The position of these anarchists was now not only that syndicalism had no defined ideology as such but that it was the opposite of anarchism. Anarchists needed to act within the unions in accordance with their libertarian ideals to ensure that they did not become an obstacle to the realisation of anarchism. Syndicalism without anarchist guidance endangered the revolution. This rejection of syndicalism formed the ideological basis of the so-called Movimiento Obrero Anarquista (Anarchist Labour Movement) which would gain support from radical sectors of the CNT in Catalonia from 1925 onwards.

Elsewhere in the regions where the CNT was strongest, repression had already become widespread. In Andalusia, the national committee, which had been formally and legally constituted in Seville on September 10, was detained in December 1923 following claims by the authorities that they were involved in a communist plot to overthrow the dictatorship, and as a result the national committee as well as the regional and local committees in Andalusia were closed down in January.[113] Following this, a new national committee was organised in Zaragoza, but this fell victim to the authorities in early June 1924.[114] In Aragón, confederal newspapers were closed and syndicalists imprisoned.[115] Alongside the imprisonments, increasing numbers of militants fled across the border to France, where, following a congress held in Lyon in early February 1924, a Committee of Anarchist Relations was established in Paris.

Meanwhile, in Catalonia a regional assembly held at Granollers at the end of December endorsed the regional committee elected at Mataró. The assembly, which had been organised to tackle the question of the conflict in Barcelona, decided that the union 'juntas' in the capital should resign and new elections should be held for both the unions and the local federation.[116] The result was a victory for the radical anarchists.[117] The Catalan CRT continued to act within the remits of its precarious legal status, and on April 4 the CRT held its final plenum before being outlawed at Sabadell. The regional committee appointed at Mataró in December resigned, and a new one, with Arnó as secretary, was elected, although it is not clear why the committee resigned.[118]

Despite adopting a less overtly pro-anarchist stance since the turn of the year, *Solidaridad Obrera* was still in the hands of the radical anarchists. On May 18, José Alberola, a teacher, replaced Felix Monteagudo as the paper's administrator, whilst an editorial on May 23, entitled "The Organisation Must Have Ideas," once again criticised those who wished to "impose an absence of ideas" on the CNT.[119] The more balanced nature of the paper allowed the syndicalists space to defend their position. Peiró argued that the period following the military coup marked a new stage in the development of the confederation and required it to develop new tactics accordingly, especially as the usual tactics associated with direct action, namely strikes, were not possible given the new political conditions. These new tactics could be found within the remit of the political motion adopted at Zaragoza, by which the confederation had agreed to intervene in "all the problems of public life."[120] Peiró seemed to be suggesting that the CNT should continue to act within legal boundaries and concentrate on organisation and education. What he did not mention was how such a policy, which would require the confederal leadership to accept labour legislation that forbade direct action and required the names and addresses of all militants to be supplied to the authorities, could avoid becoming bogged down in the material day-to-day issues which were the basis of reformism. If the confederation were to accept this, it would scarcely differ from the UGT. Surely it would make more sense to create separate groups or organisations to help propagate and clarify the anarchist message than to simply accustom the workers in the unions to such a bland form of non-revolutionary syndicalism. Meanwhile, Pestaña argued in favour of a concentration of left-wing forces through pacts of mutual understanding.[121] A united front against the dictatorship may have been desirable, but the UGT and the PSOE had rejected the CNT's call for a general strike in protest against the pronunciamento and were actively collaborating with the dictatorship. As with Peiró's proposals, the main obstacle was not necessarily the idea itself but the prospects of such polices being permitted by the dictatorship.

The collaboration of the socialists, the "spoilt child of the regime" according to historian Raymond Carr, was mutually beneficial for both the UGT, who saw in this cooperation the chance to become the only national workers' organisation, and the dictatorship, which appreciated the moderation of socialist tactics and was clever enough to see the benefit of a close relationship with representatives of the working class.[122] The socialists' collaboration also had a negative effect on the tactics of the moderates in the CNT as, despite their increasing attempts to act within the limits of legality, the dictatorship was never disposed to allow the CNT to regain its strength. The CNT was allowed to continue on a regional basis in Asturias and Galicia, and even within Catalonia militants were allowed, every now and then, to publish newspapers. However, whenever the dictatorship deemed it necessary, the papers were closed down and leading militants arrested. The dictatorship had no need to tolerate the CNT, and this would be the constant flaw in the moderates' position whilst Primo de Rivera remained in power.

If, as Peiró claimed, the military coup represented a new stage in the development of the CNT, then the ban on the Catalan CRT, introduced on May 28, 1924, following the assassination of the executioner of Barcelona, took it one stage further.[123] The confederal unions were closed, *Solidaridad Obrera* was banned, and leading militants arrested. The ban on the Catalan CRT would remain in force until 1930.

The legacy of the revolutionary fervour of 1923 would play a large part in the growing distance between anarchists and syndicalists. Although momentary and the result of a specific environment, the anarcho-Bolsheviks had an important impact on the ideological infighting in the CNT. Shocked by the extent of the confederation's compliance in the plans for armed opposition to the state and judging that the strike movements of the summer had only served to increase repression and provide the justification for the dictatorship, syndicalists now feared that anarchist domination would lead to the destruction of the confederation. This reaction is crucial to the understanding of the trajectory of the syndicalist position during the dictatorship and especially during the reorganisation of the CNT from 1930 onwards. However, given the political realities, what kind of CNT could exist? It was understandable to strive to keep the workers organised and out of socialist control, but if the CNT simply accepted the new legislation, how was it to be any different from the UGT? How could it educate workers in the need for revolution whilst not being revolutionary? Would it not simply become another socialist union, with its rhetoric out of kilter with its actions and revolution put off until the distant future and eventually forgotten amidst collaboration and cooperation with the very economic regime it set out to destroy?

The position adopted by the syndicalists would, in turn, cause a counterreaction from the radical anarchists, some of whom clearly sympathised with the revolutionary fervour of the anarcho-Bolsheviks without necessarily sharing their impatience. During the first years of the dictatorship these radical anarchists would put forward their own ideological design for the CNT. For them the CNT was a means to an end, and that end was revolution. If both weren't possible, then ideological clarity was more important than organization.

The syndicalist emphasis on the need for maintaining the confederal organisation inevitably led many of them to attempt to reach an accommodation with the dictatorship. But this would require them to sacrifice CNT principles, a fact that only increased anarchist suspicions about the reformist nature of syndicalism. With confederal activity limited to debates in the press, ideological issues became the focus of attention. The syndicalists, partly due to the experience of the previous years and partly due to the necessities of the period, now clarified the positions they had sketched out in previous years and began advocating a form of 'pure' syndicalism that was to be completely independent of political influence and which, in its relations with political organisations, would treat anarchism on a par with other socialist groups. This, in turn, would push the anarchists in the opposite direction.

6.

IDEOLOGICAL CONFLICT
IN THE FIRST YEARS OF
THE DICTATORSHIP

FOLLOWING THE BAN ON THE CATALAN CRT AND THE SUBSEQUENT repression the CNT faced throughout Spain, the CNT ceased to exist as a national organisation. In some areas, local and even regional organisations were tolerated but were forced to comply with strict legal requirements that greatly limited their activity.[1] Elsewhere the confederation maintained a precarious clandestine existence. Unions were shut down, newspapers were tolerated for short periods before falling victim to censorship and suppression, and militants were frequently detained without warning. The majority of CNT members took shelter in the Free Unions or the UGT, whilst many activists were forced into exile in northern Europe and Latin America. In Catalonia, the moderates and radical anarchists, unable to engage in normal day-to-day union issues, analysed and reevaluated their objectives and tactics in the light of the confederation's demise. Not surprisingly they reached very different conclusions.

The moderates elaborated on the ideas that they had been developing in the previous years and now openly espoused a form of 'pure' syndicalism devoid of all outside political interference, including anarchism. These moderates (henceforth referred to as syndicalists, as their opposition to the radical elements in the confederation had taken on a clearly defined ideological position) were in effect proposing a return to the principles of prewar revolutionary syndicalism as defined by the Charter of Amiens, with one important difference. Rather than being apolitical, the syndicalists now argued that the confederation needed to give weight to the political motion adopted at the Zaragoza conference of 1922 and develop a political programme that would tackle all problems relevant to the unions and their members. But the exact nature of this programme remained vague. The only apparent difference between the CNT and a political party would be that the former aimed to achieve its goal through direct action rather than by parliamentary means, although exactly what form this would take, given the limited field for action permitted by the labour legislation of the dictatorship, was never fully clarified.

In reality, the syndicalists' position represented a further retreat from the revolutionary fervour of the previous years. Significantly, the campaign in favour of a pure syndicalism was closely related to attempts to regain a legal status for the confederation. Given the existing political environment, in order to achieve this the CNT would have to tone down its revolutionary nature and soften its position on direct action. Not unsurprisingly, the moderates' position only served to stiffen the opposition of the radical anarchists, who produced their own ideological retort to the moderates' pure syndicalism: the Movimiento Obrero Anarquista (MOA, Anarchist Labour Movement), originally proposed by the Argentine Federación Obrera Regional Argentina (FORA). The supporters of the MOA did not want a labour movement open solely to anarchists but one in which ideology would take precedence over economics.

The conflict between the supporters of pure syndicalism and the MOA was predominantly limited to Catalonia and was simply a further stage in the evolution of the ideological gulf between different libertarian factions in the region evident in previous years.[2] However, the ideological debates within the confederation as a whole cannot be reduced to the simple duality of the opposing forces in Catalonia. A number of prominent anarchists, as well as the National Committee of Anarchist Relations and the newly formed Committee of Relations of the exiled anarchists in France, rejected both pure syndicalism and the MOA. They remained constant in their commitment to a form of syndicalism that responded to the economic conditions prevalent at any given time but that operated according to the principles of direct action and that had as its ultimate aim the installation of anarchism – that is, anarcho-syndicalism. This position received support from the IWMA at its second congress, in Amsterdam in 1925, which called for both the autonomy of the unions and closer collaboration between syndicalism and anarchism.

The ideological debates that gripped the confederation in Spain did not occur in a vacuum: they were part of the continued reappraisal of anarchist and syndicalist tactics in the light of the Bolshevik victory in Russia and the subsequent triumph of government repression against the libertarian movement in the countries where anarchism and revolutionary syndicalism had been strongest. The conflict between pure syndicalism and the proponents of the MOA actually originated in Argentina in the early 1920s but soon attracted the attention of militants in Spain. By the end of December 1924, the pro-MOA FORA and the pro-syndicalist Catalan CRT had become embroiled in an ideological war of words in their respective newspapers that became so serious that the IWMA felt compelled to intervene. With the appearance of a pro-MOA periodical in Barcelona in late 1925, the international dispute reverted to regional one between the syndicalists and the radical anarchists in Catalonia. Nonetheless, the ideological nature of the arguments of both sides attracted the interest of leading anarchists from abroad, in particular Errico Malatesta. However, before any conclusion could be reached, the Primo de Rivera dictatorship struck again, and in March 1926 the papers of both factions were banned and leading militants arrested.

The constant changes in the membership and location of the national committee from May 1924 to March 1926 provides ample evidence of the difficult environment in which confederal militants operated. Following the demise of the short-lived national committee in Zaragoza in June 1924, a new committee was organised in Barcelona in September. A manifesto by the new committee, dated September 20, 1924, and published in *La Protesta*, outlined the difficulties faced in maintaining the organisation under the dictatorship. (After the arrest of the committee based in Seville in December 1923, all subsequent committees were banned and operated clandestinely.)[3] The members of the new national committee were arrested by the Catalan authorities sometime in late 1924, probably November, and a new committee was established in Barcelona.[4] According to Bajatierra, the secretary of the new committee was Pestaña, although at some time later it appears that Peiró might again have become secretary.[5] By September 1925, the national committee had left Catalonia and was now based in Gijón (where the Asturian CRT was tolerated by the regional authorities), with Avelino González as secretary. Avelino González was arrested in October and sent to prison in Madrid, and the committee may simply have ceased to exist.[6] Plans were made to hold a national conference and establish a provisional committee in Galicia in early 1926, but the intervention of the government prevented the conference from taking place, and a new committee was eventually reestablished in Gijón. There it survived until June 1926, when, following an attempted revolt against Primo de Rivera in which the CNT was involved, a number of leading militants in Gijón were arrested. A new committee was created, with Segundo Blanco as secretary. However, this does not appear to have been very efficient and was roundly condemned for its inactivity at the national plenum of 1928, the first since 1925.[7]

Overall the CNT ceased to exist as an effective national organisation, and the CRTs in the areas where the confederation had been strongest were banned. The immediate task was therefore the overthrow of the dictatorship, which was seen by the majority of militants as the sine qua non for the reorganisation of the CNT.[8] Plans for an uprising had been underway almost from the first day of the dictatorship and would continue until the advent of the Second Republic in April 1931. The centre of the various conspiracies was in France, where exiled anarchists were in contact with other exiled political forces opposed to Primo de Rivera, in particular Francesc Macià's Catalan nationalists. However, such collaboration with politicians rankled many anarchists, some of whom decided that they did not need any help as any uprising against the dictatorship would be supported by the Spanish masses. In the event, when the anarchist-led uprising took place November 6–7, 1924, it was easily suppressed as little popular support was forthcoming. An armed invasion by exiled anarchists across the French border at Vera de Bidasoa was to coincide with the uprising but was prevented by the action of French border police.[9] The Vera de Bidasoa fiasco served as a severe lesson for the anarchists: the dictatorship was neither as weak as they had imagined, nor were they strong enough to threaten it on their own.[10] Simplistic insurrectionalism combined with blind faith in the masses did not work (and, indeed, outside of the disintegration caused by war such as in Russia, and in Paris in 1870, it had not presented a real threat to state power for a century). Some form of organisation was required to propagate the ideal and coordinate and unite the revolutionary masses. Moreover, quite simply, there needed to be more people to actively support the revolution.

The International Dispute between the Catalan CRT and the Argentine FORA

The realisation that the dictatorship might not be simply a passing phenomenon had already led moderates in Catalonia to adopt a more conciliatory approach towards the Primo de Rivera regime. Despite being banned, the Catalan CRT continued to operate clandestinely. A regional plenum had been held in Catalonia on June 29, 1924, which had been predominantly concerned with the plot to overthrow Primo de Rivera.[11] With the collapse of the dictatorship failing to materialise, the moderate-dominated Catalan regional committee began publication of a weekly newspaper, *Solidaridad Proletaria*, on October 18 1924 (the dictatorship would not tolerate the name *Solidaridad Obrera*). In a manifesto in the first edition of the newspaper, the regional committee claimed that *Solidaridad Proletaria's* primary aim was to counteract the campaign of slander launched by Maurín and the communists against the CNT in the pages of *La Batalla*.[12] However, it soon became clear that the newspaper had a more important goal, that of preparing the way for the legalisation of the CNT. As before, they faced strong opposition from within confederal ranks, particularly from the radical anarchists. In fact, it soon became apparent that the real target of the newspaper's criticism was not the communists but the overbearing influence of anarchism in the unions.

"Revolutionary syndicalism and anarchism each have a defined and clearly defined character. ... [T]he first is ... an instrument of economic class struggle, which bonds together workers irrespective of political or religious persuasion ... a function that does not belong to anarchism whose noble and far-reaching mission consists in ... moulding the soul of the working masses. ... The intrusion and imposition of [anarchist] affinity groups unanswerable to the unions and opinion is intolerable and cannot prosper."[13]

To emphasise the negative effect that such an intrusion would have on the CNT, *Solidaridad Proletaria* made direct reference to the conflict in Argentina between the FORA and the Unión Sindical Argentina (USA). Founded in 1901, the FORA had in 1905 adopted libertarian communism as its ultimate goal. However, at its 1915 congress, it dropped its commitment to anarcho-communism in favour of the revolutionary syndicalism of the Amiens Charter. As a result, the organisation split into two factions. The anarchists formed the FORA V, so-called as the commitment to anarchism was agreed upon at the organisation's fifth congress. The syndicalists formed the FORA IX, since the 1915 congress was the ninth. The Russian Revolution combined with fierce government repression in Argentina from 1919 onwards resulted in deep divisions within the Argentine libertarian movement. Not all anarchists remained in the increasingly sectarian FORA V, and many anarchist and syndicalist unions grouped together with the FORA IX and a number of other independent unions to form the USA, which also welcomed the 'anarcho-Bolshevik' faction of the FORA V. Initially at least, anarchists and syndicalists dominated the USA, rejecting the anarchist purism of the FORA V and embracing many of organisational and syndicalist positions favoured by both the syndicalists and anarchosyndicalists in Spain. The anarcho-Bolshevik faction should not be confused with the so-called anarcho-Bolsheviks in Spain. The Argentina anarcho-Bolsheviks favoured a form of dictatorship of the proletariat based on the unions as opposed to a party. Their distance from Russia and possibly their disbelief of FORA's criticism of the Bolsheviks led them to support the USA's entry into the RTUI. The USA was in many ways more anarcho-syndicalist than the FOR A (its founders wanted to base it on the example of the Italian USI), although the different tendencies within the movement led to factions supporting the USA's membership in both the RTUI and the IWMA, although it finally rejected both. Meanwhile, the FORA V, having discarded its Bolshevik element, joined the IWMA.[14]

The rejection of Bolshevism also brought a reappraisal of tactics and ideology by leading FORA V members, in particular Emilio López Arango and Diego Abad de Santillán (henceforth Santillán).[15] From 1922 onwards, López Arango and Santillán put forward their theories about how the relationship between anarchism and the labour movement should evolve. What they envisaged for the future was:

> An Anarchist Labour Organisation. ... Anarchism as the inspiration and organiser of the revolutionary minority of the proletariat and as an opponent and critic of reformism or authoritarianism. The purging from anarchism of all traces of Marxism which have persisted since its origins or have been introduced by syndicalism. The abolition of all economic dogmas which represent a form of preliminary legislation of the future and the conception of Anarchism as a doctrine of working-class origin and not as a scientific discovery and the monopoly of philosophers.[16]

As the main victims of the present system, the proletariat would be the vehicle for social transformation through their organisation into a truly revolutionary labour movement, one not blinded by the economic reductionism of syndicalism. Ideas had to dominate in the unions in order to ensure that the workers developed the solidarity and revolutionary fervour necessary to overthrow capitalism. For Santillán and López Arango, the quality of militants was judged to be more important than the quantity.

Santillán and López Arango developed their ideas with events in Spain very much in mind. Between 1922 and 1926 Santillán worked as the Berlin correspondent for the FORA newspaper, *La Protesta,* and, whilst in the German capital, represented the Spanish-speaking countries in the IWMA. He therefore kept abreast of events in Spain. Following the Zaragoza conference of June 1922, *La Protesta* became increasingly critical of the "syndicalist chiefs from the school of the chameleon Pestaña," whose ideas were responsible for the CNT becoming an "organisation devoid of ideology."[17] For the FORA militants, its lack of a defined political ideology meant that syndicalism could not be defined as a doctrine: it could be communist, Catholic, anarchist, et cetera, but syndicalism was "amorphous" and directionless without a guiding political philosophy.

The syndicalists of the Catalan CRT retaliated by taking the side of the FORA's opponents in Argentina. Soon after the creation of the USA in 1922, an independent anarchist organisation, the Alianza Libertaria Argentina (ALA), was formed in early 1923. The ALA supported the syndicalism of the USA and rejected the exclusivity of the FORA doctrine. In 1924 the ALA launched a campaign in favour of the admission of the USA into the IWMA and, as part of this campaign, sent a delegation to Europe to talk with member organisations of the International. One member of the delegation, Luis Di Filippo, visited Barcelona where he spoke at a number of conferences and collaborated with *Solidaridad Proletaria.*[18] The CRT newspaper then published a series of articles by the ALA on the anarchist movement in Argentina which were highly critical of the FORA. More significantly, the first article was introduced by Angel Abella, the newspaper's editor, and also blamed the FORA for the splits within the anarchist movement in Argentina and supported USA affiliation with the IWMA.[19] The FORA was the most influential of the Latin American organisations in the IWMA, and support for USA entry represented a clear threat to their position within the International. As such, Abella's introduction generated an immediate reaction from the FORA, whose president, Acha, wrote to the confederation's national committee, demanding to know whether the article represented the official position of the CNT as a whole.[20] No response was forthcoming from the national committee, and instead the Catalan CRT claimed sole responsibility for the newspaper's opinions.[21]

At the second IWMA congress, held in Amsterdam March 21–27, 1925, a commission was formed to discuss the conflict between the ALA and the FORA. However, the first item on the congress's agenda was a discussion of relations between 'Revolutionary Syndicalism and Political Parties'. The congress passed a resolution which repeated that the IWMA was independent of all political groups and dismissed the idea that political parties could have any positive role in the struggle for workers' emancipation. However, it went on to reject "the misleading definition which places on the same level parties aiming at political power and ideological associations which fight for social transformation outside every principle of authority and statism" and expressed the hope that in the future the IWMA would group around it "all the anti-state revolutionary elements from all over the world." Therefore, whilst maintaining the independence of the syndicalist organisations, the IWMA clearly envisaged close cooperation with the anarchist movement. This position supported neither that of the pure syndicalists nor that of the MOA.[22]

On the second day of the congress a discussion about the creation of an international solidarity fund degenerated into a vicious row between Carbó, representing the CNT, and Santillán of the FORA.[23] Carbó argued that if the divisions in the syndicalist movement in Argentina had been caused by the FORA then it would be better if their ideas "disappeared from the workers' movement." Santillán countered by claiming that the crisis within the CNT owed more to the absence of an anarchist spirit in its leaders than to the dictatorship of Primo de Rivera.[24]

The argument became so heated that the following day Rudolph Rocker, acting for the IWMA secretariat, was forced to intervene and request that the two delegations calm down.[25] Carbó declared that he would have kept quiet had the attacks from the FORA been limited to the press but, as Santillán had brought them to the congress, he had responded. The articles that had provoked the tension between the two organisations were, he claimed, "a personal opinion published in the paper of the Catalan Regional Confederation and not the official paper of the CNT." He challenged Santillán to tell him exactly when and how the CNT had abandoned its anarchist principles. Carbó also withdrew from the commission that was due to discuss the conflicts between the ALA and the FORA, but he rejected the FORA representative's claim that the CNT could not be impartial, adding that the CNT felt no hostility towards the FORA.[26]

On the final day of the congress, the FORA delegation read out a declaration about relations between their organisation and the CNT, calling for a public discussion on the subject. In response, Carbó presented a written statement in which he disowned responsibility for articles published in the Spanish press about the anarchist and syndicalist organisations in Argentina. He claimed that he did so because he did not know enough about the conflict in Argentina nor had he seen any note from the national committee of the CNT on the subject and because he felt that it would be to the benefit of the international movement if the conflict between the two organisations were to end.[27]

This did not occur. *La Protesta* immediately returned to the offensive against the "chameleonism" of the CNT and offered itself as a platform to all those in Spain "who wished to criticise" the confederation but "were banned from the columns of *Solidaridad Proletaria*."[28] The attacks in *La Protesta* now became more personal than ever, with Carbó joining the ranks of Pestaña and Peiró, the "pontiffs" of the CNT who, according to *La Protesta*, had forgotten the most elementary rules of anarchism.[29]

The continuation of the dispute forced the IWMA to intervene. In a letter sent to both organisations, Augustín Souchy, writing for the IWMA secretariat, stressed that such a visible conflict was causing immense damage to the International as a whole and suggested the formation of a commission composed of the secretariat and representatives of all member organisations to arbitrate the quarrel.[30] The FORA rejected the IWMA's proposal, arguing that the affair was solely a matter for itself and the CNT.[31] Nevertheless, following the IWMA's intervention, Santillán called for a restoration of cordiality between the two organisations.[32]

Ideological Conflicts in Catalonia

Rather than disappearing completely, the dispute between the FORA and the CNT was replaced by one between the syndicalists and radical anarchists in Catalonia.[33] The FORA's ideological stance had attracted the attention of the radical anarchists as early as 1923 when an article in support of the Argentine federation was published in *Tierra y Libertad*.[34] However, it was only with the rise of pure syndicalism that the radical anarchists began openly to promote the ideas of the FORA in Spain. In March 1925 *Solidaridad Proletaria* published a letter, signed by seventy-five militants, that railed against the negative effect that pure syndicalism was having upon the CNT in particular and the organisations of the IWMA in general. If the confederation was to avoid following the path towards reformism already traced by the French CGT, the letter asserted, it was vital that the predominance of ideology in the class struggle was reasserted. To ensure this the militants promised "to continue the diffusion of anarchist ideals in the syndicalist movement, with the goal that these ideas are assimilated by the working masses who in their unions and though direct action seek their emancipation... [and] resolutely combat all neutralist, reformist, or statist influences within the labour organisations."

The immediate aim was to combat the syndicalist influence in the unions. However, the long-term aim was the formation of the MOA:

> We anarchists must move towards the foundation of
> our own labour movement. ... We believe that in order
> for our activity as anarchists to be as efficient as possi-
> ble, we must ... organise our groups into a federation
> which will undertake all tasks and initiatives, [and] co-
> ordinate and unify our labour, so as to ensure that our
> work is more fruitful.[35]

The publication of the letter marked a new stage in the conflict between moderates and radicals in Catalonia, with both factions now proposing a clear shift away from the ideological basis of the confederation agreed upon at the Madrid congress in 1919. Either anarchism was to be the guiding force behind the labour movement or it was to be relegated to a role as an outside influence equal to that of other political groups. Following the publication of the letter in *Solidaridad Proletaria*, the CRT decided to suspend publication of the newspaper, an admission that, in Barcelona at least, their campaign in favour of a return to legality did not enjoy overwhelming support.[36]

Nonetheless, the conflict between the syndicalists and the supporters of the MOA continued in the pages of *Acción Social Obrera*, the paper of the confederal unions in San Feliu de Guixols (Catalonia). The main ideologue of the syndicalist position was Joan Peiró, who, as well as putting forward his arguments in the press, published a book, *Trayectoria de la CNT*, in which he summarised the ideas that he had developed in the pages of *Solidaridad Obrera* and *Solidaridad Proletaria* on the ideological and organisational direction that the confederation should follow.

For Peiró, the CNT was a class-based economic organisation with its own 'collective personality' that was independent of, and should not be confused with, that "of political parties and other socio-political schools … including anarchist groups."[37] However, the CNT could not remain apolitical as certain political decisions clearly had an impact on the confederation, a clear example being that the political situation made it impossible for the CNT to act legally. The confederation therefore needed to adopt policies towards those social, economic, and cultural issues that directly affected the functioning of the unions and their members. Just how the confederation's politics would differ from the labour policies of the other political organisations was never clarified, except that they rejected parliamentary and electoral politics in favour of the tactics of direct action.[38]

This preference for direct action was, of course, shared by the anarchists, and Peiró insisted that he remained an anarchist and that, as an anarchist, he would work to maintain the confederation's commitment to libertarian goals. However, he did not feel that it was fair for anarchists to deny the same freedom to those of different political persuasions "as long as they accept the class struggle."[39] The crux of Peiró's argument was the need for the working class to unite and form a force strong enough to take on and defeat capitalism. This required the confederation to adopt a more centralised structure and to attract as many workers as possible to its ranks.[40] As such, the confederation could not be anarchist as this would clearly alienate non-anarchist workers.

Josep Magriñà, one of the main proponents of the MOA in Spain, claimed Peiró's position was "impracticable."[41] The concept of the confederation having its own political opinion would force members to adopt a form of political schizophrenia, whereby in the unions they would support the confederation's policies whilst outside they could support those of any of the working-class or Republican parties. Yet each political group or party had a different view of the role of the unions, and these were reflected in day-to-day, tactical, and organisational policies which were, especially in the case of anarchism and communism, often mutually exclusive. For example, the defined Comintern position on syndicalism was that party members should infiltrate and dominate the unions and undermine all opponents. Besides, Magriñà concluded, the confederation already had a political programme. The Madrid conference had agreed unanimously that the aim of the CNT was libertarian communism, and libertarian ideals should "serve as guide at all times and never be hidden or ignored." Responding to Magriñà's criticism, Peiró accepted that currently the final goal of the CNT was libertarian communism, and the anarchists should act within the confederation to ensure this continued to be the case. However, they should not "deny a possible change in the ideological goal of the CNT."[42] This was exactly what the radical anarchists feared.

The supporters of the MOA were finally able to propagate their ideas openly with the appearance in November 1925 of the weekly newspaper *El Productor*.[43] Heading the editorial group was Manuel Buenacasa, whilst working alongside him were a number of young militants who would play an important role in the anarchist movement in the years to come, including José Alberola, J. Vázquez Piedra, Josep Magriñà, and Miguel Jiménez. In the first edition the newspaper outlined its principal aims: "to propagate the anarchist ideal; to review the performance of the Spanish anarchists in the syndicalist movement in recent years [the result would be highly critical]; and to promote a labour movement that is purely anarchist."[44]

In supporting the MOA, *El Productor* was not proposing that membership in the CNT be open only to anarchist militants but rather that all those workers within the confederation should share the same ultimate aim, the victory of libertarian communism, and that the daily operation of the movement should reflect this aim in both tactics and structure. The newspaper advocated a movement guided by the principles of anarchism and not simply responding to the economic materialism of syndicalism. It advocated supporting strikes on the basis of worker solidarity or as part of revolutionary preparation above those driven by wage demands, although this did not mean that campaigns and strikes for material benefits would not be pursued.[45] Pure syndicalism with its materialistic base was said to not have the ability to create in its members the required strength of purpose to tackle the state.[46] The syndicalists, it was said, had forgotten that the raison d'être of the CNT was to bring about a social revolution. The confederation should therefore serve to instil in its members the revolutionary spirit of anarchism which would prepare them for the struggle ahead and would create a feeling of solidarity based not on a transient factor such as class, itself a product of the capitalist system, but on shared ideas and goals. This would be achieved by maintaining a decentralised and democratic structure, with decisions being made from the bottom upwards, preventing the growth of bureaucracy and elitism which led to members being treated like sheep in a flock and which eventually divested them of their revolutionary élan.[47] In short, *El Productor* proposed the MOA as a means of avoiding the deviation of confederal principles which the newspaper felt the national committee and the CRT of Catalonia were attempting to enforce on the confederation. A practical objection to the policies and tactics of the 'pure' syndicalists had been transformed into an ideological position:

> It would not have been worth the effort of defending
> the idea of an anarchist labour movement in Spain –
> where such a movement has always existed – if some of
> our comrades had not begun combating it.[48]

For *El Productor*, the choice facing the CNT was whether it would continue "its markedly syndicalist direction in spite of its defined ultimate goal, grouping together all tendencies and dogmas without distinguishing between ideas and beliefs, [and] solely on the basis of class interests" or whether it had "a solid ultimate goal of libertarian communism, … a true anarchist orientation" and therefore excluded "obstructionist minorities and opposing and authoritarian tendencies" from its ranks.[49]

Anarchists against the MOA

However, there was an alternative. The supporters of the MOA suffered from a misunderstanding of the basic principles of anarcho-syndicalism which led them to confuse tactics and goals. This point was made by Errico Malatesta, the most respected and – as reading through the main anarchist publications as the time suggests – the most widely published figure in the international anarchist movement at the time. In a letter to *El Productor*, the Italian anarchist pointed out that "a labour movement with anarchist objectives is not the same thing as an anarchist labour movement."[50] *El Productor* seemed to have forgotten that the very reason that the anarchists had become involved in the labour movement was due to "the opportunities it affords for propaganda and preparation for the future – and even this aim is lost if we gather together solely with like-minded people."[51]

The problem facing the anarchists was how to ensure that the labour movement achieved its maximum potential in terms of strength and unity whilst at the same time maintaining a revolutionary spirit. Neither the MOA nor pure syndicalism provided any solution to this. Malatesta had modified his views on syndicalism expressed before the First World War in the light of events since 1917 (see chapter 2). He continued to reject the syndicalist claim that it was sufficient on its own to achieve and protect the social revolution. This was precisely due to its lack of a political stance. According to Malatesta,

> It is idealistic to hope … that politics should be excluded from the unions, since every economic question of some importance automatically becomes a political question, and it is in the political field … that the question of the emancipation of the workers and of human liberty will have to be finally resolved.[52]

Emancipation was a political goal, and syndicalism was a purely economic phenomenon. In fact, syndicalism was innately reformist because, Malatesta argued, it was simply a response to the economic environment created by the capitalist system and would naturally seek a modus vivendi with that system:

> The labour organisation easily becomes an element of
> social conservation, conciliation, and class collabora-
> tion and has a tendency to create a workers' aristocracy
> or bureaucracy ... [whereby] the interests of the or-
> ganisation are put before general interests, the achieve-
> ment of small and immediate advantages are preferred
> to that of future conquests.[53]

This "workers' aristocracy" or élite was formed by practical men,
reformists or even conservatives, who were both eager and willing to
compromise with the representatives of the capitalist society and soon
came to accept positions of responsibility within that society. They
were often members of political parties who viewed the unions as
"recruiting centres" and subordinated the workers' interests to those
of the party.[54] With the reformist socialists and the Bolsheviks having
increasing influence among the unions following the First World War,
Malatesta, although continuing to argue that it was preferable that anarchists did not assume positions of responsibility within the unions,
now accepted that it might occasionally be necessary and even useful
to do so, provided that there was a frequent change in those who held
such positions.[55]

For Malatesta, the overall mission of the anarchists in the labour
movement should be to "prevent the unions from becoming the tools
of the politicians ... preach and practise direct action, decentralisation, autonomy, and free initiative ... [and] strive to help members
learn how to participate directly in the life of the organisation and to
do without leaders and permanent officials."[56]

If the anarchists acted along these lines, Malatesta concluded, they
would maintain their contacts with the working classes and therefore
be involved in any future revolutionary movement, and they would
ensure that the unions did not come under the control of other political forces, either reformist or Bolshevik, whilst at the same time
anarchism would remain a vibrant and active force and not simply an
ideological movement.[57]

A corollary of Malatesta's position was that, if the anarchists hoped
to defend their ideals and maintain the purity of their vision from
the materialism and bureaucracy inherent in their involvement in the

unions, they needed their own independent organisation outside the unions where they could develop and debate their own specific ideas. In Italy the anarchists had formed their own specific organisation, the Unione Communista Anarchica, in April 1919, which in 1920 changed its name to Unione Anarchica Italiana (UAI). Malatesta was the leading figure in the UAI, being responsible for its programme that was adopted at the Bologna congress in 1920. The UAI's position towards the USI was spelt out by Malatesta: "The anarchists do not want to dominate the USI; they would not wish to even if all the workers in its ranks were anarchists, [and] neither do they wish to assume the responsibility for its negotiations. We, who do not seek power, only want the consciences of men; only those whose wish is to dominate prefer sheep, the better to lead them."[58] However, following the First World War leading anarchists such as Armando Borghi were among the most active militants of the USI. The difference between Italy and Spain was the strength of the anarchist movement in the latter was far greater, especially among the working classes, a point that Malatesta freely admitted. However, this did not detract from the basic sense of the Italian's arguments. Even in Spain the anarchists on their own were not strong enough to overthrow the state – a larger organisation was required.

Malatesta's critique of the MOA was endorsed by the Spanish Committee of Anarchist Relations in a manifesto published in the middle of 1924.[59] A further manifesto published at the end of the year seemed to be almost paraphrasing the Italian's views:

> It is vital that syndicalism develops and acts, in relation
> to us, in the same way and with the same indepen-
> dence that we, as an organisation, have in relation to it.
> It is necessary not to confuse an ideal that is eminently
> humane, with an idea that simply relates to class.[60]

The CNT, the manifesto continued, was a class organisation that operated within the economic framework of the capitalist system, and the anarchist organisation was a 'political' organisation that had a wider scope than the limited field of economics. Once more, the manifesto warned anarchists acting within the unions not to forget their ideology as had happened too often in the past, and to act to ensure that the CNT remained a means towards the achievements of their goals. It was this position, and not that of the supporters of the MOA, that triumphed at the national anarchist congress held clandestinely in Barcelona in 1925.[61]

At the end of 1925, the Anarchist Relations Committee of the growing community of exiled Spanish anarchists in France directly criticised the campaign launched by *El Productor* in favour of the MOA:

> This is not a suitable moment for futile discussions about theory. Nor is it the time for splits, for shouting out differences and for setting up a separate organisation. … Let's go where the proletariat is. If it is in the CNT, we will not split from it.[62]

The committee also attacked the syndicalists and stressed that "supporting the CNT does not mean following the path towards reformism along which some wish to lead the masses; as anarchists our role in the unions must be to denounce … all attempts at exploiting the credulity of the masses." The anarchists' place was in the unions, where they should seek to ensure that the confederation did not lose sight of its ultimate goal: the achievement of libertarian communism. So, despite the importance of the debates within Catalonia, the two national-based anarchist committees had both rejected the MOA. Meanwhile, a number of leading anarchists in Spain, including Mauro Bajatierra and Vicente Ballester, as well as the short-lived anarchist newspaper *Prometeo*, also rejected the MOA.[63]

Syndicalist Shortcomings Exposed

Despite the predominantly negative reaction to its campaign in favour of the MOA, *El Productor* did provide a platform for all those opposed to the syndicalists. Spurned by the criticism of *El Productor*, the syndicalists responded by launching a new weekly newspaper, *Vida Sindical*, in January 1926. The paper was not a great success, and its appearance was surrounded by controversy.[64] The local federation of Barcelona censored the editors of the paper, specifically Pestaña, Peiró,

Abella, and Arnó, for having written a letter to the government pleading for their release from prison. Suspicions were raised when five days later the authors of the letter were released, and the first edition of the newspaper appeared weeks later.[65] It would later be claimed that *Vida Sindical* and its campaign for the legalisation of the CNT were tacitly supported by the dictatorship.[66]

Certainly the main aim of *Vida Sindical* was to advocate the legalisation and the parallel reorganisation of the confederation. A manifesto in the first edition of the newspaper signed by twenty-two militants, including Peiró, Pestaña, Abella, and Arnó, promised to continue along the path which had already been traced by *Solidaridad Proletaria*. If anything, this path was now unashamedly syndicalist and more opposed to the influence of anarchism in the unions than ever.[67] The newspaper asserted that the CNT had never actually been a class organisation and had instead been "the heritage of one school: the anarchist school." This had resulted in the juxtaposition and confusion of party interests with class and union interests, the predomination of abstract ideas and short-termism, and a lack of "personal, class and union responsibility." Thus, what was needed was "the establishment of syndical independence."[68]

The admission that the CNT had never been a class-based organisation represented a complete about-turn on the syndicalists' part and a tacit admission that their position represented a deviation from the previous norm. It is not entirely clear why the syndicalists would now admit this, but one possibility is that they wanted to distance themselves as much as possible from the radicals in order to attract more moderate unions to the planned reorganisation of the confederation. This reorganisation in effect would have split the confederation in two as it was to be based solely upon the pro-syndicalist factions, and radical organisations such as the local federation in Barcelona were to be excluded.[69] Although Pestaña directed events from Barcelona, the centre of the reorganised confederation was to be in Galicia where the regional confederation was tolerated, although the more radical unions in the region were not. The syndicalists had planned to celebrate a national conference in Galicia in early 1926 at which a provisional national committee would be elected. However, following the intervention of the under-secretary of the Ministry of the Interior,

Martínez Anido, the conference was banned and the regional confederation in Asturias, which, besides the Galician CRT, was the only
regional organisation tolerated by the authorities, took responsibility
for electing a provisional committee.[70] The campaign in favour of legality came to an abrupt end when a new wave a repression in March
1926 forced the closure of both *El Productor* and *Vida Sindical* and
a number of leading militants were arrested.[71] The syndicalists' campaign depended on the authorities accepting their request to be allowed to operate legally, and the government's refusal to permit them
this liberty would continue to weaken their position and at the same
time would eventually force elements within the syndicalist faction to
advocate increasingly reformist positions.

The government's intervention introduced a temporary pause in
the continuing conflict between the two factions in Catalonia. The
ideological conflict was renewed in late 1927 when a further attempt
at reorganising the confederation was launched with the collaboration
of the newly formed Federación Anarquista Ibérica (Iberian Anarchist
Federation). Meanwhile, in the period between March 1926 and the
relaunch, the confederation's activity within Spain itself was minimal,
and in areas such as Catalonia, Aragón, Valencia, and Andalusia was
effectively nonexistent. Due to the repression in Spain, increasing
numbers of militants sought refuge in France. The relative freedom
enjoyed by the exiles allowed them to form their own national anarchist organisation, celebrate rallies in favour of the victims of persecution at home, and publish newspapers propagating their ideas.
Contacts with their French comrades would inevitably have an effect
on the Spanish anarchists, if only to demonstrate what could happen to the anarchist movement if it lost contact with the unions. The
proponents of the MOA had argued that if anarchism as a dominant
ideological force was excluded from the unions it would be reduced to
little more than an intellectual discipline, and in the French anarchist
movement they would find evidence to back their opinion.

7.

EXILE IN FRANCE: INTERNATIONAL SOLIDARITY AND NATIONAL DISUNITY

FOLLOWING THE PRONUNCIAMENTO OF SEPTEMBER 1923 AND THE subsequent ban on the CNT in May 1924, a number of anarchists were forced to seek refuge across the border in France. Each new wave of repression resulted in a further exodus and some of the most prominent confederal figures were compelled to spend some time north of the Pyrenees.[1] France had been the favourite destination for militants fleeing repression in Spain since the initial ban on the confederation in 1911. In the years that followed, a number of locally based anarchist groups enjoyed a brief existence. However, it was not until the prolonged period of exile during the Primo De Rivera dictatorship that the exiled movement finally took on a less transitory appearance. Eventually the Spanish exiles formed both an anarchist federation, the Federación de Grupos Anarquistas de Lengua Español en Francia (the Federation of Spanish-Speaking Anarchist Groups in France, FGALEF), and a syndicalist organisation, the Cuadros Sindicales (Syndicalist Cadres). However, due to internal disputes and the increasingly vigilant and repressive policies of the French authorities, the activity of the two organisations was severely limited. The influence of the exiles on their comrades in Spain was more symbolic than real. The FGALEF and the Cuadros provided hope for the future at a time when, in Spain, the CNT had all but ceased to exist and the Committee of Anarchist Relations found it impossible to function. The FGALEF played a role, although not a leading one, in the formation of the Federación Anarquista Ibérica in 1927, whilst the policy of grouping together militants within a 'host' organisation put forward by the Cuadros Sindicales, in their case the Confédération Génerale du Travail Sindicaliste Revolutionnaire (CGTSR), was later adopted by the CNT in 1929.

For the exiled anarchists there were clear lessons to be learnt from their experience in France. The pitifully weak state of the independent revolutionary syndicalist movement in the country was in large part caused by its almost total abandonment by the decadent and divided French anarchists, whilst the decline in the anarchist movement itself resulted from its failure to wrest control of the CGTU from the communists and its inability to put forward a viable alternative organisation. However, although the exiles found both the French anarchist and syndicalist movements a large disappointment, their stay in France did provide the opportunity to make contact with exiled militants from other countries forced to flee repression at home. Due to the mass exodus from eastern and southern Europe during the 1920s, Paris became the centre of the international anarchist movement. The conglomeration of exiles in Paris prompted the IWMA to promote, in a spirit of international solidarity, the formation of an emigration committee, bringing together militants from Spain, Italy, Portugal, and France, which in turn forced the French revolutionary syndicalists to finally form their own organisation (the CGTSR).

Given the duration of their enforced emigration, it is surprising that there has been so little research carried out on the Spanish exiles.[2] Again the main secondary works are those by Elorza, Gómez Casas, and Paz. Gómez Casas only briefly covers the period, whilst Paz naturally focuses on Durruti and the campaign against his deportation.[3] Elorza's extensive work once more provides the greatest detail, but his focus is more on events in Spain and the formation of the FAI. The role of the IWMA and the exiles' contacts with international groups are scarcely mentioned. There is no secondary source on the exiled movement in France before the Primo de Rivera dictatorship.

Libertarian Exiles in France before November 1924

Spanish labour had always migrated in search of work, either to northern Europe or to Latin America. Alongside the economic migrants were leading union or political figures forced to escape the periodic waves of repression that were a feature of Spanish politics in the late nineteenth century and early twentieth century. Due to its geographical proximity and the more favourable employment prospects it offered, France was the most popular destination. Although the exiled movement in France only came to prominence during the Primo dictatorship, confederation militants had been active in the country right from the initial ban of 1911. Before to the First World War, the main centre of exiled Spanish anarchists was Marseilles, where Suárez Duque (who attended the 1913 London Revolutionary Syndicalist Congress with CNT secretary Jose Negre, who was himself exiled in Paris at the time), Eusebio Carbó, and Hilario Arlandis were active prior to and during the war.[4] As well as Marseilles, there were groups of Spanish anarchists in Bordeaux, Perpignan, and Lyon, whilst during the war a Spanish Language Libertarian Federation was established in Paris.[5]

Marseilles remained the centre of activity during the Bolshevik Triennial in Spain from 1917 to 1919. In late 1919, the Employers' Federation of Barcelona complained to the Spanish authorities about the existence of an anarchist association in Marseilles that was acting as a liaison between the French anarchists and the syndicalists in

Barcelona. Correspondence was apparently carried by sailors between the two ports, with David Rey, a prominent figure in the Catalan CRT, responsible for maintaining contacts.[6] In May 1920, a rally in the city held in protest against the repression in Spain attracted a crowd of about a thousand.[7] As the repression in Spain intensified from 1920 onwards, the numbers of exiles also increased.[8] The result was that libertarian influence spread from Marseilles to other areas with a large population of Spanish labourers.[9]

By now Paris was replacing Marseilles as the centre of exile activity. A Federación Comunista-Anarquista de Lengua Española (Spanish-speaking Anarcho-Communist Federation) was formed in Paris in 1919.[10] The federation was in contact with the Groupe International de Diffusion (International Distribution Group), also based in Paris, which made copies of their domestic anarchist and syndicalist press available to exiled militants from diverse countries.[11] The federation does not appear to have enjoyed a long life, its final press release being a call to a meeting in May 1920 which also criticised the apathy of militants.[12]

Meanwhile, an exiled syndicalist organisation, the Organisation Corporative des Ouvriers Espagnols Résidant en France (Corporate Organisation of Spanish Workers Resident in France) had been established in August 1917. Initially heavily influenced by the socialist syndicalist Fabra Ribas, the organisation soon split into two factions: one socialist and the other revolutionary syndicalist. Towards the beginning of 1920, the revolutionary syndicalists broke away to form the Intersyndicale Ouvrière de Langue Espagnole en France (IOE).[13] The IOE was not a large organisation, and meetings generally attracted between one to three hundred people. No membership lists were kept, for reasons of secrecy, but according to police reports there were probably only thirty or so full-time members. The Catalan militant Bruno Lladó was the initial secretary of the IOE, being replaced by Wilkens (Jaime Salan) in late 1921, probably because Lladó was in Russia.[14] The IOE never achieved its main aim of grouping together all Spanish workers affiliated with the French CGT but was nonetheless successful in organising fund-raising events and publishing information about events in Spain and CNT manifestos. It also played an important role in informing the movement in Spain of the activities of the CNT delegation to the inaugural congress of the RTUI (see chapter 2).[15] The Intersyndicale was eventually dissolved following the expulsion from France of its leading militants.[16]

Despite this setback, anarchist activity continued to grow throughout 1923 and early 1924. In mid-1923 the anarchist group El Fructidor in Paris began publication of a pamphlet-cum-newspaper, *El Sembrador*, which appeared periodically.[17] Spanish anarchist groups based in France held in a congress in Lyon in early 1924 which agreed to the formation of a Committee of Anarchist Relations (for exiled militants) in Paris.[18] Following the Lyon congress, the new committee published a manifesto in *Liberion*, the continuation of *El Sembrador*, in which it stated its support for the positions adopted by Malatesta and the Russian anarcho-syndicalist Schapiro (both of whom opposed the MOA) towards syndicalism. More significantly, the new committee proposed the creation of an independent anarchist organisation as the best means of preparing for the revolutionary overthrow of the dictatorship.[19]

Alongside the anarchist committee in July 1924, exiled anarchists and syndicalists affiliated with the Construction Workers' Union in the French capital formed the League of Militants of the CNT in Paris.[20] The league published its first manifesto in *Iberion* (which replaced *Liberion* in June 1924), in which they called on all Spanish workers living in France to form 'leagues' that would maintain the moral and ethical strength of the CNT among the exiles and ensure that they play their part in bringing the dictatorship in Spain to an abrupt end.[21] The league's main goal was to raise funds for a possible rising against the dictatorship, the predominant preoccupation throughout 1924 for both the exiles and the remnants of the confederation in Spain.[22] As the rising failed to materialise, the league was dissolved at a meeting on September 14, 1924 to be replaced, according to a police report, by the Committee of Anarchist Relations of Paris. The report is probably referring to the Revolutionary Anarchist Committee that was established at about this time, given that the Committee of Relations already existed.[23] Not all members of the league were happy with the decision to disband, and the committee and the league existed side by side for a number of months.[24]

Both the committee and the league were involved in the failed rising of November 1924 (see chapter 6). A meeting of militants on November 19, 1924, agreed to reform the committee in order to replace those members now in Spain.[25] Although the overthrow of the dictatorship remained their main goal, the failure of the November rising forced the exiles to take stock and prepare for a longer period of exile than they had at first expected. They also had to take on more responsibility due to the difficulties faced by their comrades in Spain. At the national anarchist congress held clandestinely in Barcelona in April 1925, it was decided that, given the repression the movement faced in Spain following the failed uprising of the previous year, the Committee of Anarchist Relations would become an executive commission and be transferred to France. A secretariat of national and international relations would remain in Spain and be attached to the Catalan regional committee.[26]

Organising in Exile: The FGALEF and the Cuadros Sindicales

The lack of coordination evident during the failed rising of November 1924 showed the need to improve the existing ties between the exiles. One of the main themes discussed at the congress of Spanish-speaking anarchist groups based in France, held in Lyon on June 14–15, 1925, was the creation of a national organisation for the exiles in France.[27] In the debates over the structure of any such organisation, some delegates argued in favour of the system adopted by the Unaio Anarquista Portuguesa (UAP), in which affinity groups were able to affiliate directly with the union alongside the regional federations rather than adopt the more classically federalist structure of the Union Anarchiste Francaise (UAF), in which affiliation to the national organisation came via its regional components. However, others claimed this was too complicated given that any organisation based in France would be, so it was hoped, only temporary.[28] The congress decided that the acceptance of an overall organisational structure demonstrated a lack of faith in the prospects for an imminent revolution in Spain. Therefore, in the end it was agreed that federations would be formed wherever there were sufficient numbers and that these would elect a delegate, who would be in contact with the Committee of Relations which was to reside in Paris. Organisation thus remained at a local or regional basis and no national federation was created. In general, the congress was not a great success and was characterised by violent disagreements between delegates, predominantly in relation to the means to bring about the revolution in Spain.[29]

Beside the internal divisions in France, the exiles could not help becoming embroiled in the disputes in Spain. The Committee of Anarchist Relations issued a manifesto in late 1925 critical of both the MOA and pure syndicalism. Although the committee lamented that anarchism had never been so absent from the confederation, it argued that the anarchists should stay in and support the CNT. Their role in the unions was to propagate their ideals and not to impose them, a scarcely veiled reference to the proposed MOA.[30] This may have been one of the causes for the deterioration in relations between the Committee of Anarchist Relations in Paris and the regional committee in Catalonia. At a general assembly, which probably took place in late 1925, the Catalan committee decided that the national committee should return to Barcelona from Paris because, they claimed, the Paris committee had not fulfilled certain commitments incumbent upon it and had failed to meet a delegation sent from Spain to discuss its performance.[31]

Disagreements and disunity were constant themes in the exile movement, a point accepted by the Committee of Anarchist Relations in France in the invitation to their next congress, due to be held in Marseilles in May 1926. It spoke of the need to give "a more important character to the movement," to put an end to the quarrels and begin a constructive stage.[32] The congress, held in Marseilles May 13–16, made a number of important decisions, not only in relation to the exiles in France but also to the movement in Spain.[33] Regarding organisational issues, the congress confirmed the transfer of the Committee of Anarchist Relations back to Barcelona, finally officially founded the Federación de Grupos Anarquista de Lengua Española en Francia (FGALEF), and prepared the basis for the formation of an Iberian Anarchist Federation.[34] The newspaper *Tiempos Nuevos* became the new federation's mouthpiece.

The national committee of the CNT addressed a letter to the congress in which it stated its desire to reestablish contacts with the international revolutionary syndicalist movement and improve contacts with their comrades in France as a mean to escape the difficulties they faced at home. By now, exiled confederal militants in France had made significant progress in developing relations with other exiled movements in France. In fact, among those who attended the Marseilles congress were Armando Borghi, representing both the IWMA and the USI in exile, and Manuel de Sousa of the Portuguese CGT (CGTP). They had both come directly from a special conference of the administrative bureau of the IWMA held in Paris May 8–12, at which an action committee containing delegates from the CNT, the USI, the CGTP, the Polish anarcho-syndicalists, and the French Union Fédérative des Syndicats Autonomes (UFSA) had been set up. The main objective of the committee was to transmit the propaganda of the IWMA to the masses of exiled militants in France.[35] The Marseilles congress gave its support to the formation of the committee.[36]

The action committee was simply another name for the emigration committee, which had been formed by exiled militants from the CNT, the USI, and the CGTP in May 1926 in order to represent members who were affiliated with the UFSA.[37] The UFSA was a loose association of predominantly small unions that had been formed at a congress in November 1924 by revolutionary syndicalists opposed to the CGTU's pro-communist position. The UFSA still hoped to reunite the French working classes, already split between the reformist CGT and the communist CGTU, around the apolitical principles of the Charter of Amiens. Despite its commitment to revolutionary syndicalism, the UFSA refused to join the IWMA, as some members felt it was dominated by anarchists and therefore not apolitical.[38] This brought strong criticism from the member organisations of the IWMA, a number of whose representatives had met with the UFSA secretary, Pierre Besnard, following the IWMA's Amsterdam congress in 1925. They voiced their "evident discord" with the French revolutionary syndicalists. Undeterred, the second UFSA congress, held in Saint-Ouen in June 1925, again ratified its commitment to autonomy and independence at a national and international level.[39]

However, the meeting of the national committee of the UFSA on June 27, 1926, which gave its blessing to the formation of the emigration committee, also accepted that the new committee created "a larger problem." The emigration committee functioned under the direction of the IWMA, yet the UFSA and a number of its member organisations were also represented in the committee.[40] The UFSA was now a member of an international committee but not of the international body that presided over it. The national committee of the UFSA argued that this anomaly could not continue.[41]

At the UFSA's third congress, held in Lyon on November 15–16, the Confédération Générale du Travail Syndicaliste Révolutionnaire (CGTSR) was founded and immediately affiliated with the IWMA.[42] The attachment of the words 'revolutionary syndicalist' was meant to demonstrate that the CGTSR was continuing the legacy of the prewar CGT. However, the French syndicalists had finally accepted that their naive commitment to apoliticism was simply no longer viable. This was reflected in the adoption at its inaugural congress of the Charter of Lyon as an updated version of the Charter of Amiens. The new charter mirrored that of the IWMA by rejecting political neutrality in favour of an overtly antipolitical stance. This put ideological distance between the new confederation and the CGT and CGTU. However, in general, the CGTSR was ideologically at odds with its own reality. This was most clearly demonstrated by Pierre Besnard, its foremost spokesperson, who championed a form of industrial unionism based on national federations of labour, as opposed to small craft unions, despite the fact that the majority of members of the CGTSR were precisely such small, localised craft unions.[43]

The CGTSR was never a force to be reckoned with in France, having a membership of probably no more than five thousand.[44] Many unions of the already minuscule UFSA remained outside the CGTSR, as they opposed its membership in the 'anarchist' IWMA, whilst others, although sympathetic towards anarchism, had long since decided to stay within the CGT and the CGTU and saw no reason to change their allegiance.[45] The weakness of the CGTSR reflected the divided and disorganised nature of French anarcho-syndicalism and its almost complete isolation from the class struggle in the country, especially when compared to the anarchists in Spain. In fact, the creation of the CGTSR itself owed far more to the action of Spanish and Italian exiles and the IWMA than to the French revolutionary syndicalists.[46]

The most immediate impact of the formation of the CGTSR was upon the exiled militants in France. An early report by the emigration committee stated that, in its first two months, it had produced two tracts, one in French and the other in Italian, and was preparing a third in Polish. The apparent lack of activity by the Spanish section of the committee did not reflect its relative weakness, rather the opposite.[47] Indeed, such was the relative strength of the Spanish contingent within the CGTSR that leading militants argued that they could not be adequately represented by the committee and a further organisation was needed.[48] Therefore, following two meetings and in agreement with the emigration committee, a number of exiled CNT militants launched a manifesto in favour of the creation of the Cuadros Sindicales (syndicalist cadres of CNT militants) of Spanish workers in France.[49] The aim was to join together the thousands of ex-CNT militants exiled in France in groups that would be affiliated with the CGTSR. The Cuadros would remain loyal to the ideological heritage of the CNT, which the manifesto defined as "[not] anarchist – since if it were, all of its components would have to be so too – [yet] represent[ing] a labour movement completely addicted to anarchism and every day more inclined to support its efforts."[50]

The Cuadros were to be anarcho-syndicalist in nature and did not correspond to the ideological divisions in Catalonia. The use of the past tense in the manifesto when referring to the CNT reflected the complete lack of contact between exiled militants in France and the confederation. The militants assumed that the CNT no longer existed: "What remains today of our glorious organisation? … scarcely anything but a memory of what it once was."[51] It was hoped that the Cuadros would act as a spur to the reorganisation of the CNT, setting an example as to how the confederation might overcome its present difficulties by forming Cuadros in those labour organisations still tolerated in Spain.[52] The Cuadros would also keep alive the memory of the confederation among the exiles in France, preparing them for when they would be able to return to Spain, whilst in the meantime strengthening the ranks of the CGTSR and the IWMA.

Among the twenty-one signatories of the manifesto was Eusebio Carbó, previously the CNT's representative in France. However, the secretary of the Cuadros was Bruno Carreras, a former member of the northern CRT, who now became the CNT's representative in France.[53] By September, there were Cuadros Sindicales in twelve different regions – a figure that would eventually rise to twenty-eight. Although the number in each group was never stated, it is possible that they represented several hundred militants.[54] The creation of the Cuadros Sindicales was not warmly welcomed by all sections of the CGTSR, as some French unions suspected that the Cuadros were simply interested in Spanish affairs and would not act in the interest of the confederation in France. At a meeting of the confederal national committee called in August 1927 to discuss the issue, it was agreed that revolutionary syndicalism was an international movement and, as such, both French and Spanish members of the CGTSR had the same rights, but all members needed to accept the obligations that came with membership. That is, the Spanish sections would have to respect the decisions of the CGTSR leadership. In acknowledgment of the importance of the Spanish membership, a representative of the Cuadros was appointed to the national committee of the CGTSR, and potential conflict with the French leadership of the CGTSR was thus avoided whilst the relative strength of the Spanish within the confederation was recognised.[55]

The reaction of the FGALEF to the Cuadros was overwhelmingly negative. At a meeting of the Seine region of the FGALEF, held in Paris on February 6, 1928, to discuss the federation's forthcoming second congress, the majority of those gathered felt there was neither a role nor a reason for the existence of the Cuadros in France.[56] Carreras explained the aims of the Cuadros Sindicales at the congress of the FGALEF in Lyon February 18–19, 1928, but to no avail. After a brief discussion, almost all of those present showed themselves to be "convinced of the uselessness" of the Cuadros. The goals of the Cuadros could, the congress agreed, "be achieved by the anarchist groups since their economic goals are similar." Nonetheless, as the federation judged that the Cuadros were not "harmful to libertarian relations," it would "maintain harmonious relations" with them.[57] The FGALEF supported the entry of their militants into the CGTSR but felt that the federation and not the Cuadros should be responsible for the ideological preparation of militants. The majority of members of the FGALEF were anarcho-syndicalists, and, given that the CGTSR

and the emigration committee brought the Spanish militants together, they saw no need for any further organisation.[58] They believed that
if the workers shared their goals or wished to learn about anarchism,
then their place was in the federation.

Despite the commitment to work harmoniously with the Cuadros,
the FGALEF reaction clearly weakened the project and created a further division among the exiles. It was only following the fall of the
Primo de Rivera dictatorship that signs emerged of a possible future
relationship between the federation and the Cuadros when a general
assembly of the Seine federation on February 9, 1930, was informed
of the decision made by the FGALEF to establish "an entente" with
the Cuadros in order to intensify the production and release of propaganda in the light of events in Spain.[59] Nonetheless, in general the
exiled movement had been characterised by disunity – a fact readily
admitted by the Committee of Anarchist Relations in a manifesto in
April 1930: "The sad and lamentable spectacle that our disintegrated,
sterile, and impotent organisation offers due to its lack of cohesion
must act as a spur for us to escape from the morass in which we find
ourselves, as soon as possible."[60]

Alongside the problems caused by constant infighting, the exile
movement also increasingly fell victim to police vigilance and repression. In reality, the French authorities had never been lenient towards
the exiled militants: the leading figures of the Intersyndicale had
been expelled by 1923; the newspaper *Liberion* had been forced to
change its name to *Iberion*; the editor of *Tiempos Nuevos*, Valeriano
Orobón Fernández, had been expelled in 1925. However, from late
1926 onwards, there was a noticeable increase in crackdown on the
activities of the exiles, following police claims that they had uncov-
ered a suspected plot to assassinate the king of Spain whilst he was
visiting France in June.[61] The introduction of Ministerial Circular
100 in June 1927, which forbade exiles from involving themselves in
political activity, along with the introduction of a number of other
measures, put an end to any hopes FGALEF leaders had of running
an effective organisation. The federation remained permanently in
an embryonic state, with reorganisation a constant theme of discussion.[62] The federation's committee moved from Marseilles to Paris
and then on to Lyon during this period, giving further evidence of

a certain lack of stability. In September, the federation's newspaper, *Tiempos Nuevos*, was closed down for "reasons of state," and attempts to replace it with Spanish versions of French anarchist papers, firstly *El Libertario*, a Spanish supplement of *Le Libertaire*, and then *la Voz Libertaria*, a version of *La Voix Libertaire*, both failed due to the reaction of the authorities.[63] An order for the expulsion of the FGALEF's secretary, Juan Molina, was issued in July 1927, and he was forced to go to Belgium. The repression faced by the federation was such that, when the French Union Anarchiste Communiste decided to publish appeals in favour of the abolition of the law on 'administrative expulsions', the Spanish Federation of the Seine refused to do so in Spanish as this would attract the attention of the police.[64] For the same reason, the Federation eventually decided against publishing a paper clandestinely in France and instead opted to move the editorial team to Belgium where *la Voz Libertaria* renewed publication at the end of 1929.[65] By now, the FGALEF had little influence on events in Spain, especially following the fall of Primo de Rivera in January 1930, after which members began returning home.[66] By the time the Republic was proclaimed in April 1931, the majority of exiles had returned to Spain, although large groups remained in Lyon, Beziers, Toulouse, Paris, and Bordeaux, which was now the seat of the Committee of Relations of the French section.[67]

In reality, the exiled movement had never had a great impact on events in Spain. Repression and disunity in France meant that long before many of its militants were forced across the border to Belgium, the focus of anarchist activity had returned to Spain. The Committee of Anarchist Relations had returned to Barcelona at the end of 1925. An independent anarchist organisation for Spanish and Portuguese militants, the Federación Anarquista Ibérica had been established in 1927 at a clandestine meeting in Valencia, and, from 1928, FAI and CNT militants in Spain had begun the process of reorganising the confederation.

International Contacts

The experience of the exiles in France was not completely negative. They were able to see at first hand the rapid decline in French anarchism as well as make contact with exiled militants from other countries in which anarchists had found themselves victims of state oppression – in particular Italy, Portugal, and Russia. Throughout their period of exile the Spanish anarchists enjoyed a close relationship with the Paris-based newspaper *Le Libertaire*, whose principal director was Sébastien Faure, the senior ideologue of French anarchism.

Although originally suspicious of anarcho-syndicalism, Faure had come to accept it in the later years of the first decade of the twentieth century although he was more an anarcho-communist than anarcho-syndicalist. He had also been a close friend of Francesc Ferrer i Guardía and, like him, a proponent of rationalist education. Faure was the principal figure of the French anarchist movement at this time, being the only one of his compatriots following the First World War (in which Jean Grave had tarnished his reputation by supporting an Allied victory) to enjoy truly international prestige. The contact address of *El Sembrador* was that of the *Le Libertaire*, whilst *Iberion* was published at 14 Rue Petit (as probably was *Liberion*), the seat of the Oeuvre Internationale des Editions Anarchiste, an organisation set up under the guidance of the French anarchist Fernandel Severin following a proposal by Faure. The OIEA was established in July 1924 with the specific aim of reproducing and translating into all languages works by prominent anarchists. It operated from the International Bookshop in Paris, which quickly became a rendezvous point for exiled anarchists, in particular those from Spain. Among the original correspondents for the OIEA were two Spaniards, Leandro Olmedo and Juan Bueno. Later collaborators would include Pedro Orobón Fernández and the Italian anarchist Luigi Fabbri.[68] The Spanish and French anarchists also worked side by side when in late 1924 *La Revue Anarchiste*, with which Faure was closely associated, was closed down and replaced by *La Revue Internationale Anarchiste*, a monthly review with sections in French, Italian (*La Rivista Internazionale Anarchica*) and Spanish (*La Revista Internacional Anarquista*). *La Revista* and its successor publication *Acción* were predominantly concerned with ideological and not organisational issues.

The close ties with Faure and *Le Libertaire* were not always reflected in the relations between the Spanish anarchists and the overall anarchist movement in France. With the exception of Faure and his associates, the Spanish were less than impressed by the French anarchists. The disunity and internecine squabbles, the predominance of individualist anarchism, the detachment from the class struggle, and the general feeling that the majority of their French comrades were aloof and uninterested in the day-to-day struggle were all sources of great irritation for the Spanish exiles. In the words of Sebastià Clarà, "It is indisputable that the French anarchist movement is different from those of the other Latin countries. The French anarchist is almost always of an eclectic nature and seldom a revolutionary, which makes one assume that he is only interested in social struggles as an intellectual exercise and distances himself from them when the struggle becomes a reality."[69]

The French anarchists had nothing to teach their Spanish counterparts except the dangers that losing contact with the syndicalist movement could bring. Of course, much of the exiles' exasperation resulted from cultural and linguistic differences as well as their own impotence in the face of the dictatorship at home, but this should not detract from the pathetic spectacle that the French anarchist movement provided.[70] There were occasional triumphs, such as the campaign against the deportation of three Spanish militants, Durruti, Ascaso, and Gregorio Jover to Spain, which began in 1926 and culminated a year later with their release.[71] This successful campaign motivated thousands of workers to protest against the French and Spanish governments and, occurring at the same time as the formation of the CGTSR, raised hopes that French anarchism might finally be recovering after years of decline. However, ideological divisions and personal jealousies quickly resurfaced.

A foretaste of the problems that were to come was provided at the UAF's Orleans congress, held on July 12–14, 1926. Two exiled Russian anarchists, Volin (V. M. Eikhenbaum) and Nestor Makhno, attended the congress and asked to be allowed to join the union, promising to bring a number of valuable members. Clearly seeing the benefits of being associated with the two former Russian revolutionaries (Makhno had led the revolution in Ukraine, where his forces had defeated the white army in Russia before being defeated by Trotsky's red army), the UAF was only too pleased to welcome its new recruits.[72] Makhno was a member of the anarchist group Dielo

Trouda (Workers' Cause), made up of exiled Russian and Polish exiles, which in June 1926 had published a blueprint for the future of the anarchist movement in a booklet entitled *The Organisational Platform of the General Union of Anarchists*. The Platform was a considered response to the failings of the anarchists in Russia during and following the October Revolution when the sectionalism and confusion of many libertarians, the Russian exiles contended, had led them into the hands of the Bolsheviks. To avoid a repetition of this, the Platform proposed that the anarchists create a potent organisation, unified around a rigid programme. It asserted:

> [The] contradiction between the positive and incontestable substance of libertarian ideas, and the miserable state in which the anarchist movement vegetates, has its explanation in a number of causes, of which the most important, the principal, is the absence of organisational principles and practices in the anarchist movement. ... It is time for anarchism to leave the swamp of disorganisation, to put an end to endless vacillations on the most important tactical and theoretical questions, to resolutely move towards a clearly recognisable goal, and to operate an organised collective practice.[73]

The only means of overcoming the lack of unity was through the acceptance of the principle of collective responsibility and the creation of a General Union of Anarchists that would be based on "precise positions; theoretical, tactical and organisational ... the more or less perfect base of a homogenous programme."

Makhno outlined the basic ideas of the Platform at the Orleans congress, explaining that the main reason for the failure of the anarchists during the Russian revolution was their lack of organisation. The Platform immediately gained support from a number of French anarchists and further widened the divisions between individual and communist anarchists in the country. The former were heavily criticised by the authors of the Platform for being self-serving and maintaining the anarchist movement in a state of disunity. The anarcho-communists, due to their propensity for organisation, supported the

Russians' programme. The Orleans congress avoided a split by making certain concessions towards the Platformists. However, through the course of the following year the Platform became increasingly popular, and at the Paris congress of October 30–November 1, 1927, the Platformists gained control of the UAF, changing its name to the Union Anarchiste Communiste Révolutionnaire (UACR) to reflect the changes made to its statutes and rules in order to incorporate the principles of the Platform.

Having launched their programme, the Platformists sought to gain international support. They organised an international conference that was held on February 12, 1927 in Paris. This conference was simply a preliminary meeting, having as its stated aim the creation of a committee that would assume the task of organising an international anarchist congress to discuss the Platform. Among those who attended were Orobón Fernández (probably Pedro, brother of Valeriano), Eusebio Carbó, and Agustín Gibanel.[74] Carbó argued that, as the majority of those present were individualists and not representatives of organisations, it would not be proper for them to nominate such a committee. He also criticised the concept of basing an anarchist International on one strict programme as in his opinion it was "impossible to build an Anarchist Union based on a chapel."[75] Nonetheless, a three-man committee was set up to organise an international congress to discuss the Platform.[76]

The international congress was held in Bourg-la-Reine, Paris, on March 20, 1927 with Orobón Fernández and Gibanel again attending, alongside Bruno Carreras, who replaced Carbó. Other delegates came from France, Russia, Poland, Bulgaria, China, and Italy.[77] The Russians put forward five points to be discussed at the meeting:

1. recognition of the class struggle as the most important factor of the anarchist system;
2. recognition of anarcho-communism as the basis of the movement;
3. recognition of syndicalism as one of the principal methods of anarcho-communist struggle;
4. the necessity of a 'General Union of Anarchists' based on ideological and tactical unity and collective

> responsibility; and
> 5. the necessity of a positive programme to realise the
>   social revolution.

Luigi Fabbri immediately objected to the first proposal and suggested that it should instead be changed to "recognition of the struggle of all oppressed and exploited against state and capitalist authority as the most important factor of the anarchist system." In fact, the Italian delegation, supported by the Spanish and the French delegates, put forward a complete modification of the Russian proposals. The first point was to be modified as Fabbri proposed, the second could be accepted as it stood, and the rest were modified as follows: 3.) recognition of the labour and union struggle as one of the most important means of anarchist revolutionary action; 4.) necessity in each country of as general as possible a Union of Anarchists who have the same goal and tactics, as well as collective responsibility; and 5.) necessity of a positive programme of action for the anarchists in the social revolution.

The modifications represented a recognition of the rich diversity of the anarchist movement both ideologically and tactically and an acceptance of the need for greater coordination between national groups. As the discussion on these points was about to begin, however, police broke up proceedings and arrested all those present.

A new set of proposals for discussion was sent out by the provisional committee in April. However, these took no account of the discussion in March and simply repeated the original proposals by the committee at the March congress. This led the Italians to reject the project, as they felt that it was "in spirit very different to that of the UAI." The Italian rejection was followed by others, and, according to Ugo Fedeli, "the idea of creating an Anarchist International based on the principles of the Platform remained as nothing but an idea," and there were no further contacts between international organisations over the issue. Carbó's comments and the overall support the Spanish gave to Fabbri's objections suggest that the Spanish rejected the Russians' proposals for the same reasons as their Italian colleague. Italian anarchism already had a certain organizational unity, as well as an ideological clarity and tolerance largely thanks to the influence of Malatesta and Fabbri. Their ideas also had, as we have seen, great influence in Spain.

Although the Platform enjoyed a modicum of support among the Spanish exiles, especially from the review *Prismas* and, on an individual basis, Agustín Gibanel, the editor of *Tiempos Nuevos*, it scarcely had any impact in Spain.[78] The paucity of support may seem surprising, given the commitment to the achievement of anarcho-communism through the medium of the unions. However, the concentration on the class struggle above all else and the concomitant reductionism of the heterogeneous nature of anarchism into one limited programme found no echo from the proponents of pure syndicalism, anarcho-syndicalism, or the MOA.

The reasons for the rejection of the Platform in Spain were succinctly summarised by Miguel Jiménez, who was not only one of the principal proponents of the MOA but also the secretary of the National Spanish Committee of Anarchist Relations and a founder member of the newly formed FAI. Jiménez avoided delving too deeply into criticisms of the overtly Marxist nature of certain parts of the Platform, simply alluding to Santillán's criticism in *La Protesta* that had done so and noting that the Russians were not the only group guilty of allowing Marxism to infiltrate their ideas, a joust clearly aimed at the syndicalists.[79] Jiménez accepted that the Platform was a laudable attempt to try to solve the eternal problem of disunity within anarchist ranks but felt that the Russians' programme was critically flawed. The Platform was based around a mistaken premise about the nature of the tendencies within the anarchist movement: it divided anarchists into two distinct groups, individualists and communists, and then went on to reject the influence of the former and propose the unification of the anarchist movement around the ideas of the latter. The reality was far more complex, Jiménez argued: these different tendencies within the anarchist movement were neither contradictory nor self-contained. For example, it was possible to find elements in both groups that supported the tactics of anarcho-syndicalism. As such, he rejected the Platformists' central argument that the different tendencies were mutually exclusive.[80] Differences of opinion existed, as was inherent in an ideology based on freedom, but this did not mean that the movement was divided: "We believe that anarchism is one [unified whole] and we sustain that much of the opposition to this point put forward by those tendencies who have organised separately represents nothing but simple differences of opinion. ... [These tendencies] would benefit and enrich anarchism if they were to join together instead of serving as a cause for disunity."[81]

Rather than base any organisation around one of the specific ideological tendencies, Jiménez argued that it would be preferable simply to welcome within any such organisation members as individuals who had different views. The overriding ideology of this organisation would be anarchism in general and not that of any of the differing tendencies. Jiménez's critique was, of course, not simply an attack on the Platform, but also a defence of the all-inclusive ideological framework of the new FAI, which aimed to group together all anarchists (see chapter 8). The Platform did not embrace the diversity of the anarchist movement, which Jiménez argued was the movement's very strength: "There is no doubt that the Russian project completely satisfies those who do not support the variety, the rainbow of ideas in our movement. However, there is also no doubt that the Platform does not serve as a means of unifying anarchism and making it a movement of the masses."[82]

Unity could not be enforced on a libertarian movement – the result was bound to be the opposite of that desired. By reducing anarchism to one homogenous programme that represented solely the opinions of one tendency, the Platform would only serve to further divide the movement. To prove his point, Jiménez referred to events in France, where the Platform enjoyed its greatest popularity.

Following the victory of the Platformists at the Paris congress of 1927, a section of those who felt that the traditional ideals of anarchism were under attack broke away from the UACR to form the Association des Federalistes Anarchistes (Association of Anarcho-Federalists, AFA) in early 1928.[83] The main figure in the AFA was Sébastien Faure, and, in response to the Platform, Faure put forward his own proposals for a unified anarchist movement in *La Synthèse Anarchiste*, which first appeared as a supplement to the February 1928 issue of AFA paper *Le Trait – D'Union Libertaire*.[84] 'The Synthesis' was a simple enough idea. Three currents existed in anarchism – anarcho-syndicalism, libertarian communism, and individualist anarchism – but, far from being in opposition to each other, these currents should, Faure argued, "combine together and constitute, in amalgamating themselves ...the Anarchist Synthesis."[85] The combination of the three currents on a local, regional, national, or international level would depend upon their relative strength at each level. Thus, where anarcho-syndicalism was the major force within the anarchist movement, this ideology would predominate (but not dominate) over the others on a ratio concurrent with the extent of its majority.[86]

Due to his contacts and influence, Faure's proposal raised more interest in Spanish circles than the Platform had, and it was published in the Spanish libertarian press both in Spain and Belgium.[87] In essence, Faure was attempting to reunite the anarchist family without imposing the rigid structure proposed by the Platform, and in Spain it was treated as such.

As opposed to the situation in France, in Spain the influence of individualist anarchism was not a serious source of disruption. Although the ideas of certain individualists such as Han Ryner and Émile Armand had some impact on Spanish anarchism, this was mainly in issues such as sex and free love, areas clearly outside the remit of the unions.[88] As has been seen, the splits within Spanish anarchist circles related mainly to the relationship between anarchism and syndicalism. The attempts to foster mutual acceptance between anarchist groups therefore focused almost explicitly on the relations between anarchism and syndicalism, and, with the confederation having launched a further attempt at reorganisation in January 1928, the calls for unity were enthusiastically welcomed by militants of both sides.

The editorial board of the pro-FAI newspaper *Verbo Nuevo*, based in Belgium, described *La Synthèse Anarchiste* as "the most important document published in the last few years."[89] Josep Magriñà, another of the principal supporters of the MOA, was equally optimistic, viewing the newspaper *Despertád*, which had just begun publication in Vigo (Galicia), as the "germ of unity between the libertarian militants of the CNT, the FAI, and anarchists of all tendencies."[90] *Despertád* itself welcomed the Synthesis, which it felt should "be heard by all Spanish comrades, as except for the individualist tendency which in Spain has a very limited support, ... the events [splits in the French movement] look like they are happening here with much more intensity." To avoid this, the newspaper promised to work for unity: "The name of our thought, linked to the spirit of Faure's manifesto, has to be: FREE ANARCHIST ACCORD: mutual toleration and understanding."[91]

The Spanish anarchists were not proposing the application of Faure's Synthesis in Spain but were simply supporting the basic idea behind his work: anarchist unity. Mutual understanding and toleration between the different tendencies were vital, not only for the renaissance of anarchism in Spain but also for the relaunch of the CNT, which had begun in early 1928 and which, as had occurred during the reorganisation of the CNT of 1916–18, was heavily influenced by the anarchist groups. Support for the Synthesis represented the realisation that a united movement was required if the confederation was once more going to provide an effective and strong challenge to the power of the state and employers. However, wanting unity and achieving it were two different matters, and good intentions would not be sufficient to maintain unity when the time arrived to discuss the logistics of any understanding.[92] The Synthesis made more sense in France, where the main objective was simply to try to unite a depleted and divided movement: unity in itself was the goal. Of course, in the future the French anarchists hoped to play their part in the overthrow of the state, but, due to their weakness, this was not an immediate aim or even a remote possibility. This was not the case south of the Pyrenees. In Spain, unity would serve a greater purpose: the overthrow of the dictatorship, which might even provoke, although not necessarily immediately, a social revolution.

The desire for unity was welcome following the internecine conflicts of the previous years. However, no means had been discovered yet for overcoming the differences in opinion in relation to syndicalism. The CNT still contained supporters of pure syndicalism, anarcho-syndicalism, and the MOA. For the latter two tendencies, the experience in France had served to show what could happen if pure syndicalism was left unchallenged. Both the CGT and the CGTU had claimed to represent revolutionary syndicalism, and both had come under the control of political organizations – socialist in the first case and communist in the latter.[93] The French anarchists had prevaricated, and by the time they finally acted to create an independent syndicalist organisation, following pressure from the IWMA and Spanish and Italian exiles, it was too late. The result was that anarchism in France was very much a minority pursuit and, having lost contact with the masses, was in danger of becoming little more than the subject of café conversation. The generally pathetic spectacle offered by the French anarchists was potentially contagious. The previous anarchist International, based in the French capital, had died due to apathy, and the attempts to form a new one based on the Platform were also destined to fail. With anarchists in many countries in eastern and southern Europe forced into exile and others struck down by apathy, the international anarchist movement was in danger of following the French anarchists into the abyss. The dangers to anarchism on a national and international level if it lost contact with the labour movement had been only too clearly demonstrated in France. This experience could be repeated in Spain if the pure syndicalists won control of the CNT. It was fear of this possibility that had been the prime motivation behind the movement in favour of the MOA, and, significantly, many of the principal supporters of the MOA were among the main figures behind the newly formed FAI.

8.

ANARCHIST ORGANISATION AND SYNDICALIST OVERREACTION

In 1927, after years of delay, confusion, and debate, the Spanish anarchists finally created an independent anarchist organisation, albeit this organisation, the Federación Anarquista Ibérica (FAI), was a joint venture with their Portuguese comrades. The origins of the FAI lay in attempts by the syndicalist organisations of the two countries, the CNT and the Portuguese Confederação Geral do Trabalho (CGTP), to create an Iberian Syndicalist Confederation.[1] When this project failed, due to the ban on the Spanish confederation, anarchists from the two countries began moves towards the creation of a peninsula-wide anarchist federation, a process which culminated in the creation of the FAI. Although they played a leading role in the preparations prior to the foundation of the federation, the influence of the Portuguese in the FAI was limited. The FAI was effectively a Spanish anarchist organisation.

The goal of the federation was to unite all the diverse factions of the anarchist movement together in one organisation. Although the FAI was not therefore solely concerned with the labour movement, it soon became clear that, initially at least, the supporters of the MOA were one of the main forces behind the new organisation. The inaugural conference of the FAI in 1927 supported the principles of the MOA, but, realising that the CNT could not be forced to accept the MOA against its will, it adopted a more gradual approach instead. The FAI's tactic for ensuring that a close relationship was maintained between anarchism and syndicalism was the *trabazón* (literally 'close or organic link'). This link would be achieved by the formation of a series of joint councils in areas of mutual interest to both the FAI and the CNT, thus guaranteeing that close relations between anarchism and syndicalism in the country were maintained. Although unstated, it was clearly hoped that joint action in one area might eventually spill over into another and the CNT would slowly adopt the principles of the MOA. Although the translation of 'trabazón' into English is the same as the 'organic link' proposed by the Comintern (see chapter 4), this similarity can be misleading. The CNT was not to be forced to accept the trabazón. During a further attempt to reorganise the CNT, launched at the beginning of 1928, the confederation gave qualified acceptance to the trabazón in areas of mutual interest by agreeing to the creation of joint councils for revolutionary action and prisoners' aid, whilst at the same time stressing its independence in all union matters. As with previous attempts, the relaunch failed following the arrest of leading militants at the end of the year. Meanwhile, an attempt to create a form of international trabazón between an anarchist International and the IWMA was rejected at an international anarchist congress and the IWMA's third congress, both held in May 1928.

The close cooperation of the FAI with the CNT during 1928 inevitably brought a reaction from the syndicalists. Disturbed by the close relations between the CNT and the FAI, as well as the confederation's continued inability to reorganise, Angel Pestaña proposed the formation of a syndicalist alternative, the Union of Militants. Pestaña argued that the confederation should accept the dictatorship's labour legislation, which would involve collaboration with the state and abandoning the principles of direct action. This not only brought the expected criticism from radical anarchists but also created splits within the syndicalist tendency. The sudden collapse of the Primo de Rivera dictatorship in January 1930 thus found the confederation more divided than ever, a factor than became increasingly evident in the months before the proclamation of the Second Republic in April 1931.

The early years of the FAI, the period 1927–30, are often ignored by historians. In fact, the historiography of the FAI for this period is surprisingly limited, given the influence of the organisation. Even Gómez Casas's history of the FAI provides only a brief summary for 1927–30.[2] All too often the early life of the FAI is researched in regard to what happened during the Second Republic, and this has led to the erroneous assumption that the FAI had little impact on the CNT until the Second Republic, although this is not strictly the case, as well as to simplistic conclusions about the overall nature of the FAI.[3] The formation of the FAI must be seen in the light of the CNT's inability to organise during the Primo de Rivera dictatorship as well as the continued decline in the influence of anarchism internationally in the years following the Russian Revolution. The creation of the FAI therefore represented a defensive reaction on the part of the overall Spanish libertarian movement to the weakened state of their movement following four years of dictatorship. During these early years, the FAI sought to establish a close relationship with the CNT but did not wish to enforce its views on the confederation and accepted the limits placed on the relationship. The early FAI sought to ensure a role for anarchism within the unions rather than to dominate them, even if they hoped to persuade the CNT to adopt a more anarchist approach in its day-to-day functioning. This moderate approach during the early years of the FAI, most specifically 1927–1928, has been largely ignored.

The Proposed Iberian Syndicalist Confederation

Anarchism was introduced to Portugal in 1871 when the FRE was temporarily forced into exile due to repression in Spain.[4] However, the following years saw the rise of orthodox socialism and a decline in the influence of anarchism. The emergence of syndicalism in the early twentieth century provided a means for anarchists to reestablish contacts with the working classes. Following the 1909 National Workers' Congress, a split emerged in the Portuguese labour movement between socialists and syndicalists. The syndicalists formed the Congresso Studiale Cooperativista, in which the anarchist influence was noticeable, although the overall ideology was based on the Charter of Amiens. In an attempt to reunite the two factions, a unitary trade union organisation, the União Operaria Nacional (UON), was created in 1914. The UON was eventually replaced by the CGTP, which was founded at a National Workers' Congress at Coimbra in September 1919. The CGTP had two main objectives: to unite all workers in a single organisation and to maintain that organisation's independence from all political currents. Unlike the situations in Spain and the majority of other European countries in the postwar period, the CGTP was the only national trade union organisation in Portugal, and within its ranks could be found all the different left-wing political tendencies, although the predominant strand was revolutionary – if not 'anarcho-' – syndicalism.[5]

The first official contact between the syndicalist organisations of Portugal and Spain came at the El Ferrol congress of 1915.[6] At this congress, a Portuguese delegate, Ernesto Costa Cardozo, proposed that a committee with delegates from both countries be formed as the first step towards the creation of an Iberian confederation which, in turn, would help organise an International Federation of Workers.[7] The committee established at El Ferrol did not survive long (see chapter 2). However, contacts between the syndicalists of both countries continued. The CNT national secretary, Evelio Boal, was due to attend the September 1919 Coimbra National Workers' Congress, originally scheduled to take place in July of that year, to discuss means of improving relations with other revolutionary syndicalist organisations in advance of the creation of an International, but he was unable to do so due to events in Spain.[8]

Manuel Joaquim de Sousa represented the CGTP at the CNT's national congress in Madrid in December 1919, where he was pleasantly surprised by the warm welcome he received from his Spanish comrades.[9] In meetings between de Sousa and leading CNT members, the basis for a Latin confederation was established.[10] The CNT and CGTP were to be the initial cells of the proposed organisation, which would include the CNT, the CGTP, the Italian USI, and the French CGT.[11] The Latin confederation never got beyond the planning stage due to the unenthusiastic reaction of the CGT in France and the combination of government repression and economic decline that affected the fortunes of the organisations that were to be its members.

Despite the failure of the Latin International, the plans to create an Iberian confederation, discussed at the 1919 congress, continued. In 1922 both the CNT and the CGTP affiliated with the IWMA, albeit provisionally: the CNT at the Zaragoza conference of June 1922 and the CGTP at a national congress in Covilhã in October 1922.[12] At Covilhã, the CGTP also voted in favour of building closer ties with the CNT. Following the congress, the CGTP sent a questionnaire to the CNT, asking if they believed that "the unification of the revolutionary proletariat of the two countries in one sole organisation, an Iberian Confederation, would be convenient and useful."[13] The questionnaire was to be discussed at the CNT national congress which was scheduled to be held in June 1923, but this was postponed due to the transport strike in Barcelona.[14]

The CGTP once again took the initiative and, at the end of May or early June 1923, invited the CNT to a meeting to study the possibilities of creating a joint peninsula-wide committee for the two organisations.[15] The resulting conference of the two labour organisations was held in Évora, Portugal, in July. The CGTP was represented by Manuel Joaquim de Sousa and José da Silva Santos Arranha, and the CNT by Sebastià Clarà, Acrato Lluhi, and Manuel Pérez.[16] No record exists of the discussions held at Évora, but an editorial published in *A Batalha* (the CGTP newspaper) in early July suggests that they concerned the creation of a joint committee. The article argued that, as the two organisations were federalist, it was quite possible that the national committee of the CNT resident in Barcelona could simply become the committee of the Iberian Labour Confederation. The committee would be composed solely of militants from the region where it was based. The CGTP would constitute one or two regions within the new organisations, and, given the decentralised nature of syndicalism, these regions would still enjoy autonomy in regional affairs.[17]

Following the Évora conference, progress towards the formation of an Iberian confederation suffered a serious setback when, in September 1923, Primo de Rivera seized power in Spain. The next official contact between the CNT and the CGTP was a letter sent by the Spanish organisation in September, requesting moral support from their Portuguese colleagues in the light of events in Spain.[18] Contacts were maintained, and a further meeting between the two organisations was arranged to take place in December 1923 in Seville, the seat of the national committee of the CNT. However, shortly after arriving in Andalusia, the two CGTP delegates, Manuel da Silva Campos and Manuel Joaquim de Sousa (the national secretary of the Confederação and his predecessor), were arrested along with the members of the CNT national committee. The Spanish government claimed to have foiled a communist-inspired revolutionary uprising, although in reality the meeting had been organised to see whether the CGTP would participate in a planned insurrection that the CNT had been discussing with Republican and Catalan political forces opposed to the dictatorship. Irrespective of the government's knowledge, or otherwise, of this particular plot, mere suspicion served as an excuse for a further crackdown on the confederation in the region.[19]

The repression severely weakened the CNT and dealt a fatal blow to the project to create an Iberian Syndicalist Confederation. Although both sides continued to talk about it, there is no evidence that further discussions took place between them on the subject.[20] Avelino González (the CNT national secretary) and Segundo Blanco attended the CGTP's second congress in September 1925. However, discussion about the creation of an Iberian Syndicalist Confederation was not on the agenda, although the subject may have been raised in private conversations. In any case, the ban on the CNT meant that little, if any, progress was made by the time the military seized power in Portugal on May 28, 1926. A general strike organised by the CGTP in February 1927 failed to dislodge the military, and the Portuguese confederation was banned. The CGTP, like the CNT, continued to function underground and in exile, but the repression in the two countries effectively ended attempts to create the Iberian Syndicalist Confederation.

The Creation of the Federación Anarquista Ibérica

Despite the repression, cooperation between the libertarian movements of the two countries had continued. In 1923, the anarchists of both countries had held national congresses, which, by coincidence, had both opened on the same day, March 18, 1923. At the Madrid congress, the Spanish anarchists decided not to create a national federation and instead set up a national liaison committee: the Committee of Anarchist Relations. At the Portuguese anarchist congress in Alenquer, the União Anarquista Portuguesa (UAP) was created. At a national level, the UAP acted as a link between member organisations and a contact point with international organisations. The creation of a national anarchist union independent of the CGTP was a reflection of the difference in the relationship between anarchism and syndicalism in Portugal in comparison with Spain. This was due not simply to the greater strength of the anarchist movement in Spain but also to the fact that, in Portugal, the CGTP was the only national trade union organisation. The CGTP aimed to gather together all workers under its auspices, a goal that the Portuguese anarchists supported. The Alenquer conference accepted that there were clear differences between syndicalist organisations and anarchist groups: "The first have almost exclusively materialistic objectives, satisfying principally the selfishness of the masses, the others concern themselves with moral questions, trying to instil in the masses the greatest sense of the ideal as the only means of finding the solution [to their problems]."[21] The role of the anarchists in the unions was to instil their ideas in the masses and act to ensure that neither reformism nor communism took control of the CGTP.[22]

Relations between the anarchists of the two countries were to be discussed at both the Madrid and Alenquer conferences, although, from the brief reports that exist on the Spanish congress, the subject does not appear to have been given much attention, if any.[23] At

Alenquer, the Portuguese anarchists agreed that there should be closer "reciprocal relations between the Spanish and Portuguese anarchists," and to this effect the conference directed the committee of the UAP to contact the Spanish anarchists.[24] According to Francisco Quintal, a member of the UAP national committee, there were a number of benefits to be gained from uniting the anarchists of both countries: union would facilitate the creation of an anarchist International (which it was hoped would be created at the international anarchist conference to be held in Paris in October that year (1923) (see chapter 5), it would serve as an example for the syndicalist organisation of two countries, and it would help bring about an Iberian confederation of workers.[25]

Whilst talks continued between the two confederations about the creation of joint Iberian Syndicalist Confederation, there was little progress towards the formation of a united anarchist organisation. The first official meeting between the Spanish and Portuguese anarchists took place at the national anarchist congress in Barcelona in April 1925.[26] A delegate of the UAP arrived towards the end of the deliberations and presented a paper calling for the creation of an Iberian Anarchist Union without delay. The congress established a commission to research the feasibility of such a project, which was composed of the UAP delegate and one other who would be chosen by the Catalan anarchists.[27]

It is not clear whether this commission was ever actually set up. The Spanish Committee of Anarchist Relations was moved to France at the April congress, and it appears that, due to the repression in Spain, contacts between the Spanish and Portuguese anarchists were conducted via the FGALEF.[28] Initially the exiled Spanish anarchists were preoccupied with plots to overthrow the dictatorship, and therefore the formation of a combined federation was not discussed again until the FGALEF's inaugural congress at Marseilles in May 1926. The congress agreed to the constitution of the FAI but, given the situation in Spain, decided that the provisional Committee of Relations of the new federation would be formed by the UAP and based in Lisbon. The UAP would then, when it believed it opportune, organise an Iberian congress which would see the definitive launch of the federation.[29] The congress also agreed to send a delegate of the FGALEF to the first congress of the UAP, due to be held in July 1926.

The UAP congress was postponed following the military coup of May 18, 1926. Numerous Portuguese anarchists were detained and their journal *O Anarquista* was closed down. The congress was eventually held in Lisbon in January 1927, with Josep Magriñà attending as the representative of both the FGALEF and, according to the acts of the congress, the 'Spanish Anarchist Union' (probably the newly formed yet still embryonic Spanish national federation).[30] In the discussions on the formation of the FAI, it was proposed that the congress nominate the initial committee of the FAI, as had been agreed at Marseilles. It is not clear whether a provisional committee of the FAI was established or whether the committee of the UAP itself simply acted as such.[31] In any case, the committee was unable to fulfill the tasks it assigned itself due to intensified government repression following the failed general strike in Portugal in February 1927.[32] The organisation of the Iberian conference was thus entrusted to their Spanish colleagues.[33]

The agenda for the proposed Iberian conference was discussed at a regional plenum of the Catalan Federation of Anarchist Groups in March 1927. According to Josep Llop of the Catalan federation, the Spanish Committee of Anarchist Relations had drawn up a provisional agenda and had sent it out to the various regions for discussion. Each region had then discussed the agenda and drawn up the reports that they would present at the Iberian conference.[34]

The conference was finally held on July 24–25, 1927, in Valencia, with delegates coming from Levante, Andalusia, Catalonia, Castile, and Madrid, as well as the secretariat of relations of the National Federation of Anarchist Groups and the Catalan and Levante CRTs.[35] The UAP was represented by its secretary, Francisco Quintal, and Germinal da Sousa, the son of Manuel Joaquim. The CGTP, the IWMA, and the FGALEF were invited but unable to attend. The Valencia conference saw the creation of the FAI. The new federation had three component parts: the FGALEF, the UAP and the Spanish National Federation of Anarchist Groups. The three organisations were to be linked together by a 'Peninsular Committee'. It was agreed that one of the three would be responsible for the functioning of this committee and that this responsibility would rotate from region to region. Initially it was proposed that the committee be based in

Portugal, but the UAP declined, arguing that given the proportional strength of the Spanish within the federation, it should reside in Spain. It was eventually agreed that the committee should be based in Seville, and there it remained until the spring of 1930.[36] The UAP's decision also reflected the difficulties that it faced at home following the failure of the Portuguese general strike in February 1927. In fact, after having played such an important role in the creation of the FAI, the Portuguese anarchists had little further influence on the development of the organisation.[37] For all intents and purposes, the FAI was a Spanish anarchist organisation.

Apart from the creation of the FAI, seven other items were on the conference agenda which, taken together, demonstrate that the intention was to create an organisation that would encompass all sections of anarchist thought within Spain and Portugal.[38] Indeed, one of the main subjects discussed at the conference was the role of the single-issue groups (for example, vegetarians, Esparantists, and naturalists) within the overall anarchist movement.[39] However, it was the federation's position on the relationship between anarchism and syndicalism that would have the greatest repercussions. In discussions on the issue at Valencia, the influence of the supporters of the MOA was immediately apparent. The conference agreed that the labour movement did "not exist solely to improve the working class, but works for its emancipation, and as this is possible through anarchism, it should become an agent of anarchism."[40]

Rather than being based on class or material interests, the labour struggle, it was seen, ought to be based upon "anarchist unity" – that is, it should simply have anarchism as its ultimate goal, but the anarchist movement as a whole should play an active role in its development. The syndicalist organisations would therefore have to be linked to the anarchist movement, although neither should lose independence. The conference decided that this unity would be achieved not by merging the syndicalist and anarchist organisations, but by linking them together at the local, regional, and national levels through a series of general councils composed of an equal number of representatives from both the unions and anarchist groups. The councils would then be divided into commissions of education, propaganda, social agitation, and other areas of equal interest to both organisations. The conference also agreed to the formation of an action committee composed of members from both the anarchist and syndicalist organisations, which was to plan and prepare the overthrow of the dictatorship. So, ten years after the Bolshevik seizure of power in Russia had ushered in a period of ideological confusion and absolute decline for the international libertarian movement, the Spanish anarchists' tactic for maintaining their influence within the labour movement (the structure of joint councils), carried the same title ('trabazón') as that proposed by the Comintern in 1921. However, although the FAI hoped that the trabazón would gain the support of the majority of CNT militants, when such support was not forthcoming, the federation did not attempt, during its early years at least, to force the CNT to accept it.[41]

FAI Collaboration in the Reorganisation of the CNT

The FAI played an important role in the next attempt to reorganise the CNT, which was launched at a regional plenum of the Catalan confederation in November 1927 at Sabadell. At the plenum, a regional Committee of Revolutionary Action with members from both the FAI and the Catalan CRT was created, and the delegates agreed to hold a national conference as soon as possible.[42]

The CNT held a 'National Conference of Reorganisation' in Madrid on January 15–16, 1928.[43] In the first session of the conference, the FAI delegate proposed that the newly reorganised confederation accept the principles of the MOA. This proposal was rejected because the other delegates to the conference felt that it would be preferable to discuss ideological matters at a more opportune moment. The CNT was only at the initial stages of its reorganisation, and therefore the delegates did not have the required authority to make such a decision. The conference's preoccupation was with creating a strong revolutionary movement, and discussion of the FAI proposal was therefore postponed until the next CNT congress. The FAI delegate then presented a paper which outlined the principles of the trabazón:

> The trabazón has two objectives … to join together all those organisations that are essentially similar or have

a common goal, and to give shape ... to a *Union* once
the organisations of the *libertarian movement* are em-
bodied in one organisation. ... The trabazón does not
create a completely new organisation but links together kindred organisations in order to carry out activities
and resolve problems of common interest to both. Nor
have the General Committees, which are the organs
of the trabazón, been designed with the intention of
merging any organisations... [E]ach organisation and
its component parts will be in its proper place, without
intervening in or interfering with the other.[44]

The organisations the report referred to were the councils and
commissions of education, propaganda, social agitation, and other
areas of equal interest to both the CNT and FAI, as proposed at the
Valencia conference of July 1927. The Madrid conference gave qualified support to the trabazón by agreeing to the formation of a National
Committee of Revolutionary Action to be based in Barcelona and a
National Prisoners' Committee that would reside in Madrid. Both
were to be constituted by members of the FAI and the CNT.

The conference dismissed the previous national committee. The
new committee, with Joan Peiró once again taking on the role of secretary, was to be based in Barcelona so that it could be in close contact
with the Committee of Revolutionary Action. It was agreed that if
it proved impossible for the new committee to act, then it would be
transferred to Seville, the seat of the FAI. Following the conference
the new confederal national committee made clear in a letter to the
Spanish section of the FAI that, although it would always act in accordance with the "anarchist ideals" of its members, the reconstruction of the CNT would be based on the "union of all militants," and
each confederal member would be free to put forward his or her point
of view on all questions.[45] Although the committee did not specify
exactly what it meant by the term 'anarchist ideals', this letter suggests
that they expected that anarchism was to provide the guiding principles of the movement, a rejection of pure syndicalism. At the same
time, the commitment to freedom of expression within the unions
was a rejection of the MOA.

For its part, the FAI also accepted that its relationship with the CNT – that is, the trabazón – was limited to the areas agreed upon at the CNT's January plenum. The Spanish section of the FAI made this clear in a public letter to the Local Federation of Anarchist Groups in Valencia. The Valencian anarchists were in dispute with the Levante CRT following a meeting between the two in February 1928 at which the local section of the FAI had attempted to force the principle of the trabazón on the selection procedure of the regional committee of the CRT in Levante. The FAI response clarified that the trabazón did not extend to the actual confederal regional committee but was limited to the Revolutionary Action and Prison Committees. However, the letter concluded, the trabazón was not the federation's ultimate goal: "The trabazón ... only implies a rapprochement ... a mutual understanding with that organisation [the CNT]. By no means do we believe that this is the most adequate or practical means of realising what we have labelled the Anarchist Labour Movement."[46]

The FAI therefore accepted that the trabazón was limited to the two committees created at the January plenum of the CNT, but it was hoped that this would change in the future. In reality, the trabazón was simply a short-term tactic imposed by circumstance with the eventual goal remaining the MOA.

The operation of the trabazón and, specifically, relations between the Committee of Revolutionary Action and the national committee of the CNT, were the subject of a heated debate at the next national plenum, which was held in Madrid on June 29, 1928.[47] The confederal national committee accepted that the CNT should ensure that national committee members were "of absolute confidence from the anarchist point of view," but once this was achieved the committee should enjoy "the most complete independence," which was not the case at that time. The national committee concluded that the relationship between the different committees had to be "in revolutionary and ideological issues a close relationship," but "in internal union affairs the independence of the national committee" should be preserved.

Despite the implied criticism of its intervention in union affairs, the Committee of Revolutionary Action accepted this position.[48] The FAI delegate insisted that the trabazón be maintained, though the acts of the plenum do not specify whether he was referring to all matters or solely those concerned with the organisation of the revolution. The plenum finally agreed that the CNT national committee had to be independent in affairs solely of interest to the unions but

> [c]onsidering ... we are sympathetic to all attempts that are made to bring down the dictatorship ... [it is proposed that] whilst maintaining their independence, both the FAI and the CNT act together in order to assist in any such attempt, along with the National Committee of Revolutionary Action, created from both organisations. The three will assume the responsibility for any action and, once normality has been restored, each will return to their rightful position, and the National Committee of Revolutionary action will disappear.[49]

Once again the trabazón was accepted in principle but was limited to acting to bring about the overthrow of the dictatorship. Outside of this revolutionary task, each organisation would enjoy full independence in its own specific sphere of interest: the CNT in the unions and the FAI in the anarchist groups. Nonetheless, a letter from the national committee of the CNT to the FAI in July made clear that it wanted the anarchists to play a full role in the reorganisation of the confederation so that anarchism would remain the guiding force in its development: "We do not want to discard anarchism from the Confederation as, on the contrary, we want the anarchists to be at all times those who direct and guide the labour movement represented in Spain by the CNT. ... Therefore, those who make up the national committee want to see all the anarchists in Spain in the CNT so that it never deviates from its principles."[50]

Although the committee insisted on its independence from the FAI, it also welcomed the participation and influence of the anarchists in the unions in their capacity as workers. A clear basis for relations between the FAI and the CNT had been established, which, if not exactly what the supporters of the MOA in the federation desired, did ensure a future role for anarchism within the confederation. The reorganised CNT would not be dominated by 'pure' syndicalism. The FAI could therefore claim some success for its domestic policy in Spain.

The FAI's International Policy

The FAI's activity was not limited to the peninsula. Militants could also be found in France and Brussels, although, due to the surveillance of the authorities in France, the FGALEF's ability to act had been effectively nullified. However, the exiles in Belgium were not so restricted, and among the groups affiliated with the FAI was the Grupo Internacional de Estudios Sociales, based in Brussels, the leading figure of which was the increasingly ubiquitous Magriñà.[51] The group was responsible for the publication of *Rebelde*, a Spanish-speaking version of the Belgian monthly anarchist newspaper *Rebelle*. The first issue launched what was in effect to become the raison d'être of the newspaper, a campaign for the creation of an international anarchist organisation, the Unión Anarquista Mundial, which would then become a section within the IWMA.[52] *Rebelde* argued that this link between the anarchist and syndicalist Internationals was logical because the IWMA was an "apolitical workers' organisation" that "championed direct action" and had a "clearly anarchist goal." The newspaper invited its readers to comment on their proposal, and responses were forthcoming from leading members of the IWMA, FAI, FGALEF, CNT, and UAP.[53] For the IWMA, Augustín Souchy invited the newspaper to send a representative to the International's next congress, due to take place at the end of May 1928 in Liège, to discuss the issue.[54]

However, the link with the IWMA depended first on the creation of an anarchist International, which was the main subject to be discussed at the international anarchist congress held in Huizen (outside Amsterdam) in May 1928. The FAI did not send an official response to *Rebelde*, but the Peninsular Committee's report to the anarchist congress made clear that they fully endorsed and shared the newspaper's ideas. The congress had been organised by Dutch anarchists with the aim of creating an Anarchist Youth International.[55] Rather than simply comprising younger libertarians, the youth movements represented the more radical wings of the libertarian movement in those countries of northern Europe where anarchism was becoming little more than an intellectual pursuit.[56] The FAI rejected, in principle, the idea of creating an anarchist International that was based on a split, or splits, at a national level. Instead it called for the creation of an International made up of international federations, each representing the different tendencies within anarchism, which would in turn be linked with the IWMA through the creation of a joint commission that would represent the whole international anarchist movement.[57] The congress agreed that close collaboration with the other libertarian international organisations was desirable and proposed that the press services of the International Anti-Militarist Bureau (a libertarian antiwar organisation), the Anarchist Youth International (AYI), and the IWMA be merged. However, it rejected the FAI's proposal as "unfeasable."[58] The rejection simply reflected the differences between the Spanish anarchists and those in northern Europe who dominated the congress, the main difference being the primacy the Spanish anarchists gave to relations with the labour movement, as opposed to more theoretical issues.[59]

The decision to form an Anarchist Youth International was delayed until the next congress.[60] The FAI proposed that this congress should be organised by the French UAC with the help of the FAI (or, more probably, the FGALEF). This proposal was rejected, and eventually it was decided that the inaugural congress of the AYI would take place in Briesland, near Berlin, in May 1929. It appears that no Spanish delegate attended the congress and no further information on the AYI was published in the Spanish libertarian press until March 1931, when an uncredited article referred to a future congress due to be held in Denmark.[61] There is no evidence of further contact with the AYI, which itself does not appear to have enjoyed a long existence.

Having failed to gain support at the Huizen congress, the FAI then tried to convince the IWMA to accept its ideas at its third congress, held in Liège May 27–30. The CNT delegate at the congress was 'Frago', possibly Jean Frago, the general secretary of the Construction Labourers' Union in Paris.[62] Bruno Carreras represented the Cuadros Sindicales, and Magriñá represented the FAI but in a purely observational capacity.[63] *Rebelde*'s proposal was not directly mentioned, although relations between anarchist and syndicalist organisations were the subject of discussions on the final day. The congress unanimously approved a report on the "attitude of the IWMA to the Non-Trade union organisations that have the same ideas and methods of struggle as the IWMA." The report reaffirmed that the IWMA was an exclusively trade union organisation and, as such, no non-union organisation could become a member. However, it welcomed close collaboration with anarchist organisations, although it stated that this should be carried out at a national level. The report congratulated the CNT and the Portuguese CGT for having "found a basis of common action" with the FAI and called the attention of the other IWMA members to the example set by their Iberian comrades.[64] The report concluded that an agreement among libertarian and anti-authoritarians would be of "great moral and material help to propagate our common ideals" and entrusted the IWMA secretariat to investigate means of furthering international common action.[65]

The congress at Huizen had failed to result in the formation of an anarchist International, whilst the congress at Liège had rejected all but closer relations between anarchist and syndicalist organisations. Following this double setback, *Rebelde* accepted defeat and dropped its – and the FAI's – campaign.[66] But, despite his disappointment, Magriñà accepted that the resolutions made at Liège were "imbued with libertarian spirit."[67] Magriñà's former colleague at *El Productor*, Miguel Jiménez, was even more optimistic. For Jiménez, *Rebelde's* proposal had been precipitate in attempting to promote links between the anarchist and syndicalist organisations at an international level before these had been established at a national level. Only when the trabazón had been created nationally could it be transferred into the international arena. Furthermore, the international trabazón could only be realised following the creation of an anarchist International which would bring together all schools of anarchism outside the labour movement. The anarchist International would then be linked to the IWMA via the creation of councils and commissions in areas of mutual interest to both Internationals. In the meantime, the FAI should concentrate on strengthening its links with the CNT.[68]

However, by the summer of 1928, the reorganisation of the CNT, launched at the beginning of the year with the support of the FAI, ran into difficulties. The first serious setback came in July with the arrest of hundreds of militants, including Peiró, Buenacasa, Herreros, Pestaña, and Pedro Massoni and the editorial board of *Despertád*.[69] In most cases, the detentions did not last long and were simply a reminder by the authorities of their power. A more decisive blow came in the final months of 1928 when a construction workers' strike in Seville elicited a strong reaction from the authorities, with more than two hundred workers arrested.[70] The strike, which was supported by the CNT national committee and the FAI, was eventually put down. As well as the arrests in Andalusia, there was an increase in repression in Vizcaya, Barcelona, Asturias, and Galicia.[71] The continued repression of leading militants of the CNT and the FAI put an end to their joint efforts to reorganise the CNT.

Angel Pestaña and the Professionalisation of the CNT

The next attempt at reorganising the confederal unions was made the following year and shared a similar fate. However, it was during 1929 that a clear division emerged within syndicalist ranks, between those who held to the basic principles of revolutionary syndicalism and those who were prepared to interpret these principles loosely or even disregard them altogether. This was most clearly demonstrated in the split between Pestaña and Peiró.

In December 1928, Pestaña proposed that "the most active, enthusiastic and responsible individuals" of the confederation set up a "Union of Militants of the Confederation," whose purpose would be to advocate "the organisation in professional unions of all the workers."[72] The proposal was a delayed response to changes in the dictatorship's labour policy, which had been made following Primo de Rivera's decision to replace the Military Directorate that had ruled the country since September 1923 with a civilian one made up of technocrats. Primo de Rivera hoped that this new civilian directorate would help regenerate the country. In the economic field, this regeneration would be provided by a "Corporate Organisation of Labour," the basic structure of which was introduced by royal decree on November 26, 1926.[73] An essential part of the new corporate system was the 'Comités Paritarios' (arbitration boards), in which representatives of the unions, the government, and employer associations would work together to resolve labour and social conflicts. To play a part within this new corporate structure, the unions had to 'professionalise'. When Pestaña and his supporters spoke of "professionalising the unions," what they meant was that the CNT should work within the legal framework of the Corporate Organisation and accept the Comités Paritarios.[74] By agreeing to resolve labour disputes by arbitration, especially when this involved the direct participation of representatives of the state, the Union of Militants was therefore advocating the violation of one of the most basic principles of direct action. Pestaña and his supporters were prepared to accept this, as they were increasingly concerned about the close relationship between the state and the UGT, which openly endorsed the Comités Paritarios and had quadrupled its membership in Catalonia during the dictator-ship. What they failed to explain was how, in rejecting direct action and accepting state arbitration, which in practice greatly favoured the employers, they would differ from the other unions.

It is not clear whether Pestaña put forward his ideas at the national plenum of the CNT held in March 1929, which discussed organisa-tional issues. Given the continued impossibility of the CNT to act legally, the plenum decided in favour of the formation of Cuadros Sindicales of confederal members within the legal unions, the policy originally employed by exiled militants in France. The Cuadros would not only provide a means of maintaining some form of confederal organisation but would also propagate the CNT's ideals within the 'host' organisation. Militants would be able to join the professional unions, but on no account should they seek to lead or accept any position of authority within them since this would involve collabo-ration with the Comités Paritarios and would obscure the differences in policies between the CNT and the reformist unions. Once the po-litical situation in Spain permitted, they could leave the professional organisations and form the CNT again.

In May 1929, following the CNT's involvement in another failed attempt to overthrow the dictatorship – an attempt led by the conservative politician Sanchez Guerra, the national secretary at the time of the March plenum – Joan Peiró was forced to resign. He was replaced by Angel Pestaña, who, despite the fact that the formation of Cuadros Sindicales remained confederal policy, contin-ued with his plans to promote professional unions. Pestaña was the guiding force behind the formation of a professional organisation, the Union of Workers' Associations and Syndicates in Barcelona in September 1929, although the local federation in the city had formed Cuadros Sindicales.[75] Possibly reacting to Pestaña's duplicity, Peiró launched a scathing attack on his comrade's actions in a series of articles published in *Acción Social Obrera*, entitled "Deslinde de Campos" ("Outlining Positions"), which ran from September 1929 until January 1930.[76] In the articles, Peiró traced the evolution of Pestaña's support for the professionalisation of the unions back to a conversation between the two confederal militants whilst in prison in 1927 and to an article that Peiró had written in 1928. In both the article and conversation Peiró had argued that the absence of the CNT from the labour struggles of the period was causing the workers to forget the CNT, whilst the other labour organisations, in particular the UGT, were leading them down the path of reformism and collaboration with the state.[77] Peiró saw no way out of this situation for the CNT itself, as the arbitration and government intervention involved in the Comités Paritarios clearly conflicted with the principles of direct action, which, for Peiró, represented the "basic and essential reason for the existence of the CNT."[78] Thus the CNT had to accept that it could not exist under the present circumstances and should concentrate on the formation of Cuadros Sindicales. Pestaña and his supporters were not prepared to accept this policy. They feared the UGT would use their position in the Comités Paritarios to dominate the organised workforce, and they were not prepared to bide their time in the Cuadros. To combat the rise in the UGT's support, they argued, the CNT needed to play a leading role in the reorganisation of labour and do so immediately, rather than waiting for the fall of the regime.[79]

In December 1929, the Pestaña-led national committee published a manifesto claiming that the attempts to organise the CNT militants into Cuadros Sindicales had failed and arguing that the CNT had to take part in the immediate reorganisation of the proletariat – that is, to accept the Comités Paritarios.[80] The manifesto was disingenuous, given that leading members of the committee had long backed professionalisation and had given little support to the attempts to create the Cuadros Sindicales, the latter point being made by the local federation of Barcelona that was itself made up of Cuadros Sindicales.[81] Response to the manifesto was overwhelmingly critical, with condemnation coming from organised groups of militants from Asturias and

León, and from the CRT of Levante, the local federation of Barcelona, the Committee of Cuadros Sindicales of Alcoy, and the local federation of San Feliu de Guixols. The negative reaction to the manifesto forced the committee members' resignation.[82]

The debate between Peiró and Pestaña is significant in that it demonstrates a clear division within the syndicalists' ranks. Whereas Peiró's ideological position was essentially consistent throughout the 1920s and remained firmly within the doctrine of revolutionary syndicalism, Pestaña's ideas were, in the words of the historian Nick Rider, "often erratic and contradictory." Pestaña believed strongly in the moral exactitude of his position (as had been amply demonstrated in his critique of Bolshevism whilst in Moscow) and was often intolerant of his opponents in the CNT. Having been a radical anarchist himself during the years of the First World War, as has been seen, Pestaña had increasingly turned against the radical anarchists during the violence in Barcelona in the early 1920s, and by the final years of the dictatorship he appeared to place more faith in liberal politicians, especially the Catalan Left, than in his opponents within the CNT.[83] By 1929, Pestaña's moral pragmatism, his jealousy of the UGT's freedom to act granted by Primo de Rivera, and his suspicion of the FAI were such that he was prepared to sanction the split of the CNT that his policy entailed. It was precisely this that explains the ferocity with which Peiró attacked his colleague. Peiró, after all, had played a central role in creating the basis for cooperation between the CNT and the FAI.

Before the conflict could be resolved, or before a split became a reality, the debates over professionalisation became redundant following the resignation of Primo de Rivera in January 1930 and the partial return to constitutional guarantees under his successor, General Damaso Berenguer. There was no time for an immediate inquest into the events of the previous months. As erratic as ever, Pestaña now condemned the Comités Paritarios, which months before he had been willing to accept at the price of splitting the CNT.[84] In the months that followed, the reorganisation of the confederal unions took precedence over ideological disputes. Nonetheless, the mutual mistrust between the radicals and the syndicalists became increasingly evident.

Return to Legality – The 1930 Relaunch of the CNT

The resignation of Primo de Rivera on January 28, 1930, made the campaign in favour of the professionalisation of the CNT unions irrelevant. The CNT had played no role in the dictator's decision. In 1929, Primo de Rivera's attempt to regenerate Spanish politics through the creation of an unelected consultative assembly – which would have included political factions from the pre-dictatorship period, such as the socialists – was rejected by all but the regime's closest supporters. The extent of the opposition of the old political factions was made clear by the attempted coup launched by Sanchez Guerra, an austere seventy-year-old conservative, in early 1929. The regime had been declining and had gradually lost the support of the sectors upon which it was dependent for its survival, most significantly the king and the army.[85] Suffering from diabetes and resentful of the lack of support for his ideas, Primo de Rivera resigned after consulting senior army members and before Alfonso had the chance to dismiss him.[86] Alfonso had been closely associated with the dictatorship, as he had accepted the pronunciamento in 1923 that put an end to the constitution, so an attempt was made to distance the monarchy from the old regime's unpopularity. Primo de Rivera's successor, Berenguer, was given the task of "engineering a return to constitutional government without imperilling the king."[87] However, Berenguer procrastinated, and when he finally proposed that elections for the Cortes should be held in February 1931, the offer was met with a widespread abstention from the major political parties who had been actively conspiring against the government throughout 1930. Berenguer resigned and was replaced by Admiral Aznar, who organised municipal elections in an attempt to calm the growing opposition to the monarchy. The result of these elections in urban areas gave such a large majority to the pro-Republican forces that the king fled, fearing civil war, and on April 14, 1931, the Republic was declared.

Berenguer's quasi-dictatorship, known as the Dictablanda (Soft Dictatorship), restored the constitutional guarantees suspended in September 1923, thus allowing the CNT to reorganise legally without having to break with its principles. However, Berenguer had not foreseen the rapid return of the CNT and the increase in labour conflicts inherent in its reorganisation. Once it became clear that the authorities could not check the rise of the CNT, the government resorted to the tactics of its predecessor: censorship, mass arrests, and withdrawal of constitutional guarantees.

After six years of enforced inactivity, confederal militants set about resurrecting the CNT with understandable verve. The arguments of the past were momentarily put to aside as confederal militants focused on the day-to-day task of reorganising the unions. One of the most noticeable features of the 1930 reorganisation was the almost complete lack of direct involvement by the FAI.[88] In fact, the FAI had shown little sign of life since late 1928, with the exception of the regional federations in Catalonia and Levante.[89] In April 1930, a circular by the Peninsular Committee admitted that the functioning of the federation as a whole had been severely affected following the arrest of a member of its secretariat and the confiscation of the documents he was carrying, which included the addresses of leading members of the federation. Neither the name of the arrested militant nor the date of the arrest are recorded, but it is probable that the arrest occurred during the construction strike in Seville in the summer of 1928.[90] Following criticism of its inactivity, the Peninsular Committee was transferred from Andalusia to Catalonia, on the request of the Andalusian anarchists in late June or early July 1930.[91] In a further circular issued in August, the committee claimed that there had been a noticeable increase in FAI activity, evidenced by the appearance of a number of anarchist newspapers.[92] Nevertheless, the FAI remained relatively disorganised and was hardly involved in the reorganisation of the CNT.[93] As has been seen, the vast majority of anarchists could be found within the CNT, and it is no coincidence that the FAI was created during a period when confederal activity was banned. It is also not surprising that, during the reorganisation, the CNT took prominence over the FAI.[94]

The relative absence of the FAI in the reorganisation of the CNT did not mean that the disagreements between the radical anarchists and the syndicalists had disappeared, although initially militants of all tendencies concentrated their attention on drawing up a plan for the reorganisation of the CNT and the reopening of the unions, and differences were temporarily put aside. A regional plenum held in

Catalonia on February 16–17, 1930, agreed that the immediate task was to reorganise all the confederal committees and unions as quickly as possible, and the means for doing so at local, district, regional, and national levels were drawn up.[95] A new national committee was established to oversee the reorganisation that included Angel Pestaña (as if to prove that the conflicts of the previous year had been temporarily forgotten) and was dominated by moderates.[96] It was this committee that finally negotiated the return of the CNT to legal status at the end of April 1930.[97]

However, suspicions within the CNT concerning the aims of the national committee surfaced almost immediately with the publication of a manifesto in early April calling for a Constitutional Cortes and the reestablishment of constitutional guarantees and citizens' rights.[98] The manifesto even appeared to suggest that CNT members should work with the Republican parties in order to establish a Constitutional Cortes.[99] The reaction to the manifesto was so unfavourable that the committee had to publish a further article three weeks later that stated that the manifesto had actually been agreed upon by those who attended the February plenum.[100] As with the debates over the Union of Militants, criticism was not confined to the radical anarchists, a factor emphasised not only nationally by the newspaper *Despertád* but also internationally by the IWMA's unfavourable reaction to the manifesto.[101]

The manifesto of the CNT national committee was censured at a meeting of the IWMA administrative bureau, held in Berlin from May 29 to June 1, 1930.[102] In addition to Pestaña, who represented the CNT, delegates from the FAUD, CGTSR, NSV, and SAC attended, with Augustín Souchy and Valeriano Orobón Fernández representing the IWMA secretariat. Ostensibly the meeting had been called to organise the IWMA's next congress. The recent change in government in Spain was welcomed by all the delegates, and it was even agreed that the next congress should be held in Madrid in October 1930.[103] Pestaña read out a brief report on the situation in Spain and the rapid reorganisation of confederal forces. In the discussions that followed, Souchy and Orobón Fernández raised their concerns about the confusion that the CNT manifesto had caused and stressed that the CNT needed to try to achieve its goals through direct action and not by elections.[104] A commission made up of Orobón Fernández,

Souchy, and E. Juhel (of the CGTSR), with Pestaña as an advisor, was set up to draft a manifesto from the IWMA to the Spanish proletariat. Echoing the concerns raised at the Berlin meeting, the manifesto stated that although the confederation recognised that the "conquest and defence of the rights of association and the freedom of expression ... were indispensable conditions for the development of the labour movement," the CNT should support those who campaigned in favour of these rights by direct action and not "stop with these partial victories ... [but] continue its struggle until it achieved its ideological goals."[105] According to Orobón Fernández, the IWMA manifesto was "a clear amendment" to the disputed CNT manifesto and showed the International's lack of conformity with the line adopted by the syndicalists in the CNT.[106]

Following the IWMA meeting, both Souchy and Orobón Fernandez wrote to Carbó, expressing their fears that the original manifesto of the CNT national committee, by appearing to support the creation of a bourgeois Constituent Cortes, had given a "prize to our adversaries, the communists."[107] The fears of the two members of the IWMA secretariat were well-founded. The Partido Comunista Español (PCE) hoped to exploit the reorganisation of the CNT, following the fall of Primo de Rivera's regime, in order to increase its influence in the unions. A PCE congress held in Bilbao in March 1930 decided that the communists, under the banner of "syndical democracy," should take the lead in the reorganisation of the CNT.[108] The communists' ploy gained little support in the CNT strongholds of Catalonia, Aragón, Galicia, and Valencia but achieved notable success in Seville. Militants affiliated with the PCE in the harbour workers' section of the Transport Union in Seville organised a National Conference for the Reconstruction of the CNT on June 23, 1930.[109] Despite its grandiose title, the conference only attracted local delegates, although, urged on by the representative of the RTUI, Jacques Duclos, it agreed to create a National Committee of Reconstruction.[110] The committee helped to lay the foundations for a strong communist representation in the Andalusian capital during the Second Republic but had little impact elsewhere.

Nonetheless, the action of the communists helped maintain a semblance of unity among the main factions within the CNT. *El Productor*, the paper of the pro-MOA faction, recommenced publication in mid-June. Although Buenacasa once again used the paper to propagate his belief that the CNT should be libertarian – "the most libertarian possible" – articles of this nature were few in number, especially in comparison with those that concentrated on the communists' action in Seville or were written by militants from the Andalusian capital (or both).[111] Even *La Revista Blanca*, produced by the Urales family, who would soon become one of the main critics of the syndicalists during the Second Republic, initially seemed to actually support the position of future opponents:

"In Spain, syndicalism faces the same dangers that it faced in France ... where there is a Confederation which is a friend of the government and another Confederation which is friend of the Russian government. ... [In Spain] the Confederation must not be political, or apolitical or antipolitical. ... The Confederation should only be a workers' organisation."[112] This position can only be understood in the light of the communists' machinations.

In Catalonia, the communists, led by Maurín, initially supported the National Committee of Reconstruction. At a regional plenum of the Catalan CRT in July 1930, the representative of the Graphic Arts Union of Barcelona (either Adolfo Bueso or Helios Gómez) tried to open a discussion about the ideological direction that *Solidaridad Obrera* should have. The plenum refused to discuss the issue because they had no competence to do so, as ideological issues could only be decided at a national congress. Given that the last such congress, in Madrid in 1919, had decided that the CNT's ideology was libertarian communism, it was agreed that its newspaper should reflect this. Peiró accused the delegate of the Graphic Arts Union of belonging to a tendency within the CNT that was "vilely and despicably attacking us and have gone as far as saying that we have an agreement with the police." The plenum ended by condemning all the factions of the CNT that were trying "to produce a split" within the union.[113] Once it became clear that the PCE policy of division had failed outside of Seville, Maurín and his supporters began to criticise the formation of the National Committee of Reconstruction, fearing that the pro-communist unions in Catalonia that were still affiliated with the confederation might be expelled.[114] For their continued criticism of the established party line over this and other issues, Maurín and his supporters were expelled from the PCE in August 1930.[115] Eventually, in March 1931, Maurín and his supporters joined forces with the Partit Comunista Català (a group of dissident communists and leftist Catalan nationalists formed in 1928) to form the Bloque Obrero y Campesino (BOC), which gained a paltry three thousand votes throughout Catalonia in the municipal elections of April 1931.[116]

As the controversy over the national committee's manifesto in support of a Constituent Cortes had foreshadowed, the main source of discord between the anarchists and the syndicalists was over relations between the CNT and political parties. But, rather than the BOC, it was the creation of a leftist-orientated Catalan nationalist party, the Esquerra Republicana de Catalunya (ERC), that was to have the greatest effect on the CNT.[117] Even before the inaugural ERC congress in March 1931, the CNT had been in close contact with politicians from the different elements that merged to create the ERC: Francesc Macià's Estat Català, Lluis Companys's Partit Republica Català, and the group connected with the newspaper L'Opinió.[118] Confederation leaders in Catalonia had always had close links with prominent figures of the Catalan left. Lluis Companys and Francesc Layret had both been lawyers for the CNT (the latter was murdered by armed gunmen in the service of the Employers' Union in Barcelona in 1920), whilst during the dictatorship exiled CNT members were in close contact with Francesc Macià in the French capital.[119] The ERC's "socialised and worker-orientated" political programme and the revolutionary pretence of leading members of Estat Català paved the way for close contacts between certain CNT figures and the Catalan left throughout 1930.[120] At the end of March, leading syndicalists, including Joan Peiró, had signed a pro-Republican manifesto calling for the installation of a democratic Republic. The manifesto was later published in the Catalan newspaper L'Opinió. Due to criticism from within the CNT, Peiró later withdrew his signature.[121] From October onwards, the CNT was involved with the Macià pro-liberty committee, which campaigned for the aging Catalan leader to be allowed to return from exile.[122] Finally, in March 1931, the CNT sent an official reporter, Sebastià Clara, to the founding congress of the ERC, at which the new party promised an amnesty for political prisoners and complete union freedom in a future Republic.[123]

The CNT was also in contact with the other political groups that plotted against both Primo de Rivera and Berenguer. The Committee of Revolutionary Action, set up at the national plenum of January 1928 as part of the trabazón between the CNT and the FAI, had established an 'understanding' with the Sanchez Guerra conspiracy, although, when the coup attempt was eventually launched in January 1929, the CNT was not informed until the last moment and did not take part. The resignation of Primo de Rivera had not satisfied the opponents of the king, who held Alfonso responsible for the failures of the regime. In August the conspirators held a secret meeting in San Sebastián to discuss tactics and the future shape of the Republic.[124] Eventually a revolutionary committee was established in October and the date for the uprising was set: December 15. The rebellion failed after the garrison in Jaca (Aragon) rose three days early, forcing the conspirators in Madrid to act precipitously. The revolutionary Committee issued a rushed manifesto and was promptly arrested.

The CNT had not been represented at San Sebastián, although Progreso Alfarache and Rafael Vidiella acted as observers. The Catalan political parties involved in the Republican pact signed at San Sebastián contacted the CNT later.[125] An understanding "in principle" was reached in October, which was ratified at a national plenum in November. These contacts with politicians drew suspicions from within the CNT that leading confederal militants had formed a pact with the Republicans in which the CNT would be given full legal rights to organise and propagate their ideas in any future Republic as long as its members did not try to undermine the new political order through strikes or revolutionary activity.[126] The national committee attempted to put an end to these rumours with the publication of a manifesto at the end of October entitled "No pacts or compromises," which stated that the CNT would support any move against the monarchy but would do so on its own terms, through mass action in the streets and without requesting favours from Republicans or promising them support in future – a position that was confirmed at the November national plenum.[127] The CNT eventually agreed to support the December movement in accordance with the principles of direct action – that is, by a general strike. The government response was swift, and the strike movement was crushed.

The increase in labour unrest was an integral part of the reorganisation of the CNT, as newly reformed confederal unions struggled to force employers to recognise their right to exist and refused to accept the arbitration of the Comités Paritarios. The first major conflict of the newly organised CNT was the construction strike in Barcelona in August 1930, which finally ended in victory in September.[128] In October, the rapid reorganisation of the CNT received a sudden setback when the minister of the interior, General Emilio Mola, realising that the organisation was growing out of control, ordered the arrest of a number of leading militants.[129] In November, a dispute by dockers, who formed part of the still-embryonic transport union, led to a general strike throughout Barcelona. This time the civil governor refused to legalise the transport union, and instead the unions in the city were closed down.[130] Accepting defeat, the local federation called off the general strike after just two days.[131]

Parallel to the increase in union activity, relations between the radical anarchists and the syndicalists had been steadily deteriorating since August, when *Solidaridad Obrera* began publication. In early 1930 a group of syndicalists, including Angel Pestaña, Pere Foix, and Juan López, but not Joan Peiró, had formed the group Solidarity in order to publish a monthly theoretical review, *Mañana*, and a weekly newspaper, *Acción*, which began publication on February 15.[132] Initially, however, *Acción* attempted to represent all the tendencies within the CNT, acting as a substitute for *Solidaridad Obrera*, with articles by members of the FAI appearing alongside those of the Solidarity group. However, as soon as *Solidaridad Obrera* reappeared at the end of August, *Acción* became the mouthpiece of the syndicalist tendency. Almost immediately, the group published a manifesto, "To All the Anarchists," in which they stated that there was a need to revise anarchist tactics. In particular, they wanted the inauguration of an anarchist congress at which "clear and precise formulas as to what anarchism is and what it wants" would be agreed upon, as well as the restructuring of the Spanish anarchist movement, based on local, regional, and national federations that would act legally in a similar manner to those of the CNT rather than on a mixture of federations and affinity groups.[133] The *El Productor* group, now without their own newspaper, agreed that there was a need to reorganise the structure of the Spanish anarchist movement. However, it was the reaction of aging anarchist Federico Urales, in an article entitled "About an Intended Revision of Anarchism," that was most significant. Urales accused the Solidarity group, and Pestaña in particular, of hypocrisy. They were, after all, an affinity group themselves. They were, he claimed, guided by a desire to lead and dominate the anarchist movement and were prepared to divide it, by creating an anarchist organisation open only to those who shared their views.[134] Urales ended by calling anarchists to make their presence felt in the CNT: "The CNT, with all its defects, is the organisation that represents the aspirations of the anarchists best. ... Why don't we all come together around the CNT without each of us forgetting our particular point of view? To attempt this, on our part, we only ask one condition: no party politics, no bosses, no directive committees."[135]

Urales's reaction paved the way for increased interference in CNT affairs by the Urales family – Federico (whose real name was Juan Montseny), his partner Soledad Gustavo, and, above all, their daughter Federica Montseny – throughout the Second Republic. Previously, Urales, through his publication *La Revista Blanca*, had predominantly concentrated on intellectual anarchism, which had allowed his review to continue publication throughout the dictatorship, a factor that had raised the suspicion of CNT militants of all tendencies.[136] Although *La Revista Blanca* became more interested in labour affairs during the Second Republic, it was another Urales family newspaper, *El Luchador*, which provided the focal point for attacks against the syndicalist leadership of the CNT following the fall of the monarchy.[137]

During the months prior to this, contacts between the CNT and Republican politicians were the major cause of concern for anarchists. In a manifesto published in August, the Anarchist Regional Committee of Andalusia argued that the anarchists needed to "kill completely the state of confusion which has blossomed in the heart of our organisation [in the CNT] as a result of the seven years of dictatorship." It went on: "We anarchists must take every occasion to stress to the workers ... the advantages of their organisations being separated from politics, be they republican, socialist or communist. ... We want nothing, absolutely nothing, to do with politics. To hell with the demagogues and those who want to be [political] leaders![138]

As the social unrest associated with the reorganisation of the CNT intensified, the internal disputes within the confederation grew. By the end of November, relations between the anarchist publication *Tierra y Libertad* and *Acción* were so bad that, when the local federation in Barcelona decided the two newspapers should take turns replacing *Solidaridad Obrera*, which had again been suspended by the authorities, with one publication appearing one day and the other the next, *Tierra y Libertad* refused as it did not recognise the Solidarity group.[139] In a speech made in December, Joan Peiró called for a ceasefire between the groups but to no avail. By February the syndicalist newspaper *Acción* was speaking of a "fratricidal war" within the CNT, whilst the FAI spoke of an "eclipse of cordiality."[140]

It is difficult to trace this deterioration in internal relations as it came against a background of increasing repression against the CNT following the strike movement of December 1930 in support of the Republican uprising. The effective functioning of the CNT became increasingly difficult, with leading militants, including members of the national and regional committees, being arrested, unions closed down, and newspapers suspended or subject to censorship. The repression continued until the proclamation of the Second Republic on April 14, 1931.[141]

The CNT's attitude towards the Republicans was evident during the municipal election campaign, in which it abstained from launching its normal campaign against voting. Typically during electoral campaigns the CNT would advise workers against participating in what they considered a farce, yet this time *Solidaridad Obrera* focused instead on the campaign to release imprisoned CNT militants and reopen the unions.[142] On April 14, following the overwhelming victory of the Republicans in the towns and cities (although in the countryside, where the electorate could still be manipulated by the landowners, the pro-monarchist forces triumphed), with a crowd demonstrating outside the palace in Madrid, the king fled and the Republic was proclaimed. The CNT declared a general strike in Barcelona to demand the release of all political prisoners, but two days later called it off in order to help the new regime establish itself.[143] In Catalonia, the ERC had won an absolute majority in the elections, and Macià invited the CNT to participate in the new

Catalan regional government, offering Pestaña the position of labour advisor. The offer was refused.[144]

Nonetheless, the CNT was initially prepared to tolerate the new political regime, being guided by the popular support the Republic enjoyed among the working classes, whilst at the same time it hoped to exploit the new, more tolerant environment for its own benefit.[145] However, this new "workers' Republic" soon proved unable and indeed unwilling to make the necessary economic, labour, and agrarian reforms to back up its promises to the working classes. Whereas the syndicalists were prepared to give the Republic more time, fearful of the potential power of the Right, by the autumn of 1931 others within the CNT were not. The result was that a full-scale civil war broke out within the CNT, which eventually saw leading syndicalists, such as Pestaña, Clara, López, Piñón, and Peiró expelled from the confederation, although most rejoined at the Zaragoza congress of 1936 on the eve of the national civil war.

An analysis of the CNT's position in relation to the Second Republic is beyond the scope of this study. Nonetheless, it must be stressed that it is too simplistic to see the split of the 1930s as a logical continuation of the conflicts within the CNT throughout the 1920s. The Republic added further factors that fuelled the internal conflict: economic stagnation; a centralised labour policy enforced by the socialist minister of labour, Largo Caballero, which aimed to undermine the CNT in favour of the UGT; the rise of fascism across Europe; and the growing sense of deception among workers in city and countryside alike due to the Republic's failure to tackle the growing social and economic problems they faced. Furthermore, it is significant that the so-called *faistas* (the radical anarchists) of the Second Republic, as well as often not even being members of the FAI, did not include the leading proponents of the MOA during the 1920s.[146] Although influenced by the ideological debates of the 1920s and fearful of the demise of anarchism elsewhere in Europe, the radicals of the 1930s represented a new generation of militants who fused a basic understanding of the principles of the MOA with the activism inherited from and supported by the anarcho-Bolsheviks and propagated by the irresponsible middle-class intellectualism of the Urales family. This radicalisation of the younger members of the CNT was aided and abetted by the continued drift by Pestaña, who formed a Syndicalist Party in 1934, and some of his colleagues away from revolutionary syndicalism. However, many of those expelled, such as Joan Peiró, remained loyal to their ideological beliefs. That the witch hunt included men such as Peiró, who had played such a key role in the attempted reorganisation of the CNT in relation to the FAI from 1928 onwards, is testimony to the heated relations during the Second Republic.

A feature of the disputes between the radicals and syndicalists in the first year of the Second Republic was the *faistas'* permanent hostility to the Republic in the face of the more tolerant position adopted by the syndicalists. As has been seen, relations between the CNT and the Republicans had been a growing source of contention throughout the period of reorganisation. In this climate, the conflict between the two tendencies was now all the more intense due to the real possibility of imminent revolutionary change in Spain. The radicals feared that the syndicalists were prepared to accept a liberal Republic that guaranteed them full rights of association as a goal in itself rather than as a step towards revolutionary change. Radical anarchists had blamed the collapse of the revolutionary movement during the Bolshevik triennium of 1917–1919 on the willingness of the moderates to negotiate with political parties. With the prospect of social revolution finally at hand, they were not prepared to allow this to happen again, especially now that these parties were in government. The syndicalists themselves feared a repetition of the early 1920s when the independence of the CNT had been called into question by the actions of radical anarchist groups. The arrival of the FAI, and its close relationship with the CNT during the attempted reorganisation of 1928, only intensified their fears. Yet this could not justify the attempt by Pestaña to foist professionalism on the unions. As Peiró's criticism made clear, Pestaña had stepped outside the ideological boundaries of revolutionary syndicalism. Furthermore, with Peiró as national secretary during the 1928 relaunch, the trabazón had been limited to the Committee of Revolutionary Action and the Prisoners' Committees, and, although the FAI hoped to win support for the expansion of the trabazón into other areas in the future, in the meantime it had accepted the limits imposed. Rather than a measured reaction to the formation of the FAI, Pestaña's response only served to justify the radical anarchists'

CONCLUSION

THE GROWTH OF REVOLUTIONARY SYNDICALISM REVITALISED THE anarchist movement, providing a means to rekindle its influence in the organised labour movement. Anarchism and revolutionary syndicalism shared the same ultimate goal, the destruction of state power and the introduction of a new society based on libertarian principles, as well as the tactics required to bring this about, direct action. Both doctrines rejected the socialist claim that emancipation could be achieved through parliamentary politics. Adherents believed that participation in any aspect of the parliamentary system or government-sponsored arbitration boards would divert the workers away from revolution and towards collaboration with their enemy, the state. However, this rejection entailed a form of political abstention that created confusion and confrontation between anarchism and syndicalism. This was in large part due to the anarchist fear that the political void at the heart of revolutionary syndicalism would inevitably be filled by their political opponents, either the communists or the left-wing Republicans, and anarchist involvement in the unions would be vastly reduced, as it had been at the end of the nineteenth century. Although welcome, the resurgence in anarchist fortunes associated with the rise of revolutionary syndicalism also brought with it problems, as it created a level of anarchist dependence on the syndicalist movement. Without influence in the unions, anarchism would be a revolutionary ideology with no revolutionary force. However, anarchists believed that, as the unions were created to defend and protect the workers against the inequalities of the capitalist system, they would eventually seek a modus vivendi with that system to achieve short-term improvements. Therefore, it was the task of the anarchists to ensure that this did not happen. This would be achieved by imbuing the unions with the revolutionary spirit of anarchism and thus ensuring that syndicalism remained revolutionary.

Events in Spain and the repercussions of developments abroad conspired to make this a confrontational and divisive task. The most significant factor was the almost constant repression that the CNT faced during the period covered in this book. Between 1911 and 1931 the CNT enjoyed at most four years of unfettered existence, with the main period being between 1916 to 1919. Its rapid expansion in this period brought a violent reaction from the combined forces of the state and the Employers' Federation, and this ushered in a period of social war fought predominantly, though not solely, in Catalonia. The failure of the revolutionary period to bring about substantial improvements for the working class, the extreme violence of state and employer reaction, the resultant adoption of armed insurrection and violence by the confederation, and the later forced exile of confederal militants (whether abroad or into other labour organisations during the Primo de Rivera regime) obliged the CNT to reappraise its tactics. At the same time, the rise of Bolshevism and the decline of the anarchist movement outside Spain similarly forced anarchists to review their tactics in relation to the labour movement.

Whereas anarchism encompassed a holistic approach to life, providing solutions to social, economic, and political issues (the latter considered as the administration of society rather than the governance of the state), revolutionary syndicalism confined itself to the economic struggles of the working class. The immediate aim of revolutionary syndicalism was to gather together all organised union forces into a powerful revolutionary class association with sufficient strength to defeat the state. Revolutionary syndicalism was therefore based on class and not ideology. To avoid potential divisions, revolutionary syndicalism initially adopted a policy of political neutrality, by which membership was open to all workers, irrespective of their political beliefs, as long as they kept their political ideas outside the unions. But by stifling political debate the unions effectively denied themselves the necessary leadership to achieve their ultimate goal. This flaw at the centre of the pre–First World War revolutionary syndicalist doctrine only became apparent when a revolution became an actual possibility. Limited by its economic concerns, the syndicalist movement could initiate revolutionary protest but without political direction proved unable to bring this to a successful conclusion, in stark contrast to the success of the Bolsheviks in Russia.

If the revolution was not sparked by a spontaneous revolt of the oppressed following the classic nineteenth-century model to which many anarchists had been so attached, despite its evident failings and failures, then clearly some form of organisation was needed to provoke and maintain the revolution. This was obvious even before the Bolsheviks seized power in Russia – and essential afterwards. There were many elements of the revolutionary process in Russia in 1917 that did seem to follow the anarchist interpretations of how a revolutionary movement should evolve – the peasant seizures of land, the spontaneous creation of soviets (administrative councils), the growth of the syndicalist movement – and indeed many anarchists even supported the Bolshevik seizure of power, judging, as Copp has argued, that cooperation was necessary "if the anarchists' fundamental goal of a social revolution was to be accomplished, [and it] allowed the anarchists to focus on the Bolsheviks' 'good' side and work together with their 'revolutionary brethren' and ignore the rivalry of the past."[1] They realised their mistake too late. The mere fact of having successfully taking over the political apparatus blinded many to how this made the deeper political, social, and cultural transformations vital for a real revolutionary social transformation even more distant.

The anarchists could point to the fact that they had been right about the dictatorial tendencies inherent in Marxist theory that were pushed to extremes in Lenin's elitist doctrine, but this was cold comfort. The

Bolshevik success had shown up the evident weaknesses in anarchist revolutionary theory. There had been many anarchists active in Russia in the 1917, in the unions, in the Soviets, and elsewhere. There was evidence of "strong support" in urban areas, Copp notes, and even among the peasantry, but the Russian anarchists were unorganised: "While their individual responses were nearly always principled and often even heroic, the failure of their attempt to develop a national umbrella organisation and the contradictory responses of the anarcho-communists and the anarcho-syndicalists to the establishment of class institutions demonstrate the futility of the anarchists' efforts to band together to produce their dream of revolution."[2] Division and lack of organisation were their downfall. The Bolsheviks simply filled the political void, because no other leftist group was able to see the danger they presented to alternative visions of a socialist or workers' Russia and stop them.

Not surprisingly, given the success of the October Revolution, revolutionary syndicalist organisations across Europe and the world were initially attracted to the Bolshevik attempts to create a syndicalist International. However, once the authoritarian and politically dominated nature of Bolshevik communism became clear, with the exception of the French CGTU they immediately distanced themselves from Moscow and established an alternative International, the International Working Men's Association, the name harking back to that of the First International. The formation of the new IWMA was actually the culmination of a process that had begun at the International Syndicalist Congress in London in 1913. The new International adapted the principles of revolutionary syndicalism agreed upon at the 1913 congress to reflect the lessons learnt in the intervening years. Political neutrality was now seen to be impracticable, not simply because it dulled the effective revolutionary potential of the unions but also because it permitted members of political organisations which favoured parliamentary politics or, in the case of communists, state-centric and authoritarian politics, influence in the running of the unions. Neutrality was impossible, given that the defined communist policy towards the unions was to undermine their opponents and subjugate all initiatives to the dictates of the communist party. The IWMA statutes dropped political neutrality in favour of a more clearly antipolitical stance, declaring the association's opposition to all political parties. Nevertheless, although maintaining its institutional independence from all non–trade union organisations, the IWMA differentiated between political parties that aimed for political power and those whose ideological associations, such as anarchist groups, shared revolutionary syndicalism's rejection of authoritarianism and statism.

The IWMA welcomed all syndicalist organisations that accepted the basic principles of revolutionary syndicalism: the rejection of parliamentary or party politics; the use of direct action; a federalist or decentralised organisational structure; and the acceptance of the class struggle, though not necessarily its predominance over all other issues. As such, it welcomed members as diverse as the FORA, which supported the MOA, and the Dutch NSF, which distanced itself completely from the Dutch anarchist movement. Although anarcho-syndicalists occupied influential positions in other member organisations, such as the CGTP and the USI, the CNT was the sole anarcho-syndicalist member of the IWMA, with the possible exception of the FAUD (for which little information is available).

The CNT's departure from the revolutionary syndicalist norm of political neutrality was implicit in the motion adopted at its 1911 congress, which rejected that syndicalism *suffit à tout*. However, as the CNT was immediately banned, it did not fully elaborate its ideological position until eight years later. During this interlude, the role of anarchism within the confederation became even more prominent. The relaunch of the CNT following the El Ferrol congress was supervised by a new generation of militants imbued with faith in anarchism. During the meteoric rise in confederation membership in the following years, the first signs of discord between anarchism and syndicalism became evident. The motion on ideology passed at the Madrid congress, which confirmed that the CNT's ultimate goal was declared to be libertarian communism (that is, anarchism), was actually a compromise between the emerging moderate and radical factions. Both factions willingly committed the CNT to the "liberation of humanity morally, economically and politically" and the destruction of "the tyrannical power of the state."[3] The reference to political emancipation alongside the adoption of anarchism as the confederation's ultimate aim again went beyond the revolutionary syndicalist claim that syndicalism sufficed in itself and suggested a special relationship between the CNT and the anarchist movement. The motion essentially defined the CNT as an anarcho-syndicalist organisation.

Anarcho-syndicalism represented a synthesis of anarchist goals with syndicalist means. It reunited the collectivist and communist factions of the anarchist movement that had been split during the late nineteenth century. As has been seen, the collectivists (associated with Bakunin and the anti-authoritarian First International) had always accepted the need to act through the labour movement and shared many of Marx's basic theories on the class struggle. The anarcho-communists grudgingly came to accept the potential benefits that syndicalism offered to the anarchist movement, but they remained suspicious of the reformist nature of the labour movement. This position was perhaps most clearly expressed by the Italian anarchist Errico Malatesta, whose articles on syndicalism appeared regularly in the anarchist press in most countries, especially Spain. For Malatesta, the unions provided fertile ground for anarchists to propagate their ideas to the working class, who were now universally accepted as the most likely source of revolutionary action. However, according to Malatesta, the unions were by nature reformist, having been created in reaction to the inequalities of the existing system of economic relations under capitalism, a system with which they would logically seek a practical compromise. In short, anarchism without syndicalism would be a revolutionary ideology without any revolutionary potential, whilst revolutionary syndicalism without anarchism would provide the force but not the ideological direction. Syndicalism provided the force to destroy capitalism, but it did not necessarily have the ideas to create communism. The dichotomy between necessity and mistrust created an uneasy basis for the relationship between anarchism and syndicalism.

In Spain the anarcho-syndicalist position was defended by leading militants, such as Carbó and Orobón Fernández, as well as by the Committee of Anarchist Relations in the mid 1920s, all of whom argued that anarchism and syndicalism were two different concepts and should not be confused. Anarchism was the goal and syndicalism the means. However, this did not mean that anarchist ideals should guide the day-to-day running of the unions, which should respond to day-to-day requirements, as long as these did not break with the principles of revolutionary syndicalism. Anarchists should work against the creation of a leadership elite, work to maintain the federalist base of the labour movement, and guard against the encroachment of reformist or communist domination in the unions, without themselves seeking to dominate the unions. Despite the conflict between radicals and syndicalists in Catalonia, anarcho-syndicalism remained the defined ideological position of the CNT throughout the 1920s and 1930s.

Alongside anarcho-syndicalism there were three further ideological tendencies within the CNT during this period: the communist syndicalists, the revolutionary syndicalists, and the radical anarchists. Without becoming too bogged down in specifics, each tendency can be further subdivided. By 1930 the communist syndicalists had split between those following the Moscow policy of creating an alternative CNT and the dissident line proposed by Maurín and the founders of the BOC. The revolutionary syndicalists comprised those who remained loyal to the fundamental principles of revolutionary syndicalism, such as Joan Peiró, and those who followed the lead of Pestaña and were prepared to forget these if they felt the situation demanded it. The radical anarchists comprised those who supported the MOA and the so-called anarcho-Bolsheviks who had no clearly defined ideological position except revolutionary activism combined with blind faith in anarchism.

The communist syndicalists were a small group whose influence was limited to the early 1920s, when there was confusion over the exact nature of Bolshevism. Once the evident incompatibility between revolutionary syndicalism and Bolshevism became known, their influence quickly diminished. Following the expulsion of the CSR, the communist syndicalists would have little success in subsequent attempts to directly influence the CNT, unless one considers the cathartic effect their occasional attempts to infiltrate the CNT had on the warring factions within the CNT, most specifically in late 1923 and during the reorganisation in 1930.

The revolutionary syndicalists argued that, despite its ultimate goal being anarchism, the CNT was a purely economic organisation and should remain independent of all political currents, including anarchism. The aim of the confederal unions should be to unite all workers, irrespective of their political ideology, and educate them in the nature of the class struggle through direct involvement in it. This experience would provide the motivating force for the revolution. The failure of the strike movements of the Bolshevik triennial had shown the syndicalists that the CNT was simply not strong enough to mount an effective challenge to the power of the state. The CNT therefore needed to take stock and concentrate on ways to strengthen its ranks without provoking a reaction from the state or employers, as this would only serve to weaken the unions and distance them from their ultimate goal. They were therefore prepared to collaborate with the state, where the alternative was simply further repression, and advised against an overtly aggressive policy, given the CNT's weakness in relation to the strength of the state. The ill-defined and ultimately discarded political motion adopted at the Zaragoza conference in 1922, by which the CNT was obliged to seek solutions for all problems that affected its members, be they economic, cultural, social, or political, was an attempt by the syndicalists to provide a political basis for the CNT that would ensure its independence from political organisations in general and anarchist groups in particular. Although their initial moderation was a reaction to the failure of the 1917–19 revolutionary movement, the syndicalists later found themselves forced to adopt increasingly anti-anarchist positions in reaction to the extremist position adopted by certain sectors of the anarchist movement in Catalonia from 1923 onwards. Following the ban of May 1924, the syndicalists became even more desperate to distance the CNT from its more extreme elements in order to influence the Primo de Rivera dictatorship to restore the confederation's legal status.

This ideological acquiescence in the face of the dictatorship's resilience culminated in the emergence of a division within the revolutionary syndicalist faction. This came to the fore when certain militants, led by Pestaña, launched the campaign in favour of professionalising the unions to fit the requirements of Primo de Rivera's proposed corporate system. Whereas Peiró had seen the need to accept arbitration in one-off situations when there appeared little alternative, as in the case of the mixed commission of 1919, the acceptance of a system in which the CNT would automatically accept mediation in all disputes represented the absolute negation of direct action. This in effect represented the abandonment of revolutionary syndicalism. If it were to abandon direct action, the CNT would differ little from other reformist trade unions. This induced Peiró to launch his crusade against Pestaña and the professionalisation of the unions. In fact, as national secretary he openly embraced the collaboration between the FAI and the CNT in the attempts to reorganise the confederation in 1928, once the limits of FAI interference in the unions had been agreed upon. Although Peiró would take Pestaña's side in the fight against *faista* domination in the unions during the Second Republic, the significance of the splits in the late 1920s should not be underestimated. In acting as they had, Pestaña and his followers had shown that their brand of syndicalism was bereft of ideological principle, just as the radical anarchists claimed.

For the radical anarchists, the CNT existed to bring about the revolution. It was a means to an end, and that end was anarchism. They blamed the failure of the revolutionary movement of 1917–19 on the lack of revolutionary spirit in the workers that was the result of the syndicalist preoccupation with economic and not ideological issues. As its goal was anarchism, the CNT, they felt, should seek to instil an anarchist spirit into the workers. Therefore, as soon as circumstances permitted, the radical anarchists sought to take a more active role in union affairs. The result was an increase in anarchist interference in union affairs during the transport strike in Barcelona in 1923, which precipitated the military seizure of power in September that year. During this period, a small group of dedicated revolutionaries came to the fore. The anarcho-Bolsheviks were, above all, fanatics of revolutionary activism. Their radicalism attracted sympathy not simply from anarchists and anarcho-syndicalists alike but even from Maurín and the communist syndicalists. But their numbers were limited and their influence disappeared as they were arrested or forced into exile. Whereas the anarcho-Bolsheviks put action before ideas, the majority of radical anarchists actually blamed the lack of ideas within the CNT for its defeat at the hands of the combined forces of state and employers in the early 1920s. Angered by the syndicalists' attempts to seek a modus vivendi with the military dictatorship, which included a dilution of the principles of direct action and an apparent rejection of its anarchist heritage, these radical anarchists proposed the Movimiento Obrero Anarquista. The basic concept behind the MOA was that class unity was a myth. This had been amply demonstrated by the existence of two, and in some countries three, national union organisations claiming to represent specifically working-class goals. The existence of unions attached to the reformist socialist and communist parties demonstrated that it was more natural to organise workers according to their ideological sympathies. The radical anarchists feared that if the syndicalists successfully discarded political ideas from the unions, the CNT would lack both a sense of purpose and direction and would become easy prey to the political machinations of bourgeois or communist politics. The radical anarchists did not intend that all members of the MOA should be anarchists but that they should accept anarchism as their ultimate goal and the guiding force in the struggle between the unions and the state. The difference between the radicals and the anarcho-syndicalists was one of degree rather than ideas. The radicals wanted anarchists to play a leading role in the day-to-day affairs and decision-making of the unions, whereas the anarcho-syndicalists accepted the economic nature of the labour struggle, assigning to anarchism the educational task within the unions of preparing the workers for the struggle ahead and the implementation of the CNT's final goal, anarchism. The anarcho-syndicalists wanted to guide, the radicals to police. As with the syndicalists' political motion put forward at the Zaragoza conference of 1922, the intricacies of the MOA's polices were never fully clarified, and it is not clear how the MOA would have operated or attracted a mass membership to an ideologically exclusive organisation.

There was an evident interplay between the radical and syndicalist positions, with each move by one creating a counterreaction from the other. Both were, however, atavistic attempts to come to terms with the changes that had been brought about in the wake of the First World War. The supporters of the MOA harked back to the days of the FRE when, they claimed, the labour movement had united behind anarchist ideals. This was simply not true, however. Although anarchists had played a leading role in the FRE, the federation was not a prototype of the MOA, and membership had been open to all workers. The birth of the revolutionary syndicalist movement represented the realisation that a strong organised mass was necessary to overthrow the increasingly centralised and powerful forces of the state. The MOA simply represented ideological exclusivity, and its implementation would have led to splits in the Spanish libertarian movement. This had happened in Argentina, where the independent anarchist organisation actually supported the syndicalist alternative to the pro-MOA FORA. The syndicalists likewise looked to the past, supporting the apolitical stance of the Charter of Amiens, despite the fact that the IWMA had accepted the redundancy of such a position in the postwar era. Political neutrality had not prevented the French CGT from collaborating with the French government during the war, nor had it protected the CGTU from communist domination in the early 1920s. In France, the revolutionary syndicalists stuck rigidly to the principles of class unity for too long and became marginalised from both the CGT and the CGTU. When they eventually formed their own national organisation, following prompting from Spanish and Italian exiles, it was too late. The majority of unions sympathetic to revolutionary syndicalism had already decided to either stay in one of the other two confederations or to remain autonomous.

The demise of the French revolutionary syndicalist movement was symptomatic of the malaise the IWMA found itself in by the late 1920s. The revolutionary syndicalists had no defence against the growing trend in dictatorial government and, unlike the communists, had no state apparatus to fund their development or provide a safe haven where their militants could gather without fear of arrest. By the early 1920s, leading Russian libertarians had been forced into exile, to be followed soon after by members of the USI, which was banned in 1922 following the Fascist seizure of power in Italy. Military coups in Spain and Portugal forced militants of the CNT and CGTP to join their Russian and Italian comrades in exile. France, the preferred destination of the majority of exiles, was initially lenient towards the political activity of exiles, but this tolerance ended in 1926. A military coup in Argentina in 1930 effectively ended the militancy of the FORA, whilst Hitler's accession to power in January 1933 would later force both the FAUD and the IWMA secretariat from Germany to France. Meanwhile, the international anarchist movement was in an even worse state. Increasingly weak and irrelevant in the face of the constant repression and communist success in attracting the revolutionary wing of the working classes, the international anarchist movement withdrew into sectarianism and defeatism instead of attempting to unite and face the challenges of the post–First World War era. Attempts to create an anarchist International failed due to differences of opinion or simple indifference. The FAI's attempt in 1928 to gain approval for the creation of an international trabazón that would link an anarchist International to the IWMA was rejected by both the anarchist and the IWMA congresses of 1928. Outside the FAI's proposal, the only serious attempt to create a revolutionary anarchist International was made by the Russian anarchists. However, although focusing on the labour movement, the Platform was essentially a libertarian version of Bolshevik centralism and enjoyed little support beyond the already elitist and exclusive world of French anarchism.

Behind all these attempts at forming a coherent anarchist movement lay the fear and jealousy inspired by the Bolshevik victory in Russia and the subsequent growth of the communist movement in Europe. Previously it had been the anarchists who were the communists (albeit anarcho-communist) and the revolutionaries. Although rejecting the political domination implicit within Bolshevism, the anarchists were forced to accept the benefits of tighter organisation, as had been amply demonstrated during the 1917 October Revolution in Russia. The Russian Revolution and the revolutionary movements that briefly shone in the immediate postwar period had once again reaffirmed the central role played by the working class. Meanwhile, the Comintern had set the communist parties of the world the task of infiltrating the unions and combating anarcho-syndicalism. The anarchists not only had to defend themselves but also preserve the revolutionary syndicalist movement from Bolshevism. But, whereas the communists had the heavily financed Comintern propaganda machine behind them, the anarchists had nothing but themselves.

The pitiful state of the libertarian movement elsewhere, the experience of the exiled Spanish anarchists in France, and the intensity of the internecine conflict in Catalonia had demonstrated that anarchists needed their own organisation independent of, but not detached from, the unions. Anarchists had to accept limitations to their influence within the unions. However, given the policies towards the unions pursued by other political organisations, they could not permit syndicalism to adopt an open-door policy. What was required was an uneasy balancing act in which the anarchists worked to maintain the CNT's organisational structure, its commitment to direct action, and its ultimate goal to achieve anarchism without interfering directly in day-to-day union matters. This could best be achieved if the anarchists kept their ideological disputes concerning their position toward syndicalism outside the unions as far as possible. Hence the necessity for an independent anarchist organisation. Previously, the national anarchist congresses of 1918 and 1923 had both resisted forming such an organisation. The 1918 congress simply decided that henceforth anarchists should take a more prominent role in the CNT's activities, whilst the next national congress, in 1923, although agreeing to the formation of a National Committee of Anarchist Relations, stopped short of creating a national organisation, as this was deemed unnecessary, given the existence of the CNT. However, as the conflict between the radical anarchists and syndicalists intensified, both the national and the exiled Committee of Anarchist Relations and numerous leading anarchists came out in opposition to the MOA and argued that there needed to be clear distance between anarchism and syndicalism. The creation of the FAI therefore represented an unstated compromise among anarchists: it was an independent anarchist organisation that would be organically linked to the CNT. Although supporters of the MOA initially dominated the FAI, they accepted that they could not force their ideas upon the CNT and adopted a less radical policy instead. The trabazón established an organic link between the anarchist and syndicalist organisations in areas of mutual interest to both, which the supporters of the MOA hoped would expand into other areas. Nonetheless, the FAI accepted the limits imposed on the trabazón by the CNT, which gave the confederation autonomy in union affairs.

The FAI was created at a time when the fortunes of the international libertarian movement were at a low, a fact reflected by the constant call for unity from leading FAI militants, such as Magriñà and Jiménez. Splitting the CNT was the exact opposite of what FAI leaders wanted. Their aim was to win support for the MOA by demonstrating the benefits of close collaboration in certain fields with the CNT, in the hope that this would spill over into other areas. This position was made clear by the Spanish section of the FAI in their response to the Valencian anarchists' attempts to force the Levante CRT to accept the trabazón. For the anarcho-syndicalists, the limited implementation of the trabazón was consistent with their beliefs that the anarchist and syndicalist organisations should work closely together but that the unions should have complete independence in internal union affairs. At its 1928 congress, the IWMA had found an understanding between anarchism and syndicalism and even went as far as praising the cooperation between the FAI and CNT. The FAI's relative moderation is in stark contrast to what was to happen during the Second Republic and, significantly, to that of the syndicalists, who on two occasions in 1926 and 1929 had been prepared to split the confederation in pursuit of their ideas.

The activities of certain leading syndicalists during the reorganisation of the CNT in 1930 only served to further anarchist fears about their loyalty to the principles of revolutionary syndicalism. Initially, the reorganisation provided a momentary pause in the ideological infighting, as militants focused on reorganising the unions, on combating the communists' attempts to create a parallel organisation, and on the numerous conspiracies to overthrow the ailing monarchy. Nonetheless, the divisions were never far from the surface. Their cause was the growing anarchist suspicion of the contacts of leading syndicalists with Republican parties. Given that the anarchist critique of the defined political neutrality of the syndicalists was due to their belief in the inevitability that some other group would fill the political void, their fears are not hard to understand. Although contacts were theoretically limited to conspiracies to overthrow the monarchy, it was no secret that some Republicans, specifically in Catalonia, wished to negotiate the CNT's compliance in the consolidation of the Republic. It would soon become clear that leading syndicalists would be prepared to support such a position, albeit unofficially and with no pacts. By 1930, fears of anarchist domination and a return to the policies advocated by the anarcho-Bolsheviks in 1923 had led many syndicalists to conclude that they were happier dealing with Republicans than the FAI. Ironically, this was exactly what the radicals had claimed the limitations of their ideological position would force them to do. By distancing themselves from anarchism, the ideology embraced by the majority of the confederation's leading militants, the syndicalists were, in effect, vitiating the CNT and depriving it of its revolutionary impetus. This deviation from the revolutionary path was at the heart of the disputes between anarchists and syndicalists during the 1920s. By 1930, the syndicalists not only seemed opposed to the prefix 'anarcho-' being attached to 'syndicalism', but to the adjective 'revolutionary' as well.

Significantly, one of the two areas in which the CNT accepted the trabazón with the FAI was in the field of revolutionary action. Anarchist mistrust of syndicalism's revolutionary credentials was at the heart of the ideological disagreements that raged within the CNT throughout the 1920s and the following decade. The irony that a theoretically antipolitical organisation was torn apart by arguments concerning politics can only be understood as part of an overall assessment of the CNT's revolutionary nature. The ideological conflict that bedevilled the CNT was a further example of the reformist-revolutionary dichotomy common to other European labour movements. The inability of the PSOE and its union adjunct, the UGT, to appeal to the working classes in specific regions, most notably Catalonia, due to their state-centric and rigidly reformist approach, coupled with the general distrust the workers felt toward a corrupt political system whose labour policy ranged from blind indifference to the sufferings of the working class to violent oppression when the workers dared to protest, meant that, in certain regions of Spain, the reformist-revolutionary conflict was confined to the unions of the CNT. But while the UGT already fulfilled the role of a reformist organisation, the CNT existed to represent an alternative ideological approach to labour protest. The syndicalist policy of political neutrality had failed. A failed ideological position that meant that politics was excluded from the unions had led them to reformism and had provided the fuel for extremism on the other side.

Speaking during the Spanish Civil War, Pierre Besnard, who had been secretary general of the CGTSR and was at the time secretary of the IWMA, argued that anarcho-syndicalists had "no difficulty in agreeing that anarcho-communist groups ... should go prospecting among the labouring masses; that they should seek out recruits and temper militants; that they should carry out active propaganda and intensive pioneering work with an eye to winning the greatest possible number of workers hitherto deceived and gulled by all the political parties, without exception, over to their side and thus to the anarcho-syndicalist trade unions" but said they should do this "on the express condition that they identify with the work of the anarcho-syndicalist trade unions which they complement and reinforce, for the greater good of libertarian communism" and that "the decision-making responsibility, action and supervision of the latter should reside in the here-and-now with the trade unions as the executive agents and operatives carrying out revolutionary tasks." The anarchists should concentrate on preparing the union members ideologically for the revolution and the future society and leave the day-to-day running of the unions to the syndicalists. The connection between syndicalist and communist movements is based on one clear fact: "the anarcho-syndicalist movement represents the means whereby libertarian communism can be achieved." For Besnard, "Anarchism assists the anarcho-syndicalist movement, without supplanting it."[4]

"The workers' movement is an instrument to be used today for raising and educating the masses, and tomorrow for the inevitable clash." Nonetheless "it would be a great and fatal illusion to believe, as many do, that the workers' movement can and must on its own, by its very nature, lead to such a revolution." The anarchists, Besnard continued, "do not wish to dominate [the unions]; they would not wish to even if all the workers in its ranks were anarchists, neither do they wish to assume the responsibility for negotiations [with employers or the state]. We do not seek power, only want the consciences of men; only those who wish to dominate prefer sheep, the better to lead them."[5] The basis for common action could not be outlined more clearly. Yet internal divisions and mistrust against a backdrop of almost constant repression and ferocious ideological battle within the working-class movement as a whole conspired to make its implementation a Herculean task. Division as much as repression was the CNT's worst enemy, as it was for the international anarchist movement as a whole.

Without the force created by a unified working-class organisation, industrial capitalism – maintained by its apparatus of control, the nation-state – could not be defeated, but without some form of ideological leadership those making up this force could easily lose sight (or be made to lose sight) of its goals, blinded by the promises of liberalism. They could become disorientated and emasculated by the reformist and eventually pro-capitalist tendencies of social democracy. Together they might become the silenced partner in an imposed project ostensibly engineered to liberate them, as would occur in the twentieth century with devastating effect.

ENDNOTES

Introduction

1 Errico Malatesta, *Il Risveglio*, 1–15 October, 1927, in Vernon Richards, *Errico Malatesta: His Life and Ideas* (London: Freedom Press, 1993), 113.

2 'Libertarian' is the generic term used to describe the combination of the anarchist and syndicalist movements. For the sake of clarity, in this book the term 'anarchist movement' when not following the words 'overall' or 'global', refers to anarchists or anarchist organisation independent of, or acting outside of, unions.

3 For example, in a capitalist society the state creates laws allowing the functioning of a 'free' market (or denying the implementation of those that soften the impact of the same) and wields the tools of repression necessary to control and subjugate those most negatively affected by this.

4 Javier Paniagua, "Una gran pregunta y varios repuestos. El anarquismo Español: desde la política a la historiografía," *Historia Social* 12 (1992), 31–57.

5 For a classic Marxist analysis, see Eric Hobsbawm, *Primitive Rebels* (Manchester: Manchester University Press, 1959) and *Revolutionaries* (London: Phoenix, 1994). For classic liberal interpretations, see F. Borkenau, *The Spanish Cockpit* (London: Pluto Press, 1986) and Gerald Brenan, *The Spanish Labyrinth* (Cambridge: University of Cambridge Press, 1993).

6 For Hobsbawn, the success of "anarchism was a disaster," a "tragic farce" for Spain precisely because it got in the way of the "logical" evolution towards Marxism. Judging by his bibliography and the footnotes, this opinion comes mainly from liberal historians and Spanish Marxists – there is no evidence in his bibliography that he contemplated alternative views. He concludes, "In my view anarchism has no significant contribution to socialist theory to make." We should not be too surprised of such a view from a lifetime member of the British Communist Party. Hobsbawm, *Revolutionaries*, 71–91.

7 J. Joll, *The Anarchists* (London: Eyre & Spottiswoode, 1964); George Woodcock, *Anarchism*, (Harmondsworth: Pelican, 1963); Peter Marshall, *Demanding the Impossible* (London: Fontana Press, 1993).

8 The majority of these works focus on the years of the Second Republic and the Civil War — e.g., Julian Casanova, *De la Calle al Frente. El anarcosindicalismo en España 1931–39* (Barcelona: Critica, 1997) and John Brademas, *Anarcosindicalismo y revolución en España* (Barcelona: Ariel, 1974) – and on regional movements, e.g., Angeles Barrio Alonso, *Anarquismo y anarcosindicalismo en Asturias (1890–1936)* (Madrid: Siglo XXI, 1988); Graham Kelsey, *Anarchosyndicalism, Libertarian Communism, and the State: The CNT in Zaragoza and Aragon, 1930–1937* (Amsterdam: International Institute of Social History, 1991); José Manuel Macaro Vera, *La Utopía revolucionaria; Sevilla en la Segunda República* (Seville: Monte de Piedad y Caja de Ahorros de Sevilla, 1985); Enrique Montañés, *Anarcosindicalismo y cambio político: Zaragoza 1930–6*, (Zaragoza:

Institución Fernando el Católico, 1989); Laura Vicente, *Sindicalismo y conflictividad social en Zaragoza (1916–1923)* (Zaragoza: Institución Fernando el Católico, 1993); Eulàlia Vega, *El trentisme a Catalunya. Divergències ideològiques en la CNT 1930–33* (Barcelona: Curial, 1980); Eulàlia Vega, *Entre Revolució i Reforma: La CNT a Catalunya (1930–1936)* (Lerida: Pagès, 2004); Eulàlia Vega, *Anarquistas y Sindicalistas durante la Segunda República; La CNT y los sindicatos de Oposición en el País Valenciano* (Valencia: Edicions Alfons el Magnàmin, 1987); Dionisio Pereira, *A CNT na Galicia 1922–36* (Santiago de Compostela: Edicions Laiovento, 1994).

9   Josep Termes, *Història del moviment anarquista a Espanya (1870–1980)* (Barcelona: L'Avenç, 2011), 17.

10   According to Raymond Carr, *Spain, 1808–1975* (Oxford: Clarendon, 1982), 490, the Restoration was epitomised by the "decadent parliamentarianism" of "a conglomeration of factions without a programme." For a full critique of the Restoration system, see ibid., 489–508, and B. Martin, *The Agony of Modernisation. Labor and Industrialisation in Spain* (New York: Ithaca, 1990), 175–88.

11   Miguel Ángel Serrano, *La ciudad de las bombas: Barcelona y los años trágicos del movimiento obrero* (Madrid: Temas de Hoy, 1997), 26.

12   See Manuel Ballbe, *Orden público y militarismo en la España constitutional (1812–1983)* (Madrid: Alianza, 1985) and Paul Preston, *The Politics of Revenge: Fascism and the Military in Twentieth Century Spain* (London: Routledge, 1994).

13   The main problems were caused by inflation and a rapid decline in the cost of living for the labour force, especially in comparison with the evident enrichment of the industrialists. With 1913 prices as an index of 100, by 1918 prices had increased to 218.2 whereas wages had only risen to 125.6.

14   According to Ballbe, *Orden público y militarismo en la España constitutional*, 273, the Restoration had a "pronounced military tint." Ballbe cites Manuel Azaña, a liberal politician and future prime minister and president of the Second Republic, who wrote when General Primo de Rivera seized power in a military coup in September 1923, "Those who govern Spain openly today are those who have been in power for years," 303.

15   See Xavier Paniagua, *La Sociedad Libertaria. Agrarismo e industrializacion en el anarquismo español 1930–9* (Barcelona: Editorial Crítica, 1982), which analyses the different approaches of a number of prominent anarchists and syndicalists to envisioning the nature of a future libertarian society.

16   According to Emile Pouget, editor of the Confederación General del Trabajo (CGT) newspaper *La Voix du Peuple*, "Direct action is a notion of such clarity, of such self-evident transparency, that merely to speak the words defines and explains them. It means that the working class, in constant rebellion against the existing state of affairs, expects nothing from outside people, powers or forces, but rather creates its own conditions of struggle and looks to itself for its means of action. It means that, against the existing society which recognises only the citizen, looms the producer." Emile Pouget, *Las bases del sindicalismo* (Madrid: Tierra y Libertad, 1904). The CGT developed a theory of direct action which essentially centred around the use of strikes not only to gain material benefits

and create class consciousness as argued by Marx, but also to prepare the workers for the coming revolution, providing the training ground, revolutionary drill, and a preview of tactics for the culminating act, the general strike, which would bring about the revolution. Alongside the 'theory of the strike', a number of tactics were employed, including boycotts of the goods of employers who mistreated employees, the labeling of goods produced by good employers (an official endorsement of the products), and sabotage. These tactics were usually used in combination with strike actions.

17   Rudolph Rocker, *Anarchosyndicalism* (London: Pluto Press, 1989), 90. Rudolf Rocker was one of the leading figures in the international revolutionary syndicalist movement in the first half of the twentieth century. With his book on anarchosyndicalism, first published towards the end of the Spanish Civil War in 1938, he hoped to explain the basic tenets of the ideology to the working classes in the United Kingdom. In the book he confuses revolutionary syndicalism with anarcho-syndicalism to such an extent that there appears no difference between them. Such a definition is inaccurate and can only be understood due to the propaganda impact Rocker hoped that his work (and the heroic struggle of the CNT during the Civil War) would have on the British proletariat.

18   Ibid.

19   The basic structure of the CNT is outlined in Alexander Schapiro, "Rapport sur l'activité de la Confédération Nationale du Travail d'Espagne, 16 décembre 1932–26 février 1933," held in the archives of the International Working Men's Association (IWMA) at the International Institute for Social History (IISG) in Amsterdam, file 9.

20   Anna Monjo Omedes, "La CNT durant la II República a Barcelona: Líders, militants, afiliats," PhD thesis, Barcelona, Universitat de Barcelona, 1994, 375.

21   In giving this brief outline of the organisational functioning of the CNT, it must be kept in mind that between 1910 and 1931 the confederation was almost constantly the victim of government persecution and, as such, the procedures outlined above rarely functioned normally. In this environment, the role of the militants was especially important.

22   Revolutionary syndicalism had initially adopted an apolitical stance but would evolve a more clearly antopolitical stance following the rise of Bolshevism. 'Antipolitical' in this case does not mean no politics but implies an implicit rejection of the interference of the political parties or parliamentary politics in the emancipation of the workforce: "By calling ourselves antipolitical, we have always meant that we are enemies of parliamentary action. Nothing more." Joan Peiró, "Los partidos de izquierda y los anarquistas," *L'Opinió*, September 15, 1928. For a description of what the Spanish anarchists meant by 'antipolitical', see J. Alvarez Junco, *La ideológica política del Anarquismo (1868–1910)* (Madrid: Siglo XXI, 1991), 411–25.

23   The Asturian anarchist Ricardo Mella, who influenced leading anarchists such as Abad de Santillán, argued, "We anarchists can and must say: the revolution that we envisage goes beyond the interest of one specific class; it wants to achieve the complete liberation of humanity, from all political, economic and

moral bondage." R. Mella, "La Lucha de Clases," *Acción Libertaria* (Madrid), December 12, 1913.

24   Errico Malatesta, the most prominent anarcho-communist writer of the time (after the death of Kropotkin), argued that "among anarchists a self-styled individualist minority exists which is a permanent cause of unpleasantness and weakness." "Individualism and Communism in Anarchism," article reproduce-din Errico Malatesta, *The Anarchist Revolution (Polemical Articles 1924–1931)* (London: Freedom Press, 1995), 18–22

25   "It is nothing new to point out that in Spain anarchism, or at least the most important faction of anarchism, has an essentially class character: it is of the workers, it is proletarian." Evelio G. Fontaura, "Contra la Proletarizacion del anarquismo," *Tierra Libre*, October 25, 1930. Fontaura was one of the leading figures of the FAI at the time.

26   The late Juan Gómez Casas, a former secretary of the reformed CNT, stated in his book *Anarchist Organisation, the History of the FAI* (Montreal: Black Rose Books, 1986), 114, that the FAI's internal organisation was based on the principle of federalism: "The groups in a given locality or district formed a local or district federation. The local or district federation, in turn, joined the regional committee. The regional committee, in turn, formed the Peninsular Committee" (a form of national liaison committee). Prior to the Second Republic this structure existed more in theory than reality.

27   Dolors Marín i Silvestre, "De la llibertat per coneixer al coneixement de la llibertat. L'adquisició de cultura durant la dictadura de Primo de Rivera i la Segona República Espanyola," PhD thesis, Barcelona, Universitat de Barcelona, 1995.

Chapter 1

1   Errico Malatesta claimed that until the Bolsehvik Revolution, when people spoke of communists they were referring to anarchists. Although not entirely accurate, there is a lot of truth in this, therefore any reference to 'communism' prior to 1917 in this book means anarcho-communism. Subsequently 'communism' refers to Bolshevism.

2   See Woodcock, *Anarchism*, and the introduction to Deric Shannon, Anthony Nocella and John Asimakopoulos, eds., *The Accumulation of Freedom – Writings on Anarchist Economics* (Oakland: AK Press, 2012), 11–39.

3   Ibid., 27–28, 64–78. Iain Mackaye claims, with good reason, that Proudhon's "placing of anti-capitalism alongside anti-statism defined anarchism." Mackaye, "Laying the Foundations: Proudhon's Contributions to Anarchist Economics," in ibid., 77.

4   Henryk Katz, *The Emancipation of Labor: A History of the First International* (New York: Greenwood Press, 1992), 37.

5   The extracts of the IWMA resolution and Hins speech are quoted in Rocker, *Anarcosyndicalism*, 72.

6   Katz, *The Emancipation of Labor*, 63.

7   George Woodcock, "Anarchism" in *Encyclopedia of Philosophy* edited by Paul

Edwards (New York: Macmillan, 1967) reproduced at http://theanarchistlibrary
.org/library/george-woodcock-anarchism.html

8   Mark Leier, *Bakunin: A Creative Passion* (New York: Seven Stories
Press, 2006), 252.

9   Bakunin quoted in F. Muñoz, *Bakunin, La liberte* (Paris: Pauvert, 1965), cited
in Alexandre Skirda, *Facing the Enemy. Anarchist Organization from Proudhon to
May 1968* (Oakland: AK Press, 2002), 24.

10   The International Workingmen's Association and the International Alliance
of Socialist Democracy, approved by IWMA General Council December 22,
1868, Marxists Internet Archive, http://www.marxists.org/history/international
/iwma/documents/1868/bakunin-resolution.htm.

11   Leier, Bakunin A Creative Passion, 258.

12   *Ibid.*, 260. At Basel, Bakunin argued in favour of the abolition of the right of
inheritance as an essential condition for the emancipation of labour, whereas the
Marxist position was that inheritance was simply a by-product of the property
system and so it made more sense to attack the system itself. The significant
thing about the debate was that Bakunin used his rhetorical skills to sway opinion in his favour, thus defeating the Marxist position. This worried Marx. See
Marshall, *Demanding the Impossible*, 282.

13   Resolution on Working Class Political Action, International Working Men's
Association, London conference, September 1871, Marxists Internet Archive,
http://www.marxists.org/archive/marx/iwma/documents/1871/political
-action.htm.

14   Katz, *The Emancipation of Labor*, 136–37.

15   Cited by Augustín Souchy, a member of the secretariat of the revolutionary syndicalist IWMA formed in 1922, in "Asociación Internacional de Trabajadores",
Manaña (Barcelona) May 1930.

16   After Saint-Imier, congresses were held in 1873 (September 1–6), 1874
(September 7–13), and 1876 (October 26–29), with the final congress being
held at Verviers, Belgium, from September 6–9, 1877.

17   Skirda, *Facing the Enemy*, 26.

18   Leier, *Bakunin*, 293. A recent example that can serve for all is the otherwise highly recommendable biography of Marx by Francis Wheen. In the chapter on the
disputes in the IWMA, the author descends into a description – 'analysis' would
be too kind a word – of the conflict that wouldn't be out of place in a Murdoch
publication. Bakunin is described as a "hungry hyena" who was "scheming away
as usual" in order to "tiptoe through the back door" and "determined to hijack"
the IWMA, which one must assume, belonged to Marx. Wheen seems to believe
that to question or present alternative views was tantamount to treachery. The
fact that some of the major labour organizations of the International supported
the ideological positions put forward by Bakunin suggest that Wheen has not
quite grasped what was going on. Francis Wheen, *Karl Marx* (London: Fourth
Estate Limited, 1999), 315–47.

19   Leier, *Bakunin*, 277–78.

20   Quoted in ibid., 256.

21   Letter to *La Liberté* (1872) from Michael Bakunin, quoted by Paul McLaughlin in the unpublished article "Bakunin and Marx: An Unbridgeable Chasm?" available on the Loughborough University website, http://www.lboro.ac.uk/media/wwwlboroacuk/content/phir/documentsandpdfs/arg/McLaughlin%20-%20Bakunin%20and%20Marx%20(Loughborough).pdf. See also Paul McLaughlin, *Mikhail Bakunin: The Philosophical Basis of His Anarchism* (New York: Algora, 2002).

22   Kropotkin, the best-known proponent of anarcho-communism, concurs, seeing the relationship between economic and political institutions as a 'symbiosis' rather than in terms of Marx's theory of base and superstructure. See Marshall, *Demanding the Impossible*, 324.

23   Letter to *La Liberté* (1872) from Michael Bakunin, quoted by McLaughlin, *Mikhail Bakunin*, 13.

24   Michael Bakunin, *Statism and Anarchy*, edited by Marshall Shatz (Cambridge: Cambridge University Press, 1990), 179.

25   Michael Bakunin, "Federalism, Socialism, Anti-Theologism" reproduced in *Bakunin on Anarchy*, edited by Sam Dolgoff (New York: Vintage books, 1971), 127.

26   James Guillaume pointed out that Marx "smoked his cigarettes in his London cottage whilst many of those he insults … fought in Paris (the commune) and elsewhere." Quoted in Katz, *The Emancipation of Labor*, 99. Bakunin was "more familiar with real men and real society," says Skirda (*Facing the Enemy*, 28).

27   "'The emancipation of the workers must be accomplished by the workers themselves,' says the Preamble to our General Rules. … But the workers' world is in general unlearned, and it totally lacks theory. Accordingly it is left with but a single path, that of *emancipation through practical action*. [This] means workers' solidarity in their struggle against the bosses. It means *trade-unions, organisation, and the federation of resistance funds*." "The Policy of the International," Mikhail Bakunin, first published in *L'egalité* (Switzerland) August 1869, reproduced in Robert M. Cutler, ed., *From out of the Dustbin: Bakunin's Basic Writings 1869–1871* (Michigan: Ardis, 1985), 97–110.

28   McLaughlin, *Bakunin and Marx: An Unbridgeable Chasm?*, 7.

29   During the period between 1868 and 1910, Kropotkin was the most widely published and translated foreign anarchist author in Spain (with Reclus being the third most popular), and as such his ideas were widely known in anarchist circles in the country. The information is quoted by Termes, *Història del moviment anarquista a Espanya*, 171, who has summarised information from Álvarez Junco, *La ideológica política del Anarquismo*. The French anarcho-communist Jean Grave was second most popular, with eleven publications (seventeen editions) as opposed to Kropotkin's twenty publications (twenty-seven editions).

30   Kropotkin quoted in Lee Alan Dugatkin, *The Prince of Evolution* (CreateSpace, 2011), 67.

31   Quoted in Cutler, ed., *From out of the Dustbin*, 46–47.

32   Peter Kropotkin, *Mutual Aid: A Factor of Evolution* (New York: New York University Press, 1972), 10–11.

33 Errico Malatesta, *Umanità Nova*, September 16, 1922, quoted in Richards, *Errico Malatesta: His Life and Ideas*, 74.

34 Malatesta, *Pensiero e Voluntà*, May 16, 1925, quoted in ibid., 19.

35 McLaughlin, *Bakunin and Marx: An Unbridgeable Chasm?*, 9.

36 Friendly societies were basically mutual aid organizations or benefit clubs in which members would pay a small subscription which would entitle them to a weekly benefit in case of ill health or disability. The French ideologues Henri de Saint-Simon, Charles Fourier, and Étienne Cabet, along with Robert Owen from Wales, were the leading exponents of what Marx and Engels labelled 'utopian socialism' (as opposed their supposedly scientific approach). Although each put forward different socialist projects – Fourier and Cabet favoured the creation of communities based on their ideals, as did Owen, although he also was involved in the creation of unions and cooperatives, whereas Saint-Simon espoused a form of centralized corporate technocracy – they were linked because they all argued that social questions should predominate, that the aim of society should be to promote general happiness and welfare for all, and that the present social and political system should be replaced. A further shared component was the lack of class analysis in their projects and therefore of a revolutionary outlook to bring about change. This went hand in hand with the naïve belief that appealing to the rich and powerful on the basis of justice and fairness would lead them to change their ways. As such, the various communities established based on their theories quickly collapsed through internal squabbling or unrealistic expectations. Owen is often seen as the founder of the cooperative movement, but the self-sufficient colonies that were created based on his ideals rarely flourished. Nonetheless, it was a group of Owen's followers who improved on his ideas, especially in relation to economic policy (mainly in the provision of dividends), that would eventually create the first consumer cooperatives in the 1840s, which would form the basis of the International Cooperative Alliance. At the same time, the 1840s, in Europe, especially in France, production (or workers') cooperatives were being founded under the influence of the ideas of Proudhon. Indeed, Proudhonist mutualism was perhaps the strongest influence in the First International before the struggles between Marxism and Bakunist collectivism. See Katz, *The Emancipation of Labor*, 35. For a description of the initial growth of the cooperative movement, see Jonston Birchall, *The International Cooperative Movement* (Oxford: Alden Press, 1995). For Spain, see Jason Garner, *"Acción Cooperatista": El cooperativismo en Cataluña antes del Franquismo*, forthcoming.

37 Termes, *Història del moviment anarquista a Espanya*, 17.

38 Katz, *The Emancipation of Labor*, 105.

39 The influence of Bakunin was reflected in a speech made by Rafael Farga Pellicer, president of the FRE, about the aims of the new organisation: "We want the end of the capitalist empire, of the state and of the church, in order to build on its ruins anarchy, the free federation of free workers associations." Cited by E. C. Carbó, "La A.I.T. en España," *Suplemento de Tierra y Libertad* (Barcelona), 1931.

40 A strong attachment to class unity would also be evident in revolutionary syndicalism, although the political divisions between Marxists and libertarians,

evident within the socialist movement even during the brief life span of the IWMA, would make the unification of the Spanish workforce in one central organisation an impossible dream. However, on occasion the socialist UGT and the CNT did act together as in 1916 (see below), 1920, and during the Spanish Civil War (1936–39).

41   G. R. Esenwein, *Anarchist Ideology and the Working-Class Movement in Spain, 1868–1898* (Berkeley: University of California Press, 1989), 19.

42   César M. Lorenzo, *Los Anarquistas Españoles y el Poder* (Paris: Ruedo Ibérico, 1973), 184.

43   Termes, *Història del moviment anarquista a Espanya*, 121.

44   Josep Termes, *Anarquismo y sindicalismo en España: la Primera Internacional (1864–1881)* (Barcelona: Ariel, 1972), 251. At its height between 1872–73, FRE membership was between twenty-five thousand and twenty-nine thousand.

45   The failure of the Spanish economic development in the late nineteenth century resulted from a complex interplay of economic and political factors. In Britain an agricultural revolution sparked industrialisation which was itself led by the cotton industry. In Spain the cotton industry did not provide the impetus to industrialisation, and government protection of agriculture helped to maintain it on a subsistence basis. Spain did not have its agricultural revolution, and between 1870 and 1910 the percentage of the population active in agriculture scarcely altered from 70 percent. This, coupled with a lack of innovation in the cotton industry (itself supported by high tariffs) and the loss of key markets following the loss of Spain's last remaining colonies in 1898, resulted in economic stagnation. Other factors that had an impact on the failure to industrialise were the country's dependence on foreign capital, the structure of agriculture, and the inability of government to overcome these structural problems. See Jordi Nadal, *El Fracaso de la Revolución industrial en España, 1814–1913* (Barcelona: Ariel, 1975), 226–45; Álvaro Soto Carmona, *El Trabajo Industrial en la España Contemporánea (1874–1936)* (Barcelona: Antropos, 1989), 45–52; Jaime Vicens Vives, *Manuel de historia económica de España* (Barcelona: Editorial Vicens-Vives, 1959), 671–76. It was only with the First World War that the Spanish economy began to show signs of rapid industrialisation.

46   Álvarez Junco, *La ideológica política del Anarquismo*, 551–53, claims that he could find no reference to the Pacto after 1893. However, Miguel Iñiguez, *Esbozo de una enciclopedia histórico del anarquismo español* (Madrid: Fundación de Estudios Libertarios Anselmo Lorenzo, 2001), 450, puts the date at 1896, although he accepts that between 1893 and 1896 it "scarely exercised influence." See also Laura Vicente, *Teresa Claramunt: Pionera del feminismo Obrerista Anarquista* (Madrid: Fundación de Estudios Libertarios Anselmo Lorenzo, 2006), 116–19.

47   Álvarez Junco, *La ideológica política del Anarquismo*, 551.

48   Fernando Tarrida del Mármol, published in *La Révolte*, 3 no.51 (6–12 September). Translation by Nestor McNab, http://www.anarkismo.net/newswire.php?story_id=4717&print_page=true.

49   Ibid.

50   Translated from Rafael Núñez Florencio, "El terrorismo," in *Tierra y Libertad –
      Cien años de anarquismo en España*, ed. J. Casanova (Barcelona: Critica, 2010), 64.

51   Carlo Cafiero quotes Pisacane in "Action", reproduced in *Anarchism: A
      Documentary History of Libertarian Ideas, Volume One: From Anarchy to
      Anarchism (300CE–1939)*, edited by Robert Graham (Montreal: Black Rose
      Books, 2005), 152–3.

52   According to Juan García Oliver, its leading proponent during the Second
      Republic, the aim of 'revolutionary gymnastics' was "to create in the anar-
      cho-syndicalist militants' way of being the habit of revolutionary actions, re-
      jecting the individual actions of sabotage and terrorist attacks, directing all col-
      lective action against the structures of the capitalist system, until the complex
      of fear towards the repressive forces is overcome, achieving by means of the
      systemization of insurrectional actions, the putting into practice of revolution-
      ary gymnastics." Translated from J. García Oliver, *El Eco de los Pasos* (Barcelona:
      Ruedo Ibérico, 1978), 115.

53   Violence was of course not limited to the anarchists. As well as the People's Will
      in Russia, other groups adopted the policy of bombing and assassination, includ-
      ing the Fenians in Ireland and revolutionary groups in the Ottoman Empire.
      However, perhaps the most evident result was the repression constantly wielded
      by the state, from the 1871 Bloody Week in Paris to the incessant crackdowns on
      strikes or labour protests in the Russian Empire, Spain, Italy, and elsewhere, which
      cost the lives of far more than would fall to the propaganda of the deed.

54   Support for the tactics spread quickly. In 1877 the French anarchist Paul Brosse
      had published an article entitled "Propaganda of the Deed" in the influential
      journal *Bulletin of the Jura Federation* (of the IWMA). Even Kropotkin, the
      leading exponent of the communist tendency, not known for his support of
      violence, initially gave his support to the idea.

55   Marie Fleming, *The Geography of Freedom: The Odyssey of Elisée Reclus* (Montreal:
      Back Rose Books, 1988), 132–33. Fleming suggests that the agreements reached
      at London mirrored those taken at a secret meeting of anarchists in Vevey,
      Switzerland, the year before. She advises caution as the information comes from
      police reports, a constant problem for historians of the movement, but, given
      the similarity of the wording of the agreements of both meetings, it is proba-
      ble. Police reports on anarchism are notoriously unreliable, liable to extreme
      exaggeration, and often the result of a hidden agenda (to justify repression on
      increase in expenditure on the police forces). For ample demonstrations of this,
      see Alex Butterworth, *The World That Never Was: The True Story of Dreamers,
      Schemers, Anarchists and Secret Agents* (London: Vintage, 2011).

56   *Translated from* Rafael Núñez Florencio, *El terrorismo anarquista 1888–1909*,
      (Madrid: Siglo XXI, 1983), 188.

57   Butterworth, *The World That Never Was*, 168.

58   Examples of these attacks on the public include the attack on the audience at the
      Teatre del Liceu in Barcelona on November 7, 1893, causing twenty deaths and
      numerous injuries, and the bomb attack on a religious procession in Calle de
      los Cambios Nuevos in the same city, June 7, 1896, which killed twelve people.

About the same time in France, Émile Henry was responsible for two attacks on the public, which causes a press sensation at the time. For the Barcelona attacks, see Núñez Florencio, *El terrorismo* (2010), 65–71. For Henry, see Butterworth, *The World That Never Was*, 313–14, 326–28.

59   See Clara E. Lida, *Anarquismo y revolución en la España del XIX* (Madrid: Siglo XXI, 1972), 252–53.

60   Butterworth, *The World That Never Was*, 301.

61   Translated from Núñez Florencio, *El terrorismo* (2010), 65.

62   Núñez Florencio, *El terrorismo anarquista* (1983), 187.

63   Translated from Núñez Florencio, *El terrorismo* (2010), 63.

64   Translated from texts taken from articles published by Ricardo Mella in 1891 and 1910, quoted in Álvarez Junco, *La ideológica política del Anarquismo*, 508–9.

65   Quoted in Termes, *Història del moviment anarquista a Espanya*, 118–19.

66   Translated from Núñez Florencio, *El terrorismo anarquista* (1983), 189.

67   See Butterworth, *The World That Never Was*, 369–79.

68   Núñez Florencio *El terrorismo anarquista* (1983), 106.

69   Quoted in Butterworth, *The World That Never Was*, 313.

70   Quoted in Daniel Guerin, *Anarchism* (New York: Monthly Review Press, 1970), 78.

71   Anarchists also claimed to be socialists and tried to attend the meetings of the International, being expelled from the 1893 Zurich Congress at which it was agreed that only socialists who agreed to the necessity of political action within the context of parliamentary politics could attend future congresses.

72   Shannon, Nocella, and Asimakopoulos, *The Accumulation of Freedom*, 28–30.

Chapter 2

1   See Wayne Thorpe, *"The Workers Themselves": Revolutionary Syndicalism and International Labour, 1913–1923* (Amsterdam: IISG, 1989), 48. Thorpe provides a brief description of the growth of prewar syndicalism in Europe on pages 21–48. On the other side of the Atlantic the International Workers of the World was formed in 1905 in the United States (it also had branches in some South American countries) and the Federación Obrera Regional Argentina in 1901. Further details on the various national organizations are given in chapter 4.

2   The figures for Solidaridad Obrera come from Xaviar Cuadrat, *Socialismo y Anarquismo en Cataluña (1899–1911)* (Madrid: Ediciones de la Revista de Trabajo, 1976), 231.

3   In his introduction to the Spanish version of Fernand Pelloutier's *Historia de las Bolsas del Trabajo – los origenes del sindicalismo revolucionario* (Bilbao: Zero, 1978), 31, Max Nettlau (the anarchist historian of the period) argued that the organizational structure of the CGT "corresponded exactly" to that proposed by the FRE delegate Anselmo Lorenzo to the 1871 IWMA Conference in London, which had originally been drawn up at the FRE Conference in Valencia the same year.

4   Rather than limiting a strike to the affected sector or in some cases region of a

dispute, a general strike would spread the dispute through all branches of the industry in question and then spread to other industries with the intention of bringing society to a standstill. In France there was much discussion over the theory of the general strike (which was even seen as a scientific strike) and when and how it should be implemented. This debate must be placed within the debate over tactics within the French socialist movement and syndicalists' attempts to attract workers away from the parliamentary movement. In Spain, there was no great debate as the general strike had been an assumed tactic since the days of the FRE. Pere Gabriel, "Sindicalismo y huelga. Sindicalismo revolucionario francés e italiano. Su introducción en España," *Ayer*, no. 4 (1991).

5   The key figures in the CGT in its early years were almost entirely anarchists: Fernand Pelloutier, (1867–1901); Émile Pouget (1860–1931), assistant secretary responsible for the section of federations and editor of the CGT paper; Georges Yvetot (1868–1942), secretary responsible for the section of the Bourses following the death of Pelloutier; Paul Delesalle (1870–1948), assistant secretary for the Bourses and secretary of the committee for the general strike; Victor Griffuelhes, (1874–1923), the general secretary of the CGT. See F. F. Ridley, "The Militants and the Activist Temper," in *Revolutionary Syndicalism in France* (Cambridge: Cambridge University Press, 1970),; the first volume of Jean Maitron's *Histoire du Mouvement Anarchiste en France (1880–1914)* (Paris: Libraire François Maspero, 1975), 249–311; and the introduction to Barbara Mitchell's *The Practical Revolutionaries: A New Interpretation of the French Anarcho-Syndicalists* (New York: Greenwood Press, 1987).

6   Yvetot speaking at the CGT's 1910 congress, quoted in Ridley, "The Militants and the Activist Temper," 44.

7   The Charter of Amiens, reproduced in Thorpe, *The Workers Themselves*, 319–20.

8   Maitron, *Histoire du Mouvement Anarchiste en France (1880–1914)*, 301, argues that "the Charter resulting from the Congress of Amiens can in fact be considered as the birth of a new movement. The name of this movement is revolutionary syndicalism, it possessed a doctrine, the Charter, and it is represented in an organisation, the CGT … until then there were militant anarchists in the syndical movement, henceforward … there was only revolutionary syndicalists."

9   The ISNTUC changed its name to the International Federation of Trade Unions in September 1913.

10   Reports on the proceedings were published in Spain in *Tierra y Libertad* from November 21 to December 12, 1907. In Barcelona the Centre for Social Studies started preparations to send a delegation but their hopes were dashed due to a lack of funds. Teresa Abelló i Guell, *Les Relacions Internacionals de L'anarquisme Català (1881–1914)* (Barcelona: Edicions 62, 1987), 130. Instead it was decided that Tarrida del Mármol should travel to Amsterdam from London to represent Spain. Tarrida del Mármol, however, could not attend for personal reasons, so Spain was unrepresented. F. Tarrida del Mármol, "Los Congresos de Amsterdam," *Tierra y Libertad*, September 26, 1907.

11   Both anarchists and (revolutionary) syndicalists often referred to revolutionary syndicalism simply as syndicalism, a policy that is adopted throughout this work.

12   *The International Anarchist Congress Held at the Planius Hall Amsterdam on August 26–31 1907* (London: Freedom Press, 1907), contains a brief outline of Monatte's speech. For the full speech, see "Discurso al Congreso anarquista de Amsterdam," in *Cuadernos de Ruedo Ibérico, El Movimiento libertario español – Pasado, Presente y Futuro* (Paris: Ruedo Ibérico, 1974), 86–92.

13   *The International Anarchist Congress*, 17–20.

14   Translated from Errico Malatesta, "Sobre Sindicalismo – Los anarquistas y las leyes obreras," *Acción Libertaria* (Madrid), October 17, 1913.

15   Malatesta was referring here to the attempts of the Catholic Church to establish Catholic unions, a policy which had little success in Spain. The Uniones Profesionales was established in Catalonia after the Tragic Week of 1909 but only attracted five thousand workers at most. In 1915 an attempt to form a Unión General de Trabajadores Católicos failed as it proved difficult to prove to the workers that the unions were not simply mouthpieces of the property owners and employers. The same year a Federación Nacional de Sindicatos Católicos Libres celebrated its first congress, in which it showed itself to be dominated by extreme Catholic reactionaries. Again, this movement had little impact on the working classes. However, in 1919 the Carlists, a fanatical Catholic movement which supported the pretender to the throne and the return to the ancien régime, were instrumental in the creation of the Sindicatos Libres in Barcelona that fought on the side of the employers and state against the CNT. Most members of the Uniones Profesionales joined the Sindicatos Libres. See chapters 1 and 4 in Colin Winston, *Workers and the Right in Spain* (Princeton: Princeton University Press, 1985). Luis Rourera Ferré, *Joaquín Maurín y su tiempo* (Barcelona: Editorial Claret, 1992), 66–69, also gives a brief outline of the failure of the Catholic Church to establish a strong union base among the workforce.

16   Translated from Errico Malatesta, "Sobre Sindicalismo – Los anarquistas y las leyes obreras," *Acción Libertaria*, October 17, 1913.

17   *The International Anarchist Congress*, 21–22.

18   Revolutionary syndicalist organisations were created in a number of countries in the decade before the outbreak of the First World War: the Federación Obrera Regional Argentina (FORA) in 1904; the International Workers of the World (IWW) in 1905 in the United States; Sveriges Arbetares Centralorganisation (SAC) in 1910 in Sweden; the Industrial Syndicalist Education League in 1910 in Britain; the Freie Vereinigung Deutscher Gewerkschaften (FVDG) – Free Association of German Unions – in 1901, which broke from the social democrats and adopted a syndicalist policy based on the Charter of Amiens in 1908; and the Unione Sindicale Italiana (USI) in 1912, when revolutionary syndicalists split from the social democratic Confederazione Generale del Lavoro (CGL). The French CGT reached its height of popularity in numerical terms in 1911.

19   See "Anarquismo y sindicalismo," *Tierra y Libertad*, February 24, 1910, "Sobre sindicalismo," *El Libertario* (Gijón), October 10 and 17, 1913; *Acción Libertaria*, October 10 and 17, 1913; "Anarquismo y Sindicalismo," *El Libertario* (Gijón), May 12, 1911. In 1875 as a member of the IWMA, Malatesta visited Madrid, Cadiz, and Barcelona, and he would enjoy a triumphal lecture tour of the

country in 1891–92. In 1896 he represented a number of Spanish labour organisations at the London Congress of the Second International. His pamphlet *Entre Campesinos* was the most widely distributed anarchist text in Spain in the forty years before 1910. Álvarez Junco, *La ideología política del Anarquismo*, 367, 439; Vernon Richards, "Notes for a Biography," in Richards, *Errico Malatesta: His Life and Ideas*, 229.

20 Malatesta did not change the essence of his ideas but did emphasise more strongly that among the tasks anarchists should perform in the unions was acting "to prevent the members of unions from becoming mere tools in the hands of politicians for electoral or otherwise authoritarian ends." Errico Malatesta, "Sindicalismo y Anarquismo," *El Productor*, January 8, 1926.

21 For the debates on anarchist organisation at the Congress, see *The International Anarchist Congress*, 23–39.

22 Ibid., 28.

23 Ibid., 30.

24 Kropotkin "Letter to Nettlau" and "Anarchist Communism" quoted in M. Schmidt and L. Van der Walt, *Black Flame: The Revolutionary Class Politics of Anarchism and Syndicalism* (Oakland: AK Press, 2009), 242.

25 *The International Anarchist Congress*, 34. In 1906 Mateo Morral tried to assassinate King Alfonso XIII and his wife with a bomb. His attempt failed and he committed suicide. In the now typical repression that followed, Francisco Ferrer, director of the Escuela Moderna de Barcelona, was accused of being an accomplice as Morel had taught at the school. Once again the authorities were attempting to take advantage of a terrorist act to attack the libertarian movement in general, irrespective of their involvement.

26 Ibid., 32.

27 Ibid., 38.

28 As well as articles by Spanish anarchists, a number of syndicalist tracts by French syndicalists were translated and published in Spain. According to Álvarez Junco, *La ideología política del Anarquismo*, 555, the works of Pouget, Yvetot, Griffuelhes, and others "inundated libertarian circles between 1904 and 1911." Pere Gabriel, "Sindicalismo y huelga. Sindicalismo revolucionario francés e italiano. Su introdución en España", *Ayer* no.4 (1991), however, challenges the extent of the impact of the French syndicalism on the CNT, pointing out that most texts that were translated were by anarchists who, if not critical, were not entirely convinced by syndicalism.

29 Translated from Anselmo Lorenzo, "El Sindicalismo," in A. García Birlán, ed., *Sindicalismo. Origen, tácticas y propósitos* (Barcelona: 1934). This was originally published in 1911 under the title *El Proletariado Emancipador*.

30 José Prat, *El Sindicalismo* (Barcelona: 1909), 5–8. This pamphlet was based on a series of articles written by Prat and published in *Solidaridad Obrera* from August 22 to October 16, 1908.

31 Formed in 1908 following a split from the Liberal Party, the Radical Republican Party's anti-clerical message proved popular initially with the Catalan working class. There were rumours that the party was funded by the Liberal Party, who

saw it as a way of keeping workers away from the CNT. Ideologically vague, the party swung far from its leftist message to become a member of the right-wing government of 1934–36 responsible for the crushing of the of the 1934 risings in Asturias and Catalonia. See Nigel Townson, *Crisis of Democracy in Spain: The Radical Republican Party & the Collapse of the Centre under the Second Republic (1931–1936)* (Eastbourne: Sussex Academic Press, 2000).

32   The unions experienced considerable growth during the strike movement of 1901–1903 but declined towards the end of 1903 when an economic downturn began to undermine trade union strength. Angel Smith, "Anarchism in Barcelona, 1899–1914", *European History Quarterly* 27 no.1 (1997), 5–40. The increase in organised labour unrest in Barcelona was one of the main factors that inspired Kropotkin to publish a letter in July 1902 calling for the creation of a new International that would be a "focus of socialism and revolution." Max Nettlau, "Ojeada histórica a propósito del Congreso de la A.I.T. en Madrid," *Revista Blanca*, November 1, 1930. The Spanish anarchist Tarrida del Mármol (who was living at the time in Bromley), a close colleague of Kropotkin (also based in London), was in constant contact with Anselmo Lorenzo via letter, and it was Anselmo Lorenzo who made public Kropotkin's proposal in Spain. A. Lorenzo, "La Unión Internacional del Trabajo," *Tierra y Libertad*, September 13, 1902. The proposal came to nothing.

33   Álvarez Junco, *La ideología política del Anarquismo*, 395, 554.

34   Solidaridad Obrera had its own weekly newspaper, also called *Solidaridad Obrera*, which first appeared in October 1907.

35   The diversity of membership is demonstrated by the fact that the Carlist Ramon Sales, who would later be the leading figure in the right-wing Sindicatos Libres, was a member of the CNT in 1910.

36   The UGT was originally founded in 1888 in Barcelona, but in 1899 it had followed the PSOE to Madrid. Before the Spanish Civil War the UGT never amounted to a serious force in Catalonia, scarcely topping five thousand members. Pere Gabriel, "Sindicalismo y Sindicatos Socialistas en Cataluña. La UGT, 1888–1938," *Historia Social*, no. 8 (Autumn 1990), 47–71.

37   Translated from José Negre, *Recuerdos de un Viejo Militante* (Madrid: LaMalatesta editorial, 2010), 76.

38   Following an international outcry at the execution, the government of Antonio Maura was forced to resign. The best accounts of the events of the Tragic Week are Joan Connelly Ullman, *The Tragic Week: A Study of Anticlericalism in Spain (1875–1912)* (Cambridge, Mass.: Harvard University Press, 1968); Joaquín Romero Maura, *La Rosa de fuego: republicanos y anarquistas: la política de los obreros barceloneses entre el desastre colonial y la semana trágica, 1899–1909* (Mexico: Grijalbo, 1975).

39   Translated from Carlos Gil Andrés, "La aurora proletaria. Orígenes y consolidación de la CNT," in *Tierra y Libertad – Cien años de anarquismo en España*, 94.

40   Translated from Negre, *Recuerdos de un Viejo Militante*, 80.

41   See the series of articles entitled "Historia de las ideas y luchas sociales en España," by Angel Pestaña in *Orto* (Valencia) April–December, 1932. Fabra Ribas, who

was in exile following the Tragic Week (July 26–31, 1909), counselled his supporters that they join the CNT, but the socialist unions soon broke from the
CNT. The newspaper of the Catalan socialists lamented, "The UGT … is more
in reality than by right, excessively centralized," *Justicia Social*, April 2, 1910.

42 "Congreso Obrero Nacional," *Solidaridad Obrera*, November 4, 1910.

43 At an extraordinary meeting of delegates and juntas on January 5, 1911, the
formation of a national confederation was discussed and the new organization
was given the name Confederación Nacional del Trabajo Solidaridad Obrera.
"Solidaridad Obrera – Confederación Nacional del Trabajo," *Solidaridad Obrera*,
January 13, 1911. The last two words, 'Solidaridad Obrera', were soon dropped.

44 Ibid.

45 Ibid.

46 "Conferencia Sindicalista," *Solidaridad Obrera*, August 18, 1911. The meeting was held at the Labour Centre on August 9. The French delegates were
Desmoulins, the CGT's vice-president, and Marie, whilst the UGT delegate was
Adrian García. Previously the president of the CGT visited Catalonia in early
1910 to meet Spanish syndicalist leaders, only months before the creation of
the CNT. *Freedom*, April 1910, reporting on an article in *Voix du Peuple*. From
1918 to 1921 Desmoulins worked in Spain, having fled from military service
in France after two years on the front line. During this time he met Pestaña
and other leaders of the Catalan section of the CNT. Martial Desmoulins,
Souvenirs, ou, la fin d'une vie (Marseilles: Centre International de Reserches sur
L'Anarchisme, 1983), 20–22.

47 "Confederación Nacional del Trabajo – Primer Congreso Obrero," *Solidaridad
Obrera*, September 15, 1911.

48 An editorial entitled "El Congreso Obrero" in *Tierra y Libertad*, September 13,
1911, claimed that with the defeat of the multiple base "Syndicalism … now of
age … has adopted an antipolitical and anti-militaristic orientation, educating
its members in the principles of human solidarity and brotherhood, and teach-
ing them that their emancipation must come from their own efforts and not to
trust any type of saviour, not even those who work beside them in the workshop
or the factory."

49 Translated from José Negre, "De la Confederación Nacional del Trabajo –
Consumatum est," *Tierra y Libertad*, December 6, 1911.

50 Antonio Bar, *La CNT en los Años Rojos* (1910–26) (Madrid: Akal Editor, 1981),
279, argues that the two congresses serve to underline that the CNT was, prior
to its post-1915 reorganization, a revolutionary syndicalist organisation basing
its action on an almost dogmatic interpretation of direct action. Whilst he is
correct in drawing attention to the exaggerated emphasis in the revolutionary
potential of direct action above all other techniques, it is, as has been shown,
incorrect to ignore that the conception that syndicalism *suffit à tout*, which is the
very essence of the revolutionary syndicalist doctrine.

51 For information on the strike and the subsequent repression, see José Negre, "De
la Confederación Nacional del Trabajo - Consumatum est," *Tierra y Libertad*,
December 6, 1911. The federal committee put the number of CNT members

represented at the 1911 congress as 26,541 (from 140 unions). *Solidaridad Obrera*, September 15, 1911. Negre, in the article cited above, claimed that when it was declared illegal CNT membership was thirty-two thousand (from 130 unions).

52   A report on these meetings is reproduced in *Anarchisme et Syndicalisme: Le Congrés Anarchiste International d'Amsterdam* (Rennes: Nautilus; Paris: Editions du Monde Libertaire, 1979), 225–28.

53   The limited resources available to Cornelissen were evident from the fact that the bulletin was handwritten until April 1914. As well as news from across Europe, readers were kept up to date with the syndicalist movements in New Zealand, Japan, Australia, Argentina, Brazil, Mexico, the United States, South Africa, Canada, Cuba, and Chile.

54   The French CGT refused to attend the congress, arrogantly claiming that it was representing syndicalism within the ISNTUC and would revolutionise the socialist trade union international from within. However, the invitation from the ISEL made clear that it at least felt that the CGT's position was little more than delusion: "The International Bureau of Trade Union Centres at Berlin refuses to allow the vital questions of the general strike for expropriation, anti-militarism, and sabotage to go on the agendas for the conferences, but it would not count for much if they did, for the whole of the permanent officials are politicians; most of the delegates are conservative if not absolute reactionaries; and thus the whole business is controlled by Social Democrats." *Syndicalist and Amalgamation News*, February 1913. The CGT's position simply reflected the growing force of moderate reformism in the French confederation.

55   *Syndicalist and Amalgamated News*, February 1913. The invitation was reproduced in *Bulletin International du Mouvement Syndicaliste*, February 16, 1913, and appeared in *Tierra y Libertad* on February 26, 1913. It wasn't published in *Solidaridad Obrera* as the newspaper was still suspended as a consequence of the 1911 general strike; it did not reappear until May 1, 1913.

56   "Movimiento Social. Barcelona – Hacía la reorganización de la CNT," *El Libertario*, September 14, 1912. The process of reorganization was to start at the roots with the formation of the Local Federation of Unions in Barcelona, which would in turn move to build up a regional federation of all the unions in Catalonia, a process that would then be repeated across Spain. Progress was slow, with the Local Federation of Unions only giving notice of its formation in March 1913. "Noticias y Communicaciones," *El Libertario*, March 1, 1913.

57   The Catalan CRT drew attention to its plight, including an attack on the role of politicians (especially the socialists), to the notice of the international movement, in a manifesto published in the *Bulletin International du Mouvement Syndicaliste*, September 14, 1913.

58   "Congreso Sindicalista Internacional de Londres," *Solidaridad Obrera*, May 1, 1913.

59   "Congreso Sindicalista Internacional de Londres," *Solidaridad Obrera*, July 3, 1913. The paper also talked of the difficulties that the Catalan CRT faced in raising money to send a delegate to London. *Solidaridad Obrera*, May 17, 1913.

60   Translated from "De Suma importancia," *Solidaridad Obrera*, July 10, 1913.

61   Negre's article originally appeared in *Tierra y Libertad* in May or June 1913 under the title "Abriendo Camino" but the relevant number has not survived. Jorge Gallart cites the article in "Abriendo Camino," *Solidaridad Obrera*, June 26, 1913. Further information is given in Antonio Babra, "Sobre el Congreso Sindicalista de Londres," *Solidaridad Obrera*, July 10, 1913.

62   José Negre, "Sobre la excursión de propaganda," *Tierra y Libertad*, August 6, 1913.

63   "Congreso Sindicalista Internacional," *Tierra y Libertad*, February 26, 1913. The reaction of the paper drew the attention of the organisers and was later reproduced in the *Syndicalist and Amalgamation News*, March–April 1913.

64   The Acción y Cultura group of Badajoz proposed that "all Syndicalist and Anarchist groups should come together to found a 'New Red International'," emphasising the compatibility of the two ideologies in their eyes. Wayne Westergard-Thorpe, "The Provisional Agenda of the International Syndicalist Congress, London 1913," *International Review of Social History* 26 (1978), 33–78.

65   According to the French syndicalist Alfred Rosmer, thirty-three delegates representing some sixty organisations with a combined membership of 220,000 attended. *La Vie Ouvrière*, October 20, 1913. Approximately half of this figure were members of the Italian USI. There were also four fraternal delegates – that is, delegates representing non-economic organisations.

66   "El Primer Congreso Sindicalista," *Solidaridad Obrera*, October 9, 1913. On September 20 a meeting to discuss the London congress was held in Barcelona. *Solidaridad Obrera*, September 18, 1913.

67   Camil Piñón was selected by the Catalan CRT to represent them at London, but was unable to go due to lack of funds. Manuel Lladonosa i Vall-Llebrera, *Sindicalistes i Llibertaris, L'Experiència de Camil Piñón* (Barcelona: Rafael Dalmau, 1989), 19.

68   Anselmo Lorenzo's letter to the inaugural session was published in *Solidaridad Obrera*, October 2, 1913. His reasons for declining the invitation are given in a letter dated August 30, 1913, to García Vinas (himself a survivor of the FRE), International Institute of Social History (IISG), Amsterdam, Max Nettlau Archive, microfilm 52.

69   The bureau was formed by G. Van Erkel (president), T. H. A. Markemann (secretary), A. J. P. Hovre, M. A. Vander Hage and , T. Drerves. *Solidaridad Obrera*, November 27, 1913.

70   *Syndicalist and Amalgamation News*, October 1913; *Tierra y Libertad*, October 29, 1913.

71   The Spanish report to the congress (read out by Duque) stressed the hope that all workers should be united in one economic movement despite their theoretical differences. F. Tarrida del Mármol, "El Primer Congreso Sindicalista – Impresiones personales," *Tierra y Libertad*, October 15, 1913.

72   "Primer Congreso Sindicalista International de Londres", *Solidaridad Obrera*, October 16, 1913. See also Wayne Thorpe, "Towards a Syndicalist International: The 1913 London Congress," *International Review of Social History* 23 (1978).

73   According to Tarrida de Mármol, the Italian De Ambis and the English

representatives seemed more interested in personal grudges than revolutionary syndicalism. Nonetheless, he summed up the congress thus: "Bearing in mind the lack of experience of international congresses of both the delegates and the organisers, it can be said, with certain reserves, that the first international congress of the syndicalists was a notable success." Translated from F. Tarrida de Mármol, "El Primer Congreso Sindicalista – Impresiones personales," *Tierra y Libertad*, October 15, 1913. See also J.Suárez Duque, "Despues del Congreso," *La Voz del Obrero*, October 30, 1913.

74   J. Suárez Duque, "Autour du Congress syndicaliste de Londres," *Les Temps Nouveaux*, October 18, 1913.

75   "Primer Congreso Sindicalista Internacional de Londres," *Solidaridad Obrera*, October 16, 1913.

76   "Una Asamblea – Resurgimiento Proletario," *Solidaridad Obrera*, November 20, 1913. A further commentary on the assembly was provided by Galfe in "Crónica Internacionales – Barcelona: Reemprendiendo el camino," *Acción Libertaria* (Madrid), November 28, 1913.

77   "Circular Internacional de Información del Movimiento Sindicalista," *La Voz del Obrero*, December 20, 1913; *Solidaridad Obrera*, November 27, 1913.

78   *The International Anarchist Congress*, 14. The office was based in London and was composed of Malatesta (representing the Latin countries including Spain), Rudolf Rocker (representing the Germans), Turnr ('Anglo-saxons'), and Wilker (Scandinavians), with the Russian Alexander Schapiro as secretary. Fernando Tarrida, "Los Congresos de Amsterdam – La Oficina Internacional Anarquista," *Tierra y Libertad*, September 26, 1907.

79   Abelló i Guell, *Les Relacions Internacionals de l'anarquisme Català*, 133, states that only thirty-seven groups had joined, four of which were from Spain. The 'Fructidor' group of San Sebastián proposed the establishment of a national office in response to the call from the London bureau. *Tierra y Libertad*, May 13, 1909. The 'Futurismo' group of Barcelona, which had launched the idea of organising the scattered forces of anarchism in Spain as part of the preparation for the proposed 1909 international congress, renounced this project, complaining of the "indifference and lack of activity of the majority of [anarchist] groups." *Tierra y Libertad*, June 24, 1909.

80   The initial letter from the correspondence office of the Anarchist International to anarchist groups, requesting help for the organisation of a congress to be held in the summer of 1909,was published in *Tierra y Libertad* October 22, 1908, and a further letter published in *Tierra y Libertad* on April 22, 1909, complained that their previous call had been largely ignored.

81   Action Libre's proposal was published in *Tierra y Libertad*, August 21, 1912. See also the police report dated April 24, 1913, on Spanish anarchists in Bordeaux in the files of the French police at the Archives Nationales de France (ANF), F/7/14791. Most of the documents in the files of the ANF are typed reports on scraps of paper, which have no title.

82   Acción Libre, "A Todos los anarquistas del mundo," *Tierra y Libertad*, December 4, 1912.

83   Romanones had succeeded José Canelejas, who had been responsible for the banning of the confederation, in late 1912. Canalejas had been assassinated in November 1912 by Manuel Pardiñas Serrano, an anarchist from Huesca who appears to have had no connection with either the CNT or the organised anarchist movement.

84   *Acción Libertaria*, September 5, 1913, mentions the Andalusian Federation, then on September 12, 1913, the Basque and Valencian Federations, and finally on September 19, 1913, the Extremadura. *Acción Libertaria*, October 17, 1913, talks of moves towards a regional federation in Catalonia, which was finally formed in December (*Tierra y Libertad*, December 10, 1913).

85   "Adelante por la acción Anarquista," *Acción Libertaria*, September 12, 1913.

86   The creation of the FCRA was welcomed by both Anselmo Lorenzo and Frederico Fructidor. The latter emphasised the support the Paris congress gave for the entrance of anarchists into the unions. Anselmo Lorenzo, "El Congreso anarquista frances I," *Tierra y Libertad*, September 17, 1913; Federico Fructidor (the pseudonym of Palmiro Marbo), "La Obra de un Congreso," *Tierra y Libertad*, September 17, 1913.

87   "Le Congres Anarchiste de Paris," *Le Libertaire*, August 23, 1913.

88   The German Federation of Anarchists had previously called for the celebration of an International Anarchist Congress in June. Rudolph Oestreich, "Congreso Anarquista International – A todos los anarquistas," *Tierra y Libertad*, June 11, 1913. The manifesto by the three federations giving notice of the date for the congress was published in *Tierra y Libertad*, February 18, 1914. Alexander Schapiro was the secretary of the organization committee based in London whilst V. García (another Spanish anarchist based in London) was in charge of correspondence with Spanish-speaking nations. The exiled Spanish anarchists in France had nominated Eusebio Carbó to represent them as a delegate at the congress. Archives Nationales de France, F/7/13053, police report, August 1, 1914.

89   A short article in *Tierra y Libertad*, August 19, 1914, gave news of the "indefinite postponement" of the congress due to the war.

90   "El Congreso de Londres," *Tierra y Libertad*, May 27, 1914.

91   See M. Costa-Iscar, "Orientation Congresista," *Tierra y Libertad*, July 1, 1914; Grupo los Desconocidos, "Movimiento Anarquista," *Tierra y Libertad*, July 22, 1914; Gilimón, "El Congreso de Londres," *Tierra y Libertad*, July 29, 1914. According to *Freedom* (London) March, July, and August 1914, the Spanish had decided to send delegates.

92   Gilimón, "El Congreso de Londres," *Tierra y Libertad*, July 29, 1914. The article originally appeared in *La Protesta*, the organ of the Argentine FORA. Gilimón was expelled from Argentina and returned to Barcelona around this time. Here he was in close contact with Anselmo Lorenzo and the editorial team of *Tierra y Libertad.*

93   The French anarchist newspaper *Le Libertaire* argued that the muted Spanish response was a result of the anarchists being occupied in a pro-amnesty campaign. "L'Internationale Anarchiste et le Congrés de Londres," *Le Libertaire*, May 30, 1914. This is unlikely to be the true cause, as pro-amnesty campaigns were a

common event in Spain. In fact one such campaign was underway in early 1913 when the ISEL launched its proposal for the holding of an international congress, and this did not prevent the anarchists from showing their support.

94 A manifesto by Faure against the war, entitled "Hacia la Paz" (Toward Peace), was published in *Tierra y Libertad*, January 20, 1915. The manifesto launching the Ateneo's initiative, also entitled "Hacia la Paz," began by rendering homage to Faure's article. *Tierra y Libertad*, March 3, 1915. The organizing committee of the congress comprised López Bouza, Antonio Vieytes, D'Lom, Collado, and Manieros, *El Porvenir de Obrero*, May 13, 1915.

95 The manifesto addressed to "the Socialists, Syndicalists, Anarchists and workers' organisations " of the world called for the "end of splits and acceptance that all are to blame for the war." The agenda was as follows: 1) the quickest means for putting a stop to the present European war; 2) new tactics to follow to avoid such crimes against humanity, and 3) the dissolution of permanent armies.

96 *Tierra y Libertad*, March 3, 1915.

97 E. C. Carbó, "Congreso International de la Paz," *Tierra y Libertad*, March 24, 1915. Carbó claimed that organisations from Norway, Denmark, Sweden, the Netherlands, Italy, and Portugal were preparing to send delegates.

98 A. Schapiro, "Las Internacionales sindicales," *La Protesta (Suplemento Semanal)*, August 24, 1925. Among those invited who were unable to attend were Faure, Malatesta, and a representative of the USI.

99 "El Proletariado ante la guerra – Congreso International del Ferrol", *Solidaridad Obrera*, May 13, 1915. News of the release of the two anarchists was given in *Acción Libertaria*, May 28, 1915.

100 Reports on the congress appeared in *Acción Libertaria*, May 14, 1915; *Solidaridad Obrera*, May 13, 1915; and *Tierra y Libertad*, May 12, 1915.

101 The committee, which was to be based in Portugal, appears to have had a very short life. By the end of May 1915 *Acción Libertaria* claimed that deciding that it should reside in Portugal was tantamount to condemning it to death. *Acción Libertaria*, May 28, 1915.

102 Translated from "El Proletariado ante la guerra – Congreso International del Ferrol," *Solidaridad Obrera*, May 13, 1915. A tangible result of El Ferrol was the strengthening of the links between Portuguese and Spanish syndicalists. See chapter 8.

103 The revised statutes were published in *Tierra y Libertad*, July 7, 1915.

104 "O Congresso de Ferrol A Comissao Organizadora," *A Aurora* (Oporto), May 16, 1915.

105 *Tierra y Libertad*, July 7, 1915; "Uma Questão Palpitante," *A Aurora*, August 1, 1915. One reason for the rapid demise of the International may have been financial difficulties. The organising committee of the El Ferrol congress reported a large deficit in early August. *Acción Libertaria*, August 6, 1915.

106 Pestaña was strongly supported by Francisco Miranda and Manuel Andreu (also representing the CRT and its paper). Andreu was the first CNT national secretary following the reorganisation.

107 The initial manifesto of the relaunch was published on the front page of

Solidaridad Obrera, June 3, 1915. Subsequent editorials referring to the reorganisation included "Confederación Nacional del Trabajo," June 17, 1915; "Por la Confederación Nacional del Trabajo," July 8, 1915; "Hacia la constitución de la Confederación Nacional del Trabajo," July 22, 1915.

108   Reaction to the reorganisation by the authorities was unsurprisingly hostile. The secretary of the CNT, Andreu Negre, was one of the many who were detained during this time. *Freedom*, April 1916. His successor, Francisco Jordán, was detained in January 1917. *Solidaridad Obrera*, January 28, 1917.

109   In an article written in *La Justicia Social on* October 23, 1915, J. Bueso, who had been a member of the CNT since its birth, complained bitterly that the CNT was now "clearly anarchist." Cited in Cuadrat, *Socialismo y Anarquismo en Cataluña (1899–1911)*, 588.

110   Translated from "Sobre la Confederación Nacional del Trabajo," *Tierra y Libertad*, August 4, 1915.

111   Translated from M. Buenacasa, "Sindicalismo y anarquismo," *El Productor* (Barcelona), February 19, 1926. Francisco Jordán, secretary of the CNT from mid 1916 until February 1917, was also a member of the Catalan Federation of Anarchist Groups.

112   "Por la Internacional Anarquista," *Acción Libertaria*, June 25, 1915.

113   No list of those who attended the meeting is available, but *Tierra y Libertad* was represented at the congress by Tomás Herreros, a leading Catalan anarchist who had played a prominent part in the deliberations of the CNT congresses of 1910 and 1911.

114   "Una Circular Importante," *Acción Libertaria*, June 18, 1915.

115   "Sobre la International Anarquista," *Acción Libertaria*, September 17, 1915; "Comité Español de la International Anarquista – Continuemos", *Tierra y Libertad*, October 17, 1915. A federation of anarchist groups in Andalusia was also formed in early October. *Tierra y Libertad*, November 3, 1915.

116   *Tierra y Libertad*, November 10 and 17, 1915, and, in particular, "Rompamos el círculo," December 1, 1915.

117   With 1913 prices and wages at an index of 100, by 1918 wages had risen to 125.6 but prices had shot up to 218.2. Benjamin Martin, *The Agony of Modernisation, Labor and Industrialisation in Spain* (New York: Ithaca, 1990), 179 (table 7.3).

118   In 1915 there were 91 officially reported strikes, affecting 30,591 workers, with 383,885 days lost. By 1916 there were 178 strikes, affecting 96,882 strikers, with 2,415,305 workdays lost. In Barcelona the number of days lost to strikes rose from 191,125 in 1915 to 2,092,290 the following year. José Luís Martín Ramos, "Conseqüències socials: la resposta obrera," *L'Avenç* 69 (March 1984).

119   Following the Valencia conference, the CNT celebrated its own conference in the city, at which it was agreed that "the establishment of a unity of action between the organised proletariat of Spain is not just necessary but essential." *Tierra y Libertad*, May 17, 1916. The CNT then sent two delegates, Mauro Bajatierra and Eusebio Carbó, to the UGT's 12th Congress at the end of May, to propose a pact of action between the two unions. The result of this was the pact signed on July 17, 1916, by Salvador Seguí and Angel Pestaña for the CNT

and by Largo Caballero, Vicente Barrio, and Julián Besteiro for the UGT.

120 Martin, *The Agony of Modernisation*, 184.

121 The Restoration system functioned as a means of maintaining social peace between the different factions of the upper and middle classes. Under the so-called 'turno pacífico', power was interchanged between the two main parties, Liberals and Conservatives, which were merely groups of political bosses linked together more by support for a particular leader than any specific ideology. According to Raymond Carr, *Spain, 1808–1975*, 490, the Restoration was epitomised by the "decadent parliamentarianism" of "a conglomeration of factions without a programme." For a full critique of the Restoration system, see Carr, *Spain, 1808–1975*, 489–508, and Martin, *The Agony of Modernisation*, 175–88.

122 The manifesto was published in *El Socialista* on March 18, 1917, extracts of which are reproduced in Barrio Alonso, *Anarquismo y anarcosindicalismo en Asturias*, 170. The signatories of the pact, Seguí and Pestaña for the CNT, and Bestiero, Largo Caballero, Barrio, Anguiano, and Virginia González for the UGT, were immediately arrested.

123 The government responded to the strike by declaring a state of war throughout the country, and over two thousand strikers were arrested and prosecuted by military tribunals rather than courts of law. Ballbe, *Orden público y militarismo en la España constitutional*, 295.

124 *Tierra y Libertad*, December 21, 1917. Carlos Forcadell Álvarez, "Conflicto Social y Movilización Obrera: De la Huelga General a la Dictadura de Rivera," in *Sindicalismo y Movimientos Sociales: Siglos XIX–XX*, ed. Manuel Redero (Madrid; UGT-Centro de Estudios Historicos, 1994), 99–109, argues that throughout the early summer of 1917, in secret meetings between the leaders of the two unions, the CNT members accused the UGT of making agreements with bourgeois politicians instead of trusting a truly workers' movement.

125 At the time, of the eleven members of the National Council of the UGT, six were also members of the PSOE directorate.

126 Confederación Regional del Trabajo de Cataluña, *Memoria del Congreso celebrado en Barcelona los días 28, 29, 30 de junio y 1 de julio del ano 1918* (Barcelona: Imprenta Germinal, 1918), 134.

127 Largo Caballero's letter dated October 26, 1918 and Buenacasa's reply dated November 4, 1918, are reproduced in Amaro de Rosal, *Historia de la UGT de España 1901–1939*, vol. 1 (México: Grijalbo, 1977), 186–92.

128 The debate dominated the first sessions of the congress, after administrative details had been dealt with. *Memoria del Congreso celebrado en el Teatro de la Comedia de Madrid, los días 10 al 18 de diciembre de 1919* (Barcelona: Cosmos, 1932), 75–177. The declaration on fusion with the UGT began by stressing that the "tactics and ideas of the CNT and the UGT are diametrically opposed."

129 As the pact was contrary to the decision made at the national congress of December 1919, it was heavily criticised by many militants within the CNT, and a national plenum celebrated in Barcelona in October 1920 concluded that in signing the pact the national committee had "exceeded its functions." The plenum did not, however, decide to break the pact, believing that the UGT

was going to support the general strike. Seguí, who was one of the signatories of the pact for the CNT, later claimed that the committee took the decision to approach the UGT as the CNT was threatened with "death" and "faced by the immediate danger of a bloody repression." International Institute of Social History (IISG), Amsterdam, CNT Archive, microfilms 174 and 200; *Preámbulo y Convocatoria de la Conferencia Nacional – Zaragoza*. Just over a month after the signing of the pact, Martínez Anido became civil governor and introduced a period of repression unprecedented in its violence again the CNT which would last until 1922.

130   The CNT national committee complained of the "manifest betrayal committed by the UGT." El Comité Nacional, "La Confederación Nacional a los traba-jadores Españoles," *Acción Social Obrera*, January 1, 1921. See also Amaro de Rosal, *Historia de la UGT de España 1901–1939*, 209–38.

131   The socialists finally adopted a revolutionary position in 1934, but significantly the decision was forced on the leadership by the rank and file.

132   Translated from "En guardia – La Revolución contra la guerra," *Solidaridad Obrera*, August 30, 1916. In a similar vein: "Que haremos contra la Guerra?," *Solidaridad Obrera*, August 26, 1916, "Contra el Crimen de la Guerra," *Solidaridad Obrera*, November 14, 1916.

133   Carlos Forcadell, *Parlamentarismo y Bolchevización. El Movimiento obrero español 1914–1918* (Barcelona: Editorial Crítica, 1978) 228–29, speaks of the sponta-neous inclusion of the rhetoric and ideas of the Zimmerwald Left in the syn-dicalist press but is unable to provide any direct reference in either anarchist or syndicalist press to the congress except the article published in *Tierra y Libertad* that gives news of the celebration of the congress. This article states that due to the censorship of the Italian press report from which they gained their in-formation, they were "unclear about the nature" of the congress. "El congreso International de Suiza," *Tierra y Libertad*, November 3, 1915.

134   *Guerra di Classe*, October 23, 1915.

135   *Solidaridad Obrera* eventually published the manifesto of the Zimmerwald Left. M. Buenacasa, "La Reunión de la International – El Manifesto de Zimmerwald," *Solidaridad Obrera*, November 19, 1918.

Chapter 3

1   Salvador Seguí (Comité Asamblea Nacional de Valencia), Francisco Miranda (secretary of the CNT), and Angel Pestaña (secretary of the Catalan CRT), "Manifiesto al Pueblo Español," *Solidaridad Obrera*, May 25, 1917.

2   According to editorials in *Solidaridad Obrera* on December 5, 1917, and January 11, 1918, the bourgeois press was "distorting" and "disfiguring" the news, mak-ing it "impossible to have a concrete opinion of what is happening in Russia." A further editorial complained that "the news of the Russian revolution which we receive is more contradictory and confusing every day." *Solidaridad Obrera*, July 11, 1918. As late as May 1918, *Tierra y Libertad* was complaining about the "unending series of telegrams" giving different opinions on the revolution. "Al

Margen de la Revolución Rusa," *Tierra y Libertad*, May 22, 1918.

3   'Bolshevik' here refers to the ideology of the followers of Lenin, whereas 'communist' simply denotes allegiance to, or support of, the different international communist parties.

4   An editorial in *Solidaridad Obrera*, November 11, 1917, enthused, "the Russians are showing us the path to follow. The Russian people are victorious: we will learn from their actions so that we will triumph in our own time."

5   See Bar, *La CNT en los Años Rojos*, 436–51; Gerald Meaker, *The Revolutionary Left in Spain, 1914–1923* (Stanford: Stanford University Press, 1974), 145–51; Forcadell, *Parlamentarismo y Bolchevización*, 257–64.

6   Federación de Grupos Anarquistas de Cataluña, "Aspecto jurídico de la revolución," *Solidaridad Obrera*, December 4, 1917.

7   "Revolución y anarquía," *Tierra y Libertad*, December 26, 1917. Errico Malatesta explained that such confusion was to be expected as "[b]efore the war only anarchists called themselves communists [yet] … now everywhere tendencies more or less pro-Soviet, communist, dissatisfied, [from] party dissidents and ex-anarchists are appearing. … Each one interprets Marxism, communism, and even anarchism in a different way, trying to reconcile the irreconcilable." Translated from Errico Malatesta, "Contra el Confusionismo," *Ciencia Social*, October 1, 1920.

8   Manuel Buenacasa, "Las Ideas de Lenine," *Solidaridad Obrera*, September 13, 1918; Manuel Buenacasa, "Siluetas Pacifistas – Lenin," *Solidaridad Obrera*, November 26, 1917. Buenacasa had actually met both Lenin and Zinoviev in Lausanne in 1916.

9   M. Buenacasa, "Siluetas pacifistas: Trotzky [*sic*]," *Solidaridad Obrera*, May 30, 1918; "Un año de dictadura proletaria: 1917–1918," *Solidaridad Obrera*, December 1, 1918.

10   "La Paz y la revolución, El Comité de la Confederación Nacional del Trabajo," *Solidaridad Obrera*, November 12, 1918.

11   Bar, *La CNT en los Años Rojo*, 436–51, 525–37, provides the best overall analysis of anarchist and syndicalist reaction to the revolution. Of the books published in English, only Meaker, *The Revolutionary Left in Spain*, 103–8, 222–24, 243–48, treats the subject in any depth. See also the articles by Iwan Kurok on Russia in the anarchist publication *Acracia*, November 15 and 22, 1918, and in an article entitled "Qué hacemos pro-Rusia?" in *Guerra Social* (Valencia), December 20, 1919. Opinions in the only periodical publishing in late 1918–19 of which sufficient numbers remain (except for *Solidaridad Obrera*, which was proscribed in January 1919 and did not reappear again until 1923) – *Acción Social Obrera* – remained confused, and even as late as July 12, 1919, an article by Pedro Gaspert, "Bolcheviquismo," appears to confuse the aims of Bolshevism with those of anarchism.

12   El Comité de la Federación de Grupos Anarquistas de la Región Catalana, "Los anarquistas en nuestro puesto," *Espartaco* (suplemento), November 8, 1919.

13   For Arlandis's intervention, see *Memoria del Congreso celebrado en el Teatro de la Comedia de Madrid, los días 10 al 18 de diciembre de 1919* (Barcelona: Cosmos,

1932), 347–52. Thereafter *Memoria (1919)*. Despite admitting that he had seen few documents on the subject, Eusebio Carbó speaking at the Congress, , 352, gave unqualified support for the Bolsheviks, mainly due to the fact that the reformist socialists were criticising them. Carbó, along with Arlandis, was one of the major defenders of Bolshevism at the Madrid congress. Their views may have been influenced by their meeting with two Finnish Bolsheviks who were sent to Valencia to gain support for the CNT's affiliation to the Comintern. Archives Nationales de France, Paris, F/7/13440, police report, September 23, 1919.

14   For the information on Nin's affiliation with the CNT, see Pelai Pagès, *Andreu Nin: Su evolución política 1911–37* (Bilbao: Zero, 1975), 73–74. For more general texts on Nin, see Victor Alba, *Dos Revolucionarios: Joaquín Maurín, Andreu Nin* (Madrid: Seminarios y Ediciones, 1975); F. Bonamusa, *Andreu Nin y el movimiento comunista en España (1930–37)* (Barcelona: Anagrama, 1977).

15   *Memoria (1919)*, 355–67. Quintanilla's position was echoed by the delegate from the Madrid Toymakers Trade Union (either José Cernada or Tomas de la Llave): "At the moment, the Russian revolution has many defects; it embodies, more than anything, the Marxist principal, and we, revolutionary syndicalists, have as our base Bakuninist principals. Up to now, the Russian revolution has not managed to implant more than a type of communism, a type of socialism that kills individual energies." Translated from ibid., 346.

16   Ibid., 367. Seguí's position throughout this period was remarkably consistent, as evidenced by his intervention in the Madrid debates and at the Zaragoza conference in June 1922 as well as his articles on the subject. For example, see Salvador Seguí, "A Organizacao sindical," *A Batalha*, October 29, 1920; Salvador Seguí, "La posicion doctrinal de los sindicalistas libertarios frente a las internacionales socialistas," *Cultura y Acción*, October 21, 1922.

17   Translated from *Memoria (1919)*, 372–73. The resolution was drawn up by the national committee.

18   Ibid., 373. The resolution was drawn up by twenty-four militants, including six of the eight members of the national committee, and was not intended as an attack on Bolshevism. Rather it related to the concerns of a number of militants about what they perceived as a growing reformism within the CNT.

19   For an eyewitness account of the Canadiense strike, see Paulino Díez, *Un anarco-sindicalista de acción: memorias* (Caracas: Editexto, 1976), 34–47; Simó Piera, *Records i expèriences d'un dirigent de la CNT* (Barcelona: Pòrtic, 1975), 78–96. As secretary of the Local Federation of Unions of Barcelona, Díez was in the head of the strike committee which included Piera. For secondary accounts, see Meaker, *The Revolutionary Left in Spain*, 158ff; Murray Bookchin, *The Spanish Anarchists: The Heroic Years 1868–1936* (New York: Free Life Editions, 1977), 168ff.

20   For a description of the lockout and its effects, see Soledad Bengoechea, *El Locaut de Barcelona (1919–1920)* (Barcelona: Curial, 1998). For an overall account of the repression in Barcelona during this period, see Maria Amàlia Pradas Baena, *L'anarquisme i les lluites socials a Barcelona 1918–1923: la repressió obrera i la violencia* (Barcelona: L'Abadia de Monterrat, 2003).

21 For Asturias, see Barrio Alonso, *Anarquismo y anarcosindicalismo en Asturias*; for Seville, see Ángeles González Fernández, *Utopía y Realidad Anarquismo, anarcosindicalismo y organizaciones obreras. Sevilla, 1900–1923* (Seville: Diputación de Sevilla, 1996), 350–99.

22 The newspaper of the revolutionary pro-Moscow wing of the CGT, *La Vie Ouvriere*, was one of the three means by which the CNT had contact with the Comintern. Hilario Arlandis, "Los sindicalistas rusos lanzan la idea de una Internacional Sindicalista," *España Nueva*, January 6, 1920. The other two were via the USI or via contacts in Denmark.

23 Letters from Pestaña (in Paris) to the CNT national committee dated March 16, 17, 19, 22 and 23, 1920, Barcelona, file 1068, Archivo General de la Guerra Civil Española, Salamanca (AGGCES). In the last of these, Pestaña wrote that the police were catching up with him so he would have to leave for Moscow soon. An example of the difficulties in escaping from Spain is provided by the Catalan Anarchist Federation, which was forced to admit that it was next to impossible to send a delegate to Russia, despite the fact that they had raised the money to do so. El Comité de la Federación Anarquista de Cataluña, "A los Grupos Anarquistas de España," *Acción Social Obrera*, December 13, 1919.

24 Carbó's articles from Italy were published in the newspaper *España Nueva*, which was sympathetic to the CNT and had been printing articles by the confederation's national committee and leading militants whilst the confederation's own press was suspended.

25 After meeting with Carbó, Armando Borghi, the representative of the USI to the second Comintern congress, informed his German counterparts (Rocker and Kater of the FAUD) of the repression against the CNT in Spain, whilst passing through Berlin en route for Moscow. These early contacts between CNT and the USI and the USI and the FAUD would be of great significance during the formation the Revolutionary Syndicalist International in 1922. "A las organizaciones sindicalistas y revolucionarias de todos los países," *España Nueva*, August 21, 1920.

26 Interview with Malatesta, *España Nueva*, May 25, 1920. From the interview it was evident that Malatesta and Carbó had been in contact previously by letter. The Italian chastised Carbó for his defence of the dictatorship of the proletariat, pointing out that Carbó's belief that such a dictatorship would be "brief" was misplaced: "The best intentions clash with the logic of the facts. The formation of a government brings with it the consequences that we have warned about on so many occasions."

27 Eusebio Carbó, "La Solidaridad Internacional en Acción," *España Nueva,* June 14, 1920; *Acción Social Obrera*, June 26, 1920. The article from jail, "Cuatro palabras", was published in *España Nueva* on August 14, 1920.

28 In Berlin, Pestaña discovered that the Comintern was due to hold its second congress soon. He informed the national committee of this, and they authorised him to represent the confederation at the congress. Ángel Pestaña, *Informe de mi estancia en la URSS* (1922; Madrid: ZYX, 1968), 11–12. Hereafter *Informe*.

29 Ibid., 13.

30   Pestaña claimed that a slight variation of the paragraph relating to the critique of apoliticism was agreed on but that Lozovsky went ahead and published the original unaltered. Ibid., 23. Pestaña reproduces the statutes in his report, ibid., 15–16. It was also published in *Acción Social Obrera*, November 13, 1920.

31   *Informe*, 25.

32   Ibid., 21, claims Pestaña signed the document as Angel Pestaña "of the CNT" instead of "for the CNT," to lessen the blow: "I made like the ostrich that hides its head when faced by danger, as if such an attitude would lessen its effects." Armando Borghi, *Mezzo Secolo d'anarchi (1898–1945)* (Naples: Edizioni della Revisti Anarchismo, 1954), 244, claims that he was shown the document with the signature of Pestaña cancelled out and actually produces a photocopy of the original with Pestaña's name clearly crossed out in *La Rivoluzione Mancata* (Milan: Azione Comunee, 1964), 181. This is confirmed by both the German Augustín Souchy and the Spaniard Wilkens (the alias of Jaime Salan, who also wrote under the pseudonym Vilkins and on occasion as J. Galan), who were both present in Moscow at the time. Wilkens, "Diplomatique Bolchevique," *Le Libertaire*, February 10–17, 1922. Eusebio Carbó had met Borghi in Italy prior to the Italian's trip to Moscow, so the USI delegate was aware of the CNT's position towards the Comintern at the Zaragoza conference of July 1922. *Preambulo y Convocatoria de la Conferencia Nacional – Zaragoza, 4 June 1922*, International Institute of Social History (IISG), Amsterdam, CNT Archive, microfilm 174, 200. Hereafter *Conferencia Nacional – Zaragoza* (1922). Pestaña confirmed that he had withdrawn his signature, although he did not mention Borghi's influence. Lenin, who was greatly impressed by Pestaña, also made reference to this in an interview with Wilkens, who was touring Russia at the time. The Bolshevik leader felt that "Pestaña is committing an error in not accepting the dictatorship of the proletariat. He has not yet understood … the necessity to create a Communist Party in Spain. He will have time to reflect, and I expect that in a later congress we will be in agreement. It is a shame that he has left without giving his consent." Vilkens, "Seis meses en Rusia," *La Antorcha* (Buenos Aires), June 24, 1921.

33   Pestaña was critical of the procedures of the International, the power of the presidency of the congress, the voting system adopted in the congress, and the fact that the ten-minute rule agreed upon for each speaker in a debate was not universally observed. For example, when Pestaña argued that a revolution could not be the work of a party, as a party could only make a coup not a revolution, going as far as to claim that the Russian revolution was not made by the Bolsheviks alone but that they had only cooperated to make it happen and had needed luck to achieve power, Trotsky spent fully forty-five minutes rebuking him, and Zinoviev spent a further thirty minutes doing the same the next day. Pestaña was not allowed to defend his position. The rule limiting a speaker to ten minutes was according to Pestaña, "a mouse-trap, which allowed certain mice to pass by again and again." Pestaña also complained that the voting system in the congress went according to individual and not representation, thus favouring the numerous Russians present. *Informe*, 35–40.

34 Wilkens, "Six Mois en Russie – L'Internationale Syndicale-Politicienne," *Le Libertaire*, May 6–13, 1921.

35 It was not until November that the CNT was informed of Pestaña's whereabouts by the Italian socialist Constantino Lazzari, who traced him to Milan Prison, where he was detained for three months due to his illegal passport. "Pestaña, aparece. Pestaña, encarcelado," *España Nueva*, November 27, 1920; "Una infamia del gobierno italiano," *Solidaridad Obrera* (Bilbao), December 31, 1920. Among the documents Pestaña was carrying were papers for Malatesta. Pestaña was wanted in Spain in relation to his participation in an illegal meeting and demonstration in 1916. *España Nueva*, January 8, 1921. In January he was acquitted but remained in prison. Wilkens, "Pestaña – Victime de l'inquisition," *Le Libertaire*, February 25–March 4, 1921. According to Restituto Magrovejo, director of *Solidaridad Obrera* (Madrid), on his arrival from Italy Pestaña was "surrounded by more than 500 civil guards" and then driven to the Modelo prison where he was kept secretly for eight to fifteen days before being transferred to Montjuïc. He was not even permitted to speak to his family. Restituto Magrovejo, "Une Figure Revolutionnaire," *Le Libertaire*, June 10–17, 1921. See also Jacinto León-Ignacio, *Los años del pistolerismo. Ensayo para una guerra civil* (Barcelona: Planeta, 1981), 204; Manuel Aisa Pampols, "El Anarcosindicalismo al inicio de los años veinte en Barcelona," *Orto*, September–October and November–December 1999.

36 J. Rubio, "Dictadura del Proletariado?," *Rebelión*, February 14, 1920; Pedro Ségarra, "Bolchevismo? Sindicalismo?," *Fructidor*, March 20, 1920.

37 E. Carbó, "Una interviú con Malatesta," *España Nueva*, May 25, 1920.

38 The PCE was created on April 15, 1920 by the Juventudes Socialistas, which broke from the PSOE in order to form the party. In April 1921 a further group split from the PSOE over the question of affiliation with Amsterdam or Moscow and formed the Partido Comunista Obrero. These two parties were ordered to merge by Moscow in November 1921. Joan Estruch, *Historia del PCE (1) (1920–1939)* (Barcelona: El Viejo Topo, 1978), 14–32.

39 "La Internacional comunista – Tesis del Comité Ejecutivo," *España Nueva*, July 19, 1920.

40 In late 1920 the anarchist group Juventud Anarquista claimed that the PCE was simply a vehicle of the "old politicians" and asserted, "[They] do not confuse us, old communists, with this pseudo-communist, nascent party." La Juventud Anarquista de Barcelona, "Manifiesto a Los Anarquistas y a la opinión pública de España," Archives Nationales de France, F/7/13441, 1921. See also "Comunismo," *El Comunista Libertario*, November 13, 1920. Published in Alcoy, *Comunismo Libertario* was the forerunner to *Redención*, which began publication in February 1921 and was an official newspaper of the CNT. In a similar vein, see Pedro Sagarra, "Algo sobre el Partido Comunista Español," *Fructidor*, July 10, 1920; *Cultura Obrera* (Palma de Mallorca), November 12, 1921; Hermoso Plaja, "Pseudo Revolucionarios," *Redención*, November 11, 1921; Galo Díez, "Ya apareció aquello," *Redención*, December 23, 1921. Joaquin Maurín, initially one of the strongest supporters of Moscow in the CNT, later

severely criticised the party's policy and that of Moscow towards Spain in general. The first envoy sent by Moscow to Spain, Borodin (who could not even speak Spanish), was sent to Madrid rather than to Barcelona and contacted the embryonic PCE rather than the CNT. It was under his influence that the communists launched a campaign critical of syndicalism whilst Pestaña was still in Russia. Joaquin Maurín, *El Bloque Obrero y Campesino, Origenes – Actividad – Perspectivas* (Barcelona: CIB, 1932), 6.

41   José Peirats, *La CNT en la Revolución Española*, vol. 1 (Colombia: Carvajal, 1988), 31–36.

42   At the Zaragoza conference Joan Peiró claimed that during the period of repression following the assassination of Eduardo Dato (March 8, 1921) only five people were responsible for the functioning of five of the confederation's (regional) committees (although he did not specify which). *Conferencia Nacional – Zaragoza* (1922).

43   According to Victor Alba, D*os Revolucionarios*, 16, Maurín had gained access to the national committee via the Catalan regional committee (which he joined in November 1920 at the height of the Anido-led repression), benefitting from the detention of militants of both the CRT and CNT committees.

44   Andrew Durgan, *B.O.C. 1930–36, El Bloque Obrero y Campesino* (Barcelona: Laertes, 1996), 22; Luis Rourera Ferré, *Joaquín Maurín y su tiempo* (Barcelona: Claret, 1992), 57. For the evolution of Maurín´s political outlook, see also Antoni Monreal, *El pensamiento político de Joaquín Maurín* (Barcelona: Ediciones 62, 1984); Yveline Riottat, *Joaquín Maurín, De l'anarco-syndicalisme au comunisme (1919–1936)* (Paris: L'Harmattan, 1997).

45   Nin became national secretary despite the opposition of the Local Federation of Barcelona. El Comité Comarcal (Pamplona), "La Confederación en ridículo," *Nueva Senda*, November 10, 1921. At the same time Maurín became a member of the Catalan regional committee. F. Bonamusa, *El Bloc Obrer i Camperol (1930–1932)* (Barcelona: Córial, 1974), 9.

46   See Galfe (Joan Rovira), "Rusos y Nosotros," *Acción Social Obrera*, July 31, 1920; F. Barthe, "Sobre la dictadura innecesaria," *Acción Social Obrera*, July 27, 1920; "Comunismo," *El Comunista Libertario*, November 13, 1920; Grupo anarquista Amor y Libertad, "Kropotkine victima del sistema bolchevista?," *Acción Social Obrera*, November 6, 1920. Malatesta's criticism of Bolshevism, already made public in his interview with Carbó in *España Nueva*, was also published in article form under the title "Reformas o Revolución? Libertad o Dictadura," in *Acción Social Obrera*, October 23, 1920. *Freedom* (London), September 1920, quotes an article in *El Productor* (Seville) which also condemns the Bolsheviks and the so-called dictatorship of the proletariat.

47   Maurín later denied that delegates from the north, Castile and León, or Palencia attended. See Rourera Ferré, *Joaquín Maurín y su tiempo*, 78–9. This was contradicted in Confederación Nacional del Trabajo (*España Nueva*, April 30, 1921) and it would become evident later that a delegate from the north did attend, although it cannot be confirmed if the other delegates did so as well.

48   Nin was not happy about the selection of Leval, which he said was "imposed by

the anarchist groups." Joaquin Maurín, "La CNT y la III International," *CNT* (Mexico), 8–9, 1960. However, in reality it was Arlandis who proposed that the federation appoint a delegate.

49   Wilkens, "Ce que valent les affirmations de Rosmer," *Le Libertaire*, November 18–25, 1921.

50   Augustín Souchy, "Conferenza della Internazionale Sindicalista tenuta a Berlino del 16 al 21 Dicembre 1920," *Guerra di Classe*, January 22, 1921 (Souchy's report was also printed in "A Conferencia Preliminar da Internacional Sindicalista," *A Batalha*, February 12–16, 1921); "La Conferencia Sindicalista revolucionaria de Berlín (de Diciembre 1920)," *La Protesta*, May 29, 1921. A report on the conference in English appears in *Solidarity* ("the Official Organ of the Shop Stewards' and Workers' Committee Movement"), January 7, 1921.

51   Maurín later commented wryly that the PCE was "better known in Moscow than Spain." J. Maurín, "La CNT y La III Internacional," *CNT* (Mexico), 8–9, 1960.

52   Surprisingly, the acts of the congress were not published in Spain but were published in the revolutionary syndicalist newspaper in France, *La Vie Ouvriere* (July 22–29, 1922), whilst the documents approved at the congress were published in Portugal in *A Batalha*, December 11–22, 1921. There is an almost complete dearth of secondary material on the history of the Profintern. See Kevin McDermott's chapter on the history of the Comintern, in light of new documents, in Tim Rees and Andrew Thorpe, *International Communism and the Communist International 1919–43* (Manchester: Manchester University Press, 1998), 31–40, in which he states that the new archives made available to historians following the end of the Cold War could help sponsor research in this area, although McDermott also laments that the initial openness of the archives has since been curtailed.

53   "We didn't see much of him (Leval), for he left the other delegates immediately to unite with the opponents of affiliation." Alfred Rosmer, *Lenin's Moscow* (London: Pluto, 1971), 138.

54   "Importantes decisiones del Congreso de Moscú," *Lucha Social*, July 23, 1921.

55   Jemmy Troitzsch, "La C.N. del T. Española, no debe pertenecer a la Sindical Roja," *Nueva Senda*, January 26, 1922. Apoliticism was decried by the congress as "a paid tribute to bourgeois ideas."

56   No copy of the northern CRT's actual manifesto has survived but an extract of the manifesto was published in *La Protesta* (Buenos Aires), September 25, 1921, under the title "El Complot de Moscow." The Profintern resolution was published in *Acción Social Obrera*, August 6, 1921.

57   "La Ideología de la C.N. del T," *Nueva Senda*, November 10, 1921.

58   "La Confederación en ridículo," *Nueva Senda*, November 10, 1921.

59   "Acuerdos de la reunión extraordinaria celebrada el 14 de los corrientes," *Redención*, August 27, 1921, and El Comité Pleno de 24 delegados en Madrid, "Acuerdos de la reunión extraordinaria celebrada el 14 del mes próximo pasado," *Acción Social Obrera*, September 3, 1921.

60   *Le Libertaire*, January 7–14, 1921.

61   Vilkens, "Vilkens y los comunistas," *La Antorcha* (Buenos Aires), November

28, 1921, originally published in *Nueva Senda*. Vilkens, "Pestaña – Victime de l'inquisition," *Le Libertaire*, February 25–March 4, 1921. In Russia Wilkens was introduced to the German syndicalist Augustín Souchy by Pestaña. "Une Lettre de Souchy," *Le Libertaire*, March 25–April 1, 1921. For an overview of Wilkens's report on revolutionary Russia, see his "En Russie Sovietique," *Le Libertaire*, January 7–14, 1921.

62   Vilkens, "Seis Meses en Rusia," *La Antorcha* (Buenos Aires), June 24, 1921. It may seem a little strange that Lenin should be so honest on this matter (and it is always possible that Wilkens was exaggerating). However, on arriving in Russia, Wilkens was a staunch supporter of the dictatorship of the proletariat and the need for a communist party to direct the revolution and only changed his opinions following his experiences in Russia. J. Galan (Wilkens), "La Situation en Espagne au point de vue Communiste," *La Vie Ouvriere*, February 10, 1922, an article written in August 1920, speaks in favour of the Bolsheviks. For the reasons behind Wilkens's change, see Augustín Souchy, "Une Lettre de Souchy," *Le Libertaire*, March 25–April 1, 1921.

63   Wilkens's disenchantment with what he found and his open criticism of the regime led him to be arrested by the Cheka and imprisoned for over a month. David Berry, *A History of the French Anarchist Movement, 1917–1945* (Oakland: AK Press, 2009), 100–102.

64   Xifort may actually have attended the Profintern congress. Archives Nationales de France, F/7/13442, police report, June 22, 1923. For Durán, see his letter to *Nueva Senda* from Berlin later published in *La Protesta*, December 8, 1921.

65   "E i sindicalisti spagnoli sconfessano," *L'Avvenire Anarchio* (Italy), August 12, 1921; "La Intersindical de lengua Española en Francia a los sindicalistas del mundo," *El Trabajo* (Uruguay), September 2, 1921. The IOE was strongly criticised by Arlandis in a meeting of the Profintern Bureau on August 13, 1921, held to discuss the reaction to the Profintern in France. C. Chambelland and J. Maitron, eds., *Syndicalisme Revolutionnaire et Communisme: Les Archives de Pierre Monatte, 1914–24* (Paris: Maspero, 1968), 312–3. It is more than probable that this manifesto was also published in *Nueva Senda*.

66   "No hay Subordinación," *Lucha Social*, August 6, 1921.

67   "Equivocación Lamentable," *Lucha Social*, August 27, 1921. The article was a response to the August plenum.

68   Durgan, *B.O.C. 1930–36*, 28, admits that the failure of the newspaper for economic reasons demonstrated the weakness of the support Maurín's brand of syndicalism had at the time.

69   See Sébastien Faure, "Vous ne ferez pas cela," *Le Libertaire*, November 25–December 2, 1921. Leval spent a further four months in France following his release before returning to Spain, which explains his absence from the Zaragoza conference. International Institute of Social History (IISG), Amsterdam, Leval Archive, file 1. A letter from the Spanish ambassador in Berlin to the state commissar in Madrid informed the Spanish government of the detention of Arlandis and Nin. File 17A(3), November 17, 1921, Serie A del Ministerio de Gobernación, Archivo Histórico Nacional (Madrid) (AHN). A note added to

the file stated that the two were wanted in relation to the assassination of the former Spanish premier Eduardo Dato. Arlandis made his way back to Spain, possibly via Amsterdam (an article by him, "La CNT d'Espagne et l'ISR," dated March 1922 and written in the Dutch capital, appeared in *La Vie Ouvrière* on March 17, 1922), arriving in Spain sometime before the Zaragoza conference. News of Ibàñez's arrest was published in "Retour de Russie Ibanez est Arrete," *La Vie Ouvrière*, November 11, 1921.

70 Whilst Nin was in Moscow he was temporarily replaced as CNT secretary, but the name of his replacement is unknown.

71 Maurín read Sorel's *Reflexions sur le violence* in 1919, a year before he joined the CNT. Sorel, a retired clerical worker when he wrote *Reflexions*, had little impact on the revolutionary syndicalist movement in France and was more popular in Italy, where his focus on the replenishing force of violence attracted the fascists as much as the syndicalists. Italian revolutionary syndicalism developed within the socialist party itself as a faction of the left, and the Confederazione Generale del Lavoro, formed in 1906, remained under the influence of the socialist party. Giano Biagio Furiozzi, *Il Sindicalismo riviluzionario Italiano* (Milan: Mursia, 1977), 97–99.

72 According to French communist Alfred Rosmer, Arlandis had initially opposed the link between the Comintern and Profintern but was "easily influenced" to change his position. Rosmer, *Lenin's Moscow*, 138.

73 The manifesto is reproduced in the report of George Williams, delegate for the International Workers of the World (IWW), and cosigner. *The First Congress of the Red Trade Union International at Moscow, 1921 (A Report of the Proceedings by Geo. Williams, Delegate from the I.W.W.)* (Chicago: IWW, 1921), 35–38; "Il fallimento dell' Internazionale dei Sindicati Rossi," *L'Avvenire Anarcho*, August 12, 1921. Representatives of the following organisations signed the manifesto: IWW, USI, Allegemeine Arbeiter-Union (Germany), CNT, Federación Obrera Regional Argentina, Federación Obrera Regional Uruguaya, and Comité Syndicaliste Révolutionnaire (France), as well as the syndicalist unions of Sweden, Norway, and Denmark.

74 "Confederación Nacional del Trabajo de España – Reunión del Pleno Nacional," *Acción Social Obrera* and *Redención*, both October 29, 1921. The national committee clarification was made in a letter to the CRT of Levante which was published by "Gustavo" (Carbó) in *Redención*, February 17, 1922. Victor Alba, who was a colleague of Maurín's in the Partido Obrero de Unificacion Marxista (POUM) in the 1930s, claims that the plenum was a victory for Maurín, even pretending that "there were still not many doubts about the Bolsheviks in confederal ranks." Victor Alba, *El Marxismo en España (1919–1939)* (Mexico: B. Costa-Amic, 1973), 20. The contemporary evidence does not support this claim.

75 A note to this effect was published by the Guipúzcoa committee on October 30. It has proved impossible to locate this note. However, the basic text of the criticisms can be judged by the reactions it caused. The Sindicatos Únicos of Vitoria, Tolosa, Pamplona, Villafranca-Bessain, Elgolbar, and San Sebastián also condemned the October plenum, insisting that the delegation be disqualified. They further claimed that at the Barcelona plenum in August the regions of Andalusia

and Levante as well as the local federations of Madrid and Alcoy supported Guipúzcoa's position. "La Confederación en ridículo," *Nueva Senda*, November 10, 1921. The Levantine CRT demanded the resignation of the national committee in a manifesto in December, "Confederación Regional Levantina – Sin Eufemismos," *Redención*, December 23, 1921. Finally, in January the Sindicato Único of Pamplona published a letter in which they gave the confederation one week to disqualify the delegation, threatening that if this was not carried out they would withdraw from the CNT. El Comité del Sindicato Único de Trabajadores de Pamplona, "A Todos los Trabajadores," *Nueva Senda*, January 26, 1922. At the Zaragoza conference, La Coruña threatened to leave the CNT if it did not withdraw from the Profintern. *Conferencia Nacional – Zaragoza* (1922). *Vida Obrera*, the newspaper of the Asturian Regional Federation, criticised Guipúzcoa's actions and claimed that the April plenum was legal, though they agreed that the decision to send so many delegates was excessive. "Por la unidad Confederal," *Vida Obrera*, November 11, 1921.

76   "La Confederación Nacional del Trabajo y la Confederación Regional del Trabajo de Cataluña," *Acción Social Obrera*, November 12, 1921, and *Redención* November 18, 1921.

77   "La Internacional Sindical Roja," *Acción Social Obrera*, October 29, 1921; "La C.N.T. y la Internacional Sindical Roja – Contra una desviación reformista," *Acción Social Obrera*, November 12, 1921; "La CNT delante de la Internacional Sindical Roja – Las dos tendencias," *Acción Social Obrera*, December 3, 1921; "La CNT delante de la Internacional Sindical Roja," *Acción Social Obrera*, December 17, 1921.

78   Joaquín Maurín, "Las Dos Tendencias," *Lucha Social*, December 10, 1921.

79   The anarchist criticism of the Profintern, led by Florentino Galo Díez from the northern region, focused specifically on concrete ideological issues. See, for example, "Deslindado campos," *Redención*, October 22, 1921; "La Realidad nos Abona," January 6, 1922, *Redención*.

80   José Alverola [*sic*], "Apreciaciones sobre las dos tendencias expuestas por Maurín," *Lucha Social*, February 11, 1922. Maurín's revolutionary fervour was also unrealistic. By late 1921 the CNT was hardly in a state to mount a revolutionary assault on the Spanish state, following years of repression with its press largely censored, its leading militants imprisoned, in exile, or murdered, and with the organisation itself decimated in its Catalan stronghold.

81   Ibid.

82   For attacks on Pestaña, see Avelino González, "Deux mots pour Andrés Nin," *Le Libertaire*, December 15–20, 1922. For Leval, see Leval, "Calumnias e ideas," *Nueva Senda*, January 1, 1922. For Wilkens, see "À Propos de Wilkens," *Le Libertaire*, February 17–24, 1922; Vilkens, "Vilkens y los comunistas," *La Antorcha*, January 28, 1922. For Xifort, see Leon Xifort, "Al Comité Nacional en Particular y a todos los militantes de la CNT en General," *Nueva Senda*, June 1, 1922. For Durán, see "Acusaciones graves contra la delegación de la CGT de España a Rusia," *La Protesta,* December 8, 1921. Many of the allegations were first published in *La Vie Ouvriere*, which *Le Libertaire* strongly suggested was

funded and controlled by Moscow. "Les 'allegations' du Libertaire et les contre-verites de la Vie Ouvriere," March 17–24, 1922; "Pour ne pas dire la verite la 'Vie Ouvrière'," *Le Libertaire*, July 20–27, 1923.

83 Translated from "Confederación Regional Levantina – Sin Eufemismos," *Redención*, December 23, 1921. The CRT again questioned the legality of the April plenum and claimed that Arlandis had informed the meeting of the Levante regional committee held to discuss who to send to Barcelona as delegate to the April plenum that he had already been chosen to go to Moscow. In his response to the accusations, Arlandis singularly failed to address this point. Hilaire Arlandis, "La CNT d'Espagne et l'ISR," *La Vie Ouvrière*, March 17, 1922.

84 "Gustavo" (Eusebio Carbó), "Contra la Diplomacia Secreta," *Redención*, February 17, 1922.

85 "Sobre la Delegación a Rusia," *Redención*, March 31, 1922.

86 El Comité Nacional, "Manifiesto de la CNT a la opinión y a todos sus adherentes," *Acción Social Obrera*, March 1, 1922.

87 *Conferencia Nacional – Zaragoza (1922)*.

88 According to Xifort, Arlandis spoke for two hours. L. Xifort, "Autour de la Conférence de Saragosse," *Le Libertaire*, July 28–August 4, 1922. Leval also sent a report to the congress, extracts of which are to be found in Xavier Paniagua, "La visió de Gaston Leval de la Rusia soviética el 1921," *Recerques*, no. 3 (1974). Maurín was too ill following an attempt on his life, Nin was in Russia, and the reasons for Ibáñez's absence are not clear. Ibáñez appears to have been very much a secondary figure and by 1927 was living in Russia. See Ignacio De Llorens, "La CNT y la Revolución Rusa," *Polémica* 47–49, January 1992, Arlandis's report for the CNT on the Profintern congress was published in *Lucha Social* from May 27 to July 29, 1922. In this account he claimed that the April plenum had agreed to support in Moscow "dictatorship of the proletariat exercised by the unions of the CNT'" ("La Delegación de la CNT en Russia," *Lucha Social*, May 27, 1922) but this was not the position he adopted at Zaragoza. Leval claimed that the other delegates had told him that the April plenum had agreed that there should be an interchange of delegates between the Profintern and the Comintern and that the Profintern should be based in Moscow. Gaston Leval, "Aux membres de la CNT d'Espagne," *Le Libertaire*, February 17–24, 1922.

89 Meaker, *The Revolutionary Left in Spain*, 442, claims incorrectly that the referendum never took place. The findings of the referendum were published in an article by the national committee in *Solidaridad Obrera*, April 19, 1923. The results gave almost unanimous support for the separation from Moscow.

90 Copies of *Lucha Social*, the pro-delegation paper, held at the IISG are more accessible than those of *Redención* and *Acción Social Obrera*, which except for a few editions can only be found at the archives in Alcoy and San Feliu de Guixols. It is noticeable that much of the information in Meaker's chapters on the Profintern congress and Zaragoza comes either from *Lucha Social*, Maurín himself, or pro-Bolshevik sources.

91 Juan Gómez Casas, *Historia del anarcosindicalismo Español* (Madrid: ZTX, 1968), 138.

92 B. Lladó, "El Congreso Internacional Sindical Rojo de Moscu," *La Protesta (Suplemento Semanal)*, March 27, 1922. The article was originally written in Germany in January 1922. Lladó's articles also appeared in *Nueva Senda*. See also A. Lozovsky, *Les Syndicat et la Revoluction. Discours prononcé par A. Lozovsky au Congrès de la CGTU a Saint Étienne, juin 1922* (Paris: Petite Bibliothèque de L'International Sindícale Rouge).

93 "Sobre la Delegación a Russia," *Redención*, March 31, 1922. Paragraph 21 of the section entitled "Labor de organización" argued: "The communist groups active in the UGT should form a block with the CNT for coordinated and offensive actions. ... Those unions that have separated from the reformist organisation, who support the position of the Profintern, should join the CNT as soon as possible."

94 According to Spanish government files, Nin was "director or member of the Western Europe Office of the Profintern" and his house was a centre for the secretariat of the Third International. Letter from the ambassador in Berlin to the state commissar, November 17, 1921, and telegram from the director general of public order to the civil governor (Catalonia), File 17a(3), Serie A del Ministerio de Gobernación, Archivo Histórico Nacional (Madrid).

95 Durgan, *B.O.C. 1930–36*, 28–33, provides evidence that Arlandis and Ibáñez were members of the PCE prior to their trip to Moscow.

96 Bar, *La CNT en los Años Rojo*, 566, concludes that the performance of the delegation to the Profintern was in line with the policy agreed upon at the April plenum. This is incorrect, the delegation promised to defend the principles of Berlin which stressed the need for the strict autonomy of the syndicalist movement from any political party.

97 Meaker, *The Revolutionary Left in Spain*, 393, quotes articles by Nin from *El Comunista*, in which he claimed to be going to Russia to defend revolutionary syndicalism. See also Wilkens, "Ce que valent les affirmations de Rosmer," *Le Libertaire*, November 18–25, 1921.

98 Bruno Lladó, "El congreso Internacional Sindical Roja de Moscú," *La Protesta (Suplemento Semanal)*, March 27, 1922. Lladó also wrote an article critical of the delegation: "La Verdad sobre el Congreso de la Sindical Roja de Moscu," *Neuva Senda*, January 26, 1922. Lladó's position was supported by Leval: Gaston Leval, "Aux membres de la CNT d'Espagne," *Le Libertaire*, February 17–24, 1922. Williams, the delegate for the IWW, also claimed that while in Moscow the Spanish delegation members were tricked by the Bolsheviks, who passed on information to the delegates from "a mysterious committee somewhere in Spain" which sent "approval (or at least it is reported in communist circles) of the Profintern" which was "heralded as the approval of the whole Spanish Syndicalist movement." Williams claimed he had met several Spaniards in Berlin who denied that "this unknown committee has power to act in the way it did and have denounced it as a frame-up to stampede the syndicalists of Europe." Williams, *The First Congress of the Red Trade Union International*, 30.

99 Letter to the author from Maurín, August 8, 1965; Meaker, *The Revolutionary Left in Spain*, 389.

100 Maurín eventually joined the PCE in 1923 although he was immediately at odds with its centralised leadership and, after a period in exile in France, left in 1930 to form the Bloc Obrer i Camperol (Workers' and Peasant's Party).

101 Ramón Váquer, who had been an early supporter of the Russian Revolution, attributed the delegation's decision to sign the resolution on relations between the Profintern and the Comintern to "the dislocated head of the politician Andrés Nin," suggesting that in Catalonia Nin's preference for politics was not unknown. Ramón Váquer, "El Congreso Sindical Internacional de Moscú y los delegados de la Confederación Nacional del Trabajo de España II," *Acción Social Obrera*, August 27, 1921.

102 The subsequent anarchist attempts to control the union were perhaps more the result of the communists' attempts to link the CNT with the Bolshevik International than the actual cause of the struggle. They concluded that revolutionary syndicalism lacked ideological direction and that if they did not fill this void, then the communists would. The anarchist-syndicalist conflict has been widely covered by historians. See, for example, Antonio Elorza, "La génesis de la Federación Anarquista Ibérica," *Revista de Trabajo* (Madrid) nos. 39, 40, and 44–45 (1972) Eulàlia Vega, *El trentisme a Catalunya* and *Entre la Revolució i la Reforma*; Julián Casanova, *De la Calle al Frente. El anarcosindicalismo en España 1931–39* (Barcelona: Crítica, 1997).

103 *Conferencia Nacional – Zaragoza* (1922).

Chapter 4

1 'Antipolitical' in the sense used here and henceforth refers to the rejection of politics as defined as the governance of the state and those parties interested in working with or through the state to achieve their goals, as opposed to the administration of society through what libertarians would consider non-authoritarian means: communes, unions, et cetera.

2 Wayne Thorpe, *"The Workers Themselves": Revolutionary Syndicalism and International Labour, 1913–1923* (London: Dordrecht, 1989), provides a detailed account of the creation of the new IWMA, focusing on the general progress towards the creation of the International rather than on the specific reactions in each individual country. On the later development of the IWMA very little has been written, perhaps due to the loss of much primary material following the Nazi seizure of power in Germany, the only overall work being the brief chapter by Thorpe, "Syndicalist Internationalism before World War II," in Marcel Van der Linden and Wayne Thorpe, eds., *Revolutionary Syndicalism: An International Perspective* (Aldershot, England: Scolar Press, 1990). Maximiano García Venero, *Historia de las Internacionales en España*, vol. 2(Madrid: Ediciones de Movimiento, 1957), 376–90, provides a brief history of the IWMA but focuses almost entirely on the process leading to the creation of the International. A number of short introductory pamphlets on the second IWMA have been published, of which the best are Ramon Liarte, *A.I.T.: La internacional del Sindicalismo Revolucionario*, and C. Longmore, *The IWA Today: A Short*

Account of the International Workers Association and Its Sections (London: South London DAM-IWA, 1985). However, barring Thorpe's book on the birth of the IWMA, the best sources are all primary. See Abad de Santillán, "Preliminares de la Fundación de la Segunda A. Internacional de los T. (1912–20)," *La Protesta*, November 21, 1924; Abad de Santillán, "La Asociación Internacional de los Trabajadores – Su Historia, sus ideas, su porvenir," *La Revista Internacional Anarquista*, January–April 1925; *Solidaridad Proletaria*, March 7, 1925 (and following numbers); Augustín Souchy, "Algo sobre la historia del Origen de la Asociación I de los T," published in the *Suplemento de 'La Revista Blanca'*, May 15, 1929, and later in *Despertad*, May 4, 1929; Augustín Souchy, "Asociación Internacional de Trabajadores," *Mañana*, May 1930; A. Schapiro, "Las Internacionales Sindicales," *La Protesta (Suplemento Semanal)*, August 31, 1925. Further relevant information on the IWMA can be found in the papers of the member organisations and the copies of the Press Service of the IWMA which are kept at the IISG (International Institute for Social History) in Amsterdam.

3   The national committee's manifestos to organisations abroad informing foreign colleagues of the repression at home and calling for a boycott of Spanish goods were published in numerous foreign publications. See "La Confederación Nacional del Trabajo, al proletariado Español – La Solidaridad Internacional," *Redención*, April 9, 1921; "Il Boicottaggio della Spagna," *Avvenire Anarchico*, February 25, 1921; "Dalla Spagna," *Il Libertario*, March 17, 1921; "Una carta y un manifiesto," *El Hombre* (Montevideo), December 1, 1921; "A Espanha reaccionaria", ' "Um grito de Desespero'" and "As Persiguicoes em Espanha," *A Batalha*, March 1, October 21, and December 21, 1921; "Trabalhadores Escuta!!," *A Comuna* (Oporto), February 27, 1921; "Les ouvriers Espanols appellent au secours," *La Vie Ouvriere*, December 31, 1920. Numerous appeals were also published in *Le Libertaire* and *La Protesta*.

4   *Guerra di Classe*, May 1, 1915.

5   "L'Unione Sindicale Italiana a Consiglio Generale," *Guerra di Classe*, May 22, 1915.

6   According to the French police, delegates to go to the congress in Amsterdam were chosen at a meeting of fifty leading anarchists and syndicalists in Valencia in late July or early August, Archives Nationales de France, F/7/13440, police report, September 1, 1919. A later report states that a member of the CNT, Miguel Abos Serena, who had been living in exile in Marseilles, left to attend a congress in Amsterdam at some time in 1918. Archives Nationales de France, F/7/13440, police report, November 23, 1920.

7   M. J. de Sousa, "O II Congreso da CGT de Espanha," *A Batalha*, December 16, 1919. According to a security report sent to the Paris police by their colleagues in Madrid, the socialist Fernando de los Ríos held discussions with both Mauro Bajatierra (in Madrid) and Angel Pestaña (in Barcelona) in early September 1919 before travelling to France and England to discuss with his foreign colleagues the possibility of forming a syndicalist International. Archives Nationales de France, F/7/13440, September 8, 1919.

8   Angel Pestaña and Salvador Seguí, *El Sindicalismo en Cataluña – Conferencias dadas*

en Madrid el dia 4 de octubre de 1919 (Barcelona: Calamus Scriptorvius, 1978).

9   Archives Nationales de France, F/7/13441, report by the Naval Attache in Madrid, January 18, 1921. The fact that that most of the trips did actually occur suggests the report was well-informed.

10 Buenacasa sent a letter to Léon Jouhaux, the CGT president, in the summer of 1918 requesting that the two organisations enter into correspondence to discuss issues of mutual interest to workers of both countries. Archives Nationales de France, F/7/13440, security report from Madrid sent to the Security General in Paris, June 30, 1919. Jouhaux was scheduled to visit Spain in August 1919, but eventually did not do so. Archives Nationales de France, F/7/13440, police report, August 21, 1919. However, a CGT delegate, Antoine Desmoulins, who had visited Spain in 1911 (see chapter 1) did arrive in Barcelona in late 1919, whilst two further CGT delegates visited Valencia to work with syndicalists in the region. Archives Nationales de France, F/7/13440, police report, June 12 and November 24, 1919. At the beginning of 1920, Buenacasa wrote to Peirre Monatte, of the revolutionary wing of the CGT, requesting that the French CGT help the CNT. Monatte visited Barcelona later that year. Archives Nationales de France, F/7/13442, police report, December 28, 1921, and F/7/13441, police report, April 6, 1920.

11 The FAUD was established in 1919 out of the Freie Vereinigung deutscher Gewerkschaften (FVdG – Free Association of German Unions) which had attended the 1913 congress. See Marcel Van der Linden and Wayne Thorpe, *Revolutionary Syndicalism*, 59–80 (chapter on Germany); Helge Dohring, *Syndicalism and Anarcho-Syndicalism in Germany: An Introduction*, trans. John Carroll (Bremen: FAU, 2006). Diego Abad de Santillán wrote a brief history on the FAUD from 1922–24 for *La Protesta (Suplemento Semanal)*, December 1 and 8, 1924.

12 Santillán, "Preliminares," *La Protesta*, November 21, 1924.

13 The USI had also provisionally affiliated with the Comintern at its national congress in January 1920, due to their sympathy with the Russian Revolution. Borghi claimed that for the USI support for the Russian Revolution "was made through the intermediary of the Third International." "Conference Internationale Prealable des Syndicalistes Revolutionnaires. Compte Rendu," *Bulletin International des Syndicalistes Revolutionnaires et Industrialistes* (henceforth *BISRI*), August 1922, a position similar to that adopted by the CNT.

14 Armando Borghi, "La Memoria de Armando Borghi sobre Rusia," *Nueva Senda*, November 10, 1921. Borghi's report was originally published in *Guerra di Classe*, October 15, 1921.

15 A. Borghi, "Una intervista con Pietro Kropotkine," *Guerra di Classe*, January 4, 1921.

16 Wilkens, "Ce que valent les affirmation de Rosmer," *Le Libertaire*, November 18–25, 1921.

17 Berry, *A History of the French Anarchist Movement*, 99–100.

18 Wilkens claimed that Pestaña was actually the inspiration behind the calling of the conference. Wilkens, "Diplomatie Bolchevique," *Le Libertaire*, February 10–17, 1922.

19   Augustín Souchy, "Conferenza della Internazionale Sindicalista tenuta a Berlino del 16 al 21 Diciembre 1920," *Guerra di Classe,* January 22, 1921. Souchy's report was also printed in "A Conferencia Preliminar da Internacional Sindicalista," *A Batalha,* February 12–16, 1921, and "La Conferencia Sindicalista revolucionaria de Berlin (de December 1920)," *La Protesta,* May 29, 1921. A report on the conference in English appears in *Solidarity* ("Official Organ of the Shop Stewards' and Workers' Committee Movement"), January 7, 1921.

20   Vilkens, "Vilkens y los comunistas," *La Antorcha* (Buenos Aires), January 28, 1921. An invitation to the congress from the FAUD was discovered by the Spanish police during a raid on a "secret location." Archives Nationales de France, F/7/13441, police report, November 1920.

21   The French delegates (Victor Godonneche and Jean Ceppe) later admitted that they had been sent to hinder any moves towards the creation of a revolutionary syndicalist International and indeed left the conference after the first session. The English delegate, Jack Tanner, later joined the communists. Augustín Souchy, "Algo Sobre la Historia del Orígen de la Asociación I. de los T.," *Revista Blanca,* May 15, 1929, supplement; "La Conference internationale des Syndicalistes Revolutionnaires," *BISRI,* August 1922.

22   *Solidarity* (London), January 7, 1921.

23   A commission of three members – Rocker (FAUD), Bernard Lansink (Netherlands), and Tanner (England) – was created which would be in contact with all the revolutionary syndicalist organisations and inform them of what was occurring in other countries, as well as being a provisional council for the RTUI.

24   Wilkens, "Ce que valent les affirmations de Rosmer," *Le Libertaire,* November 18–25, 1921.

25   For more detailed accounts of the repression, see Paul Avrich, "The Anarchists in the Russian Revolution," *Russian Review* 26, no. 4 (October 1967), 341–50; John Walter Copp, "The Role of the Anarchists in the Russian Revolution and Civil War, 1917–1921: A Case Study in ConspiratorialParty Behaviour during Revolution," PhD diss. (New York: Columbia University, 1993).

26   With Borghi and other influential figures still in prison following the occupation of the factories in Italy in 1920, the two USI delegates that attended the RTUI congress, Nicolo Vecchi and Lulio Mari, were less-experienced figures within the movement and proved unable to resist the allure of Moscow. However, once Borghi and the other leading USI members were released from prison the delegation to the RTUI congress was censored. A general council meeting of the USI held in Milan in October 1921 supported the French CSR's call for the next RTUI congress to take place in western Europe, outside the influence of any party or government (although it also reaffirmed its provisional adhesion to the RTUI). "Il Consiglio Generale dell'U.S.I – Milano 5–6 Ottobre," *Guerra di Classe,* October 15, 1921.

27   Manuel Joaquin de Sousa, *O Sindicalismo em Portugal* (Lisbon: Publicacoes da AIT, 1931), 150–51.

28   "El XIII Congreso Sindicalista Aleman," *Nueva Senda,* November 10, 1921. The continued repression against the CNT at home meant that it was impossible for

the confederation to be represented in Berlin. The USI had assigned Borghi to represent them at the congress, but due to the political situation in the country at the time he was unable to attend. "Il Consiglio Generale dell' U.S.I.," *Guerra di Classe*, October 15, 1921.

29   In a letter to Armando Borghi published in *Umanita Nova*, March 7, 1922, Pestaña told his Italian colleague that the revolutionary syndicalists could not remain in the RTUI because it served the "political interests of the Russian Communist Party, not those of the world's proletariat" and claimed that the Soviet government was "more or less bourgeois."

30   Originally the conference was to be held in Paris and was to be organised by the French CSR and the USI. A. Giovanneti (USI Executive Committee), "Conferencia Sindicalista Internacional," *La Antorcha* (Buenos Aires), June 16, 1922. The acts of the conference were published in "Conference Internationale Prealable des Syndicalistes Revolutionnaires. Compte-Rendu." *BISRI*, August 1922. It was Borghi who sent the conference invitation to the CNT. *Solidaridad Obrera* (Valencia), May 18, 1922. The same newspaper also published the acts of the conference in September 1922; unfortunately not all the numbers of this paper have survived.

31   Even before the Zaragoza conference at which the CNT finally confirmed the rupture with Moscow, the SAC, FAUD, and USI had all called for the formation of an independent syndicalist International. The FAUD and SAC had been dubious about Moscow almost from the beginning, whilst the USI had finally rejected the RTUI at its fourth congress, held in March 1922.

32   Avelino González Mallada gives a description of the obstacles faced by the delegation simply to arrive at the congress in A.G.M., "La Confederación Nacional del Trabajo de España en el décimo año de la Asociación Internacional de los Trabajadores," *CNT*, January 5 and 6, 1933.

33   "Conference Internationale Prealable des Syndicalistes Revolutionnaires. Compte-Rendu," *BISRI*, August 1922.

34   Galo Díez made the position of the CNT towards the question of the International clear: "We are in favour of an absolutely autonomous International. … I declare here that we do not want to know the RTUI, we are for the creation of an revolutionary syndicalist International that is absolutely independent and autonomous. We would rather stay alone against Moscow – even if all the other centrals are adhered to it. That is the attitude of our Confederation." "Conference Internationale Prealable des Syndicalistes Revolutionnaires. Compte-Rendu." *BISRI*, August 1922.

35   *Cultura y Acción*, October 14, 1922. Rocker was the bureau's secretary whilst the other members were Borghi, Jensen, and Schapiro.

36   "Compte Rendu des Débats (del Congreso de St. Étienne de la CGTU 26-June)," *La Vie Ouvriere*, July 7, 1922; "A Saint-Étienne la Politique a triomphe du Syndicalisme," *Le Libertaire*, July 7–14, 1922. Arlandis also spoke at the congress. Veber, "Ce qui se passe dans les Syndicats," *La Revue Anarchiste*, July 1922.

37   Lozovsky, *Les Syndicat et la Revoluction*. Lozovsky had been expelled from the Bolshevik party during the revolution due to his support for independent trade

unions (see V. I. Lenin, "Concerning the Expulsion from the Party of S. A. Lozovsky, December 30, 1917," in *Lenin's Collected Works*, Marxists Internet Archive, http://www.marxists.org/archive/lenin/works/1917/dec/30a.htm). But on returning to the fold he became general secretary of the RTUI in 1921, a position he would maintain until 1937, subsequently working under Molotov during World War Two. Despite his loyalty he was eventually arrested, tortured, and executed (in 1952 along with thirteen other Jewish Bolsheviks in what is known as the Night of the Murdered Poets).

38   *La Vie Ouvriere* had supported the ill-fated Spanish delegation to the inaugural RTUI congress, opening its pages to articles by Maurín, Arlandis, and Nin but not to their opponents. In 1920 *La Vie Ouvriere* had refused to respond to or publish the communiqué they received informing them of the calling of the Berlin conference of that year, whilst it published all the documents relative to the Russian unions. Augustín Souchy, "L'Internationale Syndicaliste Revolutionnaire et la Troisième Internationale," *Le Libertaire*, September 30–October 7, 1921.

39   Berry, *A History of the French Anarchist Movement*, 144.

40   Schapiro analysed the modifications made by the RTUI and concluded that they had "not changed at all the statist and dictatorial ideology of the RTUI and have not changed in any manner the servile character of that organization towards the communist International." Translated from A. Schapiro, "Las Internacionales Sindicales," *La Protesta (Suplemento Semanal)*, August 31, 1925.

41   *Alba Social* (Valencia) and *Solidaridad Obrera* (Seville) published the resolutions of the congress in May 1923.

42   Schapiro claimed that 250,000 workers were represented in 1913. A. Schapiro, "Las internacionales sindicales," *La Protesta (Suplemento Semanal)*, August 24, 1925. In 1923 the IWMA brought together just under 1.5 million workers. Diego Abad de Santillán, "La Nueva Asociación International de los Trabajadores," *Suplemento de Tierra y Libertad*, February 1932. *De Arbeid*, January 13, 1923, puts the figures at over two million but this is probably too high, possibly representing the numbers of each member at its height – according to these figures the SAC, CNT, FAUD, and USI had all increased since the Berlin conference of June 1922, at which the official bulletin put their membership as follows 30,000, 750,000, 100,000, and 200,000 respectively (*BISRI*, August 1922) – rather than the reality in 1923 but also reflected the difficulty of assessing membership in countries such as Spain and Italy due to repression.

43   Diego Abad de Santillán, "Informe del Congreso Constituivo de la 'Asociación Internacional de los Trabajadores' y 'Estatutos de la nueva internacional,'" *Solidaridad Obrera* (Gijón), January 19, 1923; "La C.N. del T. de España y la Asociación Internacional de Trabajadores," *Solidaridad Obrera*, April 19, 1923.

44   The Berlin Declaration is reproduced in Augustín Souchy, "Asociación Internacional de Trabajadores," *Manaña*, May 1930. Hereafter "Berlin Declaration."

45   Ibid.

46   "El Congreso," *La Protesta*, March 21, 1923.

47   "Berlin Declaration."

48   "El congreso Sindicalista Internacional de Berlin," *La Protesta*, March 22, 1923.

49   Representatives from the FAUD, FORA, the Federación Obrera Regional Uruguaya, the NSF, SAC, USI, and the Bund Herrchaftlosen Sozialisten (Austria) attended, whilst the IWMA secretariat was represented by Souchy and Rocker. The CNT and the CGTs of Portugal and Mexico were unable to attend. "Conferencia plenaria de la Asociación Internacional de los Trabajadores en Innsbruck (Austria) – celebrada del 2 al 4 de diciembre de 1923," *La Protesta (Suplemento Semanal)*, February 4, 1924. Following the occupation of the Ruhr by French troops in 1923, the IWMA wrote to both the communist and socialist Internationals in Moscow and Amsterdam suggesting the establishment of a temporary international committee to help bring about "fraternization" between all the syndicalist forces of France and Germany. "Una carta de la Asociación Internacional de los Trabajadores a las Internacionales de Amsterdam y Moscú," *Solidaridad Obrera*, April 19, 1923. Neither International responded, and in May the French resolution approved at Berlin was dropped at a meeting of the IWMA Bureau. "Conferencia plenaria," *La Protesta*, February 4, 1924. Meanwhile the Bolsheviks did not invite the IWMA to the conference at Frankfurt to discuss the formation of the United Front because, according to Lozovsky, the organisation was counterrevolutionary. (Lansink, the Dutch delegate at the Innsbruck plenum, had attended the Frankfurt conference as a delegate for the NAS and had questioned Lozovsky as to why the IWMA had not been invited.) "Conferencia," *La Protesta*, February 4, 1924. Three months later the IWMA received a letter from Clara Zetkin, president of the Provisional Committee against Fascism, inviting the IWMA to participate in the committee. "Contra el fascismo internacional," *Solidaridad Obrera*, April 19, 1923. Despite reticence the secretariat accepted the offer but proposed that the fight should also be launched against "el fascismo ruso" as well. Not surprisingly, their proposal was not accepted.

50   "Declaration of Principles of Revolutionary Syndicalism (principle 2)" published in "Conference Internationale Prealable des Syndicalistes Revolutionnaires. Compte-Rendu," *BISRI*, No. 2–3, August 1922.

51   Much of the terminology used in the ten principles had an anarchist slant, for example the adoption of "the administration of things" as opposed to the "government of men" – pure Proudhonism.

52   Rocker's "Declaration of the Principles of Syndicalism," upon which the principles of the International were based, had been adopted at the founding congress of the FAUD in December 1919.

53   Sam Dolgoff, introduction to Gregory Petrovich Maximoff, *The Guillotine at Work – The Leninist Counter-revolution* (Orkney: Cienfuegos Press, 1979).

54   Andrés Nin, "El Congreso de Berlin," *La Batalla*, February 9, 1923. *La Batalla* was the "voice of the RTUI" in Spain. Nin's defence of Bolshevism outstripped even that of Maurín. On the anniversary of the Kronstadt rising he defended the Bolshevik action: "The Russian Communist Party is the only guarantor of the Revolution … so our Russian comrades see themselves inevitably obliged

to smother implacably every attempt to break their power. It is not only their right but their duty. The health of the Revolution is the supreme law." Andreu Nin, "Kronstadt," *Lucha Social*, April 29, 1922. In an ironic twist of history, Nin would later become a victim of this implacable 'right'. He was shot by the Moscow-backed communists during the Civil War in 1937.

55 Wilkens had previously stressed the same point in relation to the RTUI. Wilkens, "Una Internacional sin adherentes," *Nueva Senda*, January 26, 1922.

56 "Después del fracaso de la Conferencia de Berlin," *La Batalla*, January 18, 1923. Maurín returned to the attack in a further article, "La Confederación Nacional del Trabajo de España delante de la International Sindical Roja," *La Batalla*, April 13, 1923, in which he asked, "Will we continue detached from international relations as we have lived until now? Is it that only the adversaries of the RTUI in Spain are correct against the opinion of the unions of the rest of the world? That would be a stupid presumption!" *La Batalla* continued publishing articles calling for CNT adhesion to the RTUI and belittling the role of the IWMA.

57 "Manifiesto de la Internacional Sindical Roja – A Todos los miembros de la CNT de España," *Acción Sindicalista*, September 1, 1922.

58 "Los Sindicalistas revolucionarios de France se adhieren a Moscú," *Lucha Social*, July 15, 1922.

59 The formation of the CGTU, which occurred shortly after its members' expulsion from the CGT in February 1922, was warmly welcomed by the anarchist weekly *Alba Social* (Valencia) for rejecting the reformism of the leaders of the CGT, although the paper did warn that Moscow wanted the new confederation under its wing. "Desde France – De la Lucha Sindical," *Alba Social*, April 1, 1923.

60 Meaker, *The Revolutionary Left in Spain*, 452, incorrectly claims that Maurín did attend the congress. See Riottat, *Joaquin Maurín*, 73.

61 "Por la Organización de los Comités Sindicalistas Revolucionarios – A todo el Proletariado de la Confederación Nacional del Trabajo," *Acción Sindicalista*, November 18, 1922. The manifesto was also published on A3-sized paper, probably for distribution among the unions. A copy can be found in the archives at the CEHI in Barcelona (Centre de Documentació Centre d'Estudis Històrics Internacionals), files V (1) to VII (1).

62 The five policies had originally appeared in the manifesto of November 1922.

63 Durgan, *B.O.C. 1930–36*, 29. According to a French police report, on being created, the CSR received sixty thousand pesetas from Moscow. Archives Nationales de France, F/7/13442, police records, March 28, 1923. Previously, in the summer of 1922, the Comintern executive committee sent two hundred thousand pesetas to the PCE, some of which was to be offered to the CNT to join the RTUI, whilst the communist-syndicalist newspaper received money directly from Moscow. Archives Nationales de France, F/7/13442, police records, July 19 and August 29, 1922. Funding for the main newspaper of the pro-Moscow faction, *La Batalla*, and for *Lucha Obrera* (a joint collaboration by CSR and CNT militants) also came from dubious sources. Wilkens claimed that

the Latin Bureau of the RTUI paid for the publication of *La Batalla*. "Poniendo las Cosas en su lugar," *Acción Social Obrera*, November 1, 1924. Certainly *La Batalla*'s impressive format and financially problem-free existence could not have been supported by its scant readership (at most thousand).

64   El Comité de la CNT, "La C.N. del Trabajo de España y el frente revolucionario," *La Protesta (Suplemento Semanal)*, April 17, 1922.

65   The IWMA rejected the United Front at its plenum in Innsbruck, Austria, in December 1923 because it was felt that this was simply a manouevre by the communist parties to infiltrate the unions and take control of the working class. "Conferencia plenaria de la Asociación International de los Trabajadores en Innsbruck (Austria) celebrada del 2 al 4 de diciembre de 1923," *La Protesta (Suplemento Semanal)*, February 4, 1924. Extracts from the plenum were also published in *Solidaridad Obrera* in January 1924.

66   "O III Congreso Operario Nacional – os discursos de Joaquim Maurín, delegado da I.S.V, e Perfeito de Carvalho," *A Batalha*, October 8, 1922.

67   *Acción Sindicalista* received money directly from Moscow. Archives Nationales de France, F/7/13442, police records, August 29, 1922.

68   Luis Portela, "La ISR en España – Necesidad de una organización de combate," *Acción Sindicalista*, November 11, 1922.

69   Javier Tussell, *Historia de España en el siglo XX*, vol. 1 (Madrid: Taurus Bolsillo, 1998), 308.

70   Whilst in Moscow for the inaugural congress of the RTUI, Maurín had met Trotsky and asked him for arms to support the revolution in Spain. Trotsky refused the request, stating that if the revolution were to be successful it would have its own arms, which would be provided by the army. Rourera Farré, *Joaquín Maurín y su tiempo*, 98. Although some members of the military did conspire with the revolutionary working class, they were very few in number.

71   "Los Comités Sindicalistas Revolucionarios," *La Batalla*, February 16, 1923.

72   Maurín later admitted that the CSR had represented a "minuscule minority." Joaquin Maurín, *El Bloque Obrero y Campesino, Origenes – Actividad – Perspectivas* (Barcelona: Centro de Información Bibliográfica, 1932), 9.

73   *Acción Sindicalista*, December 9, 1922.

74   *Service de la Presse de la A.I.T*, April 15, 1923.

75   "Un Congreso Importante: La Confederación del Norte," *Cultura y Acción*, April 27, 1923.

76   El Comité (of the Catalan CRT), "Una y única replica a los Bolchevantes," *Solidaridad Proletaria*, November 1, 1924.

77   "Principales puntos tratados en la asamblea de Sabadell," *Acción Social Obrera*, May 10, 1924.

78   The CSR continued to exist until 1926 but as little more than an appendage to the PCE (and treated as such by the Comintern).

79   *La Protesta*, October 3, 1924; *Revista Blanca*, October 1, 1924; *Servicio de la Prensa de la A.I.T.*, August 27, 1924.

80   J. Peiró, "En Torno al Frente Unico," *Solidaridad Proletaria*, October 25, 1924.

81   In 1924 the Levantine CRT received a circular supposedly written for the CNT

by Trilla Valls (a communist who had come to prominence during the transport strike of May–July 1923) which announced the disappearance of the IWMA and proposed that the CNT should return to the RTUI. The Levantine CRT condemned Valls's action as a communist plot. Letter from the committee of the Levantine CRT to the national committee, November 8, 1924, Archivo General de la Guerra Civil Española (AGGCES), Regiòn Barcelona , file 1352. In 1925 the PCE organised efforts for the National Committee of the CNT to travel to Moscow, in an attempt to win CNT support for Moscow. Letter from Avelino González (then secretary of the National Committee) to Santillán, September 17,1925, International Institute of Social History (IISG), Amsterdam, Santillán Archive, file 7.

82   The first extant number that carries the motif is dated September 29, 1923. However numbers for September 24–28 have not survived.

83   *Preámbulo y Convocatoria de la Conferencia Nacional – Zaragoza*, International Institute of Social History (IISG), Amsterdam, CNT Archive, microfilms 174, 200.

84   J. Peiró, "La insensibilidad colectiva y la responsabilidad de la Confederación Nacional del Trabajo," *Cultura y Acción*, October 21, 1922; Salvador Seguí, "La posición doctrinal de los sindicalistas libertarios frente a las internacionales socialistas," *Cultura y Acción*, October 21, 1922; Salvador Quemades, "Ante los Congresos regionales," *Cultura y Acción*, October 21, 1922. Peiró also defended his position at a meeting of the Asturian Miners' Union in the same month. J. Peiró, "Por la Honrades y no por la mentira," *Solidaridad Obrera*, May 28, 1924. This suggests that the regional and local referendums took place in late October or early November.

85   "La C.N. del T. de España y la Asociación Internacional de Trabajadores," *Solidaridad Obrera*, April 19, 1923.

86   This was according to a member of the regional committee of the Aragón, Rioja, and Navarra CRT. The claims were published in Diego Abad de Santillán, "Vacilaciones e inconsecuencias de la CNT de España," *La Protesta*, May 11, 1923. The RTUI had previously claimed that the CNT had decided not to collaborate in the creation of a new International and had agreed to enter into relations with the RTUI and reestablish a "fraternal understanding," which seems to support the CRT's claims. "La CN del T de España y la Asociación Internacional de Trabajadores," *Solidaridad Obrera*, April 19, 1923.

87   Extracts from the circular and the manifesto of the national committee were published in "Las Vacilaciones del Sindicalismo Español," *La Protesta (Suplemento Semanal)*, March 5, 1923.

88   Maurín, "La Confederación Nacional del Trabajo de España delante de la International Sindical Roja," *La Batalla*, April 13, 1923.

89   El Comité Nacional de la C.N.T, "La Confederación Nacional sale al paso de una campaña de inexactitudes," *Solidaridad Obrera*, April 26, 1923.

90   *Service de Presse de la A.I.T*, April 15, 1923.

91   J. Peiró, "En torno a las Internacionales," *Solidardidad Proletaria*, March 15, 1925. The northern CRT voted in favour of the IWMA at a congress in April,

whilst the CRT of Aragón, Rioja, and Navarra followed suit at a congress in June. "Un Congreso importante – La Confederación del Norte," *Cultura y Acción*, April 27, 1923; "Celebracion del Primer Congreso de la Confederación Regional de Aragón, Rioja y Navarra," *Cultura y Acción*, July 7, 1923.

92   In 1925 Abad de Santillán questioned whether the CNT was adhering to the IWMA, concluding, "I am almost certain that in the Archives of the IWMA there is not a single letter communicating their adherence." Abad de Santillán letter to Augustín Souchy, August 18, 1925, International Institute of Social History (IISG), Amsterdam, Santillán Archive, file 4. An editorial in *Solidaridad Obrera* in May 1931 suggested that the question of the confederation's permanent affiliation should be discussed at the national congress of the CNT due to be held in Madrid in June 1931. "El Congreso Extraordinario de la C.N.T.," *Solidaridad Obrera*, May 21, 1931. However, when the congress did turn its attention to the International it was simply to discuss the papers that it was to present at the IWMA congress in Madrid immediately following the CNT congress. *Memoria del Congreso Extraordinario celebrado en Madrid los días 11 al 16 de Junio de 1931* (Barcelona: 1931).

93   In October 1924, *La Internacional*, an IWMA journal for workers in the Spanish-speaking countries, began publication. However, only one number of *La Internacional* was ever published.

94   The repression against member organisations of the IWMA was such that by February 1924 it only had four official newspapers: *l'Arbeteron* (Sweden), *A Batalha*, *La Protesta*, and *Solidaridad Obrera* (Barcelona). See Carbó interview with Armando Borghi, "Una Entrevista con Borghi," *La Protesta*, March 28, 1924. The interview first appeared in *Solidaridad Obrera*.

Chapter 5

1   See Antonio Elorza, "La génesis de la Federación Anarquista Ibérica," *Revista de Trabajo*, no. 39 and 40, 44–45 & 45 (1972); Meaker, *The Revolutionary Left in Spain*; Bar, *La CNT en los Años Rojo*. This categorisation is also generally used in works on the CNT during the Second Republic.

2   In her doctoral thesis Eulàlia Vega i Massana suggests that there were three main tendencies: the neutral syndicalists, who wanted the unions to be open to all workers and who favoured the use of direct action; the anarco-syndcialists, who agreed with the above but felt that the confederation needed ideological "content" and that this should be anarchism; and the proponents of the Movimiento Obrero Anarquista (see chapter 6). She later mentions a further tendency, the communist-syndicalists. "La Confederació Nacional del Treball i els Sindicats d'Oposició a Catalunya i el País Valencià (1930–36)," PhD thesis, Universat de Barcelona, 1986, 178–80. This analysis is supported by Monjo Omedes, "La CNT durant la II República a Barcelona : Líders, militants, afiliats," PhD thesis, Universitat de Barcelona, 1994, 63, although she describes the final group as "radical anarcho-syndicalists," and it is this which seems the most appropriate in relation to the ideological divisions in the 1920s. Previously Susanna Tavera i

García also claimed that there were three distinct tendencies within the CNT in "La ideologia política del anarcosindicalismo catalán a través de su propaganda (1930–36)," PhD thesis, Universitat de Barcelona, 1980, 249–310. These were the communist-syndicalist tendency, the radical anarchist tendency, and the moderate anarcho-syndicalists.

3   Vega, "La Confederació Nacional del Treball i els Sindicats d'Oposició a Catalunya i el País Valencià (1930–36)," 178–80; Monjo Omedes, "La CNT durant la II República a Barcelona," 63.

4   The conflict between syndicalist and anarchists, which had been brewing before the crisis sparked by the communist-syndicalists, broke out in full following the split from Moscow, when radical anarchists still wary of communist attempts to control the unions became more insistent on the need for the unions to operate according to immediately revolutionary tactics and ensure that the unions were clearly anarchist.

5   In 1912 the CGT claimed to have six hundred thousand members representing over half the active workforce in France, although, as Thorpe points out, these included reformists as well as revolutionaries. Thorpe, *The Workers Themselves*, 26.

6   It was to these militants that Maurín and Nin were referring when they spoke of 'anarcho-reformists'.

7   Although this was not clearly spelt out until 1924–25, predominantly in the pages of *Solidaridad Proletaria* and *Vida Sindical* (see chapter 6).

8   See El Comité Nacional, "Confederación Nacional del Trabajo de España II," *Solidaridad Obrera* (Valencia), May 16, 1922. The manifesto was published in at least five parts, but only the numbers with parts 2 and 5 have survived in the Hemeroteca Municipal de Valencia.

9   Lorenzo, *Los Anarquistas Españoles y el Poder*, 47.

10   Formed in October 1922, the Los Solidarios group was made up of fourteen men, including Buenaventura Durruti, Ricardo Sanz, Francisco Ascaso, and Aurelio Fernández. Abel Paz, *Durruti en la Revolución Española* (Madrid: Fundación de estudios libertarios Anselmo Lorenzo, 1996), 89–117. See also the autobiographies by Ricardo Sanz, *El sindicalismo y la política. Los 'solidarios' y 'nosotros'* (Toulouse: Dulaurier, 1966), 95ff., and Juan García Oliver, *El eco de los pasos* (Barcelona: Ruedo Ibérico, 1978), 74ff. Dolors Marin i Silvestre, "De la llibertat per coneixer al coneixement de la llibertat. L'adquisició de cultura durant la dictadura de Primo de Rivera i la Segona República Espanyola," PhD thesis, Universitat de Barcelona, 1995, 517–56, dedicates an entire chapter to Los Solidarios and Nosotros (established by the members of Los Solidaros during the Second Republic), however this is based almost entirely on the works cited above.

11   Juan Gómez Casas, *Anarchist Organisation – The History of the FAI* (Montreal: Black Rose, 1986), 58–9, provides a brief account of anarchist organisation between 1918 and 1923, although he concentrates mainly on the CNT. Further information on this period can be found in Abel Paz, *Durruti en la Revolución Española*, although this again concentrates more on the activity of Durruti than

on the regional anarchist organisations. For Andalusia, for the period 1915–17, see Ángeles González Fernández, *Utopía y Realidad Anarquismo, anarcosindicalismo y organizaciones obreras. Sevilla, 1900–1923* (Seville: Diputación de Sevilla, 1996), 232–40. In latter chapters of the book the author concentrates on the CNT, but aspects of the anarchist movement are interlaced in the text throughout.

12 Confederación Regional del Trabajo de Cataluña, "*Memoria del Congreso celebrado en Barcelona los días 28, 29, 30 de junio y 1 de julio del ano 1918*" (Barcelona: Imprenta Germinal, 1918). The committee of the CRT was made up of Camilo Piñón, Salvador Ferrer, J. Pez, Salvador Quemades, and Salvador Seguí, who was the general secretary. Among the other delegates present at the congress were Peiró, Pestaña, and Buenacasa. Previous attempts had been made to hold a national congress, but due to the continuing social unrest this had proved impossible. Furthermore, the Sans congress had been planned to take place in 1917 but was postponed due to the August general strike and the suspension of constitutional guarantees.

13 Manuel Buenacasa, *El movimiento Obrero Español, Historia y crítica (1886–1926)* (Paris: Amigos del autor, 1966), 51–52. According to Buenacasa, among the delegates who attended the congress were Carbó (Levante), Quintanilla (Asturias), Herreros (Catalonia), Galo Díez (North) either Dr. Vallina or Sanchez Rosa (Andalucía), and José Suárez (Galicia). On December 8 the Catalan CRT held a meeting at the Palacio de Bellas Artes in Barcelona, and the regional and national congress may well have occurred around this date to make the most of the fact that numerous delegates were in the city at the same time. *Acracia*, December 15, 1918. No direct reference to the national congress is made in the anarchist or syndicalist press, but this may be in large part due to the fact that *Tierra y Libertad* had been closed down in early 1919.

14 Francisco Jordán and Francisco Miranda were national secretaries between August 1916 and July 1919, and both were anarchists. Jordán was particularly vehement in his opposition to syndicalism and would eventually be expelled from the CNT. Miranda's replacement was none other than Buenacasa. Eusebio Carbó, who played a leading role at the El Ferrol congress, had previously been active in Marseilles, where he was considered an individualist anarchist, whilst both Angel Pestaña and Salvador Seguí described themselves as anarchists.

15 "A las agrupaciones Anarquistas," *Tierra y Libertad*, May 8, 1918; "La Internacional Anarquista – Pauta para su rápida organización," *Tierra y Libertad*, December 11, 1918.

16 "Actuación Anarquista – Comité de la Federación Anarquista de Cataluña," *Tierra y Libertad*, November 28, 1917.

17 The Catalan attempts to organise an international congress continued and plans were made for the holding of an 'International Anarchist Congress' in Spain, in late 1919. El Comité de la Federación Anarquista de Catalunya, "A los Grupos Anarquistas de España," *Acción Social Obrera*, December 13, 1919. No further reference is made to this proposal either in the Spanish or foreign anarchist press.

18 Grupo Juventud Acrata de Barcelona, "A los compañeros y grupos anarquistas de

España," *Acracia*, October 30, 1918; "Nueva carta del grupo 'Juventud Acrata'," *Acracia*, October 31, 1918. 'Juventud Anarquista' as another name for Juventud Acrata: *Acracia*, December 15, 1918.

19 El Grupo Acracia, "A Todos los Grupos Anarquista de España," *Acracia*, November 29, 1918.

20 The Catalan federation may have been formed in November following a meeting called by Juventud Anarquista. Grupo Juventud anarquista, "A todos los anarquistas en general," *Solidaridad Obrera*, November 9, 1918.

21 The figures are taken from, Termes, *Història del moviment anarquista a Espanya*, 304–5.

22 The Spanish constitution allowed for the suspension of constitutional guarantees whenever the security of the state required. This process was frequently used in the years prior to the Primo de Rivera dictatorship (1923–30). By this means the freedom of the press, of association, and of movement could be limited. In the case of CNT it normally resulted in newspapers being closed downs, union meetings being forbidden, movement of prominent figures restricted, as well as the arrest of leading figures and their detention without due process.

23 Anarchists constantly referred to the mixed commission when criticising the syndicalists, and the subject was still a bone of contention at the 1922 Zaragoza conference. *Preámbulo y Convocatoria de la Conferencia Nacional – Zaragoza*, International Institute of Social History (IISG), Amsterdam, CNT Archive, microfilms 174 and 200. See also Simó Piera, *Records i Experiències d'un Dirigent de la C.N.T.* (Barcelona: Editorial Portic, 1975). Piera was one of the CNT's representatives on the mixed commission.

24 The victims are named in *Tragedia y Ideas*, a booklet published by the Confederation's Barcelona Prisoners Committee (Manresa: 1923).

25 Angel Pestaña and Salvador Seguí, *"El Sindicalismo en Cataluña* (Conferencias dadas en Madrid el día 4 de octubre de 1919)" (Barcelona: Pequeña Biblioteca Calamus Scriptorius, 1978).

26 El Comité de la Federación de Grupos Anarquistas de la Región Catalana, "Los anarquistas en nuestro puesto," *Espartaco* (supplement to no. 4), November 8, 1919. A copy of the supplement is contained in Archivo Histórico Nacional, Madrid, Serie A del Ministerio de Gobernación, Legajo 21, fichero 16. Previously an editorial in the paper had argued that syndicalism was a force "lacking idealism." "Los Sindicalistas Catalanes, de Propaganda. Sindicalismo y Anarquismo," *Espartaco*, October 15, 1919.

27 A report by the French police refers to a meeting of fifty or so anarchists and syndicalists in the Valencia region in the late summer of 1919 which aimed to find a way to fuse anarchism and syndicalism. According to the report, the anarchists had abandoned their immediate revolutionary dreams due to the success of the repressive measures adopted by the authorities in Catalonia and Andalusia. Archives Nationales de France, F/7/13440, police report, September 1, 1919.

28 Salvador Seguí, *Anarquismo y sindicalismo, Conferencia pronunciada en la prisión del Castillo de la Mola (Maó – Illes Balears), 31 de diciembre de 1920* (Barcelona: 1923).

29 Max Stephen, "Son desviaciones, sin serlo, siéndolo," *La Protesta*, December 27, 1922. The article was previously published in *Tierra* (La Coruña). According to Stephen, Seguí once again spoke of "possibilist syndicalism" during the speeches at the Zaragoza conference. At a congress in Mahón (Menorca) in late 1920, Seguí argued that "[a]narchy is not an ideal that can be realised immediately ... being a perfect conception of life it will never be realised. ... Syndicalism is the advance of Anarchism." Seguí, *Anarquismo y sindicalismo*.

30 See J. M. Huertas Clavera, *Salvador Seguí "El noi de sucre". Materiales para una biografía* (Barcelona: Laia, 1974), 51–54; Antonio Elorza, introduction to *Artículos madrileños de Salvador Seguí* (Madrid: Cuadernos para el dialogo, 1976).

31 *Preámbulo y Convocatoria de la Conferencia Nacional – Zaragoza.*

32 Peiró later claimed that the resolution was predominantly his work. J. Peiró, "Hay que fijar una posición II," *Solidaridad Obrera*, May 25, 1924.

33 Max Stephen, "Son desviaciones, sin serlo, siendolo," *La Protesta*, December 27, 1922.

34 G. Leval, "La Política para los políticos," *Cultura y Acción*, October 7, 1922. In the article Leval accused Pestaña of "dreaming of a [political] ministry." For Leval's attacks on Seguí, see Gaston Leval, "Contestación a un ultimatum," *Cultura y Acción*, October 28, 1922. Seguí's response to Leval attack was succinct and to the point: "To Gaston Leval – that which only merits disdain does not require a response – S. Seguí." *Cultura y Acción*, November 4, 1922. This in turn provoked the Federation of Libertarian Groups of Aragón, Navarra, and Rioja to protest against Seguí's response, which they considered discourteous. El comité de relaciones de la Federación de Grupos Libertarios de Aragón, Navarra y Rioja, "Sobre una polémica," *Redención*, November 30, 1922. According to the Madrid-based anarchist periodical *Tierra Libre*, the National Committee of the CNT had previously issued a public reprimand to Seguí due to his contacts with politicians. "Por la no re-eleción de los funcionarios Sindicales," *Tierra Libre*, July 21, 1922.

35 "La Política de la Confederación," *Redención*, July 22, 1922.

36 Letter from Orobón Fernández to Pestaña, August 9, 1930, Archivo General de la Guerra Civil Española, Región Barcelona, File 1068.

37 Orobón Fernández was beset by respiratory illness, which eventually would claim his life in 1937 at the age of thirty-six. He came to prominence at the age of eighteen at the Madrid congress of 1919 where he drafted a report on National Federations of Industry. From 1926 until 1931 he worked within the secretariat of the IWMA. Both Rudolf Rocker and Max Nettlau held him in the highest regard. Salvador Cano Carrillo, "Orobón Fernández," *Ruta* (Caracas), February 1, 1976. See also José Luis Gutiérrez Molina, *Valeriano Orobón Fernández: Anarcosindicalismo y Revolución en Europa* (Madrid: Libre Pensamiento, 2002) and the section on Orobón in Paniagua, *La Sociedad Libertaria*, 177–82.

38 V. Orobón Fernández, "Soviets o Sindicatos?," *Solidaridad Obrera* (Bilbao), December 3, 1920. This position was supported by *Vida Obrera*, the paper of the Asturian Regional Federation: "The CNT supports the period of force called

the *Dictatorship of the Proletariat* with the difference that this is exercised by the unions and not a political party." "Por la Unidad confederal," *Vida Obrera*, November 11, 1921. This is not to pretend that all anarchists accepted this point of view. In 1920 a former secretary of the national committee, Francisco Jordán argued in a pamphlet that anarchists could never accept the concept of a dictatorship. He did not, however, manage to resolve the problem of the transition phase from pre- to post-revolutionary society, and the evident holes in his theory did not convince many. Francisco Jordán, *La Dictadura del Proletariado* (Madrid: grupo redactor de Espartaco, 1920). Jordán was yet another leading CNT militant to die at the hands of the gunmen of the Free Unions.

39   Por la Federación Comunista Libertaria el Comité, "La Federación Comunista Libertaria, a sus comradas y a la opinión pública," *Acción Social Obrera*, January 28, 1922. My italics.

40   "La Federación de Grupos Acratas de Levante al pueblo productor en general," *Redención*, July 6, 1922.

41   Antonio Peña bemoaned the 'syndicalisation' of some of his comrades who had allowed the anarcho-syndicalist movement to become "simply syndicalist." Antoine Pena, "Mouvement International – En Espagne," *La Revue Anarchiste*, March 3, 1922. For similar opinions, see *Espartaco*, January 1920, and 'A todos los anarquistas de España', *El Productor* (Seville), July 25, 1920.

42   Antonio Peña, "Mouvement International – En Espagne"; El Comité de la Federación Anarquista y los sindicatos únicos de la provincia, "Nuestro Congreso," *El Comunista Libertario*, November 6, 1920. The article also claimed that the Catalan proposal had been supported by *El Productor* (Seville), *Nueva Humanidad* (Torredelcampo), and other papers. *El Productor* had argued that to avoid being marginalised the Spanish anarchists should follow the examples of their colleagues in France and Italy and create their own national organisation. "A todos los anarquistas de España," *El Productor* (Seville), July 25, 1920.

43   The Anarchist Labour Group of Alcoy called for all the anarchist groups in the Levante region to join together to form a Levantine Federation of Anarchist Groups which would initiate a campaign of propaganda and prepare for the national anarchist congress. El Grupo Labor Anarquista, "A todos los anarquistas de la región levantina," *El Comunista Libertario*, January 22, 1921. Gallego Crespo argued that the only way to overcome the period of ideological confusion that had reigned in the CNT since 1919 was to group together all the libertarian forces outside syndicalism, from where it would be possible to study the errors of the past and be better prepared to push for the revolution that would bring about the triumph of libertarian communism. Juan Gallego Crespo, "Cartas a Magdalena," *Redención*, July 30, 1921.

44   The letter was printed alongside a report on the congress in *Le Libertaire*, April 8–15, 1921.

45   *Nueva Senda*, October 19, 1921.

46   Such a congress was proposed by Asturian Federation of Anarchist Groups, "Federation de Agrupaciones Anarquistas de Asturias," *Vida Obrera*, November 25, 1921.

47 It is possible that Lladó was chosen as delegate by the Madrid anarchists, as he was in contact with the Madrid-based paper *Nueva Senda*. Lladó's opinions on the relationship between anarchism and syndicalism in Spain presented at the congress mirrored that of the report sent to the congress by Madrid anarchists. Both claimed that the CNT had been created by anarchists and that anarchists must remain in the unions to "maintain the true spirit of revolutionary syndicalism." The report was read out on the sixth day of the congress. *La Antorcha* (Buenos Aires), March 24, 1922. News of the Madrid federation's inaugural meeting: El Comité, "Federación Local de Grupos Anarquistas de Madrid," *Acción Social Obrera*, January 28, 1922.

48 Malatesta, Schapiro, and the Russian anarchists Alexander Berkman and Emma Goldman were due to attend but were ultimately unable to do so. As well as Lladó, representatives came from Sweden (Bjorklund), Italy (Fideolio), France (Mauritius, Fister, and two others), Bulgaria (Rasudin), England, the United States (Kelly and Volgin), Norway and Denmark (Hansen represented both), the Netherlands (Meyer, De Ligt, and one other) and the host nation, Germany, which had twenty delegates.

49 From late 1919 onwards, national anarchist organisations were formed in a number of countries, especially in those countries that had close contacts with the Spanish anarchists. In April 1919 the first national congress of the Unione Communista Anarchica was held in Italy (in 1920 it changed its name to Unione Anarchica Italiana (UAI) according to "Movimiento Internacional," *Acción Social Obrera*, August 7, 1920). In France the Federation Comuniste Revolutionnaire Anarchiste (founded in 1913) had collapsed during the war and the Union Anarchiste Française was created at a congress in November 1920. "Le Congrès Anarchiste," *Le Libertaire*, November 28, 1920; *Acción Social Obrera*, December 4, 1920. Independent anarchist organisations were formed in Argentina and Portugal in 1923.

50 E. Cancho, "La Sindical Roja está traicionando a la Confederación Española," *Nueva Senda*, January 26, 1922.

51 Full reports on the congress can be found in *Freedom* (London), March and April 1922; *La Antorcha* (Buenos Aires), February 10 to March 24, 1922; and *Le Libertaire*, January 20–27 to March 10–17, 1922. The version in *Antorcha* was written by Rudolph Rocker and is the most complete report.

52 *La Revue Anarchiste*, January 1922.

53 Quotes from the resolutions are taken from the report in *Freedom*, April 1922.

54 Ibid.

55 International Institute of Social History (IISG), Amsterdam, CNT Archive, Fedeli Archive, file 76 (1). The congress had been called by the French Anarchist Union (UAF) following a meeting of about two hundred militants from different countries at Saint-Imier to celebrate the fiftieth anniversary of the first congress of the anti-authoritarian IWMA. "A Bienne et a St-Imier – Vers une Internationale Anarchiste," *Le Libertaire*, September 22–29, 1922. The meeting took place on September 17, 1922. The two hundred militants came predominantly from France, Italy, and Switzerland. Anarchists in Barcelona were

informed of the congress by the UAF; the only Spanish delegate was Wilkens. Archives Nationales de France, F/7/13442, police records, November 16, 1922; Archives Nationales de France, F/7/15995, police records, February 28, 1922.

56 The agenda of the congress did appear in *Redención*, June 28, 1923, but no Spanish delegates attended. The congress was attended by two delegates of the Dutch Anarchist Union, one from the International Anti-Militarist Office, two from the International Anarchist Union, one from China, and two representing France. Haussard, "Unión Anarquista Universal – Circular a las organizaciones del mundo," *Solidaridad Proletaria*, October 23, 1924.

57 "Le Congress International Anarchiste," *Le Libertaire*, October 12–19, 1923. The article is simply a brief report on the congress; a more detailed report is promised by the paper but never appeared.

58 Haussard, "Unión Anarquista Universal – Circular a las organizaciones del mundo," *Solidaridad Proletaria*, October 23, 1924. An International Anarchist Committee was set up in Paris in 1925 in which the Spanish were represented by Gibanel. Archives Nationales de France, F/7/13443, police records, June 1925. This is probably the 'International Anarchist Union' which according to Magriñà held a congress in Paris in 1925. Magriñà, "La Organización Anarquista," *Prismas*, December 1927.

59 Letter to Max Nettlau from Lucien Haussard, July 23, 1937, International Institute of Social History (IISG), Amsterdam, Nettlau Archive, microfilm 153.

60 The invitation from the UAF was published in "Congreso Internacional Anarquista," *Acción Social Obrera*, October 26, 1922.

61 "La Federación Anarquista del Norte a los Anarquistas Españoles," *Redención*, December 21, 1922.

62 "Opiniones acerca del Congreso Internacional Anarquista," *Redención*, January 11, 1923. The Madrid anarchists suggested that a national congress should be held prior to any decision being made on the international congress. F. L. de Grupos Anarquistas (Madrid), "Congreso Nacional Anarquista," *Solidaridad Obrera* (Valencia), January 13, 1923.

63 La F. L. de G. A. de Madrid, "A la Agrupación Libertaria de La Felguera," *Nueva Senda*, April 6, 1922. According to the article, the original proposition by the group from La Felguera was published in *Nueva Senda*.

64 A manifesto by the Asturian federation appears in *Vida Obrera* in November 1921. This could have been written following an inaugural congress. "Federación de Agrupaciones Anarquistas de Asturias," *Vida Obrera*, November 25, 1921; El Comité de la Federación de Grupos Acratas de Levante, "La Federación de Grupos Acratas de Levante al pueblo productor en general," *Redención*, July 6, 1922.

65 "Movimiento Anarquista – España," *Realidad* (a free anarchist paper in Valencia), July 16, 1922; El Comité, "La Federación Anarquista del Norte a los anarquistas españoles," *Redencion*, December 21, 1922. The meeting took place on December 10. In a letter to the 'Anarchist secretariat' in Barcelona, the Andalusian Anarchist Federation claimed that eleven thousand groups had been recently formed in the region, representing two hundred thousand members. Archives Nationales de France, F/7/13442, police records, February 10, 1922.

66 "A todos los individuos, Grupos y Regionales Anarquistas La Federación Anarquista de Levante," *Redención*, August 10, 1922; "A todos los grupos acratas de la Región Levantina," *Redención*, October 12, 1922.

67 "A los grupos acratas de toda España," *Redencion*, August 31, 1922.

68 El Comité Provisional de la "Unión Anarquista" de Barcelona, "Aviso," *Acción Social Obrera*, September 30, 1922.

69 Paz, *Durruti en la Revolución Español*, 91.

70 The Liberal-dominated government had found out that Martínez Anido had organised a false attack against himself to justify further repression in Catalonia and was planning a massacre of syndicalist militants, and the civil governor was forced to resign. The conference was organised by the Los Solidarios group. Ibid., 90.

71 La Comisión de Relaciones Anarquistas, "A los compañeros y grupos anarquistas de la Región Catalana," *Acción Social Obrera*, February 10, 1923. The regional congress was to take place on March 18 but must have been held earlier as the national congress opened on this date.

72 Los Anarquistas de Zaragoza, "Una Proposición – Hacia el Congreso Nacional Anarquista – A los libertarios de España," *Solidaridad Obrera* (Gijón), January 19, 1923; *Redención*, January 11, 1923.

73 Buenacasa had previously proposed that the national committee of the CNT should convoke a meeting of all the anarchist militants involved in syndicalism to discuss the problems arising from the relationship between anarchism and syndicalism. Manuel Buenacasa, "Lo más urgente," *Cultura y Acción*, October 14, 1922. Galo Díez responded to this initiative by suggesting that it would ne most logical for an anarchist conference discuss the issue. Galo Díez, "En torno a una iniciativa," *Cultura y Acción*, October 28, 1922.

74 The other eight subjects for discussion were relations with political parties, the dictatorship of the proletariat, international relations, the anarchist press, propaganda, a campaign for justice for political prisoners, agriculture, and relations with Portuguese anarchists. "Congreso Nacional Anarquista," *Redención*, March 1, 1923. No official report of the congress appeared in the Spanish anarchist press, although a less-than-flattering account was published in the Madrid-based independent paper *El Sol*. Ramón Gómez de la Serna, "El Congreso Anarquista Español" and "El Terrible Congreso Anarquista," *El Sol*, March 21 and 22, 1923, respectively.

75 Only one number of *Crisol* has survived. According to Valeriano Orobón Fernández (writing under the pseudonym of Valetin de Roi), the editorial board of *Crisol* was made up of Liberto Callejas, Felipe Alaiz, Fortunato Barthe, and Torres Tribo, whilst the administrators were Ascaso and Montes. "Jover y la Represión Española," *La Antorcha* (Buenos Aires), January 7, 1927. Alongside *Crisol* and *Tierra y Libertad*, which began publication again on January 20, 1923, after four years absence, a further anarchist newspaper, *Fragua Social*, appeared during this period. However, no numbers have survived.

76 El Comité de Relaciones Anarquistas de España, "A todos los Anarquistas," *Solidaridad Obrera*, April 10, 1923. The Catalan Commission of Relations correspondence address was that of *Tierra y Libertad*.

77   Mauro Bajatierra, "Del Congreso Nacional Anarquista – Constitutión de Grupos," *Redención*, April 12, 1923. A similar argument is given by José Vilaverde, the Galician delegate at the congress. José Vilaverde, "Consideraciones sobre la vida pasada y futura de la CNT," *Sindicalismo*, April 25, 1934.

78   Translated from F. Caro Crespo, "Inquietudes revolucionarias – La C.N. del Trabajo," *Redención*, March 22, 1923.

79   According to José Vilaverde the majority of the delegates at Madrid agreed that the unions were of "incalculable value for the revolution" as all revolutions that aim to overthrow the capitalist system "must have as their aim the absolute liberation of the entire proletariat." José Vilaverde, "Consideraciones sobre la vida pasada y futura de la CNT II," *Sindicalismo*, April 25, 1934.

80   For an assessment of the action of Los Solidarios, see Marín i Silvestre, "De la llibertat per coneixer al coneixement de la llibertat," 517–56. See also García Oliver, *El eco de los pasos*; Sanz, *El sindicalismo y la política*; Paz, *Durruti en la Revolución española*.

81   Núñez Florencio, *El terrorismo anarquista*, 126, stressed this point. Julián Casanova, "La Cara Oscura del anarquismo," in *Violencia política en la España del siglo XX*, ed. Santos Juliá (Madrid: Tauros, 2000), 67–104, agrees, arguing that with the arrival of the CNT, "discussion about an anarchist subculture gave way to the language of class" (page 82).

82   The assassination of Prime Minister Dato in March 1921 was carried out with the full knowledge and support of the national committee of the CNT. See Rourera Ferré, *Joaquín Maurín y su tiempo*, 70–72. Likewise the murder of Bravo Portillo, who was head of one of the gangs of pistoleros in the pay of the Employers' Federation, was welcomed by both Maurín and Camille Piñón (a leading syndicalist). Joan López, a prominent member of the syndicalist tendency in the late 1920s had been actively involved in the *pistolerismo*, whilst Angel Pestaña, who later turned against the use of violence, was also in contact with the action groups that carried out attacks through to 1923 (see Pestaña's autobiography, "Lo que aprendi en la vida," in Angel Pestaña, *Trayectoria Sindicalista* (Madrid: Ediciones Tebas, 1974), 41–49. The violence was indicative of the social tension in Barcelona and a logical reaction of those who saw their colleagues shot down and the perpetrators not only escaping justice but being protected by the authorities.

83   El Comité, "A los anarquistas de España," *Tierra y Libertad,* May 30, 1923. A note from the committee in *Cultura y Acción*, June 9, 1923, informed militants that it had finally started functioning normally.

84   Los comités de Relaciones Anarquistas de Cataluña y España, "Los Anarquistas y el movimiento actual," *Cultura y Acción* June 29, 1923; *Acción Social Obrera*, July 7, 1923; *Redención*, July 12, 1923. The president of the new committee was José Ruigerado.

85   An image of the intensity of the conflict in Barcelona is provided by a call by the national committee for an absolute boycott of all products imported to or exported from Catalonia, due "to the magnitude of the actual conflict in Barcelona," which was having a negative effect on the functioning of the

organisation. El Comité de la CNT, "A todas las regionales, comarcales, sindicatos, y a todo el proletariado en general," *Redención*, July 5, 1923.

86 Piñón is quoted in Manuel Lladonosa i Vall-Llebrera, *Sindicalistes i Llibertaris,
L'Experiència de Camil Piñón* (Barcelona: Rafael Dalmau, 1989), 40. During the
strike, *Solidaridad Obrera* sold fifty-three thousand copies an issue and could
apparently have even increased this amount had the printing machines been able
to produce more. "Un rato de Historia," *Sindicalismo*, May 5, 1933. Also during
the strike, Piñón was targeted at least twice by the gunmen of the Sindicatos
Libres; Piñón suggests that one attack was set up by Primo de Rivera himself.

87 The main information on the strike is provided in Manuel Lladonosa's brief
essay based on his interviews with Camil Piñón: Lladonosa, *Sindicalistes i
Llibertaris*, 40–47. Adolfo Bueso also gives a brief account in his autobiography:
Bueso, *Recuerdos de un cenetista*, vol. 1 (Barcelona: Ariel, 1978), 176–77. See
also Jacinto León-Ignacio, *Los años del pistolerismo. Ensayo para una guerra civil*
(Barcelona: Planeta, 1981), 280–90.

88 According to Magriñà, the transport strike had shown "the failure of syndicalism
and … the ideological chaos of anarcho-syndicalism." J. Rosquillas (pseudonym
for Magriñà), "Replica y Recortes," *Acción Social Obrera*, August 23, 1924.

89 "Manifiesto," *Tierra y Libertad*, May 30, 1923.

90 *Tierra y Libertad* was never able to completely clarify the point. It stopped publication at the end of May 1923, according to Santillán, on the orders of the
confederation. Santillán refers to an article in the *Tierra y Libertad*, "A callar to-
can," which unfortunately is not in the editions of the paper that have survived.
D. Abad de Santillán, "En Torno a la Confederación Nacional del Trabajo," *La
Protesta (Suplemento Semanal)*, June 8, 1925.

91 "Una Entrevista con el Secretario General de la C.N. del T. Companero
Giménez," *El Libertario* (Buenos Aires), August 10, 1923. It is not clear who
Giménez was, although he could possibly have been Miguel Jiménez, a prominent Catalan anarchist. In a number of early articles Jiménez, or the relevant
newspaper, spells his name Giménez. Juan Manuel Molina, who was active in
the Committee of Anarchist Relations at the time claims that during this period
he was elected as a delegate of the national committee of the CNT and that
Antonio Sesé, a radical anarchist who would later be a proponent of the MOA,
was the actual secretary of the national committee. Jaume Fabre and Josep M.
Huertas, "D'un temps, d'una FAI," *Avenç* 39 (June 1981), 16–21.

92 "Actas de las sesiones celebrados por el Pleno Regional de Cataluña, en Barcelona,
el dia 29 de julio," *Solidaridad Obrera*, August 24, 1923.

93 García Oliver, a leading anarchist in the region, criticised "the cowardice,
the duplicity and the infamy" of Roigé (and the leaders of the metalworkers'
union) during the strike. Letter from García Oliver to Pestaña, May 30, 1928,
Archivo General de la Guerra Civil Española, Región Barcelona, file 1068.

94 Piñón, in his role as president of the transport union, visited the civil governor (Barber), his replacement (Manuel Portela), and the captain general of
Catalonia, General Primo de Rivera. Both Barber and Portela hoped to negotiate a settlement but were initially frustrated by the employers' refusal to

negotiate. However, Primo de Rivera, by now a favourite with the Catalan employers, was not so conciliatory and ordered Piñón to get the strikers to return to work as they were being unpatriotic. Lladonosa, *Sindicalistes i Llibertaris*, 43–45. According to Pestaña, the leaders of the unions involved in the transport strike had been forced to accept arbitration to bring the strike to an end. Angel Pestaña, "La danza de los principios," *Solidaridad Obrera*, December 20, 1923.

95   León-Ignacio, *Los años del pistolerismo*, 287–88. In Catalonia the employers were closely involved with Primo de Rivera, who would lead the coup in September 1923. *La Protesta*, a Carlist newspaper which began publication in Barcelona in April 1923, claimed that there was a pact between the Madrid government and the CNT against the Catalan bourgeoisie. "Tramando la muerte de Barclona. El gobierno y los alias del Sindicato Único," *La Protesta*, June 24, 1923. An article that covered the social conflict in Barcelona printed in bold on the front page on July 15, 1923, "The Regime – enemy of the army and the people – is the most responsible." *La Protesta* also frequently published pictures of leading CNT members it accused of being involved in terrorism, giving information on their address or workplace or both, a tactic commonly used to this day in places as a means of identifying possible targets for reprisal attacks.

96   García Oliver, *El Eco de los Pasos*, 633, gives information about the decision made at the plenum. There is a certain amount of disagreement about the veracity of García Oliver's claims. León-Ignacio, *Los años del pistolerismo*, 292, claims that the plenum refused to support assaults on banks but that the transfer of the committee to Seville was a victory for the anarcho-Bolsheviks, whereas González Fernández, *Utopía y Realidad*, 437, claims that the plenum supported the assaults whilst agreeing with León-Ignacio about the significance of the transfer of the committee. As León-Ignacio's work contains certain minor errors and less source material, González Fernández's argument seems more convincing. On the second point, the transfer of the national committee, González Fernández quotes from an article in the liberal newspaper *La Unión*, in which Pestaña complained bitterly about the decision. However, other contemporary material suggests differently. "De Organización – Practicas abusivas," *Solidaridad Obrera*, August 4, 1923, claims the committee was moved due to "the asphyxiation" that it was suffering in Barcelona as a result of the intervention of certain militants," a point that seems to be echoed by García Oliver in a letter to Pestaña five years after the events (as opposed to his autobiography published fifty-five years later) in which he claimed that "Roigé kicked the National Committee out of Catalonia to avoid us dominating it." Letter from García Oliver to Pestaña, March 25, 1928, Archivo General de la Guerra Civil Española, Región Barcelona, file 1068. Other press comments on the plenum give no information about the decisions made. For example, "La Confederación Nacional del Trabajo de España a todas las Federaciónes Regionales, Comarcales, Locales, Sindicatos y companeros," *Cultura y Acción*, August 11, 1923, simply gives notice that the plenum took place. According to Juan Ortega, the Committee of Anarchist Relations was represented at the plenum by a member of the group Juventud Anarquista from Barcelona. "La Verdad. Es un Delito?," *Acción Social Obrera*, April 17, 1926.

97 As if to emphasise the domination of revolutionary activism over ideology among the anarcho-Bolsheviks, Adame would soon join the PCE.

98 Barrio Alonso, *Anarquismo y anarcosindicalismo en Asturias*, 259.

99 Candido Prado, *Al Servicio de la Verdad* (Madrid: 1930), provides evidence that the strike had been prolonged deliberately to create the atmosphere for a military coup. Francisco Cambó, the leader of the bourgeois Catalan nationalist party La Lliga Regionalista, which actively collaborated with Primo in his seizure of power, later wrote: "The Spanish dictatorship was born in, and created by, the atmosphere in Barcelona, where the syndicalist demagogy had reached a persistent intensity." Francisco Cambó, *Las Dictaduras* (Madrid: Espasa-Calpe, 1929); Candido Prado and Cambó are cited by M. Teresa González Calbet, *La Dictadura de Primo de Rivera. El Directorio Militar* (Madrid: Ediciones el Arquero, 1987), 34, 37. The Lliga supported Primo's early moves against the CNT but soon fell victim to a series of anti-Catalan decrees issued by the dictatorship.

100 Spanish attempts to expand its empire in Morocco had long been the cause of troubles at home. In July 1921 a force of twenty thousand men had been defeated by a few thousand Moroccans at Annual, near Melilla. A report was ordered on the causes of the defeat, but Primo de Rivera rose before it could be published. It was rumoured that the king had encouraged the commander of the defeated army, Silvestre, to undertake the suicidal advance that preceded the rout.

101 "A los trabajadores," *Solidaridad Obrera*, September 29, 1923, gives note of the rejection by the UGT. The initial invitation was published the previous day. The UGT effectively sanctioned open collaboration with the military dictatorship when, in October 1924, it agreed to accept a position on the newly created State Council. Talks between the socialists and the Military Directorate (the government during the early years of the dictatorship) had begun as early as October 1923. Primo de Rivera made it clear that he favoured working with the socialists by offering them positions on the industrial councils established by the dictatorship. In June 1924, as part of ongoing moves to give a civilian veneer to the military dictatorship, a Labour Council was established, including three socialist representatives (Largo Caballero, Lucío Martínez, and Santiago Pérez Infante). On September 13, 1924, the military dictatorship created the State Council, a consultative body. Largo Caballero was elected by the UGT Labour Council to join it. José Andrés-Gallego, *El Socialismo Durante la Dictadura 1923–30* (Madrid: Ediciones Giner, 1977), 70–119.

102 A law unused till then, introduced in March 1923, was enforced, which required unions to maintain membership records and books of accounts as a condition for legal existence. Elorza, "La génesis de la Federación Anarquista Ibérica," 125–26; González Calbet, *La Dictadura de Primo de Rivera*, 205–9.

103 The civil governors were to repeat these orders every two weeks. Gómez Casas, *Anarchist Organisation*, 71.

104 Los Sindicatos Únicos de Barcelona de todos los trabajadores [the local federation], "El cierre de los sindicatos," *El Diluvio* (Barcelona), October 14, 1923. The federation argued that "today the unions are unable to do anything but

administer their membership fees … the powers that be have issued an edict in which the leaders of the unions are held responsible for acts that may be carried out in isolation, both at work or in public life." However, closing the unions down did not mean that the federation renounced its mandate to represent the workers: "Those who in Barcelona are members of the Confederation, are able to maintain the necessary cohesion to maintain our strength in the face of the employers demands … despite the suspension, the juntas that you elected and who have made this decision make it known that they have not deserted their posts and will be in constant contact with you."

105 Peiró argued that the local federation's decision (with which he disagreed) was prompted by the desire to protect members from the authorities. J. Peiró, "Precisa que nos Conozcamos Bien," *Solidaridad Obrera*, February 8, 1924. According to Buenacasa, speaking at the Catalan regional assembly held at the end of December, *Solidaridad Obrera* was closed down because the paper was carrying out a campaign against this decision and was refusing to publish articles that supported the position of the local federation. "Asamblea Plenaria de los Sindicatos de la Confederación Regional del Trabajo de Cataluña (Granollers, 30 Diciembre)," *Lucha Obrera*, January 1, 1924. According to Pestaña, the federation immediately transformed itself into a revolutionary committee and began the search for arms. Angel Pestaña, "No son los principios," *Solidaridad Obrera*, December 30, 1923.

106 For example, the anarchists that published the newspaper *El Productor* (1925–26) were part of a legally constituted union in Blanes (Catalonia).

107 The editorial board of the paper was made up of militants of the CSR (Arlandis and Maurín) and the CNT (Viadiu and Alaiz, who would later become a prominent member of the radical anarchist tendency during the Second Republic). The first number of *Lucha Obrera* appeared on December 4, 1923, and the last on January 1, 1924.

108 One of the national committee delegates claimed that in reality the CRT had not existed since the regional plenum at Manresa on September 8–9. For the Manresa plenum, see "Sintesis de los acuerdos más importantes tomados en el pleno de Manresa," *Acción Social Obrera*, September 22, 1923.

109 "Reseña del Pleno de la Confederación del Trabajo de Cataluña celebrado en Mataro el día 8 de diciembre," *Acción Social Obrera*, December 15, 1923.

110 See Germinal Esgleas, "La Crisis del Sindicalismo en Cataluña," *Solidaridad Obrera*, December 22, 1923, in which he argued that "the present crisis of syndicalism can only be overcome by ideas."

111 "Nuestro Proposito," *Solidaridad Obrera*, November 29, 1923.

112 Translated from "El anarquismo se basta por si solo," *Solidaridad Obrera*, December 4, 1923. In a similar vein, see also "Ante todos las ideas," *Solidaridad Obrera*, December 14, 1923. This position was also supported by Buenacasa in a series of articles in January and February 1924: "Las secciones y los individuos," *Solidaridad Obrera*, January 30, 1924; "El Individuo en el sindicato," *Solidaridad Obrera*, February 8, 1924; "Cambiando de Disco," *Solidaridad Obrera*, May 17, 1924.

113 Letter from the civil governor of the province of Seville to the under-Ssecretary of the Ministry of the Interior, January 29, 1924, Archivo Histórico Nacional, Madrid, Serie A del Ministerio de Gobernación, file 58(A) 22. The national committee in Seville was made up of Paulino Díez (a militant sent from Barcelona to oversee the committee), Ramon Mazón, Manuel Pérez, Pedro Vallina, and Pedro Calderón.

114 The secretary of this national committee was José García Galán, and the other members were José Montuenga Golvano, Angel Benito García, Angel Peribanez Ranera, and José Torregrosa García. Official telegram from the Civil Governor (Zaragoza) to the Under-Secretary of the Ministry of the Interior, June 4, 1924, Archivo Histórico Nacional, Madrid, Serie A del Ministerio de Gobernación, file 58(A) 22.

115 Letter from the civil governor of Seville to the under-secretary of the Ministry of the Interior, January 29, 1924, Archivo Histórico Nacional, Madrid, Serie A del Ministerio de Gobernación, file 58(A) 22. The government files for this period, which are neither complete nor well organised, also show that there was widescale repression against syndicalists in Aragón in 1924. The paper of the Aragón CRT, *Cultura y Acción*, was closed down in the first days of the dictatorship. See, for example, the telegram from the under-secretary of the interior to the civil governor in Zaragoza, July 4, 1924, Archivo Histórico Nacional, Madrid,, Serie A del Ministerio de Gobernación, file 58(A) 22.

116 "La Magna Asamblea Regional celebrada en Granollers el domingo proximo pasado," *Acción Social Obrera*, January 5, 1924; "Del Pleno de la Barceloneta al De Granollers," *Lucha Obrera,* January 1, 1923. At the assembly, Buenacasa was appointed editor of *Solidaridad Obrera.* Here he was joined on the editorial board by fellow anarchist Felix Monteagudo. At the end of January both were arrested, and Buenacasa was replaced by another anarchist, Hermoso Plaja, in February 1924.

117 *Solidaridad Obrera*, January 29, 1924, gives the results of the elections for the new committee of the local federation.

118 "Principales puntos tratados en la asamblea de Sabadell," *Acción Social Obrera*, May 10, 1924.

119 "Insistiendo: En la organización debe haber ideas," *Solidaridad Obrera*, May 23, 1924.

120 "Hay que fijar una posición, II," *Solidaridad Obrera*, May 25, 1924.

121 Angel Pestaña, "Fijando una posición," *Solidaridad Obrera*, April 27, 1924. The proposal was a response to plans by Primo de Rivera to set up his own party (the Unión Patriótica) by which he aimed to give a civilian aspect to the military regime. The party was to be the only political organisation tolerated by the dictatorship.

122 The spoilt child reference: Carr, *Spain, 1808–1975*, 572.

123 Bueso, *Recuerdos de un cenetista*, vol. 1, 177–78, claims that the assassination of the executioner was actually carried out by agents of Martínez Anido. The speed with which the unions were closed down and leading CNT militants detained on the very same night as the assassination would tend to support the theory that the authorities had been waiting for an excuse to act.

Chapter 6

1   In the areas where the CRTs remained legal, they had to present their accounts and membership books to the civil governors every fifteen days. Even within a specific region the level of repression could differ, for example, although the Galicia CRT was tolerated in some areas, in others, such as El Ferrol, it was banned. See chapter 3 of Dionisio Pereira, *A CNT na Galicia 1922–36* (Santiago de Compostela: Edicions Laiovento, 1994); Barrio Alonso, *Anarquismo y anarcosindicalismo en Asturias*, 272–73.

2   There was an attempt to create an Andalusian Syndicalist Party, but this never got beyond the planning stage. M. Torres, J. Saenz, Vicente Ballester et al., "A proposito de un partido," *El Productor*, February 12, 1926.

3   "The persecutions and imprisonments do not stop for even an instant. Every day there are new arrests, whilst no comrades are released." "De España – Dos notas de la Confederación Nacional del Trabajo: Nuevo traslado del Comité Confederal," *La Protesta*, October 31, 1924.

4   "La Confederación Nacional del Trabajo y El Productor," *El Productor*, February 12, 1926. A letter from the Regional Committee of the North dated November 8, 1924, notes the recent change in address of the national committee. Archivo General de la Guerra Civil Española, Barcelona, file 1352,. *El Productor*, the paper of the pro-MOA faction, claimed that the national committees created in Catalonia toward the end of 1924 were irregular, including members who were either not union members or did not work, and did not enjoy the support of the local federation of Barcelona. "La Confederación Nacional del Trabajo y "El Productor", *El Productor*, February 5, 1926.

5   Letter from Mauro Bajatierra to Santillán, January 14, 1925, International Institute for Social History, Amsterdam, Santillán Archive, file 6. According to Jose Peiró, the son of Joan Peiró, in his introduction to Juan Peiró, *Trayectoria de la CNT* (1925; repr., Madrid: Ediciones Júcar, 1979), 23, Peiró was the national secretary of the CNT during this period.

6   Letters from Pi Sierra to Santillán October 24, 1925 and November 6, 1925, International Institute for Social History, Amsterdam, Santillán Archive, file 7.

7   "Acta del Pleno Nacional celebrado en Madrid los días 15 y 16 de Enero de 1928," *La Protesta*, April 25– 27, 1928.

8   The CNT was involved in plotting against the dictatorship with political forces throughout the years of its existence, with militants from all tendencies involved. For information on the different conspiracies, see the extract of Joan Peiró's speech to the 1931 CNT extraordinary congress reproduced in Peirats, *La CNT en la Revolución Española*, vol. 1, 47–50.

9   For a description of the preparations and the rising itself, see Paz, *Durruti en la Revolución española*, 126–29.

10   Following these events there was an increase in government repression against the anarchists, most noticeably in Barcelona. J. Elizalde, an anarchist based in Barcelona, claimed in a letter to Pierre Ramus (pseudonym of the Austrian anarchist Rudolf Grossman, 1882–1942) that following the failed rising in Barcelona there only remained "a total of 146 individuals, almost all young

men of 18 to 25 years." Letter from Elizalde to Pierre Ramus, January 15, 1925, International Institute for Social History, Amsterdam, Ramus Archive, file 191.

11   Letter from Peiró to Pestaña, April 26, 1933, Archivo General de la Guerra Civil Española, Barcelona, file 1352.

12   "Manifiesto del Comité Regional de Mataró sobre legalización de los sindicatos," El Comité Regional, *Solidaridad Proletaria*, October 18, 1924.

13   Ibid. From January 1925 onwards, articles critical of the communists in Spain and the Bolshevik Revolution were increasingly replaced by articles arguing in favour of legalisation and 'pure' syndicalism.

14   Following the emigration of thousands of Spanish workers to Argentina from the 1880s until the early twentieth century, many of whom were anarchists, contacts had been maintained between the movements from the two countries. For a history of the FORA written by one of its leading figures, see Diego Abad de Santillán, *La FORA – Ideologia y Trayectoria del Movimiento Obrero Revolucionario en la Argentina* (1933; repr., Buenos Aires: Anarres, 2005). For a general history of anarchism in Argentina, see Juan Suriano, *Auge y caída del anarquismo en Argentina, 1880–1930* (Buenos Aires: Capital Intelectual, 2005). Antonio López, *La FORA en el movimiento obrero* (Buenos Aires: Centro Editor de América Latina, 1987) focuses more directly on the FORA, whilst Andreas Doeswijk, *Los anarco-bolcheviques rioplatenses, 1917–1930* (Buenos Aires: CeDInCI editores, 2014) covers in detail the divisions within Argentine anarcho-syndicalism during this period. A brief history in English is provided by the chapter on Argentina by Ruth Thompson in Van der Linden and Thorpe, eds., *Revolutionary Syndicalism*, 167–84.

15   Diego Abad de Santillán (real name: Sineso Baudilio García Fernández) was born in Spain (León) but grew up in Argentina. As with many other anarchists Abad de Santillán initially welcomed the Russian Revolution, believing that the programme of Lenin and Trotsky was "anarchy itself." "Anarquismo y maximalismo," *España Futura*, April 1919. For an account of Abad de Santillán's life, see his autobiography, *Memorias (1897–1936)* (Barcelona: Planeta, 1977), and Antonio Elorza, introduction to Abad de Santillán's *El Anarquismo y la revolución en España: Escrits 30–38* (Madrid: Ayuso, 1976). López Arango was also a Spanish exile, having been born in Asturias.

16   E. López Arango and D.Abad de Santillán, *El anarquismo en el movimiento obrero* (Barcelona: Cosmos, 1925), 199–200.

17   See "Las Vacilaciones del Sindicalismo Español," *La Protesta (Suplemento Semanal)*, March 5, 1923; "Un Programa anarco-sindicalista," *La Protesta (Suplemento Semanal)*, October 1, 1923; Abad de Santillán, "Vacilaciones e inconsecuencias de la CNT de España," *La Protesta*, May 11, 1923; "Paradojas del Sindicalismo," *La Protesta*, December 12, 1924. The FORA attacks on the CNT had been partly inspired from sectors in Spain that provided the paper with its information. The address of Galo Díez, whom Santillán met at the Revolutionary Syndicalist Congress in Berlin in June 1922, is one of only three Spanish individuals contained on a list of contacts in the Santillán archives. The other two names were those of Catalan José Prat and Asturian

Ricardo Mella. International Institute for Social History, Amsterdam, Santillán Archive, file 6.

18   Previously a member of the Alianzea Libertaria Argentina, Jaime Rotger had met with members of the CNT and the Committee of Anarchist Relations in 1923 whilst visiting Barcelona. The 1924 delegation was made up of Rolando Martel, who visited France, and Luis Di Filippo, who visited Spain and represented the Unión Sindical Argentina at the 1925 IWMA congress at Amsterdam. "De nuestra delegación en Europa," *El Libertario* (Buenos Aires – the paper of the ALA), March 15, 1925. Di Filippo was considered part of the 'anarcho-Bolshevik' tendency within the Argentine libertarian movement. This group, led by García Thomas, supported the affiliation of both the ALA and the USA with Moscow, although eventually both organisations decided on being 'independent' internationally so did not affiliate with any International. So, ironically, the syndicalists, led by Pestaña (among others), whose prestige within the movement was in part due to his stand in Moscow against the Bolsheviks, now used information from a supporter of Moscow to attack the radicals, an example of how dangerous it is to try to simplify too much the similarities in the internal disputes within national libertarian movements. For a detailed description of the splits in the Argentine anarchist movement in the 1920s, see Doeswijk, *Los anarco-bolcheviques rioplatenses.*

19   "Sobre el movimiento obrero anarquista en la Argentina – introducción a un proceso revolucionario," *Solidaridad Proletaria*, October 18, 1924.

20   Letter from Acha (secretary of the federal committee of the FORA) to the committee of the CNT, December 5, 1924, International Institute for Social History, Amsterdam, Santillán Archive, file 7,]. In a letter to Max Nettlau, Santillán complains bitterly about the articles published in *Solidaridad Proletaria*, adding that they had caused "us to break all relations with the Spanish." Letter from Abad de Santillán to Max Nettlau, October 31, 1924, International Institute for Social History, Amsterdam, Nettlau Archives, microfilm 1. See also "Sobre el entredicho con la Confederación Nacional del Trabajo de España," *La Protesta*, February 21, 1925.

21   Letter from Acha to Santillán, February 12, 1925, International Institute for Social History, Amsterdam, Santillán Archive, file 7.

22   Resolutions adopted by the second congress of the International Working Men's Association, March 21–27, 1925, Amsterdam, *Press Service of the IWMA*, July 1, 1925.

23   The official report of the congress was published in *La Protesta (Suplemento Semanal)* from June 29 to August 31, 1925. Unofficial reports on the congress were also published in *Solidaridad Proletaria*, May 23, 1925, and *La Protesta*, April 23–30, 1925. Less-detailed commentaries appeared in *Tiempos Nuevos*, April 2, 1925, and *La Revue Internationale Anarchiste*, May 15, 1925. A four-page official report on the congress can be found in International Institute for Social History, Amsterdam, Santillán Archive, file 4. The resolutions adopted by the second congress of the IWMA were published in the *Press Service of the IWMA* in April 1925.

24 "Informe official del segundo congreso de la Asociación Internacional de los Trabajadores, celebrado en Amsterdam del 21 a 27 de Marzo de 1925 [second day of sessions]," *La Protesta (Suplemento Semanal)*, July 6, 1925.

25 In a letter to Max Nettlau written just after the congress had ended, Santillán claimed that had it not been for Rocker's intervention "we would have publicly distanced ourselves from the rest," and he said that a split within the organisation had been a real possibility. Letter from Santillán to Nettlau, April 15, 1925, International Institute for Social History, Amsterdam, Nettlau Archive, microfilm 1.

26 "Informe" [fifth day of sessions]," *La Protesta (Suplemento Semanal)*, July 17, 1925. Due to the amount of work undertaken at the congress, the commission was only able to meet once and achieved very little.

27 "Informe [seventh day of sessions]," *La Protesta (Suplemento Semanal)*, August 31, 1925.

28 "Cosas de España – Los neutros del Sindicalismo," *La Protesta*, April 15, 1925. Later in the month the Catalan CRT published a manifesto in which it said that *Solidaridad Proletaria* would no longer publish anything that referred to 'personalisms' (personal attacks) or articles by individuals rather than organisations critical of the CRT, a veiled reference to the radical anarchists. El Comité, "Manifiestos del Comité Regional sobre la Carta Abierta a los Anarquistas," *Solidaridad Proletaria*, April 25, 1925. See also "Cuestiones Internacionales – Incoherencias Doctrinarias," *La Protesta*, April 4, 1925; "La Camaleonización del Sindicalismo Español," *La Protesta*, April 5, 1925.

29 "Los jornadas internacionales de la FORA – En torno al Congreso de Amsterdam," *La Protesta*, April 22, 1925; "El Pleito Internacional – Profesionales de la Mentira," *La Protesta*, April 26, 1925. Carbó responded by criticising the absurd "all or nothing" policy of the FORA militants. E. C. Carbó, "El Eclipse de la Cordialidad," *La Revista Internacional Anarquista*, April 15, 1925. Carbó's criticism of the FORA cannot be seen as a defence of the syndicalists' position. He had made this clear in his report on Spain presented at the Amsterdam congress: "I am not a supporter of pure syndicalism – as behind this formula I can only see a reformist spirit. ... Nor [do I believe] that syndicalism is ever sufficient in itself." "Informe presentado por el Delegado de la C.N.T., Eusebio C. Carbó, en el Congreso de la A.I.T. celebrado en Amsterdam en Marzo de 1925," International Institute for Social History, Amsterdam, Santillán Archive, file 6. Later even Valeriano Orobón Fernández fell victim to *La Protesta*'s wrath following an article he wrote on the Amsterdam congress in *Tiempos Nuevos*. See Orobón Fernández, "Para el diario 'La Protesta': Una precisa calificación a sus insolventes redactores," *El Libertario* (Buenos Aires), October 31, 1925; "Contumaces en la Calumnia," *Tiempos Nuevos*, September 10, 1925.

30 Letter from the Augustín Souchy to the CNT and the FORA, July 13, 1925, International Institute for Social History, Amsterdam, Santillán Archive, file 4.

31 Letter from Nuerta of the FORA to Santillán, September 5, 1925, International Institute for Social History, Amsterdam, Santillán Archive, file 4.

32 D. Abad de Santillán, "En Torno a la Confederación Nacional del Trabajo

– Por el Restablecimiento de la Cordialidad," *La Protesta (Suplemento Semanal)*, June 8, 1925.

33   The Unión Sindical Argentina (USA) was soon weakened by internal divisions, and the socialists and communists eventually left to form their own organisations. Given the acrimonious nature of the previous disputes between the USA and the FORA, a reconciliation proved impossible, and the Argentine libertarian movement remained divided until a military coup in 1930 effectively emasculated the FORA.

34   Rodela, "Mas allá de la lucha de clases," *Tierra y Libertad*, January 20, 1923. The attention of Miguel Jiménez and Josep Magriñà, who would both become leading defenders of the MOA in Spain, had already be drawn toward the FORA in late 1924. Miguel Jiménez, "Cuestiones Internationales," *La Protesta*, November 2, 1924; Magriñà, "Blasfemias ingenuas," *Acción Social Obrera*, November 8, 1924.

35   "Carta Abierta – A los camaradas anarquistas," *Solidaridad Proletaria*, April 4, 1925.

36   "La obsession antianarquista de Pestaña," *La Protesta*, September 13, 1925.

37   Peiró, *Trayectoria de la CNT*, 99.

38   Joan Peiró, "Misión política del sindicato," *Vida Sindical*, January 23, 1926. Nick Rider, "Anarchism, Urbanisation and Social Conflict in Barcelona, 1900–1932," PhD thesis, University of Lancaster, 1987, 456, feels that Peiró's "image of how the CNT should develop was something like that of an anti-state, a partially autonomous socialist society developing within capitalism, a broadly based movement, strongly organised on a multitude of levels, that could be present in all aspects of social life, steadily increasing its capacities, learning how to satisfy more and more of its needs and occupying positions of power." The overall idea is reasonably clear, but the practicalities and specifics of how such an organisation would function are not (especially in relation to the political situation in Spain at the time).

39   Peiró, *Trayectoria de la CNT*, 56.

40   J. Peiró, "Nuestro Sindicalismo II," *Acción Social Obrera*, January 26, 1925.

41   Magriñà, "Incoherencias," *Acción Social Obrera*, March 21, 1925.

42   J. Peiró, "Amables aclaraciones para el compañero 'Magriñà'," *Acción Social Obrera*, April 11, 1925.

43   With the exception of the aforementioned letter, the radical anarchist point of view had been given little space in *Solidaridad Proletaria* and had scarcely been published since the disappearance of *Solidaridad Obrera*.

44   "Lo que debe ser El Productor," *El Productor*, November 7, 1925.

45   M. Buenacasa, "Nuevas aportaciones," *El Productor*, March 5, 1926; Magriñà, "El movimiento Anarquista," *El Productor*, December 11, 1925; Miguel Jiménez, "El movimiento obrero anarquista," *El Productor*, February 26, 1926.

46   E. Labrador, "La reorganización anarquista," *El Productor*, January 15, 1926.

47   As well as espousing the benefits of the MOA, *El Productor* accused the national committee of acting in a dictatorial manner, representing personal and not collective opinions, and being totally ineffective. Ramón Domínguez, "Lo que

debe desaparecer de la C.N. del T.," *El Productor*, March 5, 1926; M. Jiménez; "El Movimiento Obrero anarquista," *El Productor*, February 26, 1926; A. Parera, "Aclaraciones," *El Productor*, February 5, 1926.

48 M. Buenacasa, "Sindicalismo y anarquismo," *El Productor*, February 19, 1926.

49 Miguel Jiménez, "El movimiento obrero anarquista," *El Productor*, February 26, 1926.

50 Enrique [*sic*] Malatesta, "Sindicalismo y anarquismo," *El Productor*, January 8, 1926. Malatesta complained that the title was badly translated and should have been 'The Labour Movement and Anarchism.' Errico Malatesta, "Ancora su movimento operaio e Anarchismo," *Pensiero e Volontà*, March 1, 1926. This article provoked a reaction from Santillán, who criticised the Italian for his faith in "class unity" and "the pure workers' movement" (pure in the sense that it was not stained by political differences), which "does not exist and cannot exist." Diego Abad de Santillán, "El movimiento obrero puro," *El Productor*, January 29, 1926.

51 Errico Malatesta, "Ancora su Movimiento operaio e Anarchismo," *Pensiero e Volontà*, March 1, 1926.

52 Errico Malatesta, *Pensiero e Volontà*, February 16, 1925.

53 Enrique [*sic*] Malatesta, "Los anarquistas en el movimiento obrero," *Solidaridad Proletaria*, April 18, 1925.

54 Errico Malatesta, "Sindicalismo y Anarquismo," *El Productor*, January 8, 1926.

55 Errico Malatesta, "La conduite des anarchists dans le mouvement syndical," *Le Libertaire*, March 12, 1925. The article was the report that Malatesta was due to present at the 1923 International Anarchist Congress as the delegate for the UAI.

56 Errico Malatesta, "Sindicalismo y Anarquismo," *El Productor*, January 8, 1926.

57 A similar position to that argued by Malatesta, but from a more syndicalist perspective, was provided by the veteran Asturian syndicalist Eleuterio Quintanilla, in a series of articles in *Noroeste* (Gijon), a regional newspaper, in January 1926 (see "La crisis del proletariado español. Sindicalismo no es anarquismo," January 9, 1926, and "La crisis del proletariado español. Política social y sindicalismo," January 13, 1926).

58 Errico Malatesta, *Umanità Nova*, March 14, 1922.

59 El Comité de Relaciones Anarquistas, "Un manifiesto Anarquista," *El Libertario* (Buenos Aires), June 10, 1924.

60 "A los anarquistas," *Tierra* (Havana), November 13, 1924; *El Libertario* (Buenos Aires), December 15, 1924.

61 A report on the congress is contained in the archives of the French police in Paris. Archives Nationales de France, F/7/13443, 1925.

62 "Manifiesto del Comité de Relaciones de los Grupos Anarquistas de lengua española en Francia," *Acción (Suplemento al numero especial)*, December 1925.

63 Mauro Bajatierra, "Algo sobre orientación sindical," *Solidaridad Obrera* (Gijón), April 30, 1926; Vicente Ballester, "En torno a una encuesta," *Solidaridad Obrera* (Gijón), April 9, 1926; "Nuestros propositos," *Prometeo*, March 13, 1926.

64 *El Productor* claimed that it sold six thousand copies as opposed to the six

hundred sold by *Vida Sindical.* "El Internacionalismo en España," *El Productor,* June 26, 1926. According to Buenacasa, the supporters of *El Productor* represented 80 percent of confederal militants, although this questionable statistic more likely refers to opponents of the pure syndicalists than to supporters of the MOA. Letter from Buenacasa to Santillán, May 11, 1926, International Institute for Social History, Amsterdam, Santillán Archive, file 6.

65   "Nuestra opinión sobre las cartas publicadas en el numero anterior," *El Productor,* December 11, 1925.

66   The accusations are contained in a letter written by a large group of militants detained in Barcelona prison in November 1931. Arturo Parera, Miguel Terren Manero, et al., "Contra el Confusionismo," *Solidaridad Obrera,* November 20, 1931.

67   Adrián Arnó, Miguel Corney, Ladislao Bellavista, Luis Coll, José Banet, Manuel Pedemonte, Ramón Molist, Juan Gascón, Francisco Lleonart, José Quinta, Joan Peiró, Angel Pestaña, Jenero Minguet, Camilo Piñón, Antonio Calomarde, Enrique Bono, Ramón Porquet, N. Marco, José Vidal, Juan Renold, Optimo, Angel Abella, "A los trabajadores y al lector – La Confederación Nacional del Trabajo es un organismo proletario de clase y no de partido político," *Vida Sindical,* January 15, 1926.

68   "Al comenzar nuestra tarea. Orientaciones y rectificaciones," *Vida Sindical,* January 15, 1926.

69   Rafael, "Latgazos," *El Productor,* January 29, 1926.

70   Dionisio Pereira, *A CNT na Galicia,* 36–46. The Asturian and Galician CRT were vastly smaller than they had been prior to the dictatorship and had little influence on CNT militants elsewhere in Spain or abroad.

71   An uprising against the dictatorship was eventually launched on June 1926, in which leading figures in Asturias, including Quintanilla, were involved. The attempt, known as the sanjuanada (as it occurred on Saint Juan's Day), failed. See Angeles Barrio Alonso, *Anarquismo y anarcosindicalismo en Asturias, 1890–1936* (Madrid: Siglo Veintiuno, 1988), 288.

Chapter 7

1   Among those who spent time living in exile were Eusebio Carbó, Pedro and Valeriano Orobón Fernández, Manuel Buenacasa, Joan Peiró, Simó Peira, Camille Piñón, Maura Bajatierra, Augustín Gibanel, Josep Magriñà, Labrador, Floreal Ocaña, Buenaventura Durruti, and Juan Molina. It is impossible to know the exact figure of CNT militants who spent time abroad during this time, but the figure would have been at least several thousand. Numerous Spanish-language publications were produced during this period in France or French colonies: *Brisas Libertarias* (Marseilles, 1912–13), *Ciencia Social* (Marseilles, 1920), *Solidaridad Obrera* (Paris, 1920), *España Libre* (Paris, 1920), *El Sembrador* (Paris, 1923), *Liberion* (Paris, 1924), *Iberion* (Paris, 1924), *Tiempos Nuevos* (Paris 1925–27), *La Revista Internacional Anarquista* (Paris, 1924–25), *Acción* (Paris, 1925–26), *Prismas* (Béziers, 1927–28), *El Libertario* (Paris, 1927), and

La Voz Libertaria (Limoges, 1929), whilst so-called Spanish tribunes – that is, a page or column written in Spanish – appeared in several French libertarian publications: for example, *Le Reveil du Bâtiment* (Lyon), *Le Travaileur du Bâtiment* (Paris), and *Le Flambeau* (North Africa). Other papers published information for the exiles in French: *Le Libertaire* (Paris), *Le Progrès* (Lyon), *Le Combat* (Nord Pas-de-Calais), *L'Upsurge* (Paris), and *L'en-dehors* (Paris).

2   At their height there were twenty-eight Cuadros operating in France ("Los Cuadros Sindicales de los Emigrados Españoles en Francia afectos a la CNT de España," *Acción*, September 6, 1930) and at least seventy anarchist groups (Archives Nationales de France, F/7/13443, police records, June 9, 1925). The exiled anarchist periodical *Tiempos Nuevos* sold upwards of five thousand copies. Archives of the Cabinet of the Prefect of Police, Paris, BA1900, report on 'the Anarchist Movement' dated July 31, 1928.

3   Elorza, "La génesis de la Federación Anarquista Ibérica"; Gómez Casas, *Anarchist Organisation*, 82, 100–106; Paz, *Durruti en la Revolución española*, 156–205.

4   A Spanish-language libertarian newspaper, *Brisas Libertarias* had began publication in August 1912. Gaetan Antansonti was the paper's director, and Angel Fernández and Jesús Flores were its editors. Arlandis was a contributor. It does not appear to have survived long, and only two numbers are held at the Bibliothèque Nationale de France (BNF). Alongside the group Brisas Libertarias, there was a further anarchist group, 'antipatriotas', active in the city. According the French police, José Negre had arrived in Paris in 1912 and had published a "very anarchist" paper, although no information about the name of the paper was given. "Compt-Rendu de Renseignements Speciaux," March 13, 1920," Archives Nationales de France, F/7/13441.

5   Sebastiá Clarà was the secretary general of the federation in Paris which maintained correspondence with the libertarian press in Spain and provided a contact point for militants living in France. Susanna Tavera i García and E. Ucelay da Cal, "Conversa amb Sebastià Clarà un líder cenetiste català," *Avenç* 6 (October 1977), 11–18. In April 1913 there were twenty-nine Spanish anarchists active in the Gironde region (the most important group being Action Libre of Bordeaux), sixty-five in Perpignan; a thirty-three more in the rest of the département of Pyrenées-Occidentales, twenty-three in the département of Basses-Pyrenées, and five in the group 'Nada' of Lyon. Archives Nationales de France, F/7/14791, police records, April 1913.

6   The association contained both French and Catalan militants. Spanish authorities informed the French police of these claims. Archives Nationales de France, F/7/13440, police records, November 24, 1919. According to the French police, two Spanish anarchists, Juan Durán and Fernando Vela, directed "the revolutionary organization" of minority syndicalists in Marseilles. This could be a reference to the syndicalist opposition within the CGT, which would latter break away to form the CGTU. Archives Nationales de France, F/7/13441, police records, May 11, 1921.

7   Among those who had organised the rally were J. S Duque and Narcisse Blanco, the directors of a bimonthly libertarian journal, *Ciencia Social*, which began

publication in August. The paper folded after five numbers due to lack of funds. Among the collaborators was Leopoldo Bonafulla, and number 5 contained the obligatory article by Malatesta critical of the Bolsheviks. The paper received copies of libertarian papers from Spain, including *La Razón* (Cadiz) and *El Productor* (Seville).

8   A report by the French police in early 1921 claimed that the Catalan CRT was encouraging unemployed members to look for work in France. Archives Nationales de France, F/7/13441, police records, January 18, 1921.

9   Sinibaldo Campanula, "Breve reseña sobre el Proletariado Español en Francia," *Tiempos Nuevos*, November 12, 1925. Another centre of activity was Toulouse, where in December 1920 Spanish anarchists and syndicalists held a congress. Letter from minister of interior to the minister of war, December 6, 1920, Archives Nationales de France, F/7/13441. Centres for 'Social Studies' were set up by Spanish anarchists in Lyon in December 1919 (Archives Nationales de France, F/7/13060, police records, December 1919) and Saint-Étienne in early 1921 (*Le Libertaire*, April 15–22, 1921). A Spanish Syndicalist Defence Committee was active in Beziers from 1922 (*Nueva Senda*, July 27, 1922) and in 1923 published a booklet by Restituto Mogrovejo on the crimes of Spanish authorities during the revolutionary period in Spain: "Los crimenes de un Régimen," *Redención*, April 28, 1922.

10   *La Bandera Roja* (Barcelona), December 7, 1919, a revolutionary anarchist paper directed by Manuel Casanovas García, contains a manifesto by the federation.

11   "Groupe International de Diffusion," *Le Libertaire*, December 14, 1919. Spanish libertarian newspapers were dispensed at the weekly meeting of the Anarcho-Communist Federation. Among the newspapers made available were *Solidaridad Obrera* (Bilbao), *El Productor* (Seville), *Espartaco* (Madrid), and *Rebelión* (Cadiz) from Spain, *Avvenire Anarchico* (Italy), and *Le Reveil de Geneve* (Switzerland). Anarchist groups in Provence also made available copies of *El Comunista*, *El Productor*, *La Guerra Social* (Valencia) and *Espartaco* to militants in their region. *Le Libertaire*, November 2, 1919. In 1923 copies of *Solidaridad Obrera* (Barcelona) were being sold at a number of outlets in Paris. *Le Libertaire*, June 22–29, 1923.

12   *Le Libertaire*, May 2, 1920.

13   Report from the chief of the General Information Service to the Prefect of Police, November 7, 1921, and from the Ministry of the Interior to the Ministry of War, January 29, 1921, Archives of the Cabinet of the Prefect of Police, Paris, BA2156.

14   Other known members were Josep Robusté, Felipe Martínez, Cosme Aranguren, Pedro Font-Walls, Pablo Martín, and Francisco Pellicer-Monferrer. Archives of the Cabinet of the Prefect of Police, Paris, BA2156, November 9, 1922.

15   The IOE also launched a campaign to raise money for the publication of a version of *Solidaridad Obrera* in Paris, which was to be directed by Restituto Mogrovejo. *Ciencia Social*, October 1, 1920, mentions the campaign to raise money for the paper, whilst *Solidaridad Obrera* (Bilbao), November 5, 1920, claims that the paper had started publication. No numbers have survived.

Mogrovejo had previously been the director of *Solidaridad Obrera* in Madrid. Another Spanish-language paper, *España Libre*, which represented socialist, syndicalist, and libertarian tendencies (similar in style to *España Nueva* of Madrid) also began publication in 1920. The editorial board was made up of Pitte Llaneza y Gil, Del Teso, and Alonso Feliciano, who were in close contact with the Madrid-based paper. The paper folded following the expulsion of the three members of the editorial board in October 1920. Report sent from the minister of the interior to the minister of war, January 29, 1921, Archives Nationales de France, F/7/13441.

16   Report from the head of the Service of Administrative Research and Sports to the Prefect of the Police, November 15, 1924, Archives of the Cabinet of the Prefect of Police, Paris, BA2156. The IOE had previously issued a warning to militants not to come to France due to the repression they would face from the French authorities. El Comité de la IOE, "A todos los organismos revolucionarios," *Acción Social Obrera*, January 14, 1922.

17   The first reference to *El Sembrador* is contained in *Le Combat* (Organe Anarchiste du Nord et du Pas-de-Calais), July 1923. The paper gives the address of the paper as 9 Rue Louis-Blanc, the same as *Le Libertaire*.

18   El Grupo Fructidor, "Aux anarchistes & aux ouvriers de langue espagnole," November 30–December 7, 1923, *Le Libertaire*. Once more the address of the paper was the same as *Le Libertaire*. No numbers of *El Sembrador* remain, whilst only one number of *Liberion* and two of *Iberion* have survived. José Martín was the director of *Iberion*. In a raid on the office of *Iberion* on November 18, 1924, the police discovered two books containing the list of 490 subscribers to the paper, either individuals or organisations. Archives Nationales de France, F/7/14791, police records, November 19, 1924. For the Lyon congress, see El Comité de Relaciones Anarquistas, "A todos los grupos anarquistas de lengua española," *Solidaridad Obrera* (Barcelona), February 8, 1924.

19   The manifesto was reproduced in *El Libertario* (Buenos Aires), June 10, 1924.

20   Letter from the sub-secretary to the minister of state, October 27, 1924, Archivo Histórico Nacional, Madrid, Serie A del Ministerio de Gobernación, Legajo 42A (11).

21   La Liga de Militantes de la CNT de España, "A todos los españoles residentes en Francia," *Iberion*, August 14, 1924.

22   In April 1924 Peiró and Arnó were sent to Paris by the Catalan CRT to discuss a possible rising involving the confederation and Catalan separatists. Their mandate was simply to "give everything with the aim of putting an end to the dictatorship." When they returned to Spain in June, Carbó was given full responsibility by the CNT to maintain relations with political groupings in France that were plotting to overthrow Primo de Rivera. In the end, the prevarications and delays of the political forces resulted in many anarchists distancing themselves from the negotiations with political figures, and plans began for a rising organised solely by libertarian forces. To this end a Revolutionary Anarchist Committee was established in Paris. The eventual outcome was the failed rising of November 1924. Letters from Peiró to Pestaña April, 17 and

26, 1933, and from Gustavo (Carbó) to Perico (Peiró), August 14 and 18, September 17 and 24, 1924, Archivo General de la Guerra Civil Española, Barcelona, file 1352.

23   The Revolutionary Anarchist Committee was composed of Alfonso Miguel Martorell (former secretary of the Federation of Anarchist Groups of Barcelona in 1920), Paulino Sosa, and García Drego Parra. Archives Nationales de France, F/7/14791, July 1925. An executive commission for the Committee of Anarchist Relations also functioned during this period. Among its members were Phillippe Sandova or Sandoval (a pseudonym for Juan Nojo), Ruiz García (Cantaclaro), Juan Navarro, and Ricardo González. Sandoval was probably also a member of the League of CNT Militants. Archives of the Cabinet of the Prefect of Police, Paris, BA2156, November 15, 1924.

24   Report from the head of the Service for Administrative Research and Sports to the Prefect of the Police, November 15, 1924, and reports on various meeting of the league, September 1, 11, 15, 19, and 24, and October 20, 1924, Archives of the Cabinet of the Prefect of Police, Paris, BA2156. One of the main complaints of members was that the executive committee often operated as it pleased and did not follow the directives of the CNT, an early example of the tensions that would latter arise between the CNT and leading sections of the exiled anarchist movement in relation to the various plots to overthrow the dictatorship.

25   Archives Nationales de France, F/7/13442, police records, November 19, 1924.

26   In a letter to John Brademas, Miguel Jiménez states that at roughly this time a secretariat was established in Barcelona with Buenacasa as general secretary. John Brademas, *Anarcosindicalismo y revolución en España* (Barcelona: Ariel, 1974), 36. Patricio Navarra, José Piedra Vázquez, and one other (whose name Jiménez could not remember) were the other members.

27   "Congreso de los Grupos Anarquistas de lengua española residente en Francia celebrado en la ciudad de Lyon los días 14 y 15 de junio de 1925 – Acta in extenso," International Institute for Social History, Amsterdam, Fedeli Archives, file 120 III. Fedeli, an Italian anarchist who lived in Paris at the time and who was in contact with Spanish exiles in the city, wrote a report on the congress (using the pseudonym Hugo Trene) for *La Tempra* (the paper of the Italians exiled in Paris), July 20, 1925, in which he emphasised the lack of order and solidarity at the congress, a point that was also mentioned in the report of the French police on the congress. Archives Nationales de France, F/7/13443, June 9, 1925.

28   In Portugal local groups would unite to form regional federations which were independent of each other. (There were three independent organisations: the Federation of the South Region, the Anarchist Federation of the Central Region, and the Committee of Anarchist Organization and Propaganda of the North.) The groups affiliated directly, and not via the regional federations, with the UAP, being linked together by a national committee of relations. The UAF had a more straightforward, 'bottom-upward' structure, with local groups linked together in regional federations which came together to form the national union. See Francisco Quintal, "El movimiento anarquista en Portugal," *La Revista Internacional Anarquista*, May 15, 1925.

29 The Lyon congress, in agreement with the decisions of the Barcelona congress of April 1925, accepted that the anarchists were not sufficiently strong enough on their own to overthrow the dictatorship in Spain. The congress thus accepted in principle the necessity of a "pacto circumstantial" with political groups that shared their aims of overthrowing Primo De Rivera. The only forces that fit this qualification were Francesc Macià's Catalan nationalists. However, a manifesto released by the committee in December 1925 warned of the dangers of trusting politicians and nationalists, suggesting they had changed their view on Macià. "Manifiesto del Comité de Relaciones de los grupos anarquistas de lengua española en Francia," *Acción (Suplemento al numero Especial)*, December 1925, a copy of which is in International Institute for Social History, Amsterdam, Fedeli Archives, file 130. At their Marseilles congress in May 1926 the exiles overturned the decision made at Lyon and rejected making pacts with any political organisations. The only organisation with which they would work with was the CNT. This was problematic because at a secret plenum held in Madrid in October 1925, the CNT had decided in favour of collaboration with political forces in order to bring down the Primo de Rivera regime and replace it with a Republican one. The reports on the plenum came from Armando Borghi, who represented the IWMA in Madrid. Letter from Borghi to Nettlau, June 18, 1931, International Institute for Social History, Amsterdam, Nettlau Archive, microfilm 6; letter from Borghi to Rocker November 4, 1931, International Institute for Social History, Amsterdam, Rocker Archive, file 64; "Posizioni Anarchiche," an article published in April 1945 and reproduced in Armando Borghi, *Armando Borghi: Un pensatore ed agitatore anarchico* (Pistoia: Agitatore Anarchico, 1988), 324–34.

30 El Comité de Relaciones Anarquistas de Francia y España, "A todos los grupos y compañeros y a los revolucionarios del mundo entero," April 1925, a copy of which is in Archives Nationales de France, F/7/13443, 1925.

31 *El Productor* stated that the committee had been disqualified by the anarchists in France but does not say why. "Para los Compañeros de Francia y particulamente para el compañero Regino Equinoa," *El Productor*, January 2, 1926; "Por una sola vez," *El Productor*, February 19, 1926. Given that the national secretariat based in Catalonia (created at the 1925 Barcelona congress) was made up of supporters of the MOA, it is possible that the criticism of the MOA by the committee based in France led the anarchists in Barcelona to react. The 'Barcelona-Paris' incident was briefly discussed at the next congress of the exiled anarchists. "Congreso de la Federación de Grupos Anarquistas de Lengua Española en Francia – Celebrado en Marsella los días 13, 14, 15 y 16 Mayo 1926," a copy of which is in International Institute for Social History, Amsterdam, Fedeli Archives, file 120. The exact date of the anarchist committee's return to Spain is not clear. A manifesto published in the special supplement of *Acción* in December 1925 carried solely the name of the Committee of Anarchist Relations of France instead of 'of France and Spain', suggesting that the committee had returned to Spain before this date.

32 "Convocation pour le Congrès anarchiste que aura lieu les 13, 14, et 15 de Mai 1926, A Marseilles – France," Archives Nationales de France, F/7/13443, 1925.

33 "Congreso de la Federación de Grupos Anarquistas de Lengua Española en Francia – Celebrado en Marsella los días 13, 14, 15 y 16 Mayo 1926," in International Institute for Social History, Amsterdam, Fedeli Archives, file 120.

34 The congress also agreed to the transfer of the Committee of Anarchist Relations in France from Paris to Marseilles.

35 It is not clear who represented the CNT at the IWMA conference, although Pedro Orobón Fernández (brother of Valeriano Orobón Fernández who had been expelled from France in 1925) was present and wrote a brief report of the meeting. "Apontamentos acerca do Congresso da AIT," *A Batalha*, May 21, 1925. See also "Resoluciones del Bureau Administrativo de la A.I.T.," *Servicio de la Prensa de la AIT*, May 24, 1926.

36 M. J. de Sousa, "Impresiones sobre el Congreso," *Acción*, May 1926.

37 Le Comité d'Emigration de la CNT d'Espagne, de l'USI d'Italie et de la CGT du Portugal, "Aux camarades émigrés de France," *L'Insurgé* (a French anarchist paper published in Paris), May 1, 1926.

38 Pierre Besnard, who played a leading role in the relations between the Comité de Défense Syndicaliste and the IWMA, left the CDS in June 1923 and at the same time abandoned the secretariat of the IWMA as part of his attempt to detach the CGTU from Moscow and unite it around a policy of independence from the Internationals. This policy failed, so he and other leading revolutionary syndicalists formed a Minority Syndicalist Committee within the CGTU in November 1923 and then the UFSA in November 1924. See "Comité de la Minorité Syndicaliste Révolutionnaire," November 15, 1923, and "Manifeste de la UFSA et de la Minorité Syndicaliste Révolutionnaire au pays syndicaliste," November 20, 1924, both *La Bataille Syndicaliste* (newspaper of the revolutionary syndicalist minority and, from November 1924, of the UFSA).

39 Besnard spoke of the meeting at the Saint-Ouen congress. "La Conference Nationale de l'UFSA," *La Bataille Syndicaliste*, July 15, 1925.

40 Alongside the exiled organisations in the emigration committee were the UFSA, the National Federation of Construction and Public Works' Workers, the Construction Union of the Seine, and the Construction Union of the XIII arrondissement, demonstrating the level of immigrant labour in the construction industry.

41 Huard and Besnard (secretaries of the UFSA), "Le Mouvement Syndicaliste Autonome," *La Voix du Travail*, August 1926. *La Voix du Travail* was the paper set up by the IWMA in accordance with the decisions made at the May meeting of its administrative bureau to propagate revolutionary syndicalism in France, although it was under the direction of Pierre Besnard, the secretary of the UFSA.

42 "Compte Rendu analytique de Congrès des Syndicates Autonomes de France, Lyon 15–16 Novembre 1926," *Le Combat Syndicaliste*, December 1926. Representatives of the IWMA, the Portuguese CGT (Miranda), the Nederlandsch Syndicalistisch Verbond (Lansink Jr.), the SAC (Severin), and the FAUD (Buth) were present at the congress. "Le Congrès Constitutif de la C.G.T. Syndicaliste-Revolutionaire," *Le Libertaire*, November 26, 1926.

43 Besnard's views were soon to be championed by leading moderates in the CNT.

For an outline of Besnard's ideas, see the section on Besnard in Paniagua, *La Sociedad Libertaria*, 117–39, and Wayne Thorpe, "Anarchosyndicalism in Inter-War France: The Vision of Pierre Besnard," *European History Quarterly* 26, no. 4, (1996), 559–90.

44 Maitron, *Histoire du mouvement anarchiste en France*, vol. 2, 71.

45 At its congress in Paris in 1930 the Union Anarchiste Communiste Révolutionnaire, as the old UAF now called itself, actually recommended that anarchists should stay in the CGT or the CGTU in support of "union unity."

46 This point was argued by Manuel Pérez in "La AIT y los Anarquistas," *Rebelde*, July 1928.

47 "Le Travail du Comité D'Emigration," *La Voix du Travail*, October–November 1926.

48 Report by the Prefecture of Police, July 31, 1928, Archives of the Cabinet of the Prefect of Police, Paris, BA1900, claimed that in the Paris region, where the majority of exiled militants were based, the Italians and Spanish were the largest groups. The Spanish movement was "the most important and the most solidly organised."

49 A brief history of the Cuadros Sindicales was given in two reports by its committee: "Rapport de los cuadros sindicales de emigrados españoles adherentes a la CNT," *Despertád*, July 13, 1929; "Los Cuadros Sindicales de los emigrados españoles en Francia afectos a la CNT de España," *Acción*, September 6, 1930.

50 Translated from D. Parra, S. Cortés, E. Carbó, B. Carreras, L. Callejas, et al. ('Por la Comisión Organizadora'), "Los trabajadores españoles refugiados en Francia, por la Confederación Nacional del Trabajo," *Tiempos Nuevos*, March 31, 1927.

51 Ibid.

52 See B. Carreras, "Puntualizando," *Acción Social Obrera*, July 9, 1927. A national plenum of the CNT in March 1929 adopted the creation of Cuadros Sindicales as a means for confederation militants to maintain some form of organisational structure whilst the confederation itself remained banned.

53 As the prominent figure in the Cuadros Sindicales, Carreras traveled widely within France and abroad, often under the pseudonyms Truchero Kero and Manuel Cervello y Lucio.

54 Comité de Paris (Sección de Estadistica), "Cuadros sindicales de emigrados en el extranjero," *El Libertario* (the continuation of *Tiempos Nuevos*), September 25, 1927; "Los Cuadros Sindicales de los emigrados españoles en Francia afectos a la CNT de España," *Acción*, September 6, 1930.

55 *La Voix du Travail*, August 1927. The meeting took place in Lyon on August 14–15.

56 Archives Nationales de France, F/7/13061, police records, February 15, 1928. The Lyon congress was also discussed at a meeting of militants in Barcelona in January 1928. Archives Nationales de France, F/7/13443, police records, February 7, 1928. A 'González' said there was no point sending a delegate to the congress as the federation was "anti-syndicalist." However, rather than being anti-syndicalist, the federation was simply anti-Cuadros.

57 "Boletin de la FGALEF – Nuestro Pleno Nacional," *Prismas*, March 1928. This

position was consistent with the decision made at the Marseilles congress to refuse to recognise the Alianza Revolútionaria (Revolutionary Alliance). The Alianza was a short-lived organisation that had been set up by exiled militants to bring together the Spanish syndicalists and anarchists resident in France. The federation opposed the establishment of the Alianza, deeming it unnecessary, which was essentially the same view they had toward the Cuadros.

58   According to the Portuguese anarchist M. J. de Sousa, the "principal and almost sole tendency in the Federation was anarcho-syndicalist." M. J. de Sousa, "Impresiones sobre el Congreso," *Acción*, May 1926.

59   Report sent by president of the council of the Ministry of the Interior to the minister of Foreign Affairs, February 11, 1930, Archives Nationales de France, F/7/13444.

60   Translated from "El Comité de Relaciones de la Federación de Grupos Anarquistas de Lengua Española en Francia, a todas las agrupaciones y compañeros residentes en este país," *La Voz Libertaria*, April 10, 1930.

61   Between 1921 and 1927, ninety-two Spaniards were expelled from France for political reasons. Report on "Les Emigres Espagnols en France, 1927," Archives Nationales de France, F/7/13443. From January 1 to October 10, 1927, fifty-eight were expelled. Archives Nationales de France, F/7/13518, police records, 1928.

62   The reorganization of the FGALEF was the subject of a lively debate at the Lyon congress of February 1928, was again the subject of a letter sent by the FGALEF's Committee of Relations in August 1929, and had been the central point of discussion at a meeting of the Seine Region of the FGALEF in February 1927, which also had noted that it was impossible to publicly propagate their ideas due to their position as "foreigners" in France. "Boletín de la FGALEF," *Prismas*, March 1928; "FGALEF – Comité de Relaciones," *Acción Social Obrera*, August 10, 1929, "Hacia la Reorganización del Movimiento Anarquista Español en Francia," *Tiempos Nuevos*, February 1927.

63   On the cessation of *Tiempos Nuevos*, see "Noticiario Internacional," *El Libertario* (Buenos Aires), November 15, 1927; "La Expulsión del Administrador de Tiempos Nuevos," *El Libertario* (Paris), September 25, 1927. *El Libertario*, which was published by the group Sin Pan of the Seine Federation, only produced one number. *La Voz Libertaria* shared a similar fate. Its first and only number, produced in France, came out on March 1, 1929. Almost immediately the two anarchists charged with its publication, Tomas Espinossa and Avelino Samlios (who was known by his pseudonym Sakuntala), were arrested by the authorities. Archives Nationales de France, F/7/14720, no date. See also "Arrestation a Limoges de deux camarades Espagnoles," *La Voix Libertaire*, March 16, 1929.

64   Police report on "Réunion de la Commission Administrative de 'L'Union Anarchiste Communiste," October 9, 1928, Archives Nationales de France, F/7/13061.

65   At a meeting of the Seine Region of the FGALEF on August 18, 1929, a proposal by Sakuntala (Samlios) to publish an underground paper was rejected as

this would attract the French authorities. Instead it was decided that *La Voz Libertaria* should be published in Brussels, with Erguido-Blanco as administrator and Labrador as director. Archives Nationales de France, F/7/13444, police records.

66 At a general assembly of the Seine Region of the FGALEF, held on February 9, 1930, many of those in attendance made clear their intentions to return to Spain as, following the collapse of the dictatorship of Primo de Rivera, the new government under General Berenguer had granted a general amnesty. Later in the year a number of anarchist militants in Paris reported having been invited to return home by their compatriots in Spain due to imminent possibility of a revolution. Archives Nationales de France, F/7/13444, police records, February 11, 1930, and October 25, 1930.

67 See the report on France at the Madrid conference of the FAI in June 1931 in "Los Grandes Comicios del Anarquismo," *Tierra y Libertad*, June 20, 1931. Previously a meeting of the Seine Region of the FGALEF on March 22, 1931, had rejected a proposal to create a union between the federation and the UACR, a union intended to strengthen the movement, although it was agreed that the federation should establish a close relation with its French counterpart. "Crónicas de nuestro movimiento," *Tierra y Libertad*, March 28, 1931.

68 Report of the OIEA from the chief of general information and games service to the Police Prefect, August 13, 1924, Archives of the Cabinet of the Prefect of Police, Paris, BA 1899.

69 Translated from Sebastià Clarà, "El movimiento obrero en Francia," *Solidaridad Obrera*, March 19, 1931. Clara was one of the many Catalan militants that spent a long period in exile in France. Ricardo Sanz, who was in Paris during the preparation for the November 1924 rising as delegate of the revolutionary committee in Barcelona, was equally dismissive: "Our French comrades, except rare and honourable exceptions, were useless both collectively and individually. The individuals who were of any use to the cause of the international proletariat could be counted on the fingers of one hand. The rest, worthless." Translated from Ricardo Sanz, *El sindicalismo español antes de la Guerra Civil (Los Hijos del Trabajo)* (Barcelona: Petronio, 1976), 186. Juan García Oliver talks of the "decadent French pure anarchists" in *El eco de los pasos*, 83–84. Augustín Gibanel in "Nosotros y el Sindicalismo de Aquí," *Tiempos Nuevos,* April 1925, accuses the French syndicalists of xenophobia. At a meeting in Paris of the Construction Workers' Union, Sandoval, a prominent figure in the Seine Region of the FGALEF, accused the French anarchists of being "rabidly sectarian." Archives Nationales de France, F/7/13443, police records, February 6, 1925. See also "Desde Francia," *Alba Social* (a communist libertarian weekly of the Local Federation of Valencia), April 1, 1923, which blamed the inability of the anarchists to successfully defend their ideas in the CGTU on the predominance of individualism in the movement. In a similar vein, see also Manuel Pérez, "Sobre el movimiento obrero anarquista," *Le Reveil du Batiment*, February 1928, and Peiró and Magriña's articles welcoming the formation of the CGTSR, both of which criticised the unnecessary delay in creating their

own confederation: J. Peiró, "La III CGT de Francia, considrada desde España," *Acción*, February–March 1927; R. Magriñà, "Salud a la CGTSR," *Tiempos Nuevos*, December 1926.

70   In 1922 the UAF had about four hundred members. Report on the Anarchist Movement in France, January 1922, Archives Nationales de France, F/7/12948. According to Floreal Ocaña of the Seine Region of the FGALEF, by 1928 the UACR only had 180 members. Floreal Ocaña, "Movimiento obrero anarquista?," *Acción Social Obrera*, December 8, 1928.

71   Paz, *Durruti en la Revolución española*, 162–90.

72   "Congrès national de l'Union anarchiste Francaise – Orleans," July 1926, Archives Nationales de France, F/7/13056.

73   The Platform was originally written in Russian. A version in French (translated by Volin) was published in June 1926 under the title "La Plate-forme organisationnelle des communiste libertaires." The first Spanish version was published in *Prismas* in August 1928, although a questionnaire by Dielo Trouda related to issues raised in the Platform was published in the June issue.

74   Alongside the Russians, those who attended came from France (Odeon, who represented the French Anarchist Youth, and Dauphin-Meunier), Bulgaria (Pavel), Poland (Ranko and another), Italy (Fedeli, under the name Hugo Trene), and China (Chen). International Institute for Social History, Amsterdam, Fedeli Archive, files 33, 175.

75   International Institute for Social History, Amsterdam, Fedeli Archive, file 175, February 12, 1927. File 175 is Fedeli's personal archive. Carbó's comments are not in Fedeli's general account of the conference in file 33, which is a draft work entitled *Historia del Movimiento Anarquista: Principios y métodos de organización*. Carbó's comments were later echoed by Malatesta, who, whilst welcoming the intentions of the Russian anarchists, criticised the idea of forming a general union with a defined and rigid ideology that would be enforced by an executive committee, writing that this would be tantamount to a "government of a church." "A proposito della Piattaforma," *Il Risveglio* (Geneva), October 1927.

76   The three members of the committee were Makhno, Chen, and Ranko.

77   The account of the congress that follows is taken from Fedeli's unpublished work *Historia del Movimiento Anarquista: Principios y métodos de organización*, International Institute for Social History, Amsterdam, Fedeli Archive, File 33. The delegates according to Fedeli were from Italy (Fabbri, Camillo Berneri and Trene [Fedeli]), the Russian group (Archinoff, Makhno, and others), Bulgaria (Pavel), France (two delegates: Odeon and Severin Fernandel), and Poland (Ranko and Waleki). Chen, Dauphin-Meunier, and other individualists, who represented no one but themselves, also attended.

78   Agustín Gibanel recommended that all those Spanish anarchists who understood French should "acquire the Platform and discuss it in their groups." Gibanel claimed that support for the Platform originally came from the exiled groups in Lyon who introduced their comrades in Beziers (where the journal *Prismas* was published) to the Russians' ideas at a meeting. "A proposito de un proyecto de organización," *Acción Social Obrera*, May 14, 1927. Gibanel was then sent by

those groups that supported the Platform to Barcelona to meet officials of the FAI in either late 1929 or early 1930. However, the FAI rejected the Platform and had no interest in the programme. Agustin Gibanel, "Fuera de Valija I & II," *Cultura Libertaria*, March 11 and 18, 1932. For support in France, see R. Verter, "La Plataforma de Organización General de los Anarquistas," *Acción Social Obrera*, June 1, 1929. J. Manuel Molina, the secretary of the FGALEF at the time, told Gómez Casas in a letter that the Platform had "very few defenders" as the Spanish anarchists "viewed any modification or revision with reservation." Gómez Casas, *Anarchist Organisation*, 106, citing letter from Molina to Gómez Casas, December 31, 1975.

79   Miguel Jiménez, "La Plataforma," *Acción Social Obrera*, July 6 and 13, 1929. Santillán's reaction had previously been published in *La Protesta (Suplemento Semanal)*.

80   Miguel Jiménez, "La Trabazón, la Sintesis y la Plataforma," *Cultura Proletaria* (New York), April 12, 1930. The articles in *Cultura Proletaria* were published with the intention of clarifying the FAI's ideological base to the Spanish exiles living in the United States prior to the affiliation of the Spanish-speaking anarchist groups of the United States with the FAI.

81   Miguel Jiménez, "La Plataforma," *Acción Social Obrera*, July 13, 1929.

82   Ibid.

83   The AFA rejected the rigid statutes and regulations adopted by the UACR at the Paris congress of 1927. *Le Trait – D'Union Libertaire* (the paper of the AFA), January 1, 1928. For a history of the splits within the anarchist movement in France caused by debates over the Platform, see Maitron, *Le Mouvement anarchiste en France*, 80–86.

84   Faure's *Anarchist Synthesis* was greatly influenced by, if not simply an elaboration of the synthesis proposed earlier in 1924 by the Russian anarchist Volin, "De la Synthèse," *La Revue Anarchiste*, March and May 1924. Faure openly admitted that he had not discovered anything new and paid homage to the work of Volin as well as similar works by Fabbri.

85   S. Faure, "La Synthèse Anarchiste," *Le Trait – D'Union Libertaire*, March 1, 1928.

86   Faure represented this idea with the use of fractions. For example, if in one location for every individualist there were two communists and four syndicalists, this would be represented as "I. C2. S4," and therefore the syndicalists would have four times as much influence in that area as the individualists and twice as much as the communists.

87   *Despertád*, July 14, 1928; *Verbo Nuevo*, April 10–25, 1928.

88   It is important not to see the different factions of the anarchist movements as absolute wholes in themselves. Many anarchists who may have accepted certain parts of the anarcho-individualist doctrine in their private lives also operated in the unions and affinity groups in line with either anarcho-syndicalist or anarcho-communist positions. Furthermore, certain aspects of anarcho-individualism were shared by the other tendencies of anarchism (for example, the emphasis on non-state, rational education). However, it must be stressed that the influence of the extremist egoistic form of anarcho-individualism associated with

Max Stirner and Nietzsche did not enjoy great support in Spanish anarchist circles from 1917 onwards. Articles by Stirner did not appear in the Spanish press. His classic work, *The Ego and Its Own*, was not published in Spain until after the Civil War. And the only syndicalist who was known to have at one point supported Stirner's ideas was Salvador Seguí, who, as has been seen, later became a force for moderation in the CNT. Pure anarcho-individualists rejected both membership in unions and anarchist organisations and thus by definition stayed outside of unions. In general, anarcho-syndicalists of the period and those who survived to write autobiographies or accounts of the CNT did not even mention the influence of anarcho-individualism or denied it had any influence at all. In her doctoral thesis, Marín i Silvestre, "De la llibertat per coneixer al coneixement de la llibertat," 202ff., has argued that anarcho-individualism was a force in the 1920s and 1930s within the overall libertarian movement. However, whilst accepting that certain individualist ideologues, such as Han Ryner and Émile Armand, had an influence, this was of a limited nature and did not directly impact the unions. Moreover, there is a danger in assuming that if an anarchist showed an interest in the work of a specific individualist anarchist this would make him or her an individualist or would have an guiding impact on his or her opinions in other matters. However, the best known of those whom she interviewed – Joan Ferrer, José Pierats, Josep Llop and Juan Molina – could by no means be considered as anarcho-individualists. The criticism of individualism in works by anarchists from the radical Abad de Santillán and López Arango, *El anarquismo en el movimiento obrero*, 143–44 (in relation to Russia), to the syndicalist Joan Peiró, *Trayectoria de la CNT*, 171, the relative paucity of articles in relation to those of syndicalist and communist theorists, and the lack of any reference to individualism in reports, articles, and books by CNT members speaks volumes.

89   "Un manifiesto de Sebastian Faure," *Despertád*, July 14, 1928.

90   Translated from Magriñà, "Unidad," *Verbo Nuevo* (Brussels), April 25, 1928. *Despertád* was a continuation of a regional paper, *Despertar Marítimo*, but from the relaunch in March 1928 its scope was evidently more national, demonstrated by the quality of its contributors. A further example of the newly discovered unity among the exiles was the decision of the three libertarian papers *Prismas*, *El Sembrador*, and *Rebelde* to voluntarily close down in order to pool their finances so that the FGALEF could publish *La Voz Libertaria*.

91   "Un Manifiesto de Sebastian Faure," *Despertád*, July 14, 1928.

92   The French individualist anarchist Émile Armand argued that, although a worthy attempt, the Synthesis provided no means of creating unity. Anarchists did not differ in their ultimate goal but in the tactics to achieve it. Therefore it was impossible to weld the different tendencies together in a compact organisation. The anarchists should aim simply to build an 'entente' between the different tendencies based on comprehension and toleration. Armand's individualism had few supporters among the Spanish exiles, and thus his position did not draw much attention, although Federico Pizana (Federico Morales) from Béziers was a notable supporter. See Federico Pizana, "Sintesis o Entente," *Verbo Nuevo*, May 29, 1928.

93   The Paris congress of 1929 formally acknowledged the subservience of the CGTU to the French communist party. Berry, *A History of the French Anarchist Movement*, 148.

Chapter 8

1   The fact that moves were made toward the formation of both an anarchist and a syndicalist organisation has caused much confusion. Edgar Rodrigues (pseudonym of António Francisco Correia, "An-Arquia: Uma Visao da Historia do Movimento Libertario em Portugal," https://we.riseup.net/assets/160397/ Edgar%20Rodrigues%20hist%C3%B3ria%20do%20movimento%20 anarquista%20em%20portugal.pdf, traces the prehistory of the FAI from a meeting of militants in 1923 without mentioning the fact that this meeting was actually between the CNT and the CGTP. This confusion was shared by many militants active at the time. Mariano Prat claimed that the idea of creating an Iberian anarchist federation was launched in 1920 soon after the Madrid congress of the previous December. Mariano Prat, "Por la Concreción y por las Convicciones," *Acción Social Obrera*, October 5, 1929. Manuel Buenacasa, *El movimiento Obrero Español*, 252, claimed the FAI was created as a result of an initiative by Evelio Boal (the secretary of the national committee at the Madrid congress) in agreement with Manuel Joaquim de Sousa. According to 'Optimos', the issue of a peninsula-wide confederation had been the subject of debate in the newspaper *Cultura Proletaria* (Mallorca) in 1921–22. Unfortunately, very few numbers of this paper survive, none of which refer to this. 'Optimos', "Pro Constitución de la F.A. Iberica y F.I. Anarquista, Respuesta a la Encuesta," *Rebelde*, August 1928. Whatever the exact truth, it is clear that discussion on the proposed Iberian Syndicalist Confederation began in 1919 and that with the formation of the Committee of Anarchist Relations in Spain and the União Anarquista Portuguesa in 1923 talks began over the formation of a joint anarchist organisation.

2   Lorenzo, *Los Anarquistas Españoles y el Poder*, 5, claims that "the FAI was not known until 1929," whilst Peirats, *La CNT en la Revolución Española*, 41, states that "until 1931 the FAI did not have a decisive influence." Gómez Casas, *Anarchist Organisation*, 116–19, covers the period after the inaugural conference in 1927 to the birth of the Second Republic in April 1931 in only four pages. Although he makes use of letters from FAI militants written decades after the events, he scarcely refers to the primary material available, including the FAI papers published abroad – in particular, *Rebelde*.

3   Although outside the scope of this book, the role of the FAI within the CNT during the Second Republic is of interest due to the confusion among historians as to the actual nature of the federation. The FAI is often seen as an extremist radical anarchist organisation that sought to enforce its ideological direction on the operation of the CNT from both outside and within the confederation. The truth is more complex. Many of those associated with the increased radicalisation of the CNT during the Republic (e.g., Durruti, García Olivera, Federico

Urales, and Federica Montseny), although labelled *faistas*, were not actually members of the federation, especially during the pivotal years 1931–33 when leading syndicalists were expelled from the party. See Vega," La Confederació Nacional del Treball i els Sindicats d'Oposició a Catalunya i el País Valencià (1930–36), 290–92. Juan Lopez and Domingo Torres, leading members of the syndicalist tendency, were present at the founding conference of the FAI, and many other syndicalists, including Peiró, were also members. See Brademas, *La Confederació Nacional del Treball*, 34. For a brief survey of the historiography of the FAI, see the first chapter of Gutiérrez Molina, *La Idea Revolucionaria*, 9–20.

4   Anselmo Lorenzo, *El Proletariado militante* (Toulouse: MLE-CNT en Francia, 1946), 165–70.

5   See Joao Freire, *Anarquistas e Operarios – Ideologia, oficio e practicas socais: o anarquismo e o operariado em Portugal, 1900–1940* (Porto: edicoes Afrontamento, 1992). For a contemporary account, see "Subsidios para a historia do Movimento Sindicalista em Portugal de 1908 a 1919," in *A Batalha Porta-voz da organizacao operaia Portuguesa Almanaque para 1926* (Lisbon: Seccao editorial de a Batalha, 1926), 53–78.

6   The UON delegate at the El Ferrol congress was Manuel Joaquim de Sousa.

7   "El Proletariado ante la Guerra – Congreso Internacional del Ferrol," *Solidaridad Obrera*, May 13, 1915.

8   M. J. de Sousa, "O II Congreso da CGT de España," *A Batalha* (CGTP newspaper), December 16, 1919; "Por Coma das Fronteiras," *A Batalha*, May 26, 1920. The Coimbra congress, originally scheduled for July 1919, was postponed due to a railway strike in Portugal.

9   "A verdadeira harmonia iberica," *A Batalha*, December 25, 1919.

10   Boal and Seguí were among the CNT's representatives at these meetings. The members of the national committee based in Seville in December 1923 claimed that it was Seguí who had initiated the moves towards the creation of an Iberian Labour Confederation. "A Revolucão Iberica," *A Batalha*, January 1, 1924. *Solidariad Obrera* (Seville) agreed in "Portugal – Una Confederación Ibérica," March 31, 1923.

11   "Por Coma das Fronteiras," *A Batalha,* May 26, 1920. Following the Madrid congress the CNT sent delegates to France (Pestaña), Italy (Carbó), and Portugal (Vicente Gil) to raise support for a boycott of Spanish goods as well as discuss the Latin International.

12   "O III Congresso Operario Nacional," *A Batalha*, October 7 and 8, 1922. Initially the decision was only provisional, but in a referendum held in 1923 the unions of the CGTP supported affiliation with the IWMA and not the RTUI by 104 to 6, with 5 abstentions. "Confederacão Geral do Trabalho," *A Batalha*, September 30, 1923.

13   Acrato Lluhi, "Confederación Ibérica del Trabajo," *Solidaridad Obrera*, May 6, 1923; Santillán, "La confederación ibérica del trabajo," *La Protesta*, June 21, 1923.

14   "Para el Próximo Congreso Nacional," *Solidaridad Obrera* (Gijón) June 22, 1923; *Cultura y Acción* June 29, 1923. Even before the scheduled national

congress, the northern CRT had made clear that it supported the formation of an Iberian federation. "Congreso de la Confederación Regional del Norte," *Solidaridad Obrera*, April 27, 1923. In an interview with *A Batalha*, Lorenzo Isasa, former secretary of the northern CRT, argued that the two organisations should form a "spiritual and material union." "Uma Confederacão Iberica?," *A Batalha*, March 16, 1923.

15 It has proved impossible to locate the number of *Solidaridad Obrera* that contains the invitation. Information about the invitation was provided by Jaime Aragó, "Confederación Nacional del Trabajo IV – Catalanismo o Sindicalismo," *Acción Social Obrera*, September 11, 1926.

16 Rodrigues, *An-Arquia*, 96, claims that J. Ferrer Alvarado attended and not Acrato Lluhi. However, according to a contemporary account by Juan Ortega, the CNT's delegates for the meeting were Clara and Acrato Lluhi, and they left for Portugal in June 1923. Lluhi had previously shown an interest in, and knowledge of, the negotiations between the CNT and the CGTP. It is possible that 'Acrato Lluhi' was a pseudonym for Ferrar Alverado (or vica versa). Juan Ortega, "La Verdad, es un delito?," *Acción Social Obrera*, March 26, 1926. Pérez was a Spaniard, although at the time he was living in Portugal.

17 "Semente que Germine – A Confederacão Iberica," *A Batalha*, July 6, 1923. It has proved impossible to find any precise date for this conference. However, according to Juan Ortega, the delegates from the CNT left Barcelona the day after a meeting of militants in Barcelona which was celebrated on the same day as the CRT's plenum at Lleida (Lérida). The plenum lasted from June 29 to July 1 so the delegation would have arrived in Portugal sometime in the first week of July. The conference would have taken place within days of their arrival. Juan Ortega, "La Verdad, es un delito?," *Acción Social Obrera*, March 26, 1926.

18 The letter was discussed at a meeting of the CGTP Confederal Council. "Confederação Geral do Trabalho," *A Batalha*, September 30, 1923.

19 For information on the proposed insurrection, see Díez, *Un anarco-sindicalista de acción*, 106–7. Previously Díez, who was the national secretary as the time, had met the Catalan nationalist leader Francesc Macíá and leading Basque and Republican politicians at Font-Romeu (France) to discuss the rising. Following these discussions the CNT invited the CGTP delegates to visit Seville. The two CGTP delegates were not released until March 2, 1924, despite the fact that the Portuguese government had written to the Spanish government informing them that they had known about the delegation's trip, that legal passports had been assigned to the two delegates, and that they had known the purpose of the visit and had no objections to it. The CGTP delegates pointed out that the meeting was a result of the decisions made publicly at Covilhã, whilst both the arrested members of the CNT and the CGTP pointed out the farcical nature of the charges given their relations with the communists, the size of the delegation, and the fact that two delegates of the national committee of the CNT had visited Catalonia on December 20, in support of a campaign to legalise the unions there. See "Uma Revolucão Iberica," *A Batalha*, December 27, 1923; "Foram Presos," *A Batalha*, December 28, 1924; "Revolucão Iberica," *A Batalha*, January

1, 1924; Rafael Pena, "A Revolucão Iberica," *A Batalha*, January 8, 1924; "Ja e tempo," *A Batalha*, January 31, 1924; "Enfim," *A Batalha*, March 4, 1924.

20 See, for example, Quintanilla, "Una Confederación sindical Ibérica," *El Noreste*, January 29, 1926; Jaime Aragó, "Confederación Nacional del Trabajo IV – Catalanismo o Sindicalismo," *Acción Social Obrera*, September 11, 1926.

21 Theses adopted at the Alemquer conference on "The position of the anarchists towards revolutionary syndicalism": "A Conferencia Anarquista da Regiao Portuguesa," *A Comuna* (journal of the UAP), March 25, 1923.

22 The CGTP had so far avoided much of the ideological conflict that befell the CNT in the early 1920s between the communist and revolutionary/anarcho-syndicalists. Support for Moscow was limited, as the vote on affiliation to the IWMA had shown. The communists eventually set up their own trade union federation in 1926 after the CGTP congress of 1925, held in Santerem, had decided that delegates "holding political positions" were not allowed to be members. The UAP supported Malatesta's opinion that the unions had to be open to all so as to allow the anarchists the widest possible audience for its propaganda and therefore rejected the MOA. El C. N. de la União Anarquista Portuguesa, "Nuestra Respuesta," *Rebelde*, March 1928. See also 'Malatesta e o anarquismo portugues', *Ler Historia*, no. 6 (1985), 35–49.

23 "Convenience of a close relationship with the Portuguese anarchists" was the tenth and final item due to be discussed at the Madrid meeting. "Congreso Nacional Anarquista," *Redención*, March 1, 1923. A later editorial in the newspaper complained that not enough attention had been given to the subject by the anarchists in Spain and called on the newly formed Committee of Anarchist Relations to look into the possibilities of a closer relationship with their Portuguese comrades. "Por la Federación Peninsular Anarquista," *Redención*, June 21, 1923.

24 "A Caminho … A Conferencia de Alemquer marcou uma nova fase no movimento anarquista em Portugal," *A Comuna*, April 1, 1923. According to the acts of the first conference of the Central Region of Portuguese anarchists, an initiative committee set up at the Alenquer conference had sent an invitation to their Spanish comrades to send delegates to the conference. "Tese votadas na Conferencia Anarquista da Região do Centro," *A Comuna*, June 29, 1924. No delegates were sent as the Spanish anarchists were attending their own congress at the same time.

25 Francisco Quintal, "Anarquistas Ibericos," *A Comuna*, August 12, 1923. The FAI itself announced its hope that the syndical organisation would follow their lead and create an Iberian Federation of Labour, in a report presented at a national plenum of the CNT in January 1928. "La Federación Anarquista Ibérica a la Confederación Nacional del Trabajo," *Acción Social Obrera*, April 13, 1929.

26 Archives Nationales de France, F/7/13443, 1925 (no exact date given).

27 At the Lyon congress of the exiled Spanish anarchist groups in June 1925, relations with Portugal were not discussed. The delegates were preoccupied with the prospects of revolution in Spain. "Congreso de los Grupos Anarquistas de Lengua Española residentes en Francia celebrado en la ciudad de Lyon los días 14

y 15 de junio de 1925," International Institute for Social History, Amsterdam, Fedeli Archive, file 120.

28   Following the closure of *El Productor* and *Vida Sindical* in early 1926, the accompanying intensification of government repression in Spain included the censorship and checking of incoming mail. "A Causa da Revolucão em Espanha," *O Anarquista*, May 16, 1926.

29   "Congreso de la Federación de Grupos Anarquistas de Lengua Española en Francia Celebrado en Marsella los días 13, 14, 15, y 16 Mayo 1926," International Institute for Social History, Amsterdam, Fedeli Archive, file 120. The decisions of the congress were also reproduced in *O Anarquista*, June 20, 1926.

30   The Spanish National Federation of Anarchist Groups was set up sometime in late 1926, though it probably existed in name only and remained little more than an embryonic organisation until the anarchist Valencia conference of July 1927, at which it became the Spanish section of the newly formed FAI. Gómez Casas, *Anarchist Organisation*, 66, claims that the federation was created at the 1923 anarchist congress. This appears to be incorrect. The reports on this congress make clear that only a Committee of Relations was created, whilst no mention is made of such an organisation at any time until 1927. Furthermore there is no reference in the libertarian press to any congress or conference at which such an organisation might have been established. According to a series of articles published by *El Productor* (which briefly renewed publication in 1930), the surge in reorganisation that led to the formation of the FAI began following the Marseilles congress. "Antauen – Servo II – La Federación de Grupos Anarquistas de España," *El Productor*, June 28, 1930; "Antauen-Servo III – La Federación Anarquista Ibérica," *El Productor*, July 5, 1930. A letter from the Spanish Committee of Anarchist Relations to the delegates of a FGALEF plenum in September 1926 claimed that "the Spanish Anarchist Union will soon be a reality." "FGALEF – Extracto de las actas y acuerdos tomados en el Pleno de Delegados Regionales celebrado los días 5, 6 y 7 de Septiembre de 1926," International Institute for Social History, Amsterdam, Fedeli Archive, file 120. This union would most probably be the National Federation of Anarchist Groups.

31   The acts of the UAP congress were published in the first number of the *Boletim Informativo* of the UAP, April 1927.

32   Following the rising, the anarchist and syndicalist press was decimated, and the CGTP and its federations were closed, with its offices destroyed by police. A large number of militants were imprisoned or deported to the Portuguese colonies of West Africa or Asia, where they would remain for a number of years. See Arnaldo Simoes Januario, "Desde el destierro," *Rebelde*, August 1928; "Los deportados portugeses a la isla de Timor," *El Libertario* (newspaper of the FAI), September 17, 1932.

33   In its second circular, issued in early 1928, the Peninsular Committee stated that the UAP had not been able to carry out the tasks entrusted to it due to the repression in Portugal, and that, after consultation with the other respective regions, including the FGALEF, it was agreed to relieve them of their duties.

Comité Peninsular, "Circular N. 2: A Los Individuos, Grupos y Federaciónes de la Federación Anarquista Ibérica," *Rebelde*, February 1928.

34   Letter from J. Llop to J. Peirats reproduced in Gómez Casas, *Anarchist Organisation*, 107. A short extract form the acts from the plenum of the Catalan regional federation was published in *Tiempos Nuevos*, June 1927.

35   "Sintesis del acta de la Conferencia Nacional celebrada en Valencia en los días 24 y 25 de julio de 1927," *La Protesta*, November 1927. The report was later reproduced by José Peirats in *Ruta*, July 22, 1937.

36   Gómez Casas, *Anarchist Organisation*, 116, states that the committee remained in Seville only a short time before moving to Barcelona and that in the Catalan capital it was made up of Germinal de Sousa, Noja Ruiz, and Jiménez. The evidence suggests this might not be the case. Until March 1930 the circulars from the Peninsular Committee were written from Seville, and Ruiz was in prison in Valencia for much of the period. The latest definite date for the Peninsular Committee being in Seville is a response to an opinion poll by the newspaper *Despertád* dated March 1930. See "La FAI contesta a la encuesta iniciada por el semanario Despertád," *Despertád*, June 7–21, 1930. The FAI first gave news of the transfer to Barcelona in a circular in July: El C.P. de la F.A.I, "Puntualicemos," *Acción Social Obrera*, July 26, 1930. Jiménez was the general secretary of the Spanish National Federation of Anarchist Groups in 1927 which was responsible for the organisation of the Valencia conference, and de Sousa was a leading figure in the UAP, so it is possible that the three mentioned by Gómez Casas were part of the organisational committee that helped arrange the Valencia conference.

37   In 1928 the UAP committee was forced into exile in the Portuguese West African colonies by the military dictatorship. An attempt to reorganise forces in Lisbon in 1929 failed, and by 1931 the UAP had been disbanded and replaced by the Federación de los Anarquistas Portugueses exilados en el extranjero y en las colonias (Federation of Portuguese anarchists exiled abroad and in the colonies, FAPE). A subcommittee of the FAPE was based in Barcelona, and the Portuguese involvement in the FAI in the following years was predominantly limited to the exiled movement in Spain. See Comité de Relaciones de Anarquistas Portugueses residentes y refugiados en el Extranjero, Sub-comité (Barcelona), "De Portugal – Los libertarios portugueses emigrados y refugiados en el extranjero," *Acción*, March 7, 1931.

38   Marín i Silvestre, "De la llibertat per coneixer al coneixement de la llibertat," 427–28, states that the anarchists that she interviewed who were active within the FAI during the dictatorship insisted that the FAI was primarily created as a means of "coordinating the [anarchist] groups in Spain and Portugal" and to provide "solidarity, and reenforce [anarchist] culture and action."

39   The eight items on the agenda were: concerning the Iberian Federation (that is, the creation of the FAI); the Labour movement; the Internationals; the important problems of anarchism and characteristics and development of the movement; cooperatives; prisoners and persecuted; propaganda and culture; and the dictatorship. For a brief description of the debates at the conference, see Miguel

Jiménez's letter to John Brademas, in Brademas, *Anarcosindicalismo y revolución en España*, 34–39.

40 Translated from "Sintesis del acta de la Confederación Nacional celebrada en Valencia en los días 24 y 25 de julio de 1927," *La Protesta*, November 1927.

41 In interviews with Marín i Silvestre, FAI members of the period state that during the dictatorship the FAI did not have the "decision making capacity" that it would have during the 1930s. Marín i Silvestre, "De la llibertat per coneixer al coneixement de la llibertat," 428.

42 No record of the CRT regional plenum has been found. However, the history of the Committee of Revolutionary Action was briefly discussed at the national plenum held in Barcelona on June 29, 1928. "Confederación Nacional del Trabajo – Acta del Pleno Nacional celebrado en Barcelona el dia 29 de junio de 1928," *La Protesta*, August 31–September 2, 1928.

43 "Confederación Nacional del Trabajo Acta del Pleno Nacional celebrado en Madrid los días 15 y 16 de enero de 1928," *La Protesta*, March 25–27, 1928. Delegates from the Cuadros Sindicales (Carreras), the FAI, the Catalan CRT, the Catalan Committee of Revolutionary Action, the Levante CRT, the Local Federation of Anarchist Groups from Alicante, the CRT from Castile, and the local labour federation of Seville attended. According to the national committee, the areas in which the confederation was best organised were Catalonia, Levante, and Andalusia. The plenum was originally scheduled to take place in Barcelona. Orobón Fernández had been delegated by the IWMA to represent it at a 'National Conference of Reorganisation' in Barcelona in January but had to cancel after a letter from him to Federico Urales (a leading figure in anarchist circles in Barcelona), containing information about his trip, arrived already opened. The police had evidently opened the letter, and this may have been the cause for the change of venues. Letters from Orobón Fernández to Max Nettlau, December 22, 1927, and January 25, 1928, International Institute for Social History, Amsterdam, Nettlau Archive, microfilm 57.

44 The FAI report does not appear in the acts of the congress. A slightly modified version was published in *Acción Social Obrera*, April 6 and 13, 1929, under the title "La Federación Anarquista Ibérica a la Confederación Nacional del Trabajo."

45 Letter from the National Committee of the CNT to the Spanish Section of the FAI, March 15, 1928, International Institute for Social History, Amsterdam, FAI Archive, microfilm181.

46 El Comité Nacional – FAI. Sección Española, "Carta abierta para la F.L. de G.A. de Valencia," *Prismas*, April 1928.

47 The local federation accused the Levantine CRT of being "republican syndicalists" and enemies of the FAI. The Levantine CRT claimed that the local federation was trying to impose its ideas on the regional syndicalist organisation. The dispute was the result of a misunderstanding by the local federation of the agreements made at Madrid in January which limited the trabazón to the Action and Prisoners' Committees. This point was clarified by the Catalan anarchists Miguel Jiménez and Josep Llop. See Federación Local de Groupos Anarquistas

de Valencia, "Escisión," *Prismas*, March 1928; La Confederación Regional Levantina (el Comité), "Restableciendo la Verdad," *Prismas*, May 1928. For the Catalan intervention: M. J. H. and J. Ll. V. (Jiménez and Llop), "Aclaración que se impone," *Prismas* June 1928.

48   According to Elorza, *La génesis de la Federación Anarquista Ibérica*, 211–12, the Revolutionary Action Committee was controlled by anarchists and was made up of Armando Artal, Pedro Canet, Santiago Alonso, and Antonio Blanco.

49   "Confederación Nacional del Trabajo Acta del Pleno Nacional celebrado en Barcelona el día 29 de junio de 1928," *La Protesta*, August 31, and September 1, 2 and 4, 1928.

50   Letter from the National Committee of the CNT to the FAI, July 27, 1928, International Institute for Social History, Amsterdam, Nettlau Archive, FAI Archive, microfilm 181.

51   Magriñà stated in a letter to Rudolf Rocker that those behind the publication were "anarcho-syndicalists militants of the CNT," though he gave no names. Letter from Le Groupe du "Rebelde" (signed by Magriñà) to Rudolf Rocker, March 17, 1928 International Institute for Social History, Amsterdam, Rocker Archive, file 189. Working alongside Magriñà on the paper were Wolney Solterra and Portos.

52   El Grupo Internacional de Estudios Sociales, "A todos los Grupos y Camaradas," *Rebelde*, January 1928.

53   Gibanel warmly supported *Rebelde*'s campaign, whilst Peiró, although not committing himself on the newspaper's campaign, warmly welcomed the appearance of the paper. *Rebelde*, January 1928. Many of Magriñà's former colleagues from *El Productor* responded to the survey but did not support their colleague's position. Alberola, T. Cano Ruiz, and Buenacasa all argued that the IWMA was a workers' and not an anarchist organisation, even though it supported anarchist goals, and that therefore the anarchists should organise independently of it. José Alberola, "Respuesta a la Encuesta," *Rebelde*, June 1928; T. Cano Ruiz, "Respuesta a la Encuesta," *Rebelde*, March 1928; M. Buenacasa, "Anarquistas y Trabajadores," *Rebelde*, April/May 1928.

54   Souchy's personal opinion was that "there must be an understanding and agreement between the forces of anarchism and syndicalism," but he warned that, although a link between anarchists and syndicalists might appear natural to the Spanish, not all members of the IWMA enjoyed such close contacts with the anarchists in the country. He felt that the best way forward was for the first steps toward closer ties to be made on a national and not international basis. Augustín Souchy, "Carta de la I.A.T. [*sic*]," *Rebelde*, April/May 1928 (the letter is dated March 15, 1928). A more categorical critique came from the Russian Alexander Schapiro (based in France), who pointed out the error of *Rebelde* in referring to the IWMA simply as an apolitical organisation: "The IWMA is not only apolitical, it is syndicalist and can only permit syndicalist organisations to be members." A. Schapiro, "AIT y Organización Anarquista," *Rebelde*, April/May 1928.

55   "International de La Jeunesse Anarchist – Appel à tous les jeunes anarchistes," *Rebelle* (Brussels), November 1927.

56   A Federación Ibérica de Juventudes Libertarias was established in 1932, although until the outbreak of the Civil War its influence and size were limited.

57   Comité Peninsular de la FAI, "La Federación Anarquista Ibérica a la internacional de juventudes Anarquistas – Holanda," *Rebelde*, June 1928; *La Protesta*, June 12 and 13, 1928.

58   The origins of the AYI could be traced back to 1923 when anarchists from Austria, Holland, Sweden, England, Germany, Belgium, Denmark, and other northern European countries celebrated the first of what would become an annual meeting at Easter. In 1927 it was decided to celebrate an international congress to create the Anarchist Youth International. El Delegado de la FAI, "La I.J.A.," *Rebelde*, June 1928. Two Spanish delegates attended the congress, Solterra for the FAI and another for the FGALEF.

59   Netherlands, which was the seat of the Anarchist Youth International, provides a classic example of the divisions between anarchist and syndicalist organisations. Dutch anarchists rejected the national syndicalist movement, NSV, because they considered it reformist. Magriñà had been informed of this attitude by the secretary of the Dutch anarchist youth in autumn 1928. See R. Magriñà, "Desde el destierro," *Rebelde*, September 1928.

60   The Huizen congress did agree to a declaration of principles which were to form the basis of the future International, a copy of which was found in the possession of Tómas Espinossa and Avelino Semlios, the editors of *La Voz Libertaria*, who were arrested by the French police in March 1929. Archives Nationales de France, F/7/14720, police records, March 11, 1929.

61   In a letter attached to the invitation, M. Stephens, secretary of the AYI, complained of the lack of interest in the International from outside Holland. For the congress in Denmark, see "Tribuna libertaria," *Solidaridad Obrera* (La Coruña), March 14, 1931; "Una encuesta y un congreso," *El Productor*, June 21, 1930.

62   Jean Frago was in close contact with the exiled Spanish anarchists in Paris, the largest section of which worked in the construction industry. Archives Nationales de France, F/7/13443, police records, February 5, 1925.

63   The full list of delegations is as follows: FORA (Maurice and Fabbri); Belgian Metalworkers' Federation (Krenzt and Chalent); FAUD (Betzer and Schmitz); CNT (Frago); CGTSR (Huart); NSV (Lansink, Jr.); the USI emigration committee (Cremonini); SAC and the Norwegian NSF (both represented by Jensen); and the IAC (De Jong and Muller-Lehring). The Portuguese CGT and the Uruguayan FORU were unable to attend, the former nominating Souchy to represent them and the latter Magriñà. A number of other groups also attended, including the German Federation of Construction, the Dutch federation of factory committees, the groups behind the papers *Verbo Nuevo* and *Rebelde*, and the Polish Anarchist Group based in Paris. The list appears in *Rebelde*, June 1928. Orobón Fernández attended as a representative of the IWMA secretariat. "El Congreso de la Asociación Internacional de los Trabajadores," *Despertád*, October 13 and 20, and November 3, 1928, was the report of the FORA delegation. Magriñà also wrote a very general report on the congress. R. Magriñà, "Impressiones y apuntes," *Rebelde*, June 1928.

64 The CGTP actually had made no agreement with the FAI whatsoever, a point that they pointed out later to the IWMA by letter. "La AIT y las organizaciones anarquistas," *Rebelde*, July 1928.

65 "Resolutions of the IIIrd International Congress in Liege, Belgium, at Whitsuntide 1928," *News Service of the IWMA*, July 6, 1928. The resolutions were published in Spain in *La Revista Blanca*, August 1 and 15, 1928.

66 "Fracaso?," *Rebelde*, July 1928.

67 R. Magriñà, "Las ideas y el sindicalismo V," *Acción Social Obrera*, December 8, 1928.

68 Miguel Jiménez, "Respondiendo a una encuesta," *Rebelde*, March, April/May, and June 1928; Miguel Jiménez, "De la colaboración a la unidad," *La Protesta*, October 26, 1928.

69 In total eighty militants were arrested in Catalonia, fifty-five in Valencia, sixty-seven in Madrid, and twenty-nine in Bilbao, and numerous more were detained across the country. R. Magriñà, "Noticias de España," *La Protesta*, September 4, 1928.

70 "La dictadura del sable," *Le Reveil du Bâtiment*, January 1928. A circular by the Peninsular Committee published in *Despertád* in December 1928, but dated November 1928, gives news of the forced inactivity of the committee as well as defending the committee from criticism from the FAI. *Despertád*, December 15, 1928. Two further circulars, both dated December 1928, talk of the repression in Seville: "Bajo la Dictadura Militarista y Católica" and El Comité Peninsular de la FAI, "A Todos los Trabajadores," *Rebelde*, January 1929.

71 El Comité (de la CNT), "A los trabajadores y a la opinión pública," *Le Reveil du Bâtiment*, September 1928. See also "Bajo la Dictadura Militarista y Católica" and El Comité Peninsular de la FAI, "A Todos los Trabajadores," *Rebelde*, January 1929, and the circular by the Peninsular Committee in *Despertád*, December 15, 1928.

72 Angel Pestaña, "En torno a la Unión Moral – Tercer Objetivo II," *Acción Social Obrera*, December 1, 1928. The article was the final of a series by Pestaña on the three objectives of the Moral Union which appeared under the title "En torno a la Unión Moral" in *Acción Social Obrera*: "Primer Objetivo," September 29, 1928, October 20 and 27, 1928; "Segundo Objetivo," November 10, 1928; "Tercer Objetivo," November 17 and December 1, 1928.

73 Jacinto Toryho, "Historia y significado político-social de los Jurados Mixtos," *Tiempos Nuevos*, September 1, 1935. See also E. Guerrero Salom, "La Dictadura de Primo de Rivera y el Corporativismo," *Cuadernos Económicos del ICE*, no.10 (1979), 111–32.

74 This was persuasively argued by J. Peiró in "Desvaneciendo Nebulosas," *Acción Social Obrera*, January 4, 1930.

75 See Peiró's articles: "Para que la Unión Moral?," *Acción Social Obrera*, September 1, 1928; "La lucha entre tendencias," *Acción Social Obrera*, July 6, 1929; "Es Preciso Personalizar," *Acción Social Obrera*, December 14 and 28, 1929; "Desvaneciendo Nebulosas," *Acción Social Obrera*, January 4, 1930.

76 For an overall view of Peiró's critique of Pestaña's policies, see the whole series of

articles entitled "Deslinde de Campos" which appeared in *Acción Social Obrera* between September 21 and October 19, 1929.

77   The article in question was entitled "Alea jacta est" and appeared in *Despertád* on May 20, 1928. Unfortunately, this edition is not in the archives of the International Institute for Social History, Amsterdam. However, Peiró retraces his basic arguments in a later article: J. Peiró, "Quien Sabe?," *Acción Social Obrera*, August 20, 1929.

78   J. Peiró, "Deslinde de Campos III – Oportunismo Suicida," *Acción Social Obrera*, October 5, 1929. See also J. Peiró, "Deslinde de Campos II. La Acción Directa y Los Congresos de la CNT," *Acción Social Obrera*, September 28, 1929.

79   Pestaña outlined his ideas in a series of articles in *Despertád* under the title "Situemonos." It was not until number 4 that he finally exposed that he felt that the CNT should accept the labour legislation. Pestaña, "Situemonos I–VII," *Despertád*, June 1 to November 25, 1929. At no point does Pestaña respond to Peiró's criticism of the dangers of 'professionalism' with any degree of satisfaction, and he even suggested in number 5 that as "organisations are abstract things, 'containers' and 'contents'," the CNT's principles could be changed at any time. Peiró had argued previously that the libertarian principles of the CNT could be changed if a congress so decided, but what he objected to was that it should be anarchists that were responsible for such a change.

80   El Comité, "El comité de la CNT ante las dificultades del momento," *Despertád*, December 7, 1929.

81   La Federación Local de Sindicatos Únicos (Barcelona), "A los Trabajadores y en particular a los militantes de la CNT," *Acción Social Obrera*, January 11, 1930. Cuadros had also been created in Valencia, Alcoy, and other areas. Vega, *La Confederació Nacional del Treball i els Sindicats d'Oposició a Catalunya i el País Valencià*, 153, argues that the CNT was able to reorganise so quickly in 1930 as "the cuadros sindicales were perfectly organised," suggesting that the national committee's claims were questionable.

82   "Los Militantes Asturianos y Leoneses de la CNT, de España, ante una polémica," *Acción Social Obrera*, December 28, 1929 (the article was signed by forty-five militants from the two regions, including Quintanilla and Segundo Blanco (a former secretary of the national committee). Las Federaciónes Locales de San Feliu de Guixols, Palámos y Palafrugell y los sindicatos de Llagostera, Cassa de la Selva y Calonge, "Un acuerdo," *Acción Social Obrera*, January 11, 1930; El Comité Regional (Aragón, Rioja and Navarra), "Dos palabras al Comité Nacional," *Acción Social Obrera*, January 11, 1930; La Federación Local de Sindicatos Únicos (Barcelona), "A los Trabajadores y en particular a los militantes de la CNT," *Acción Social Obrera*, January 11, 1930. The response from the Cuadros Sindicales of Alcoy was published in *Despertád*, December 21, 1929.

83   For the most detailed discussion of the differences between Peiró and Pestaña, see Rider, *Anarchism, Urbanisation and Social Conflict in Barcelona*, 443–59. The evolution of his position can also be traced in the selection of articles compiled by Antonio Elorza in Angel Pestaña, *Trayectoria Sindicalista* (Madrid: Ediciones Tebas, 1974).

84 In his interview with General Mola, minister of the interior, in April 1930, Pestaña said that the Comités Paritarios were a "monstrosity," "absurd," not "part of our [the CNT's] customs," and "were guided by the employers." Mola quoted in Bernardo Pou and J. R. Magriñà, *Un año de conspiración* (Barcelona: Ediciones Rojo y Negro, 1933), 49.

85 Primo de Rivera's continued attempts to reform (and reduce the number of officers in) the artillery corps from 1926 onwards brought increasing opposition from the military, which was clearly demonstrated in 1929 when a military tribunal found Sanchez Guerra innocent of any charge in relation to the failed coup attempt.

86 Jordi Casassas Ymbert, *La Dictadura de Primo de Rivera (1923–30). Textos* (Barcelona: Anthropos, 1983), 37–39, argues that by 1929 Primo de Rivera was faced by a divided army, growing labour unrest, opposition from liberal and pre-Republican political parties, students, intellectuals, and economic stagnation. To these problems the dictatorship had no answer. The ideological foundation of the dictatorship, based on the regeneration of Spain, was "simplistic, variable, contradictory and confused," and in reality the regime survived due to the popularity of its leader. Tussell, *Historia de España en el siglo XX*, 552–53. When this popularity began to wane, his most important allies, the king and the army, began to distance themselves.

87 Carr, *Spain*, 591.

88 The FAI itself had refused to become embroiled in the discussions over the Union of Militants and the professionalisation of the unions. El Comité Peninsular de la FAI, "A Todos los Individuos y Organismos Adheridos a La Federación Anarquista Ibérica," *Despertád*, August 21, 1929; *Cultura Proletaria* (New York), September 7, 1929. The circular was dated August 1929. The Peninsular Committee did, however, respond to Pestaña's claims that their policy was to interfere in the daily running of the confederal unions, stating that the trabazón was limited to the areas previously agreed upon at the national plenum in January 1928. El Comité Peninsular, "La Federación Anarquista Ibérica ante la Confederación Nacional del Trabajo," *Acción Social Obrera*, December 21, 1929. Pestaña had made his allegations in Angel Pestaña, "Unas Preguntas," *Acción Social Obrera*, June 15, 1929.

89 Evelio G. Fontaura (pseudonym of Vicente Galindo), "Que hace la F.A.I.?," *Acción Social Obrera*, March 15, 1930. The Levante Federation of Anarchist Groups even claimed that the existence of the FAI had been "a fiction." El Comité de la Federación de Grupos Anarquistas de Levante, "A la opinión libertaria," *Tierra y Libertad*, May 31, 1930.

90 The detained member might have been Vázquez Piedra, a former member of the editorial team behind *El Productor* who was arrested in Valencia whilst travelling from Seville to Barcelona. See Magriñà, "'Movimiento internacional," *La Protesta*, September 4, 1928. In a letter to Gómez Casas, Jiménez claimed that Vázquez Piedra had been a member of the national secretariat of the Spanish National Federation of Anarchist Groups prior to the Valencia conference at which the FAI was created. Gómez Casas, *Anarchist Organisation*, 108.

91 El C.P. de la F.A.I, "Puntualicemos," *Acción Social Obrera*, July 26, 1930. An example of the problems of communication between regions was that the influential Andalusian anarchist Mefistofeles (obviously a pseudonym) only discovered in early 1931 that the Peninsular Committee had left Seville. Mefistofeles, "Sindicalista, Anarquista," *Solidaridad Obrera*, March 12, 1931. According to the Levantine federation the decision to transfer the Peninsular Committee to Barcelona had been made without consulting the other regional organisations.

92 El Comité Peninsular, "A todos los anarquistas de la penisular," *Acción*, August 23, 1930. *Tierra y Libertad* and *El Productor* (Barcelona) and *Redención* (Alcoy) had all reappeared in the months following the fall of the Primo dictatorship.

93 Writing in early September, the Portuguese anarchist Meridional claimed that Magriñà, now a member of the CRT of Catalonia, had told him that the FAI was "moribund." Meridional, "Como de interpreta la fai?," *Tierra Libre*, September 13, 1930.

94 This point was made by Evelio Fontaura in "Existe una organización peninsular anarquista?," *Tierra Libre*, October 4, 1930. An example of the FAI's influence was the appointment of Manuel Sirvent, a member of the Peninsular Committee of the FAI, to the national committee of the CNT in June. A joint manifesto by the FAI and CNT in support of social and political prisoners was published in May 1930, suggesting that the trabazón was still in operation. *Acción*, May 3, 1930.

95 El Comité, "La Confederación Nacional del Trabajo a los Comités Federales, a los sindicatos y militantes," *Acción* (Barcelona), February 22, 1930.

96 The membership of this committee remains unclear. Apart from Pestaña the only other known member was Pedro Massoni. Angel Pestaña, "Impressiones y comentarios de viaje," *Sindicalismo*, April 21 to May 19, 1933.

97 El Comité (de la CNT), "El Gobierno y la Confederación Nacional del Trabajo," *Acción*, February 2, 1930. The legalisation of the CNT followed an interview between Pestaña and General Despujol, the governor of Barcelona, on February 18, and then between Pestaña, another CNT member, and General Mola, the minister of the interior, following a national plenum held in Blanes (Catalonia) on April 17–18.

98 El Comité, "Nuestra Posición en el Momento Actual," *Acción Social Obrera*, April 5, 1930.

99 "El manifiesto de la CNT," *Despertád*, April 12, 1930.

100 El Comité, "Aclaración al Manifiesto de la CNT," *Acción Social Obrera*, April 26, 1930. The most vehement criticism came in a letter signed by nine Catalan militants who argued that the committee had clearly stepped outside the remits of the Zaragoza 'political motion' in placing so much emphasis on the parliamentary path to liberation. Antonio Blanco, Luis López, et al., "Nuestra Protesta. Lo que ha sido, lo que es y lo que será … La Confederación Nacional del Trabajo," *Acción Social Obrera*, April 26, 1930. *Redención*, the weekly periodical of the anarchists in Alcoy, published an article by Malatesta which argued that there was little difference between bourgeois constitutionalism and dictatorship. The article did not specifically refer to the CNT and may have been written previously

but provides the basic arguments for the anarchist criticism of the CNT manifesto. Errico Malatesta, "Constituyente y Dictadura," *Redención*, April 19, 1930.

101 An editorial in *Despertád* agreed that the emphasis of the manifesto on the parliamentary procedure was "unfortunate" and could lead to "confusion." "El Manifiesto de la CNT," *Despertád*, April 12, 1930.

102 Reports on the meeting were published in *Redención*, July 29, 1930; *Acción Social Obrera*, August 2, 1930; and *Le Combat Syndicaliste*, June/July 1930. The report in the paper of the CGTSR is the most extensive, although the version published in *Redención* gives more information on the discussions specific to the situation in Spain. See also *The Press Service of the IWMA*, July 14, 1930.

103 The Spanish government initially authorised the congress. However, the rapid rise in confederal support led to rethinking this, and at the beginning of October numerous confederal militants were detained, and the IWMA congress had to be postponed. Letter from Orobón Fernández to Max Nettlau, July 22, 1930, International Institute for Social History, Amsterdam, Nettlau Archive, microfilm 57. The congress was eventually held in Madrid in June 1931.

104 Pierre Besnard, the spokesman for the French CGTSR, whose ideas would become closely associated with the syndicalist tendency in the CNT in the years that followed, agreed with Souchy and Orobón's criticism of the manifesto. Pedro Besnard, "Hagamos concordar los esfuerzos," *Redención*, June 7, 1930.

105 "La Asociación Internacional de los Trabajadores al proletariado Español," *Despertád*, July 5, 1930.

106 Letter from Orobón Fernández to Carbó, August 2, 1930, Archivo General de la Guerra Civil Española, Barcelona, file 886.

107 Souchy felt that the CNT should proceed with caution whilst it reorganised, given the fact that a dictatorship still existed, but by giving such clear support for the calling of a Constituent Cortes the national committee was "superfluous and even a little dangerous." Letter from Souchy to Carbó, May 16, 1930, Archivo General de la Guerra Civil Española, Barcelona, file 886.

108 Manuel Adame, *El C.N. de Reconstrucción y la politica sindical del Partido* (Madrid: Ediciones Frente Unico, n.d.). Adame, a former member of the CNT, was one of the leading figures in the National Committee of Reconstruction.

109 Joan Peiró and Sebastià Clara were sent from Barcelona to try to convince the Transport Union members not to go ahead with the conference, but they were unsuccessful. Peiró and Clara, "Desde Seville – Obedencia a la consigna de Moscú" and, by the same two authors, "Lo que estaba previsto," *Acción*, June 14, 1930; "Contra una baja maniobra," *Acción*, June 21, 1930; La Federación de Grupos Anarquistas (de Andalucía), "Desde Seville – A la Opinión, A todos los Trabajadores y al Pueblo," *Acción*, July 6, 1930; *El Productor*, June 28, 1930.

110 According to Mefistofeles and Rodia, only fifteen people attended the conference. Mefistofeles, "Como se fragua el acuartelamiento hispano-moscovita," *Acción*, July 6, 1930; Rodia, "De color rojo," *Acción*, July 19, 1930.

111 Manuel Buenacasa, "Las ideas y las tacticas del movimiento obrero," *El Productor*, July 5, 1930. The paper also launched a questionnaire on the state of the CNT at the time ("Nuestra encuesta," *El Productor*, June 14, 1930), but this

did not attract responses from leading militants, and the paper stopped publication in mid-July.

112   "Para nuestros periódicos y nuestros compañeros," *Suplemento de"La Revista Blanca"*, June 1, 1930.

113   The report of the plenum is reproduced in Pou and Magriñà, *Un año de conspiración*, 68–82. Susana Tavera, *La ideologia política del anarcosindicalismo catalán*, 260, claims that the delegate was Bueso. However, in his autobiography, Bueso, who has a tendency to exaggerate his role in certain events, does not mention this, confirming the suspicion that José Peirats, *Figuras del movimiento libertario español* (Barcelona: Picazo, 1977), 74, is correct when he claims that the delegate was Helios Gómez. This suspicion is reaffirmed by the savage attack on Helios Gómez, who at the time was working for the communist paper *Mundo Obrera*, by Valeriano Orobón Fernandez, "Por qué se marcha Gómez del anarquismo," *Accion*, August 23, 1930. Helios Goméz had previously announced his departure from the anarchist movement earlier that year in an article "por qué me marchó del anarquismo," June 1930, reproduced on HTTP://NOTICIASAYR.BLOG-SPOT.COM.AR/2014/10/POR-QUE-ME-MARCHO-DEL-ANARQUISMO-HELIOS.HTML. He then joined the BOC but was soon expelled.

114   For their initial positive attitude, see "La Reconstitución de la C.N.T," *La Batalla*, June 27, 1930. For their change of opinion, see "Contra todo intento de escisión," *La Batalla*, August 15, 1930; "Por la unidad sindical," September 5, 1930, *La Batalla*. Maurín's U-turn brought ridicule from the syndicalists. See Noy, "Guerrillero – Los reconstructores y los antireconstructores," *Acción*, March 14, 1931.

115   See Durgan, *B.O.C. 1930–36*, 36–46. Maurín's criticism of the Committee of Reconstruction was simply a tactical dispute. More important was his ideological rejection of the overall classic revolutionary Marxist policy towards Spain adopted by the PCE. He argued that the Spanish bourgeoisie was neither strong enough nor organised enough to bring about its own revolution and thus it would make more sense in Spain for the Left to ally itself with the nationalist forces, most specifically the Catalanists and the Basques, and the rural labourers.

116   Ibid., 73. During the Second Republic the influence of the BOC did increase, especially in Lleida (Lérida) and Girona.

117   Previously Catalan nationalism had been dominated by the Francesc Cambó's bourgeois Lliga Regionalista de Catalunya.

118   Estat Català, formed in 1922, had initially adopted a policy of insurrectional separatism but had abandoned this during 1930 in exchange for an autonomous regime within a future Spanish Republic. This smoothed the way for the merger with the autonomist, rather than pro-independence, Partit Republicà Català. See Albert Balcells, *Catalan Nationalism* (London: MacMillan Press, 1986), 89–92.

119   The CNT had maintained contacts with the exiled Catalan leader from 1924. In 1925 Estat Català, the CNT, and the PCE formed a 'Free Alliance Action Committee' in Paris. The CNT eventually withdrew from the committee when it realised that Macià was only interested in liberating Catalonia and not the whole of Spain.

120 Tavera (1980), *La ideologia política del anarcosindicalismo catalán*, 18. Amadeu Aragui claimed that the ERC was "not interested in administration, but revolution" (*El Diluvio*, April 7, 1931) whilst Jaime Aiguader argued that the Catalonia he foresaw was not of old Europe but one of which "Soviet Russia is an anticipation" (*El Diluvio* April 7 1931) – both are cited in Rider, *Anarchism, Urbanisation and Social Conflict in Barcelona*, 542–44. Macià's insurrectionalism had always been attractive to certain sections of the CNT, whilst in his book on the events of 1930–1931 Jaime Aiguader claimed that Catalonia had "to make a pact with the proletariat if it wanted its integral freedom" and that without the working class "the Spanish revolution [i.e., the Republican revolution] is not possible." Jaime Aiguader, *Cataluña y la Revolución* (Barcelona: Arnau de Vilanova, 1931), 144–45.

121 "Manifest d'Intelligencia Republicana," *L'Opinió*, May 2, 1930. Alongside Peiró, Pere Foix and Josep Viadiu also signed the manifesto and later withdrew their support.

122 The CNT members on the committee were Peiró, Massoni, and Clara. CNT leaders also took part in a number of mass meeting with other Republican and Catalanist figures in favour of a general amnesty for political prisoners throughout the year before the proclamation of the Second Republic. Aiguader, *Cataluña y la Revolución*, 117–18.

123 Susanna Tavera i Garcia and E. Ucelay da Cal, "Conversa amb Sebastià Clara un líder cenetiste català," *Avenç* 6 (October 1977), 11–18.

124 Alongside Estat Català, the pro-Republican conspiracy involved the socialists and a number of liberal and even conservative parties or factions: the Alianza Republicana, Partido Radical Socialista, Izquierda Republicana, Federación Republicana Gallega, Acció Catala, Acció Republicana de Catalunya, and Derecha Liberal Republicana.

125 In June, Captain Alejandro Sancho Subirats, who was part of a pro-anarchist group within the army that formed part of a revolutionary committee in Catalonia, contacted the regional CRT about their possible participation in a revolutionary movement. Throughout the summer both the CNT and the FAI maintained contact with conspirators, who included politicians. However, the planned plot collapsed when Magriñà, representing the Catalan CRT, discovered that the committee was actually receiving money from the army. However, members of both FAI and the CNT maintained contact with Sancho Subirats, and eventually, tired of the Republican procrastination, the libertarians and soldiers planned their own rising in October. The government found out about the plot and arrested the conspirators, including Subirats, who later died in prison. Pou and Magriñà, *Un año de conspiración*, 83ff.

126 "La Confederación Nacional del Trabajo toma acuerdos," *Acción*, November 15, 1930. Peiró, speaking at the CNT's national congress in Madrid in June 1931, stated that during the negotiation with Sanchez Guerra, the conspirators had asked the CNT to give them six months of social peace in order to consolidate any future regime, whilst the conspirators of 1930 requested three months. Peiró's intervention in the congress is reproduced in Peirats, *La CNT en la Revolución Española*, 47–50.

127   El Comité (de la CNT), "Ni pactos ni compromisos – La actuación clara de la CNT," *Solidaridad Obrera*, October 30, 1930. This point was stressed again on the eve of the municipal elections in an editorial in *Solidaridad Obrera*, "Ni pactos ni conferencias," April 11, 1931. For the negotiations between the CNT and the Republicans, see Pou and Magriñà, *Un año de conspiración*, 160ff.

128   The strike began when the company Foment d'Obres i Construcció sacked six workers who had been reorganising the union within the company. The company insisted on dealing with the dispute in the Comité Paritaro for the industry and refused to acknowledge the CNT. By September the strike had spread throughout the rest of the Construction Workers' Union, involving thirty-seven thousand workers. In sympathy, rubbish disposal workers also went on strike. The civil governor, General Ignasi Despujol i de Sabater, put pressure on the employers to concede to all the union's demands, and the six workers returned to work. Vega, *La Confederació Nacional del Treball i els Sindicats d'Oposició a Catalunya i el País Valencià*, 161–62; Rider, *Anarchism, Urbanisation and Social Conflict in Barcelona*, 532–33.

129   El Comité [de la CNT], "La Confederación Nacional del Trabajo a todos los organismos adheridos y a los trabajadores en general," *Acción*, November 23, 1930. Among those arrested were Alfarache, Pestaña, Sirvent, and Sebastià Clara. Valeriano Orobón Fernández had also been arrested on his return to the country in September.

130   Elorza, *La génesis de la Federación Anarquista Ibérica*, 438; Rider, *Anarchism, Urbanisation and Social Conflict in Barcelona*, 523.

131   "Lo que ha terminado, ha terminado," *Acción*, November 23, 1930.

132   The Solidarity group had initially been formed in 1928 by militants of the different tendencies (including Pestaña, Peiró, Buenacasa, Jiménez, Magriñà, Alberola, Quintanilla, and Germinal de Sousa) with the aim of publishing a newspaper, *Revista Obrera*. Magriñà, "Opiniones y comentarios," *Despertad*, November 17, 1928; "Revista Obrera," *Despertad*, December 29, 1928. However, the disputes between Pestaña and Peiró and between Pestaña and the FAI put an end to this proposal. The new group, constituted in early 1930, was made up of syndicalists who supported the ideas of Pestaña.

133   El groupo Solidaridad, "A todos los anarquistas," *Acción*, August 23, 1930.

134   Previously one of the leading members of the Solidarity group, Juan López, had written a series of articles arguing that the different tendencies within the CNT should form their own groups and define their positions. "Las tendencias deben agruparse y definirse," *Despertad*, January 23, 1929–March 23, 1929. Writing from Argentina, Gaston Leval warned that this would only serve to further divide the libertarian movement ("Las tendencias no deben agruparse," *Despertad*, May 17, 1929).

135   Federico Urales, "Sobre una pretendida revisión del anarquismo," *La Revista Blanca*, September 15, 1930.

136   Urales was able to publish *Revista Blanca* as the review avoided commenting on the situation in Spain. This brought criticism from anarchists that he was "compromising too much" with the dictatorship. Letter from Abad de Santillán to

Nettlau, April 27, 1927, International Institute for Social History, Amsterdam, Nettlau Archive, mircrofilm 1. In 1928–29 Urales provoked the wrath of both the FAI and the CNT by launching a fund-raising scheme for detained militants but refusing to hand the money over to the Prisoners' Committee, which was made up of militants from both organisations in line with the trabazón. See Teresa Abelló and Enric Olive, "El conflicto entre la CNT y la Familia Urales-Montseny, en 1928. La lucha por el mantenimiento del anarquismo puro," *Estudios de Historia Social* 32–33 (1985), 317–32. See also the letters from Federica Montseny to Nettlau of March 9, 1929, and March 1, 1929, as well as Orobón Fernández's criticism of Urales in a letter to Nettlau of September 19, 1929, all in International Institute for Social History, Amsterdam, Nettlau Archive, microfilm 52. Ricardo Sanz complained that many prisoners' families never received money from the Urales family. Sanz, *El Sindicalismo español antes de la Guerra Civil*, 170–71. Sanz's Los Solidarios colleague García Oliver, who was happy to use Urales's newspaper *El Luchador* to attack the syndicalists during the Second Republic, later stated that the influence of the Urales family on the CNT was "very disruptive." *Colección de Historia Oral El movimiento libertario de España (2) Juan García Oliver* (Madrid: Fundación Salvador Seguí, 1990), 15–16.

137   An editorial in the first issue of *El Luchador*, January 9, 1931, warned against the negative impact that political parties had on union activity. "El Luchador ante las sociedades obreres," *El Luchador*, January 9, 1931. *El Luchador*'s vitriolic campaign against the syndicalists would not really start until May 1931.

138   El Comité Regional Anarquista de Andalucía, "A las federaciónes y grupos anarquistas de Andalucía," *Tierra Libre*, August 23, 1930. *Tierra Libre* began publication in August as a replacement for *Tierra y Libertad*, which, after a brief existence in May 1930, was banned and did not reappear until November 1930.

139   "Una Justificación," *Acción*, December 13, 1930.

140   According to J. Ferrer Alvaro, Peiró had called for the truce at a meeting held on December 15. "Una Tregua," *Acción*, February 19, 1931; "Ni esta guerra, ni aquella paz," *Acción*, February 26, 1931; El Comité Peninsular, "Fijando actitudes," *Solidaridad Obrera*, January 25, 1931.

141   In the final national plenum before the collapse of the monarchy, held on March 28–29, the reports from the different regions gave witness to the difficulties they had faced following the failed republican rising of December 1930. "Se reunió el Pleno Confederal durante los días 28 y 29 de marzo, tomándose importantes acuerdos sobre la legalización de los Sindicatos y otras cuestiones de actualidad," *Solidaridad Obrera*, April 3 and 4, 1931. In March 1931 there were still forty-four members of the CNT detained in Barcelona Prison, including Magriñà, Alfarache, and Pestaña.

142   "Solidaridad Obrera y los políticos," *Solidaridad Obrera*, April 10, 1931; "El voto de los trabajadores," *Solidaridad Obrera*, April 1, 1931.

143   "La vuelta al trabajo," *Solidaridad Obrera*, April 16, 1931.

144   Feran Soldevila, *Història de la proclamació de la República a Catalunya* (Barcelona: Curial, 1977), 72.

145 For the CNT's initial position towards the Second Republic, see Julian Casanova, *De la Calle al Frente. El anarcosindicalismo en España 1931–39* (Barcelona: Crítica, 1997), 13–31.

146 Buenacasa remained in exile in France but did attempt to intervene in the conflict between the radical anarchists and the syndicalists with the publication of a book, *La CNT, los Trienta y la FAI* (Barcelona: Alfa, 1933), calling for more tolerance within the CNT. As has been seen, Magriñà had been very active in the various plots and plans to overthrow the dictatorship. However, although he continued to be active during the Second Republic and was often called upon to give propaganda speeches, he does not appear to have involved himself directly in the condemnation of the Trientistas, many of whom he worked with in the Catalan CRT and in the years 1928–31, and he even supported Peiró's proposed restructuring of the CNT based on National Federations of Industry at the 1931 Madrid congress. Miguel Jiménez and José Piedra Vázquez were also notably less active during the 1930s. The former concentrated on his work as a teacher at the *ateneo* in Carmel (Barcelona). The more radical sections of the CNT centred around the likes of García Oliver and Durruti. Meanwhile the FAI secretariat that had been involved in the conspiracies against the monarchy in 1930 – Elizalde, Hernandéz, and Sirvent – were expelled from the organisation for having "exceeded their functions" by working with political parties. "Los grandes comicios del anarquismo – Magnas resoluciones de la conferencia de Madrid," *Tierra y Libertad*, June 20, 1931.

Conclusion

1 Copp, "The Role of the Anarchists in the Russian Revolution and Civil War," quoted in *KSL: Bulletin of the Kate Sharpley Library*, no. 73 (February 2013).

2 Ibid., page 212 in Copp's thesis.

3 *Confederación Nacional del Trabajo, Memoria del Congreso celebrado en el Teatro de la Comedia de Madrid, los días 10 al 18 de diciembre de 1919* (Barcelona: Cosmos, 1932).

4 Pierre Besnard, *L'Anarcho-Syndicalisme et l'Anarchisme, Rapport de Pierre Besnard, Secretaire de l'A.I.T. au Congrès Anarchiste International de 1937* (May 30, 1937), translated by Paul Sharkey, Libcom.org, https://libcom.org/library/anarchosyndicalism-anarchism-pierre-besnard.

5 Ibid.

INDEX

Española (OARE) 12, 35, 36
Orobón Fernández, Pedro 202, 205, 337n35
Orobón Fernández, Valeriano 151–152, 200, 205, 236–237, 252, 314n37, 318n75, 328n29, 331n1, 350n43, 352 m.63, 357n103&106, 360n129, 361n136
Ortega, Juan 321n96, 346n16&17
Owen, Robert 271n36

P

Pallás, Paulino 41
Pardiñas Serrano, Manuel 283n83
Parera, Arturo 98, 107, 330n47, 331n66
Parra, Diego 335n23, 338n50
Partido Comunista Español (PCE) 84, 96, 99–100, 104, 107, 109, 111, 129–131, 134, 237–239, 292n38, 293n40, 294n51, 299n95, 300n100, 307n63, 308n78, 309n81, 322n97, 358n115
Partido Obrero de Unificación Marxista (POUM) 296n74
Peira, Simó 331n1
Peirats, José 344n2, 349n34, 358n113
Peiró, Joan 74, 106, 111, 134, 150, 161, 166–167, 172, 178, 180–181, 186–187, 224, 229–233, 238–239, 241–245, 253–255, 267n22, 293n42, 309n84, 312n12, 314n32, 323n105, 325n5, 326n11, 331n67, 334n22, 335n26, 340n69, 343n88, 345n3, 351n53, 353n74, 354n79, 357n109, 359n121&122, 360n132, 361n140 362n146
Pellicer-Monferrer, Francisco 333n14
Pelloutier, Fernand 49, 274n3, 275n5
Pérez, Manuel 217, 324n113, 338n46, 340n69
Peribanez Ranera, Ángel 324n114
Pestaña, Ángel 73–74, 92–101, 105–107, 109, 111, 116–117, 122–123,

134, 142–143, 148, 150–151, 161, 166, 172, 176, 178, 186–187, 215, 229–233, 236–237, 241–245, 253–255, 279n46, 284n106, 285n119, 286n122, 287n1, 290n23, 291n30&32, 292n35, 293n40, 295n28, 297n82, 301n7, 302n18, 304n29, 312n12, 314n34, 319n82, 321n94, 323n105, 326n11, 327n18, 331n67, 334n22, 345n11, 353n72, 354n79, 355n84, 356n96, 360n129, 361n141
Peña, Antonio 315n41
Piera, Simó 289n19, 313n23
Pisacane, Carlo 37, 273n51
Pizana, Federico (pseudonym for Federico Morales) 343n92
Piñón, Camil 160–161, 244, 281n67, 312n12, 319n82, 320n86, 321n94, 331n67
Plaja, Hermoso 292n40, 324n116
Portela, Luis 131
Portos 351n51
Pou, Bernardo 358n113
Pouget, Emile 266n16, 275n5, 277n28
Prat, José 59, 277n30, 326n17
Primo de Rivera, Miguel (General) 5, 14, 15, 76, 78, 136, 140–141 162–163, 167, 171–173, 177, 190–191, 200–201, 215, 218, 230, 233, 234, 237, 240, 248, 254, 266n14, 320n86, 321n94&95, 322n99, 324n121, 334n22, 336n29, 340n66, 355n85&86, 356n92
Prismas 207, 341n73, 341–342n78, 343n90, 341n73, 341–342n78, 343n90
El Productor 181, 182, 183, 186, 188, 229, 237, 241, 315n42, 325n4, 329–330n47, 330–31n64, 333n11, 336n31, 348n28, 348n30, 351n53, 357–358n111
Profintern (Red Trade Union International, RTUI) 84, 93–111, 135, 294n52, 295n64, 296n72,

Support **AK Press!**

AK Press is one of the world's largest and most productive anarchist publishing houses. We're entirely worker-run  & democratically managed. We operate without a corporate structure—no boss, no managers, no bullshit. We publish close to twenty books every year, and distribute thousands of other titles published by other like-minded independent presses from around the globe.

The Friends of AK program is a way that you can directly contribute to the continued existence of AK Press, and ensure that we're able to keep publishing great books just like this one! Friends pay $25 a month directly into our publishing account ($30 for Canada, $35 for international), and receive a copy of every book AK Press publishes for the duration of their membership! Friends also receive a discount on anything they order from our website or buy at a table: 50% on AK titles, and 20% on everything else. We've also added a new Friends of AK ebook program: $15 a month gets you an electronic copy of every book we publish for the duration of your membership. Combine it with a print subscription, too!

There's great stuff in the works—so sign up now to become a Friend of AK Press, and let the presses roll!

Won't you be our friend? Email friendsofak@akpress.org for more info, or visit the Friends of AK Press website: www.akpress.org/programs/friendsofak